The Birth of a Great Power
System 1740–1815

The Birth of a Great Power System 1740–1815

H.M. Scott

PEARSON
Longman

Harlow, England • London • New York • Boston • San Francisco • Toronto
Sydney • Tokyo • Singapore • Hong Kong • Seoul • Taipei • New Delhi
Cape Town • Madrid • Mexico City • Amsterdam • Munich • Paris • Milan

PEARSON EDUCATION LIMITED

Edinburgh Gate
Harlow CM20 2JE
United Kingdom
Tel: +44 (0)1279 623623
Fax: +44 (0)1279 431059
Website: www.pearsoned.co.uk

First edition published in Great Britain in 2006

The right of H.M. Scott to be identified as author
of this work has been asserted by him in accordance
with the Copyright, Designs and Patents Act 1988.

ISBN 0 582 21717 2

British Library Cataloguing in Publication Data
A CIP catalogue record for this book can be obtained from the British Library

Library of Congress Cataloging in Publication Data
Scott, H. M. (Hamish M.), 1946–
    The birth of a great power system 1740–1815 / H.M. Scott. — 1st ed.
        p. cm.
    Includes bibliographical references and index.
    ISBN 0-582-21717-2 (pbk.)
    1. Europe—History—1648–1789. 2. Europe—History—1789–1815.
3. Europe—Politics and government—1648–1789. 4. Europe—Politics and
government—1789–1815. 5. Great powers—History—18th century. 6. Great
Powers—History—19th century. I. Title.
    D299.S33 2005
    940.2'53—dc22
                                                                2004063798

10 9 8 7 6 5 4 3 2 1
09 08 07 06 05

Set by 35 in 10/13.5pt Sabon
Printed and bound in Malaysia

The Publishers' policy is to use paper manufactured from sustainable forests.

To Bruce P. Lenman

Contents

Maps

Publisher's acknowledgements

We are grateful to the following for permission to reproduce copyright material:

Pearson Education Limited for Map 1, based on M.S. Anderson, *The War of the Austrian Succession, 1710–1748* (Pearson Education Limited, 1995), Maps 2, 3, 5 and 7, based on Michael Hochedlinger, *Austria's Wars of Emergence, 1683–1797* (Pearson Education Limited, 2003) and Maps 6, 9 and 10, based on Derek McKay and H.M. Scott, *The Rise of the Great Powers, 1648–1815* (Longman Group Limited, 1983); Cambridge University Press for Map 4, based on H.M. Scott, *The Emergence of the Eastern Powers, 1756–1775* (Cambridge University Press, 2001) and Oxford University Press for Map 8, based on P.J. Marshall, *Oxford History of the British Empire: Vol 2 – The Eighteenth Century* (2001, by permission of Oxford University Press).

In some instances we have been unable to trace the owners of copyright material, and we would appreciate any information that would enable us to do so.

Author's acknowledgements

In 1983, jointly with Derek McKay, I published a substantial and pioneering survey of international relations entitled *The Rise of the Great Powers 1648–1815*, which enjoyed considerable scholarly and commercial success. The present study originated as a projected second edition of 'my' parts of that book, which I naively believed could be produced in a year or so. Five years later the outcome is very different both from my own plans and from our original study, and should be seen as a successor to it. Though in a few places the structure and even the material of the 1983 book has been retained, in almost all respects this is an entirely new book. Three principal differences can be indicated at the outset. It seeks to give more attention to events in northern, eastern and south-eastern Europe than is usual in a study written from a British or West European perspective, believing that such events, and the experiences of supposedly minor states, were important for the emergence of the great power system as a whole; it sets out, far more than the original study, to analyse the reasons for particular policies and courses of action being adopted and to provide where relevant the domestic contexts for foreign policy decisions; and, finally and most importantly, it is not merely longer and more detailed but explicitly a book with an overarching thesis, embodied in the programmatic title and summarised in the 'Introduction'.

Revisiting one's own intellectual past is a fascinating if occasionally unsettling experience. Since I originally wrote, the contours of the subject have changed very considerably, while the pace at which important new research has been published is little short of astonishing, particularly on the period from the 1770s onwards. 'International History' has fully emerged as a distinctive subject in recent decades, while the domestic and ideological dimensions of relations between states have received appropriate attention, often for the first time, and these shifts of emphasis are reflected in this study. Much of the credit belongs to the distinguished American scholar, Paul W. Schroeder, who in the past decade has spearheaded a renaissance in the study of diplomatic history. Though the pages which follow occasionally set out a rather different interpretation to that which emerges from his own seminal *The Transformation of European Politics 1763–1848* (Oxford, 1994), my profound debt to that study and to its author, for his generous friendship and wise advice over the past decade, is very real. Over a much longer period Derek Beales and Tim Blanning have encouraged and stimulated me by their friendship and by their own massive contributions to our knowledge of these decades; Derek put me further in his debt by reading several chapters and commenting constructively and incisively on them, while Tim generously sent me his extensive notes on Paul von Mitrofanov's rare and neglected study of Leopold II's foreign policy which were important for Chapters 8 and 9 of this book. Daniel Baugh generously allowed me to draw on his profound knowledge of these decades. The whole text has been read, much to its benefit, by Michael Hochedlinger, Derek McKay, Brendan Simms and Peter Wilson: I am grateful to them all for their consistently helpful and always well-informed suggestions, which have contributed substantially to the final revision of the text. My gratitude to Derek McKay is particularly great, not only for his unusually extensive comments and generous willingness to allow me to use some material which he originally wrote, but for his warm friendship, encouragement and criticism over the past thirty-odd years, since we were graduate students together. Any errors or misconceptions which remain are of course entirely my own responsibility.

Andrew MacLennan, *doyen* of History editors in Britain, first commissioned me to write both the original version of this book and its successor: I remain grateful for all his wise advice and good fellowship. His successor, Heather McCallum, was supportive and sympathetic when the project expanded beyond its original limits and generously allowed me the time to complete it, while the final production was efficiently supervised by Casey Mein, Melanie Carter and their colleagues at Pearson. Successive versions of the text were typed speedily and efficiently by Yvonne Campbell and Nancy E.M. Bailey. My debt to Nancy is particularly great, as she is not merely a remarkably swift and accurate typist who can cope with my handwriting, even where foreign names are involved, but also a hawk-eyed critic of logic and presentation: she has contributed far more to this book than she will ever know.

I owe most to two people. During the final stages of writing Julia Smith has sustained and supported, and at times tolerated, a distracted author, besides critically listening to him thinking out aloud many of the intellectual and organisational problems involved in writing a survey of this kind; more importantly, she has constantly reassured me that life is about much more than writing books. The second obligation is a much more longstanding one. Over the past quarter of a century, Bruce Lenman's personal friendship and intellectual comradeship have been very important to me. Being old enough to remember when research in British universities primarily concerned intellectual enquiry rather than the winning of grants or the guaranteeing of publications, I have been even more grateful for his remarkable and continuing ability to make me think critically about what I am doing and to point me in new directions, sometimes without fully realising he is doing so. Many of the ideas set out in the pages which follow first took shape in our conversations, and it is only right that the book should be dedicated to him.

H.M. Scott

Dates, distances and place names

During the second half of the eighteenth century, the Russian calendar was still eleven days behind that used throughout the remainder of Europe; in this study all such dates have been given in the New Style which prevailed elsewhere. Distances are given in kilometres, rather than old-fashioned British 'miles'. Personal and proper names are an obvious problem in a study which ranges so widely and across lands where there have been frequent subsequent changes of political geography. I have adopted a solution which is pragmatic rather than linguistically correct. An established English form is used where it exists or existed at the period covered by this study: thus 'Vienna' rather than 'Wien', and 'Danzig' rather than 'Gdansk'. Otherwise I have employed the version which is most familiar to historians, with the present-day name given in brackets on the first mention if this seems appropriate.

Introduction: Europe's emerging Great Power System

The treaties which underpinned the Final Coalition against Napoleon in 1813–14 and the peace settlement which followed at Vienna set out a novel role for what were styled the 'great powers'. The coalition's four leading members agreed in the treaty of Chaumont (February 1814) not merely to defeat Napoleonic France but also 'to obtain for themselves and for Europe a General Peace, under the protection of which the rights and liberties of all Nations may be established and secured'. Four months later the allies concluded a settlement in Paris with Louis XVIII, newly-restored to the French throne, which provided for all outstanding problems to be settled by an international congress. A secret article, however, laid down that the final decisions should remain firmly in their own hands. These seem to have been the first important occasions upon which rights and obligations of this kind were articulated. In the months and years which followed, the leading states shaped the general settlement reached at Vienna and then sought to uphold it by a series of great power meetings: the celebrated 'Congress System' of the decade after 1815.

The dominance of the great powers over the wider international system was assumed, while their right to supervise the actions of the smaller states and to determine the fate of the continent as a whole was asserted. Europe's five leading powers – Austria, Britain, Prussia and Russia who had combined to defeat Napoleon in 1813–14, together with France who was readmitted to the political élite after the restoration of the Bourbon monarchy – claimed and actually exercised an ascendancy over the other states which appeared novel and would endure for a century to come.[1] The political leadership of 'the powers of the first order', as they were styled by Viscount Castlereagh, Britain's foreign secretary, was accepted

[1] See the succeeding volume in this sequence: F.R. Bridge and Roger Bullen, *The Great Powers and the European States System 1814–1914* (2nd edn., London, 2004).

by all the continental states, whether tacitly or explicitly. With the tentative addition of the newly-unified Italy from the 1860s, this European great power system would survive down to the First World War (1914–18), when first the entry of the United States of America and Japan, and then the enhanced power and ambitions of Russia under its new Soviet régime, would establish a world system which, with important modifications, has endured until our own day.

Though the explicit emphasis on the role of the great powers in 1813–15 and immediately thereafter was unprecedented, the ideas which underpinned it were much more familiar. They had emerged over the previous two generations, during which the notion of a small élite of leading states exercising collective political dominance became established. This study aims to identify the elements in this crucial period in the evolution of the modern European international system, and to explain how it came about. Three interlocking developments provide its dominant themes. These would only become fully evident during the final stages of the wars of the French Revolution and of Napoleon (1792–1815), but had taken shape over the preceding decades and can be identified as: firstly, an expansion in the number of great powers and, as a corollary, the extension of their control over the wider states-system; secondly, the completion of Europe's diplomatic network, with the full incorporation of Russia (1760s–1780s), its tentative extension to include the Ottoman Empire in the 1790s and 1800s, and the reincorporation of France after the upheavals and warfare of the 1790s and 1800s; and finally the establishment of the term and concept of 'great power' and, more importantly, of the strengthened domestic régimes which underpinned this notion. Each had significant origins before 1739–40, examined in earlier volumes in this sequence. But the central premise of the present study, encapsulated in its title, is that the crucial changes were located in these decades.

In the first place, this period saw significant alterations in the status and political role of individual states. France, Europe's leading monarchy in 1739–40, declined sharply as a result of defeats in the Seven Years War (1756–63) (see Chapter 4) and the domestic problems which both accompanied and were intensified by this decline, and experienced a significant political eclipse during the next generation. Powerless on the continent, the French Bourbon monarchy could do only marginally more to weaken Britain's new-found leadership overseas (Chapter 8). Yet France's demographic and economic resources were enormous, while its relative strategic position was highly favourable. French power revived notably during the 1790s, under the contrasting régimes of the Revolutionary period

(Chapter 9), and from the end of that decade down to the close of the Napoleonic Wars it dominated Europe and shaped its politics in a novel way, in so doing contributing to the final establishment of a great power system (Chapters 10 and 11).

France was always potentially early modern Europe's strongest state, and her power stood permanently at the heart of its international system. Her decline after 1763 also contributed to the key political development of these decades: the emergence of what its most distinguished analyst, Paul W. Schroeder, has styled the 'flanking powers', Britain and Russia, who were in different ways to dominate the nineteenth century. Each enjoyed significant strategic advantages over its rivals and allies: Britain through her island situation, Russia by virtue of her inaccessibility to attack and her frontiers to the south and east which lay beyond the reach of her continental rivals. Britain's success, achieved by stripping first France and Spain, and then the other European states as well, of their colonial possessions and in this way acquiring raw materials, captive markets and commercial opportunities for her nascent industries, was achieved mainly through the deployment of her naval strength and the adoption of a strategy of insularity, even at times of outright isolation, from continental Europe. Only in the final stages of the Napoleonic Wars did Britain's military, financial and political commitment to the struggle against the French Leviathan assume significant proportions (Chapter 11).

Russia's rise was quite different in nature, resting as it did on massive territorial gains (Chapters 6, 7, 10 and 11) in eastern Europe and in the areas around the Black Sea, which moved her empire westwards and southwards. Yet territorial extent was not the same as political power. While the Russian empire's achievement was due to formidable military strength – its army was the largest in Europe until the novel mobilisation of the French Revolutionary régimes – it rested on a precarious infrastructure which at times proved unable to cope. That was also true, though to a lesser extent, of the two German great powers, whose rivalry after the 1740s facilitated Russia's drive westwards.

This period saw Austria's continuing political decline, evident before 1740. It was both relative and absolute: relative as Prussia and Russia challenged her traditional ascendancy, absolute in that the distinctive domestic structure of the Monarchy inhibited the mobilisation of enough of its relatively abundant resources to sustain a great power role. The notable reforms introduced by Joseph II during his hectic personal rule (1780–90) enabled more of this potential strength to be realised in the quarter-century of warfare after 1787. Yet Austria's great power position was always flawed by structural limitations upon the effectiveness with which resources could be directed to support her extended commitments. Prussia's enduring problem was exactly the reverse. Until the substantial territorial gains in 1815 greatly enhanced her political potential (Chapter 11), the Hohenzollern monarchy always lacked the demographic and economic resources to support the leading European position secured by Frederick the Great's dynamic policies during the first half of his long reign (1740–86) (Chapters 2 and 4) and by the formidable Prussian army, supported as it was by a relatively efficient administrative system. Throughout the period down to 1815, Prussia's troubled international trajectory frequently appeared to bear out the long-surviving French minister Talleyrand's celebrated aphorism that, while a great power in name, she was essentially a second-rank state in fact – an analysis which Frederick the Great himself appeared to share.

Talleyrand's remark highlighted one important characteristic of the emerging great power system: that international leadership rested not merely on resources and administrative, military and, where appropriate, naval power, but on the willingness of the established élite to treat a newcomer as one of their number, as Prussia and Russia were after the Seven Years War. Their political rise signalled one key development of this period (Chapter 6): the increase of the great powers from three to five, the number it would remain until Italy's incorporation a century later. It also underlined that the dominance of these states over the wider system was based upon cooperation as well as conflict, though the latter has conventionally attracted more attention.

That cooperation rested upon the second key theme which can be identified at the outset: the completion of a network of resident and reciprocal diplomacy which in its essentials would last to the present day. Here, there were crucial developments before the period examined in this study, with the origins of modern resident diplomacy in the Renaissance and the extension of reciprocal diplomatic representation across much of Europe during the long personal rule of France's Louis XIV (1661–1715) (see pp. 121–3). In important respects, however, the decades covered by this study were vital. Above all, the network of embassies was completed: this is why the beginnings of Ottoman involvement during the 1790s and 1800s and the full incorporation of Russia a generation earlier were so significant (Chapter 5). These developments advanced the establishment of a distinctive diplomatic culture throughout the whole of Europe. Paul W. Schroeder has made clear that what unified the international system at this time was the acceptance of norms of conduct: what Michael Oakeshott styled the 'constituent rules of a practice or a civic association – the understandings, assumptions, learned skills and responses, rules, norms, procedures, etc., which agents acquire and use in pursuing their individual divergent aims within the framework of a shared practice'.[2] It was facilitated by the eighteenth-century spread of this diplomatic culture, French, Francophone and aristocratic in tone, concessive and negotiatory in nature.

Some – though far from all – of the brutalities of power politics were mitigated by the actions of the diplomats and foreign ministers, who usually sought tactical, small-scale territorial gains rather than pursuing complete victory and large-scale annexations. Of course – and more importantly – this also reflected the indecisiveness of warfare during the *ancien régime*. It was why the new decisiveness of Revolutionary and Napoleonic warfare was such a fundamental challenge to established norms of international conduct (Chapters 9, 10 and 11). It also explains why the new approach to diplomacy adopted by French Revolutionary régimes (pp. 275–9) and, even more decisively, by Napoleonic France (pp. 302–5) was so alarming to the established powers. The Congress of Vienna was at one level a re-assertion of older modes of diplomatic conduct and political cooperation, as well as the beginning of a novel approach to international relations.

There was much more continuity in the final theme of this study: the establishment of the concept of a 'great power', a term which decisively established itself during this period (pp. 117–21). Central to this notion was the idea that the possession of human and material resources and, crucially, the ability to mobilise an ever-increasing proportion of these, were the foundations of international power. No attempt is made in this book to explain the domestic underpinnings of that political strength, since this would inflate it beyond acceptable proportions, and also because such discussion is readily accessible elsewhere.[3] But considerable attention is paid to financial strength, and military and naval power, since these were important determinants of international rivalry.

Between 1740 and 1815 more and more of Europe's resources were successfully mobilised to support and sustain international competition, culminating in the massive efforts made by both sides during the final phase of the Napoleonic Wars. It was made possible by the economic and

---

[2] Paul W. Schroeder, *The Transformation of European Politics 1763–1848* (Oxford, 1994), p. xii.

[3] See below, pp. 382–4, for a list of the major surveys of national history.

demographic expansion experienced by Europe, particularly from the 1730s, and by the ability of continental states to tap these reserves, which itself had been enhanced by administrative reforms before and during this period. The outbreak of the French Revolution in 1789 contributed indirectly to this increased extraction by both France and her enemies. The threat which first the revolutionary régimes and then the Napoleonic state represented to the old European order rested ultimately upon the novel capacity of these governments to mobilise men and, to a lesser extent, economic resources on a wholly new scale to support their foreign and military policies. Cultural capital decisively gave way to material wealth as the foundation of state power. It was also one further reason for the reduced role of smaller, much less well-endowed states in international relations, a trend facilitated much more importantly by the growing control exercised by the great powers over the whole system. In the 1740s medium-sized states such as Bavaria, Saxony and particularly Sardinia played a significant and independent role, but by the 1790s and 1800s (if not actually earlier) they were reduced in importance: they had themselves become the objects of the rivalries of the great powers, rather than active if minor participants in these struggles.

Civilian-minded international historians have sometimes underestimated and even ignored military factors, believing that these were minor influences upon international affairs. By contrast, this study gives considerable attention to military and naval warfare, persuaded that it was a catalyst for many of the wider political changes. The leading foreign minister of the age, the Austrian statesman Wenzel Anton von Kaunitz, put the point squarely to Maria Theresa in the final stages of the Seven Years War: 'No one would disagree [he wrote] that the mainstay of the [Habsburg] Monarchy, the security and prosperity of the land and loyal subjects, rests principally in the quality and strength of the military.' The great powers accepted war as a norm and employed it routinely, still convinced that it was more usual than peace. At least until the early 1790s it was universally seen as a rational instrument of state policy: in the words of a German officer at the very beginning of the period under study, 'What makes a monarch powerful and respected is a strong army that he maintains in peacetime and is thereby able to confront his enemies at any time.'

This period was dominated by two extended periods of general warfare, which shaped political rivalries: those of 1739/40–1763 (with fighting in North America but a precarious peace in Europe between 1748–56) and 1792–1815. Both of these were decisive conflicts, which contributed to the prolonged peace which followed and also imposed enduring burdens upon hard-pressed domestic régimes. The Seven Years War saw Britain's decisive victory over her French and Spanish rivals overseas, while within Europe – though no territory changed hands – the relative position of the leading states had been transformed (pp. 144–50). The Revolutionary and Napoleonic Wars were even more decisive, both for France who had manifestly been defeated and for the victorious great powers who were able to re-shape Europe's political geography in their own interest. The long period of peace after 1815 – exactly like that after 1763 – owed much to the mutual exhaustion of the belligerents and to a shared desire to promote domestic recovery.

The intervening decades (1763–92) saw only bilateral conflicts among the leading states, with the single and short-lived exception of the War of American Independence after 1778. Yet European rivalries were strongly influenced by the enduring legacies of the earlier fighting and especially the Seven Years War. The generation after 1763 saw significant attempts, in all the major states with the partial exception of France, to confront soaring deficits and to overhaul rickety domestic infrastructures which had been exposed as inadequate. These were accompanied by a wide-spread desire for peace, not yet seen as an end in itself, but as a necessary period of consolidation and preparation for inevitable future aggression. Warfare – and warfare on an increasing scale and, ultimately, of a wholly novel decisiveness – was central to the processes by which the European states of 1740 became the great powers of 1815.

CHAPTER 1

The European states in 1740

France

In the mid-eighteenth century France was clearly Europe's leading state. Though her dominance was less complete than during the later seventeenth century, it was still considerable. It rested upon her abundant demographic and economic resources, far superior to any other single country, together with the ability of the French monarchy to mobilise men, materials and cash from her large population, rich agriculture and buoyant commerce: the contemporary yardsticks for international power. Louis XIV had ruled over three times as many subjects as his Spanish or English counterparts, and while territorial expansion and political consolidation had allowed France's principal eighteenth-century rivals, Austria and Britain, to catch up, this had merely reduced the substantial French lead. At mid-century France's population was around 25 million; half a century later it had risen to almost 30 million. This was twice that of Austria and almost three times that of Britain. Only Russia, among Europe's leading powers, could rival France's demographic strength during these decades.

The French economy was also strong and vibrant, advancing impressively during the eighteenth century. The grain-growing plains of northern France were especially productive, and peasant agriculture prospered, reflecting the country's favourable climatic and geographical location. The commercial sector had also flourished, deliberately encouraged by state policy, particularly during the ascendancy of Jean-Baptiste Colbert, Louis XIV's celebrated economic and financial minister. Though the decades around 1700 had witnessed a significant economic decline, largely due to the warfare of the period, the return of peace after 1714 had been followed by renewed expansion. This had been especially striking along the western seaboard, which became the most dynamic sector in the economy. By the 1730s commerce was expanding so rapidly, encouraged by favourable government policies, that it appeared that France might soon overtake her British rival as a trading nation.

These abundant resources had made France early modern Europe's leading power. During the seventeenth century a strengthening of royal government had significantly increased the King's ability to raise revenues and soldiers, which were then used to enhance France's international position. Though the tax system had glaring faults, at least to later observers, it provided the ruler with far greater revenues than any other government enjoyed. It has been fashionable during recent decades to question the extent of Louis XIV's power and to highlight the real and undoubted limitations upon absolute monarchy. At the time, however, the French King's régime had been the envy of most European rulers, who copied his administration, fiscal system, army, palaces and style of monarchy. During the second half of his long reign, Louis XIV had been almost continuously at war, fighting powerful coalitions in the Nine Years War (1688/89–97) and War of the Spanish Succession (1701–13/14). France's survival against considerable odds testified to her intrinsic military and financial strength. During the 1690s the French had fielded around 300,000 men, and raised considerable sums through taxation and borrowing both during this war and its successor. This massive effort had significant and enduring consequences. During the generation after the Spanish Succession conflict, the fiscal and financial pressure had contributed significantly to France's pacific foreign policy. When Louis XIV died in 1715 the interest-bearing public debt was slightly over 1700 million *livres*. This figure was increased by a further 700 million *livres* by the disastrous failure of John Law's efforts in 1718–20 to introduce a paper currency, reduce the national debt and expand the credit market. By the 1730s, however, the economic expansion under way assisted in a financial recovery, and the national debt had been reduced.

These were among the key achievements of the long ministry of Cardinal Fleury (1726–43), which saw a notable resurgence of French power. The former tutor of the young Louis XV (1715–74), who had succeeded his great-grandfather at the age of five, Fleury achieved his position through his influence over the teenage king. He retained power through his own skill and the success of his policies. Though he never held the formal title, Fleury was the most politically long-lived and, probably, the most successful first minister of eighteenth-century France, dying in office in his ninetieth year. Subtle and determined, and ruthless when necessary, he followed fundamentally cautious and pacific policies: in many ways he resembled his English counterpart, Sir Robert Walpole (see below, p. 18). Fleury provided stable and effective government, while continuing a rapid and important build-up of the French navy begun in the early 1720s (essential after two decades of damaging neglect) and presiding over a noted commercial and financial recovery. He also restored the Bourbon monarchy's prestige within France and its diplomatic leadership of Europe.

For the two decades after the peace settlement of 1713–14, France had been eclipsed politically. Economic and demographic decline, partly caused by the extended wars of Louis XIV's final decades, together with their financial and fiscal legacies, had made peace and recovery essential. The problem of the French succession had been even more important. The extreme youth of Louis XV, born only in 1710, had made a Regency essential and this had lasted until 1723, while the risks to the young King and thus to the French succession posed by childhood illnesses were considerable. Only in 1729, with the birth of a first son to Louis and his Polish wife, Maria Leszczyńska, was the succession secured in the male line. These internal preoccupations had produced a muted and pacific French foreign policy during the later 1710s and 1720s, when Versailles acquiesced in and, partly, supported a period of British ascendancy.

During the 1730s, however, Cardinal Fleury had ended France's dangerous isolation and had regained the leading European position which French population and resources always justified. This was accomplished more through successful diplomacy, exemplified by French mediation of the Russo–Austrian War with the Ottoman Empire (see below, pp. 21, 23), rather than by military force, though the Cardinal was always prepared to fight when this was essential and involved few risks. France's recovery was largely accomplished by the so-called War of the Polish Succession (1733–38), in which she successfully attacked a weakened Austria. It was a conflict fought principally in the Rhineland and the Italian peninsula, far from the country which gave it its name: though the fighting did ensure that the Saxon ruler Augustus III (1733–63) succeeded his father on Poland's throne and in this way consolidated the Russian yoke (see below, p. 28). Fleury's main objective in this struggle was the duchy of Lorraine on France's north-eastern frontier. Its duke since 1729, Francis Stephen, was the intended husband of Charles VI's daughter, Maria Theresa, heir to the vast Habsburg inheritance. France was unwilling to see this border-duchy, a traditional focus of her anxieties, pass to a member of the ruling family of her Austrian adversary. Lorraine in enemy hands endangered France's eastern frontier and for this reason had been occupied on several occasions, most recently during the War of the Spanish Succession. Military and diplomatic pressure upon Vienna during the War of the Polish Succession forced Francis Stephen to renounce his homeland of Lorraine, receiving in exchange the Italian Grand Duchy of Tuscany, whose Medici dynasty had died out in 1737. He ruled this as a personal possession, and not as part of the sprawling Habsburg Monarchy, and never forgave France for evicting him from his beloved Lorraine. This passed to Stanislas Leszczyński, the father-in-law of Louis XV and also former King of Poland (1704–09); efforts to restore him to the Polish throne during the 1730s had been unsuccessful. Leszczyński's acquisition of a ruling dignity indirectly strengthened the position of his daughter, the Queen of France: earlier there had been suggestions that, as the child of a monarch without a throne, she was not a suitable bride for Louis XV. When Leszczyński died in 1766, the territory was integrated into the French monarchy.

Fleury's acquisition of the reversion upon Lorraine further strengthened France's eastern frontier and so completed the work of her diplomacy since the Peace of Westphalia in 1648. Seventeenth-century French foreign policy had been dominated by efforts to reduce her strategic vulnerability, with her Habsburg enemy encircling her territory and no defensible frontier. A series of annexations during the second half of the century had closed the 'gates' into French territory one by one. Foremost among these gains had been areas of Alsace (1648), Roussillon (1659), Franche-Comté (1679) and Strasbourg (1681), together with a series of small annexations from the Southern Netherlands (1668; 1679), then under Spanish rule. These had created more defensible frontiers, and their value had been enhanced when the master fortress-builder, Marshal Vauban, had fortified them. Louis XIV's annexations had been successfully defended in the wars of 1688–97 and 1701–14, which had demonstrated that France's strategic position was far stronger. Her frontiers had hardly been breached during the Spanish Succession conflict and would not be breached again before the French Revolution. Against that, however, eighteenth-century France faced far stronger obstacles beyond her own frontiers to any future expansion, for example, in the Southern Netherlands, now ruled by Austria but with Dutch garrisons in the so-called 'Barrier' fortresses, and in Milan, ruled directly from Vienna, than when these areas had been under Spanish sway. This compact territorial position, which contrasted sharply with that of some of her rivals, was a further source of France's international strength.

That power ultimately rested upon abundant demographic and economic resources, supported by a relatively efficient administrative system; her impressive army, much reduced in size since its seventeenth-century heyday, but still the continent's leading military force; and her traditions of political leadership, rooted as these were in the age of Louis XIV. In 1757 the Cardinal de Bernis, then France's foreign minister, would declare that her objective should be to 'play in Europe that superior role which suits her seniority, dignity and grandeur'. Such ideas would long be influential within France's military and diplomatic establishment, for whom she was primarily a continental military power whose principal enemy was Austria. This exemplified a wider point about the eighteenth-century states system. It was precedent-conscious and rooted in political traditions which were the product of past events and previous conflicts. Europe's leading states in 1740 and the relations between them were influenced in important ways by developments during previous decades. In the case of the French monarchy the dominant traditions were anti-Habsburg and therefore continental. During the quarter-century after 1740, however, such assumptions would be seriously challenged by the demands of a world-wide struggle with the rising British state.

Spain

France's international position had been strengthened by the accession of Louis XIV's younger grandson to the Spanish throne at the beginning of the eighteenth century, which removed the threat from the south, from across the Pyrenees. Philip V (1700–46) was Spain's first Bourbon king. He had established his hold over Spain itself during the War of the Spanish Succession, but at the end of this struggle his inheritance from the last Habsburg monarch was partitioned. Madrid lost almost all its haphazard and far-flung empire in Europe, which had been difficult to defend or administer, but retained the far larger possessions overseas. Though the Philippines were an outpost of Spanish commercial imperialism in the Far East, the extensive overseas empire was primarily located in the Caribbean and on the mainland of Central and South America, where only the vast Portuguese colony of Brazil and extensive unsettled areas in the interior were not under Spanish rule. On the North American continent, Florida was a Spanish outpost and the source of tension with the new British colony of Georgia during the 1730s. The economic potential of this vast empire was enormous, though it was never fully realised. Its size alone made the Spanish monarchy potentially a leading European state.

Madrid secured trade and, more importantly, income in the form of the royal share of the profits from gold and silver mining. During the first half of the eighteenth century, however, commerce with Spanish America grew only modestly, while the Crown's income from treasure was usually less than that enjoyed by the last Habsburg King. It was nonetheless significant for the monarchy and was to increase from the later 1740s. The overseas empire, however, imposed heavy costs upon its Bourbon ruler, principally for defence and government, and these mounted as British pressure grew. It proved more and more difficult to protect the theoretical monopoly of trade with the empire from interlopers.

At mid-century, metropolitan Spain contained some nine million inhabitants; by the 1790s this figure would rise to 11.5 million. Her agriculture was more backward and her trade less buoyant than that of her powerful Bourbon neighbour. Philip V's reign saw a series of reforming initiatives, largely on French models and sometimes implemented by French specialists. The cumbersome Councils through which Habsburg Spain had been governed, and the aristocrats who had dominated them, were eclipsed by a more streamlined central government of secretaries of state and a new administrative nobility. Regional autonomy was reduced, taxation was spread more evenly geographically, while the post of intendant was imported from France, where these administrators had been the loyal representatives of central government in the provinces. After initial failures, the system of intendants was successfully established in 1749. The armed forces were overhauled and, by the 1730s, an army of some 70,000 created, while a respectable navy was built up, principally during the ministry of the experienced and hardworking José Patiño (1726–36), who temporarily disguised the monarchy's fundamental financial weakness.

The new Bourbon administrative élite provided the impetus behind these policies despite monarchical weakness. Philip V was notably vacillating and ineffective. A victim of mental illness, he was also a slave to sexual and religious excess. For long periods he withdrew from government and refused to meet ministers. During the 1720s and 1730s the resulting vacuum was filled by his Italian second wife, Elisabeth Farnese. Patiño's dependence upon the Queen, to maintain himself in power, ensured that her dynastic ambitions were adopted by Madrid, thereby weakening Spain's foreign policy. Farnese believed that her two sons by Philip V, Charles and Philip, would not succeed to the Spanish throne, which would pass to the surviving son of the King's first marriage, the subsequent Ferdinand VI (1746–59). The Queen was determined to secure ruling titles and incomes for these two children, and looked to her native Italy to find these. During the 1730s Spanish troops fought there, as part of the War of the Polish Succession, and successfully conquered an appanage for her elder son, who became Charles VII (1738–59) of Naples and Sicily (subsequently the 'Kingdom of the Two Sicilies'). During the War of the Austrian Succession (1740–48) Madrid would devote considerable resources to securing an Italian principality for the younger son, Philip.

The renewed preoccupation with the Mediterranean could be, and was, justified in Madrid as an attempt to recover its traditional position in the Italian peninsula, lost at the end of the Spanish Succession War. Farnese's dynastic ambitions, however, ensured that Spain did not benefit from the surgery performed at Utrecht during the generation after 1713. Scarce financial and human resources were committed to Italy and not to the overseas empire, which was itself coming under British pressure. Despite the modest improvements brought about by its new élite, Bourbon Spain was a weakened and vulnerable power living uneasily on the substantial trophies of a glorious imperial past. This was at the heart of her fundamental dilemma in foreign policy. Alliance with Bourbon France and *rapprochement* with Hanoverian Britain each had their attractions and their advocates in Madrid, yet both had obvious drawbacks. During and immediately after the War of the Spanish Succession, the young Philip V had depended upon France's support and had in effect been a satellite. This had been widely resented, and a deliberate and successful attempt had been made by Madrid to assert its political independence.

Cooperation with Britain, by now Spain's principal colonial rival, had its attractions. The problem was that the British had conquered Gibraltar and the Mediterranean island of Minorca during the Succession struggle, and had retained them at the peace. Minorca was a particularly important naval base, and London appeared unwilling to return either, as Spain periodically demanded. Succeeding generations of British statesmen, from the Earl of Stanhope to William Pitt the Elder and even the Duke of Bedford were prepared to return either or both of these, provided they secured an appropriate gain in return, but were unable to obtain the price they wanted from Madrid. This was an enduring source of Anglo-Spanish tension and thus a factor promoting a Spanish alignment with France. That was also suggested by dynastic loyalty and by the need for support from the much stronger French monarchy in the colonial confrontation with Britain. Bourbon cooperation, evident in the First Family Compact signed in 1733, was more essential than ever when Spain and Britain went to war in 1739 (see below, pp. 39–44). Yet, throughout the eighteenth century, the undoubted special relationship between the two leading Bourbon monarchies did not exclude periods when Madrid exhibited considerable political independence from France. Spain was never again to be the political satellite she had been during the Succession conflict.

Britain

Britain was the pre-eminent opponent of the Bourbons. She had emerged as a major European state during the wars of 1688–1714, through her leadership of the coalitions against Louis XIV. Central to this was the succession of the Dutch Stadtholder William III to the British thrones after his successful invasion in 1688–89. Britain's enlarged European role at this period came from William III's fears of the threat of French hegemony and his determination to employ British resources to defeat this. This brought the 'British state' decisively onto the continental stage as a military power as well as a diplomatic and naval one, during two hard-fought wars which set limits to France's dominance. During this struggle, England, which ruled Wales and Ireland, concluded an incorporating union with Scotland in 1707, creating a 'British state' for the first time. It was to be another hundred years before a parliamentary union with Ireland was imposed in 1801. William III's aims were pursued, after his death in 1702, by the government of Queen Anne (1702–14), and largely accomplished in the settlement which ended the War of the Spanish Succession. The Peace of Utrecht provided that the thrones of France and Spain were never to be united in one person, and partitioned the Spanish monarchy, while creating more effective obstacles to French power in the Southern Netherlands and in north Italy. Britain gained Gibraltar and Minorca, and secured the slave contract, the *asiento*, together with the right to send an annual ship of 500 tons to the fair at Porto Bello on the Isthmus of Panama. The actual territorial gains made at Utrecht were relatively small, but colonial possessions were to be less important sources of Britain's dominance during the eighteenth century than trading stations, commercial concessions and naval might.

In other ways, too, the wars of 1688–1714 had been crucial for Britain's spectacular eighteenth-century emergence as a European and world power. During the 1690s she had acquired a modern financial system, as the need to fund William III's campaigns brought about nothing less than a financial revolution, which owed much to the example of the Dutch Republic. A National Debt (1693) and the Bank of England (1694) were created, and these were underwritten by the parliamentary and constitutional settlement which had followed the 1688–89 revolution. This established the cheap and reliable credit system which financed Britain's eighteenth-century wars, which was so widely admired on the continent and was one source of her commercial, industrial and political supremacy. Investors could put their funds in government loans, confident that these would be repaid since they were guaranteed by parliament, and both the merchant community and the landed interest invested heavily in government stock. Credit was important to Britain's war-effort during the eighteenth century. During the Spanish Succession conflict it had provided just over 30 per cent of expenditure, while by the American War this figure rose to 40 per cent. Yet taxation, more than borrowing, financed warfare at this period, as would become particularly clear during the wars of 1792–1815.

Here again, the 1690s had seen a crucial change. In 1692 the Land Tax, a direct charge on landed property, was introduced. During the wars of 1688–1714 it provided most revenue; thereafter its contribution was eclipsed by indirect taxation, in the form of customs dues and, in particular, the Excise. A dramatic expansion of the fiscal bureaucracy facilitated the collection of the revenue and provided the infrastructure of the British fiscal–military state. Even more unusual, however, was the willingness of the English landed classes to pay direct taxation to support the struggle with France, in sharp contrast to the French nobility's tenacious defence of its fiscal privileges. The Hanoverian aristocracy and gentry not merely paid the Land Tax; they helped to assess it and even to collect it, through their unpaid role in local government. It was one source of Britain's unrivalled financial power, which enabled allies to be subsidised, armies to be paid for and a powerful fighting navy to be created.

The long struggle with Louis XIV had also seen Britain's emergence as Europe's leading naval power, which she was to remain until 1815 and beyond. During the Spanish Succession War the British fleet had achieved complete mastery, and this dominance had been consolidated at Utrecht. The navies of France and Spain had been swept from the seas, while the Dutch fleet acted largely as Britain's junior partner. The Utrecht settlement also contributed to Britain's increased dominance of Europe's strategic coasts and islands, which allowed her to police the main trading routes, to dominate those to America and the East, and to dispatch ships to all the waters round the continent. In the south, Britain's command of the western Mediterranean was secured by the acquisition of Gibraltar and Minorca, the division of Spain's former Italian possessions between the non-naval powers of Austria and Sardinia,* together with the alliance

* The duchy of Savoy-Piedmont secured the royal title it had long craved through its possession of Sicily (1714–1720) and subsequently Sardinia (1720 onwards), by which name it is usually referred to in this book.

with Portugal. In northern Europe friendship with the Dutch Republic and with Denmark allowed access to the Baltic and contributed to eventual predominance there.

For almost two decades after Utrecht, Britain was the leading European state. Naval predominance was a significant element in this, as British fleets dealt with rivals and enforced London's policies in the Baltic and in the Mediterranean. Though the French and Spanish navies were rebuilt during the 1720s and 1730s, they possessed no more than a defensive capacity, while the neglect of the Russian fleet after Peter the Great's death in 1725, and its consequent decline, removed the main barrier to British dominance of the Baltic. Britain's ascendancy, however, was insecurely based. Her small population (between seven and eight million at mid-century, less than one-third that of France), lack of a sizeable standing army and important interests beyond Europe meant that she could never dominate the continent as Louis XIV had done. London was also obliged to devote attention to the threat from the Jacobites, as those who favoured a restoration of the House of Stuart were styled. By the 1730s, Jacobitism itself did not seriously challenge the Whig ascendancy, though Walpole chose to pretend otherwise. But it provided an obvious lever against Britain and, until mid-century, governments lacking a large standing army had to be alive to threats of foreign help for the Stuarts. Until the early 1730s, successive British ministries used their naval, financial and diplomatic muscle to exert more influence than any other state. Yet they only managed to do so because France, the strongest continental power, was passive and no other state was asserting itself effectively.

The wars of 1688–1714 had also created what became Britain's eighteenth-century foreign policy, that of opposition to France pursued through alliances with continental states – particularly the Dutch Republic and Austria – which were subsidised or given other financial help to put their own armies into the field. The substantial and direct military contribution against Louis XIV proved to be exceptional; British troops did not fight on the European mainland in substantial numbers again until the final phase of the struggle with Napoleonic France. In all other respects, however, William III's policies were continued by his eighteenth-century successors, with the single important exception of the quarter-century after the Utrecht settlement. Then, Whig doctrines of opposition to France pursued through alliances with continental powers were discarded by the Whigs themselves, in favour of friendship with a weakened France and dependence upon naval power and diplomacy for security: ideas which were associated with the Tory approach.

These doctrines were followed in spite of the accession of the Elector of Hanover to the British throne as George I (1714–27) upon Queen Anne's death. This finally assured the survival of the constitutional monarchy created after 1689, and made it difficult for Britain to ignore the continent, as many in parliament continued to urge. In the longer perspective, the Personal Union which linked Kingdom and Electorate until 1837 would strengthen Britain's involvement in European affairs, which had been growing since William III's accession a quarter-century before. British and Electoral ministers voiced the doctrine that King and Elector were different rulers, with separate governments and distinct priorities. But since the same man occupied both thrones, continental observers recognised it for the political fiction that it was. Europeans soon appreciated that the Hanoverian succession necessarily made British political and military strategy more 'continental' in focus, and Britain's own political élite largely accepted this. This integration was strengthened by the policies pursued by Hanoverian monarchs. Both George I and George II (1727–60) exploited their position in order to protect their Hanoverian homeland. But until the 1740s Britain did not adopt an actively anti-French policy. Internal and dynastic preoccupations created the *entente* (see below, pp. 37–8) and this only broke down after 1731. It was one important source of Britain's political leadership of Europe at this period.

During the 1730s, however, France's diplomatic recovery was partly facilitated by Britain's own passivity. The leading figure behind London's policy was Sir Robert Walpole, whose policies mirrored those of his French counterpart Fleury in his search for peace and prosperity, and for the stability which would enable the Hanoverian dynasty and the economy to flourish. This led him to remain neutral during the War of the Polish Succession after 1733. In that year, Walpole was involved in the most serious crisis of his long ministry over the Excise Bill and was also preparing for a general election in 1734. Against this background, any increase in the Land Tax was unthinkable. Walpole's personal influence was sufficient to prevent the King and the other ministers from taking the country into war. The costs, however, were considerable. The War of the Polish Succession facilitated France's re-emergence as Europe's leading power (see above, p. 10), and also contributed to a weakening of Austria, who resented British inaction. Walpole's success, moreover, was essentially short term. In the later 1730s there was a significant deterioration in relations with Spain, and this was to lead first to open war (see below, pp. 39–44) and then, three years later, to contribute to Walpole's own political demise.

The Dutch Republic

The second of the 'Maritime Powers', as the Anglo-Dutch alliance was styled at this time, was a waning force by 1740. During its seventeenth-century Golden Age, the Dutch Republic had been a major state, with a powerful navy and the strongest economy in Europe. But it had spent its power in the long struggle against Louis XIV's France, which had been led by William III, Dutch Stadtholder (1672–1702) and British King (1689–1702). Warfare had been near-continuous between 1672 and 1713, and this had forced the Republic to spend vast sums on an army as well as its navy. This necessitated heavy taxation and even heavier borrowing: by 1713 the public debt of Holland, the dominant province, stood at 310 million guilders (double what it had been a quarter-century before) and consumed over 70 per cent of tax revenue. By 1715 the Republic was virtually bankrupt. The War of the Spanish Succession was the last major conflict in which the Dutch played the role of a leading state, fielding an army over 100,000 strong and subsidising its allies. The peace of Utrecht proved to be a turning-point in the Republic's European position. The ruinous legacy of the struggle with France led to a precipitate reduction in the size of the army, which during the eighteenth century was maintained at a peacetime establishment of around 30,000, though this in itself did little to solve the basic financial problem. The navy's position was even worse, since for many years the provincial admiralties received no subsidies from the federal government and the fleet was allowed to decay. By 1719, and despite the considerable reductions in the military establishment, the dominant province of Holland faced an annual deficit of almost nine million guilders on its ordinary expenditures and revenues. Two decades of peace marginally reduced this debt, but it was again forced upwards by renewed military expenditure during the 1740s.

The Republic's financial predicament was the principal source of the cautious and soon explicitly neutralist foreign policy pursued during the eighteenth century. The decentralised and republican government which prevailed during the 'second Stadtholderless period' (1702–47) reinforced this outlook. The dominant merchant oligarchs wanted peace above all, so that trade could flourish and the Republic's financial position be restored. The Dutch had become a leading state during the previous century because of their commercial and manufacturing supremacy in European and world markets, together with the strength of their financial institutions. It soon became clear, however, that the economic basis of their power was being undermined, and this exacerbated the legacies of the wars against Louis

XIV. The 1720s and 1730s saw the beginning of a structural decline in the Republic's economic system which weakened its ability to cope with existing financial commitments.

This deterioration was partly relative: the Dutch were overtaken by the spectacular growth of the French, and especially the British, economies during the middle decades of the eighteenth century. But the Republic's decline was also absolute, as its primacy in world trade crumbled away. This had driven the remaining sectors of the economy, and its collapse from the 1720s onwards had wide-ranging repercussions. The fisheries and associated manufacturing declined sharply and the urban economy disintegrated. However, the picture was not one of unrelieved gloom. Commerce to the Baltic declined less sharply, and the Republic dominated Europe's carrying trade at least until the 1730s and, in some measure, far beyond. During the decade 1721–30, 42 per cent of ships passing through the Sound into the Baltic were still Dutch and only 20 per cent British. The import and re-export of items such as sugar, coffee, tobacco and tea from the Far East and the Americas actually expanded. But this was exceptional. By mid-century it was becoming clear that the Republic's economic power was failing, and with it the ability to play a European role.

This took some time to become apparent to its enemies, and especially its friends in London and Vienna, who continued to treat the Dutch as a leading state until the 1750s. It exemplified the way in which the eighteenth-century states system was slow to adjust to changes in relative power. The Republic was to be involved in the warfare of the 1740s, but thereafter it adopted a deliberately neutralist stance more in keeping with its new position as a second-rank state. Its adoption of a much-diminished international role was aided by the so-called 'Barrier' established in 1713–14, which consisted of fortresses in the Southern Netherlands, now ruled by Vienna – which were garrisoned by Dutch troops – and by periodic French assurances that it only aimed to neutralise this region. Both helped to reduce the Republic's anxieties about its vulnerability and the threat from France. The Barrier Treaty also made the Southern Nether-lands into an economic satellite of the Dutch and of their British ally.

Austria

The second element in Britain's anti-French alliance system was Austria, as the lands of the Habsburgs ruled from Vienna were coming to be known. During the half-century before 1740 Austrian power had risen impressively. Between the 1680s and 1720s Austria had freed herself from the twin Ottoman and French dangers, with the vital help of the Maritime Powers and the German princes together with the military genius of Prince Eugene of Savoy. Until the close of the seventeenth century, Vienna had been only 80 miles from territory controlled by the Ottoman Empire, whose armies besieged the city for the last time in 1683. Its relief in that autumn had provided the springboard for a decisive Habsburg counter-attack, which pushed Ottoman power back. These campaigns, in which Austria had come to be joined by Poland, Venice and, after 1695, Russia, were ended by the Peace of Carlowitz in 1699. The Ottoman Empire ceded vast tracts of territory: all of Hungary and Transylvania apart from the Banat of Temesvár (Timisoara) were now controlled by the Habsburgs. Austria had made further spectacular gains after a second successful war against the Ottoman Empire in 1716–18. This had been ended by the Peace of Passarowitz by which Vienna secured the Banat of Temesvár and northern Serbia with the key strategic city of Belgrade, which commanded the crossing of the Danube. These striking gains were reduced two decades later by Habsburg defeats in the Russo-Austrian War of 1735/37–39 against the Ottoman Empire, and many of the territories gained in 1718 were handed back in the Peace of Belgrade. The settlement at Carlowitz marked the effective limits of Austrian expansion in the Balkans until 1878, when Bosnia–Herzegovina was to be occupied.

The victories over the Ottomans during the 1680s and 1690s and the creation of a vast Danubian empire ruled from Vienna had raised Austria to the ranks of the leading states which would dominate Europe until World War I. She was coming to be recognised as a major power, an integral part of the emerging European states system. Britain and the Dutch Republic viewed her as a vital factor in anti-French coalitions, and their subsidies and loans had made possible Austria's participation in the wars of 1689–1714 against Louis XIV. The extinction of the Spanish line in 1700 had made the Austrian branch the guardian of Habsburg family interests, and it had benefitted substantially from the partition of the Spanish inheritance in 1713–14. Austria made striking gains in the Utrecht settlement, securing the Southern Netherlands, the crucial gain of Milan, which was ruled directly and conferred a strong position in northern Italy, together with the Spanish enclaves on the coast of Tuscany, and Naples and Sardinia (though these two possessions were subsequently lost). Vienna was now clearly dominant in the Italian Peninsula and – except between 1796 and 1814 – would remain so until the second half of the nineteenth century. Its position was further strengthened when Maria Theresa's husband Francis Stephen secured Tuscany with the status of

Grand Duke in exchange for Lorraine (see above, p. 11). This was governed directly and, on his death in 1765, became a Habsburg secundogeniture, being ruled by Maria Theresa's second son Leopold (1765–90) and his descendants. This second Italian satellite strengthened Austria's grip on the peninsula and particularly its northern half. Yet the anticipated wealth from the lands in Italy never materialised.

It was symptomatic of a wider problem. By the first half of the eighteenth century Austria had assumed the role she was to play over the next two centuries: that of the great balancing power between East and West, with interests in the Balkans as well as in Germany and Italy. Her territories sprawled through central Europe, where the Habsburgs ruled over the Austrian duchies (the heartlands of the dynasty's power which lay along the Danube), the so-called 'Lands of the Bohemian Crown' (Bohemia, Moravia, Silesia and Lusatia), and the Kingdom of Hungary together with Transylvania. The Utrecht settlement added the former Spanish territories of the Southern Netherlands, Milan and Naples, though these were difficult to administer and a tempting target for her enemies to attack: during the 1730s the Austrians were driven from Naples. The Austrian Netherlands (as they became after 1713–14) were to prove a heavy financial and military burden, as Vienna's main enemies became France and, after 1714, Bourbon Spain. The reconquest of Hungary had provided enhanced security: the kingdom now resumed its late medieval role as a buffer state protecting central Europe against Muslim power. Yet the Ottoman threat had been reduced, not removed. Throughout the middle decades of the eighteenth century, Vienna remained anxious about a further attack.

In the Holy Roman Empire (Reich) the Habsburgs filled the elective post of Emperor, which had been in practice hereditary in the family since the fifteenth century, although it was to be lost temporarily during the 1740s. The imperial dignity, however, by the eighteenth century conferred limited income, some real power and rather more prestige. The early modern period had seen some of the larger territorial rulers consolidate their own authority and, in so doing, reduce that of the Emperor: Bavaria and Saxony had both become more significant during the seventeenth century. While the Empire's legal institutions remained important, the authority of the Habsburgs within 'Germany' (very broadly the area over which the Empire extended) was much reduced. The Peace of Westphalia (1648) was a crucial point in this process and, during the following century, Vienna's position within the Empire had been further weakened. Several of the leading states, Hanover, Saxony and especially Brandenburg-Prussia (see below, pp. 48–50), had grown in political and military power,

and their rise was reinforced by their wider territorial and political con-
nections, together with the fact that all three now possessed their own
royal titles outside Germany, which made them believe themselves to be
almost equal in status with the Emperor. This advanced the crucial distinction between the Habsburgs as rulers of the Empire and as rulers of
their own dynastic possessions which was to be particularly important
during the eighteenth century.

Austria's fundamental problem was that she was a leading state in
terms of her territorial extent and her political commitments, but not in
terms of the resources available to defend these. No other power was
involved at so many points on the map of Europe, or faced so many
challenges to her position. Her striking territorial gains between 1699 and
1718 had led her rivals and enemies to exaggerate Habsburg power. In
fact it was already clear that Vienna's commitments were too extensive to
uphold alone. Austria could usually cope with the Ottoman Empire when
she had no other involvements, though the disastrous war of 1737–39
was an important exception. Any military conflict with a European power,
which during the first half of the eighteenth century normally meant France,
quickly made Austria dependent upon outside support. During the confrontations with Louis XIV and XV, successive Emperors had had to
rely heavily on military and financial support from one or both of the
Maritime Powers. The lack of such subsidies during the 1730s contributed
significantly to the military reverses during the War of the Polish Succession. The Habsburg Monarchy's weak financial and administrative structure flawed its position as a major power, though its tenacity in defending
dynastic and territorial interests and its resilience were to be impressive.

At Maria Theresa's accession in 1740, 'Austria' remained a dynastic
union of separate and diverse provinces with little in common except the
ruler and each with their own administrative structures, exactly as she
had been a hundred years before. By the end of the Thirty Years War
(1618–48) the independent political power of the great nobles and clerics
in the Austrian and Bohemian territories had been curtailed, though certainly not destroyed. During the next century the ability of successive
rulers to extract taxation and recruit troops was severely limited by the
enduring power of the territorial Estates, which frequently controlled and
collected taxation, and by Vienna's lack of effective central institutions
and administrators to challenge their dominance. The Habsburg Monarchy's infrastructure was ramshackle even by the standards of the age,
while its army was poorly organised and badly equipped. A significant
proportion of Austria's forces were still raised privately by old-style noble

military entrepreneurs and not by the government in Vienna. These colonel-proprietors exercised enormous power over their troops and ensured that, until the 1740s, the Habsburg army resembled a federation of regiments rather than a modern-style unified force. In other European states the seventeenth and eighteenth centuries saw a significant increase in the range and effectiveness of government authority, which facilitated the raising of men and money to wage war. No such evolution was evident before the mid-eighteenth century in the central European Habsburg territories, where the provinces and their wealth were almost completely controlled by the great ecclesiastical and secular landlords. The Monarchy's financial and therefore military weakness was starkly apparent during the 1730s in the unsuccessful wars with Bourbon France and Spain, and with the Ottoman Empire, and would again be evident after 1740.

These structural weaknesses meant that Austria's actual power did not reflect her territorial extent, which was greater than any European rival. Her eighteenth-century position as a great power was always to be fragile. Charles VI (1711–40) had failed to introduce the fundamental administrative and financial reforms which, it was recognised, were badly needed. This was because the last male Habsburg was instead preoccupied with the succession. By the early 1720s it was clear that his heirs would be his two surviving daughters. The novelty of a female succession made Charles increasingly concerned about the future of the Monarchy's far-flung territories, and so he persuaded the Estates in most of his possessions to agree that his own daughters should take precedence over those of his elder brother, the Emperor Joseph I (1705–11). This had been laid down in the so-called Pragmatic Sanction, which created an entail out of the far-flung Habsburg inheritance. During the 1720s and 1730s Charles VI sought wide-ranging international guarantees, at the cost of significant political concessions. The succession of Maria Theresa posed two further problems: whom would she marry and who would become Emperor, a dignity to which a woman could not be elected? Both were apparently solved by her marriage to Francis Stephen (see above, p. 10). The fragility of these dynastic arrangements – which mirrored Austria's financial and administrative shortcomings – would become evident when Charles VI died unexpectedly in late autumn 1740.

Russia

Russia was clearly the dominant state in northern and eastern Europe in 1740. Her rise, and the spectacular territorial expansion at the expense of the Ottoman Empire and then Poland which accompanied it, was the central political development of the eighteenth century. It was not a linear process. Periods of success and expansion were interspersed with spells of disengagement from European politics: only under Catherine II (1762–96) did her emergence as a European power become irreversible.

The decisive step had been Peter the Great's decision to become part of the anti-Swedish coalition in 1700. Until his reign (1682/96–1725) Russia had been largely isolated. During the sixteenth and seventeenth centuries European observers had considered Muscovy (as she had then been known) only slightly less barbarous than the Ottoman Empire. The lure of international commerce had produced intermittent and temporary western diplomatic missions there, but permanent and reciprocal representation had not been established. Sweden and Poland, at that period major states, lay along Muscovy's western frontier and had both prevented contacts with western Europe and blocked expansion. To the south, in a similar way, the Ottoman Empire and its Tartar vassals blocked the path to the Black Sea. Seventeenth-century Muscovy's one port had been Archangel, on the White Sea far to the north and open only briefly during the summer. Yet the products of Russia's forests and plains were in considerable demand in western Europe, especially the much-prized naval stores.

Russia's eighteenth-century rise may have been inevitable, given her abundant population (some 18 million by the 1740s) and strategic invulnerability. Yet it came about when it did because of her impressive military victories over Sweden in the Great Northern War (1700–21). During the first decade of this struggle the Russian army was rebuilt impressively and an important series of administrative reforms introduced. These were shaped by military requirements, and succeeded in releasing more of Russia's vast reserves. With the help of foreign experts, Peter worked feverishly to reform his army, built a Baltic navy for the first time (his one real innovation), and then restructured his central administration on Swedish lines. The cavalry was increased in size and effectiveness, new garrison and line regiments were created, and the artillery was renewed. Above all, a unified territorial recruitment system was consolidated, in place of the haphazard mixture of peasant conscripts and volunteers who had previously filled the ranks. Though these arrangements were imperfect, they proved enduring and were to be the basis of Russian military and naval recruitment until the second half of the nineteenth century. It was a relatively efficient way of creating and reinforcing a powerful army from a country with a backward economy and a large population. The strength of this peasant army, in spite of shortcomings in the high command and particularly in logistics, was the basis of Russia's emergence as a European power.

That military potential had been first revealed to contemporaries during the Great Northern War. In 1709 Peter and his rebuilt army had defeated Sweden's Charles XII at Poltava, probably the most decisive battle of the entire eighteenth century. It ensured that Russia would win the Great Northern War, established a dominant position for her on the Baltic and its eastern shores and reduced Poland–Lithuania to the status of a Russian client. The peace of Nystad (1721) brought massive territorial gains around the Gulf of Finland at Sweden's expense: Livonia, Estonia, Ingria, Kexholm and part of Karelia. The acquisition of the Baltic provinces restored direct access to the sea, lost a hundred years before, and did something to facilitate trade with western Europe. These new priorities had been highlighted by the building of a new capital, St Petersburg, in the Neva estuary with access to the Gulf of Finland. The fighting had a second major consequence: it made Poland a Russian satellite. When the anti-Swedish coalition had originally been formed, the Polish King Augustus II (1697–1733), also the Elector of Saxony, not Peter the Great, had been its leading figure. Charles XII's initial successes, however, had led to Augustus's deposition and the election of Stanislas Leszczyński as King. After Poltava, Augustus had been restored to his Polish throne by Russia, who now dominated her western neighbour, which had been almost as much a victim of the fighting as Sweden. The Russian Emperor was the *de facto* guarantor of a constitutional settlement in 1716 between Augustus II, who was both a Russian puppet and an elective monarch, and the numerous nobility, which contained one or two very powerful families. Peter's reign established an invisible empire in Poland, and this would survive until the kingdom was partitioned out of existence during the 1790s.

The Great Northern War had also seen Russia's rapid emergence from diplomatic isolation. Peter's search for allies and for European technology led to closer links with the west, while his victories gave Russia a new-found importance in European eyes. He rapidly created a western-style diplomatic service and established embassies throughout Europe. By 1725 there were no fewer than 21 permanent Russian missions (including consulates) abroad, though this number was to decline slightly during the eighteenth century. The dramatic expansion of Russian diplomacy far outstripped the supply of noblemen with the knowledge of Europe's languages, history and political culture required to fill these embassies, and a shortage of trained personnel long hindered the country's full incorporation into the diplomatic network. Yet the decisive break had been made with the isolated and xenophobic Muscovite past. Russia henceforth maintained substantial and permanent links with other European courts, despite enduring problems over language and ceremonial.

This participation, however, was a different thing from full membership of the international system. Peter's victories had made Europeans aware of Russia's power, but he had not secured admission to the ranks of the continent's leading states. That would take another generation and would only be achieved during the Seven Years War of 1756–63 (see below, pp. 147–8). This was due both to developments within Russia, and to the slowness of other European nations to recognise the new force in the north. With the single exception of the Baltic fleet, his policies were continued by his successors. The army, the real agent of Russia's emergence, was maintained and even expanded, while the new administrative institutions were also continued. To a surprising extent, Peter's achievement had been a personal one, and he had been assisted by only a handful of trusted collaborators. The dangers of such a narrowly-based régime became clear after his death. His successors were far less able, and resistance to his reforms re-emerged, while the limitations in the effective range of government were increasingly evident. Russia was an enormous and thinly-populated country, and beyond its European provinces distances were vast and administrators few. Its remarkable seventeenth-century expansion meant that Russian territory sprawled across much of the Asian continent and bordered China. The huge *guberniya* ('government') of Kazan, for example, contained some 2.5 million people, but in the early 1770s it was ruled over by a mere 80 officials. In these circumstances, it is scarcely surprising that the authority of central government was remote and frequently ineffective. The men who controlled Russia's foreign policy after 1725 at first lacked Peter's wide-ranging European vision. This was certainly true of A.I. Ostermann, the leading minister of the Empress Anna (1730–40), who aimed primarily to consolidate and extend Russia's influence among her immediate neighbours.

In 1740 Russia's role in the states-system remained ambiguous. During the 1720s and 1730s only Prussia and Austria, her neighbours in the eastern half of the continent, were really willing to accept her as a full member of the international order. The two leading western powers, France and Britain, were determined to shut her out of Europe. Indeed, during the first half of the eighteenth century, the French *barrière de l'est* ('eastern barrier'), originally a network of alliances with Sweden, Poland and the Ottoman Empire directed against Austria, was turned against Russia, Vienna's ally for a generation after 1726. During the middle decades of the eighteenth century, no leading state would ally with Russia on terms of equality or conclude dynastic marriages with her: two of the litmus tests of full membership of the international system. During the decades after 1725 it became clear that Peter's achievement had been to make his country dominant in northern and north-eastern Europe. He had not pushed Russian influence very far into central Europe, while he had been far less successful in the south, suffering a severe setback at the hands of the Ottoman Empire on the Pruth in 1711. It would be half a century after his death before Russia became a leading European power.

Poland

One source of Russia's political advance was the control exercised since the early eighteenth century over her western neighbour Poland (strictly speaking the 'Polish Lithuanian Commonwealth'). The Kingdom of Poland was an invaluable buffer state which protected a long stretch of Russia's exposed frontier from direct attack, yet enabled her own troops to move westwards with ease: it was the glacis which St Petersburg craved. Eighteenth-century Poland was a large territorial area, bigger even than France though lacking defensible frontiers, with a population at mid-century approaching 12 million. Throughout much of the early modern period Poland had been the region's leading state, with a particularly powerful army, and had been in the forefront of the earlier struggle with the Ottoman Empire. In the sixteenth century, the monarchy had become elective, while the power of the numerous nobility and especially the leading families increased. Two centuries later Poland's archaic constitution, symbolised by the celebrated *liberum veto*, which theoretically enabled any member of the Diet to overturn an entire session's legislation, weak monarchy and powerful magnate class had made it an arena for great power rivalry. Her increasingly powerful neighbours were beginning to support one or more of the noble factions, intervening in exactly the same way as in eighteenth-century Sweden (see below, pp. 30–1) to secure their own ends.

Since 1697 Poland had been ruled by the Wettins, the Electoral House of Saxony, first Augustus II (1697–1733) and then his son Augustus III (1733–63), whose election had been secured by Russian and Austrian soldiers, confirming the country's satellite status. Augustus II had dreamed of creating a new power in central Europe and tried to establish a viable union, rather than merely a dynastic connection. His aim had been a consolidated and integrated Saxon–Polish Kingdom, ruled by the Wettins as hereditary absolute monarchs, but he had been forced to abandon his schemes due to opposition from Russia and, to a lesser extent, resistance from his Polish subjects. His son instead aimed to exploit the Kingdom in the interests of the Electorate. Poland was a convenient source of revenue for Saxony (whose public finances were in disarray) and also provided the prestige of a Wettin royal title. Augustus III ruled from Dresden, spending no more than two out of the first twenty years of his reign actually on Polish soil. This exploitation coupled with neglect contributed to Poland's political decay. Its army had been limited to a paper strength of 24,000 in 1717, to facilitate St Petersburg's control, and by the 1760s would be around half that number. Mid-eighteenth-century Poland's military weakness symbolised her diminished status and evident vulnerability, surrounded by increasingly aggressive neighbours. Her struggle to survive provides a central theme in the chapters which follow.

The Scandinavian states

Sweden's losses to Russia in 1721 had signalled that she had become a second-class state, of Baltic rather than European significance. During the seventeenth century, the Swedish monarchy had acquired an extensive and widely-scattered trans-Baltic empire through successful military imperialism. This had been achieved in spite of a shortage of demographic and economic resources, and her success had owed much to the weakness of her rivals at that period. The Great Northern War had ruthlessly exposed the exiguous resources available to defend Sweden's overseas territories, and defeat had been accompanied by substantial demographic losses and severe economic decline. In the peace settlements of 1720–21, she was effectively expelled from Germany, retaining only Wismar and part of western Pomerania including the important port of Stralsund as mementoes of her faded imperial past. All her other conquests had been ceded, though Stockholm continued to rule over most of Finland. The loss of Sweden's possessions on the European mainland made direct intervention there difficult. Yet Stockholm only slowly renounced her European pretensions – in contrast to the situation in Denmark (see below, p. 31) and continued to mount occasional expeditions to recover former imperial territories: two against Russia, in 1741 and 1788, and one against Prussia in the Seven Years War.

These *revanchiste* ambitions epitomised Sweden's occasionally painful adjustment to the status of minor power. The Great Northern War had imposed considerable and enduring burdens. Sweden's population had declined by 10 per cent, that of Finland – where no direct taxation was collected for six years – by as much as 16 per cent. Trade was at a low ebb, the country prostrate and the state bankrupt: the loss of the Baltic empire halved annual income. Recovery was soon under way, but it took time to accomplish. By mid-century Sweden–Finland had a combined population of 2.3 million, while trade had also picked up. The problem of the state finances, however, was never really solved and this condemned eighteenth-century Sweden to impotence. The funds needed to build up the army and navy could not be raised from the country's own resources. The solution was familiar from earlier Swedish history: that of seeking foreign subsidies and using them to strengthen the armed forces. Stockholm was receiving subsidies for some two-thirds of the period 1721–72, with a resulting loss of political independence. This arrangement worked well for a time, but was weakened by the renewed Anglo-French rivalry from the 1730s.

The Great Northern War had discredited the absolutism established by Charles XI after 1680. The death of the warrior-king Charles XII (1697–1718) without an heir of his own body had facilitated a constitutional revolution and once again made the Swedish monarchy elective. The Constitution of 1720 limited the powers of the Crown and gave effective authority to the noble-dominated council (*råd*), the Estates (*riksdag*) and, increasingly, the powerful bureaucracy, which together ruled during the 'Age of Liberty' (1719–72). From the 1730s, the political equation was further complicated by the serious party conflict between the Hats and the Caps. Before long, foreign powers were subsidising one or other side in an attempt to control the country and its foreign policy. The Hats, who were to be the dominant alignment from the 1730s until the early 1760s, favoured a policy of revenge upon Russia and the recovery of some of the lands lost in 1721, and were therefore supported by France. Their political opponents the Caps were to be backed by Russia and, for a time, Britain.

The psychological adjustment for the political élite was most difficult of all. Almost overnight, Sweden had gone from being a leading European and the dominant Baltic state, to a second-rank power at best, one which was at the mercy of Russia and even Denmark, her traditional rival on the other side of the Sound. In these circumstances it is not surprising that there was considerable nostalgia for past imperial splendours and, periodically, attempts to recover some of the vanished territories and lost glory. The wars of 1741–43, 1757–62 and 1788–90 were all expensive gambles which ignored political and financial realities and ended in humiliating failure. Unlike Poland, Sweden did not dissolve completely into internal chaos and suffered only minor territorial losses until the Napoleonic Wars. Yet she shared Poland's fate of repeated and increasing foreign intervention in her domestic politics. This strengthened the loss of political independence which was to be the leading characteristic of the Age of Liberty.

By contrast, Denmark adjusted very successfully to her diminished status. The Danish kingdom comprised Norway, Iceland, Greenland, the Faroe Islands and the duchy of Schleswig (occupied during the Great Northern War, though international recognition had not been secured) in addition to Denmark, and contained around 700,000 inhabitants at mid-century, one-third the population of its Swedish rival. The peace settlement which ended the Great Northern War had marked Copenhagen's abandonment of any idea of recovering the territories earlier ceded to Sweden in 1645 and 1658 and so regaining a foothold on the Swedish mainland across the Sound. During the eighteenth century Denmark renounced all notion of territorial gains (with the single exception of the strategically-crucial area of Holstein: see below, p. 153) and instead aimed merely to defend and retain her existing possessions. Copenhagen adopted neutrality and sought the accompanying economic benefits through a policy which aimed to encourage the development of trade and shipping.

Denmark was a relatively poor country, and such income was therefore more important. It came from two principal sources. The first was the celebrated Sound Dues, levied on all commercial shipping passing through the narrow channel which led into the Baltic. With the eighteenth-century expansion of population and economic activity, this traffic and the resulting profits which went directly to the Danish monarch, both increased sharply. At the very end of the century, almost 8 per cent of the Crown's total revenues came from the Sound Dues. Between 1730 and 1800 the number of ships passing annually through the Sound more than doubled, from some 4,000 to 10,000, and their average tonnage increased by almost a half. The second source of this prosperity was participation in Europe's carrying trade, which also expanded significantly during the eighteenth century. Denmark's share was considerable – as much as one-fifth during the 1720s and 1730s – and would rise during wartime, especially if the Dutch Republic, which continued to dominate this commerce, were involved in the fighting, as it was after 1780 and again after 1795. Copenhagen therefore remained neutral in every war before the Napoleonic era, upheld the principles of neutral commerce and prospered.

This did not mean that security was neglected: on the contrary, self-defence took priority over economic opportunity. Denmark's statesmen long remembered that Charles XII had died besieging a Norwegian fortress. They understood that Norway was the most obvious target for Swedish statesmen seeking territorial compensation, and feared further aggression, particularly after Gustav III's *coup* in 1772 restored the Swedish Crown's authority. Copenhagen was also anxious about the complex and potentially dangerous problems posed by Schleswig and Holstein which lay on its southern frontier. This concern increased sharply from the early 1740s, and would eventually lead Denmark into alliance with – and dependence upon – the Baltic's dominant power, Russia (see below, pp. 154–5). Yet neutrality served Copenhagen well. A respectable fleet provided defence in home waters against any Swedish threat. For the first three-quarters of the eighteenth century, Denmark was the Baltic's strongest naval power, though manning the ships remained a problem. The army was far weaker, and land defence to the south periodically caused serious anxieties. Yet Denmark adjusted more successfully than any other country to the situation facing all minor states within an international system in which the leading powers were more and more dominant.

The Ottoman Empire

In 1740 the Ottoman Empire played an important role in continental politics, but it was outside the network of reciprocal diplomacy and on the fringes of the states-system. It had secured a major success in the previous year when the Peace of Belgrade, which concluded its war with Austria and Russia, restored most of the territory lost to the Habsburgs in the settlement at Passarowitz two decades before. This included the prize acquisition of the city of Belgrade itself, which controlled passage across the Danube and thus the invasion route to central Europe. The war had seen a notable Ottoman recovery: its army in particular had performed creditably. Yet the successful campaign against the Austrians in 1738–39 was to prove the last the Ottoman army would win against European forces without an ally. The balance of military advantage was swinging in favour of the Christian powers. Although there were to be occasional significant periods of recovery throughout the eighteenth and well into the nineteenth centuries, a new pattern in relations between the Ottoman Empire and its European neighbours was becoming established.

During the fifteenth and sixteenth centuries Ottoman power had first waxed impressively and then stabilised. Uniquely successful military imperialism had created a vast and far-flung territorial empire. The Ottomans – like their Austrian and Russian adversaries – were involved at many points on the map: against Poland and Russia to the north of the Black Sea, against Persia (Iran) in the east, and in the Indian Ocean as well as in Arabia and North Africa. During the seventeenth century this sprawling empire had come under mounting pressure, and at its close had suffered the first serious territorial losses to its European neighbours. With hindsight it is clear that the Peace of Carlowitz of 1699 (see above, p. 21) marked merely the beginning of the long retreat of Ottoman power which lasted until the early twentieth century. It was also viewed in Constantinople as a decisive point: significantly it is with the Carlowitz settlement that the empire began to keep a record of its international commitments to European states. Whether this retreat amounted to the decline of the Ottoman Empire is less clear: its resilience was impressive and its capacity for recovery was to be evident periodically. Yet a change was apparent in the relationship between the Sultan and his Christian neighbours during the eighteenth century. Europe, which had been on the defensive for more than two centuries, was beginning to force the Ottoman Empire back. The collapse of the Sultan's own authority, accompanied by fiscal and military decline, and the resulting political vacuum in the Balkans, were to form the basis of the 'Eastern Question' of the nineteenth century.

Two developments underlined the adjustment in relations between Constantinople and the European states. The Peace of Carlowitz had been the first settlement which had been negotiated by a member of the Ottoman chancery and not by the military commanders. During the early decades of the eighteenth century the European states began to treat the *Reis Efendi* (sometimes known as the *Reis ül-Küttâb*, literally, 'Chief of the Clerks', a leading chancery official) as the Empire's foreign minister, and this necessarily increased his responsibility for Ottoman diplomacy. More importantly, the territorial cessions made at Carlowitz themselves called in question the basic tenets of the Empire. Until the close of the seventeenth century relations with the infidel states of Europe had been viewed solely through a traditional Islamic pattern of thought which assumed a unified Muslim polity, the *Dar al-Islam* ('abode of Islam') in a state of continuous conflict – the *jihad* or holy war – with the infidel, the *Dar al-Harb* ('abode of war'). Carlowitz, with its assumptions of European equality, indicated that the zenith of Ottoman territorial expansion had been passed and highlighted the political advantages to Constantinople through establishing diplomatic relations with the leading continental states. As the reverses mounted up, the survival of the Ottoman Empire came to depend upon the rivalries apparent within the European states-system.

Though permanent representation of the continent's leading countries at the Porte (as European diplomacy styled the Ottoman Empire) had begun during the sixteenth century, this had been completely one-sided, as the Sultan did not send missions of his own. These would have been incompatible with the basic Islamic assumption that there was a permanent state of war with the infidels, in which only brief truces for tactical purposes were permitted. The Ottoman Empire had benefitted indirectly from this non-reciprocal diplomacy. It ensured that any negotiations would take place in Constantinople, close to the heart of Ottoman government, and would be conducted in Turkish not by European diplomats but by the dragomans (interpreters) who remained the Sultan's subjects and were thus not completely free from his control. These tactical advantages were a by-product of the Ottoman Empire's refusal to acknowledge the equality of its European adversaries, and not a deliberate strategy.

During the eighteenth century both the theory and the practice of Ottoman relations with Europe changed because of repeated military defeats and growing Russian pressure. Increasingly, Muslim jurists elaborated interpretations of Islamic law which took account of the new political and military realities and so permitted extended truces with the infidel, which the Carlowitz settlement was recognised to be. They also developed the notion of safe conducts which were essential if formal and more regular diplomatic relations were to be established. Diplomatic immunity – one of the essential foundations of permanent relations – had never been established in Constantinople, where foreign representatives were usually imprisoned in the Castle of the Seven Towers when war broke out, a practice which was only finally abandoned in the nineteenth century: as late as 1798 the French representative was incarcerated on the outbreak of hostilities. Foreign diplomats were viewed as hostages for their monarchs' good behaviour, not privileged representatives whose persons and property were guaranteed and therefore protected by the host government. The eighteenth century saw significant modification of this strict attitude, brought about by the capitulations issued to permit Europeans to trade, which began to incorporate western formulas concerning the rights of consuls. This undermined strict Islamic theory, and made possible the sending of the first permanent Ottoman embassies during its final decade (see below, pp. 126–8) and the early stages of the Empire's incorporation into Europe's network of reciprocal diplomacy. A second development at this period also prepared the way for the dramatic changes during the 1790s. This was the significant increase in the number of temporary Ottoman embassies sent to European capitals: at least 26 were despatched during the eighteenth century, usually with a very specific purpose such as the conclusion of a treaty of friendship.

The century after Carlowitz saw the Ottoman Empire realign itself. From being the permanent and bitter enemy of Christendom it gradually moved towards becoming an accepted member of the European states-system. Too much should not be made of this more peaceable trajectory, however. Contemporaries, in an age when religious belief remained the basis of life, continued to view the Ottoman Empire as an Islamic predator and to fear its armies, still capable of occasional impressive victories. The traditional fear and hatred were only slowly removed. The Sultan's diplomats were exotic outsiders in the capitals to which they travelled, more gawped at than accepted, while the religious, linguistic and cultural barriers remained huge. At most they were to be marginally lowered during the eighteenth century, and even this may have been less evident to contemporaries than it has been to later historians. Ottoman gains in the Peace of Belgrade, and the military recovery which brought these about, suggested that the Empire remained a threat to Europe. The 1739 settlement was important in one final respect. It opened three decades of peace on the Ottoman western border – the longest unbroken period without warfare in the entire history of the Empire – during which successive sultans employed diplomacy rather than military force and explored a new dispensation in their relations with Europe. Indirectly this was to be of considerable importance since, during the decisive mid-century wars, neither Austria nor Russia was to be diverted by its traditional rivalry with the Sultan.

The States-System in 1740

Though important in European politics, the Ottoman Empire would not become a full member either of the international system or of the diplomatic network before the nineteenth century. While the network of resident embassies and the states-system overlapped significantly, they were not identical. Indeed, until the final years of the Napoleonic era, there was no single international system covering all of Europe. There were three separate 'systems', as contemporaries styled the zones of interaction between the leading states. These were geographically distinct, though to some degree overlapping. Two of these were regional in nature. The first extended across northern and eastern Europe and was focussed upon the Baltic.

There Russia was clearly the leading power, having gained the upper hand over Denmark, Sweden, Poland and the north German states, above all Brandenburg–Prussia. The second lay on Europe's remote south-east fringe, extending from the Balkans to the northern shores of the Black Sea, where the rising powers of Russia and Austria confronted the Ottoman Empire. The third and most important system comprised the rest of Europe, to the west of the Carpathian mountains and the river Oder. During the second half of the seventeenth century, France had become predominant within this system. From the 1690s, however, three states had emerged to rival French power: Austria, Britain and, temporarily, the Dutch Republic. The latter's decline during the half century after Utrecht removed it from the ranks of the leading powers, though simultaneously Russia had begun to emerge. The dominant system in western, southern and central Europe largely determined international rivalries.

These three systems were never entirely separate, and during the eighteenth century the degree of interaction increased as events within one area influenced the other two. Certain states were always involved in more than one region: Austria was part of the main system and also integral to the rivalries of south-eastern Europe against the Ottoman Empire, as was Russia who was also involved around the Baltic, where Britain too was concerned. Despite these overlaps, however, the three systems remained largely distinct in 1740. This separation had been evident in the early eighteenth century when there had been very little contact between the Great Northern War and the contemporaneous conflict over the Spanish Succession. As the century progressed, the barriers between these three political zones gradually broke down and a truly European states-system finally emerged under the pressure of the struggle against the French Revolution and Napoleon.

The generation before 1740 had seen one further change in the nature of international relations. During the first half of the eighteenth century, a more fluid states-system was coming into existence, with several leading states which appeared to be almost equally matched, in contrast to the earlier dominance of first Spanish and then French power within the main system. This process was assisted by France's passivity and internal preoccupations during the two decades after 1713–14 (above, pp. 9–10). During the next half century, Russia's full emergence and Prussia's sudden breakthrough during the generation of warfare after 1740 (covered in Chapters 2–4) did two related things. They turned a three-power system (France, Austria and Britain) into a five-power one, the forerunner of the Pentarchy which would dominate international relations during the nineteenth century. Secondly, the fact that Russia and Prussia were located in northern and eastern Europe extended the states-system's geographical extent, gradually incorporating areas which had hitherto lain on its periphery and so slowly integrating the two minor regional systems. It was an extended process, prolonged by the extent to which Anglo-Bourbon rivalry during and after the Seven Years War came to be focussed overseas, and not completed until the early nineteenth century.

The two decades after 1713–14 had been generally a period of peace among the leading states of western and central Europe, with fighting largely confined to the northern and south-eastern fringes. Britain, France and Austria had acted conservatively and, on the whole, attempted to settle their differences by negotiation. Crucially, all three had been pre-occupied with their own domestic problems. The heavy indebtedness everywhere, a legacy of the Spanish Succession conflict, made each government anxious for peace to facilitate recovery. Half-a-century later, exactly the same factors would promote a general desire for retrenchment and the avoidance of further fighting after the Seven Years War (see below, pp. 144–50), as it would again after 1815. A century earlier there had been an additional factor promoting the search for peace. This was the fear, common to France, Britain and Austria after 1713–14, about the future of the succession to their thrones. Britain's first Hanoverian king sought to strengthen his own régime, which was far from popular, and was openly challenged by a Jacobite rising in 1715 and by periodic conspiracies thereafter, while Charles VI wrestled with the problems of a female heir to the Habsburg inheritance. Dynastic insecurity was most acute in France where, until 1729, the future of the Bourbon line hung on the frail shoulders of Louis XV. The weakness and insecurity felt in what was potentially the strongest and most dangerous of the states did much to preserve peace.

It was also one origin of an important *rapprochement* with France's major enemy in the wars of 1689–1714, Britain, where the new Hanoverian dynasty had similar priorities. The Anglo-French *entente* (1716–31) lasted for 15 years and was as remarkable as the subsequent Diplomatic Revolution of 1756 (see below, pp. 81–92). It was the principal exception to the general pattern of rivalry, hostility and periodic warfare between the two states which prevailed from 1689 until 1815 and beyond. The *entente* was always precarious: it was never popular in either country, which remained rivals. Many French ministers, diplomats and soldiers, particularly those who had served Louis XIV, felt that it betrayed France's true interests and only benefitted the Regent Orléans and his British ally. The political élites of both states included men who had grown to maturity during the fighting between 1689–1714 and sometimes even participated, and this strengthened hostility, but it did not prevent an important period of cooperation.

The *entente* had certainly helped both Orléans and George I, stabilising their régimes and in particular depriving the exiled Stuarts of French support. Without such backing the Jacobites did not pose a real threat. In a wider sense, the alliance helped propel Britain into the leading role in Europe and, to some extent, made France dependent upon London. It also contributed to preserving the Utrecht settlement, which until the later 1720s was defended by British naval and financial resources backed by French military power. Many problems had been left unsettled in 1713–14. Those in the Italian peninsula proved the most intractable and were not to be finally resolved until 1748. Until the later 1720s, however, the *entente* was central to the defence of the Utrecht settlement, which was the dominant issue in continental diplomacy. Problems had been solved by cooperation and negotiated agreement between the leading states, and the Barrier was never tested, due to the passive policies adopted by France.

More importantly, these years had seen a significant diplomatic realignment, with a steady weakening of the *entente* and a *rapprochement* between London and Vienna. The conclusion of the Second Treaty of Vienna, signed in 1731, destroyed the Anglo-French alliance. Negotiated in secret, it appeared to resurrect the Austro-British axis which had fought France under Louis XIV. This alienated Fleury, who during the next decade built up French power and reasserted France's diplomatic leadership (see above, pp. 10–11). The 1730s also saw the first important breach in the peace of Utrecht with the establishment of Farnese's elder son, Charles, as King of Naples and Sicily, from which the Austrians had been expelled. It modified, rather than overturned, the situation created in 1713–14. The Utrecht settlement was finally to be overthrown by the Prussian attack on Austria at the end of 1740. The principal agent of this transformation was not one of the leading powers but the electorate-kingdom of Brandenburg–Prussia, which might not even have ranked among the second-class states at the death of its King Frederick William I in May 1740 but which – within a generation – was to emerge as a great power.

CHAPTER 2

The War of the Austrian Succession, 1740–1748

During the quarter century after 1739 the leading European states fought one another with a ferocity unknown since the Spanish Succession struggle. They contested first the War of the Austrian Succession (1740–48) and then, after a brief armed peace, the much more decisive Seven Years War (1756–63). At stake was not only the future shape of Europe but also control of a great part of the world overseas and, in particular, its trade. The two wars undermined British and French dominance of European politics, which had persisted since the peace of Utrecht. They also enhanced the diplomatic importance of eastern Europe, as the political centre of gravity moved sharply eastwards. Russia was brought decisively onto the European stage, Prussia became a leading state and Austria's very right to be one was for a time questioned. Two dominant rivalries emerged: that between Britain and France, at times supported by Bourbon Spain, overseas and that between Austria and Prussia in central Europe. The traditional primacy of continental issues in international relations was slowly undermined by extra-European ones. Although many statesmen, even in London and Versailles, remained blind to the latter, it is symptomatic of the change that the first conflict was purely colonial in nature.

The Anglo-Spanish War of 1739–1748

In 1739 Britain went to war against Spain in a manner superficially reminiscent of the days of Hawkins and Drake, the legendary seamen of the age of Elizabeth I a century-and-a-half before. Once again British seamen and merchants tried to seize control of trade with Spanish America. This produced a wider conflict with France for dominance of all the commerce between Europe and the outside world. In contrast to earlier and brief

Anglo-Spanish wars in 1718–20 and 1727, Spain was not the principal aggressor and her ambitions in the Mediterranean were not the cause. The conflict's origins lay instead in British efforts to trade with Spain's extensive American empire, and Madrid's desire to limit and even extinguish such commerce.

At the heart of Anglo-Spanish disputes was the *asiento*. By the terms of the peace of Utrecht, modified three years later in 1716, the English South Sea Company had secured the contract (*asiento*) to supply 4,800 slaves annually to Spanish America for 30 years. It was also allowed to send an annual ship to the region's trade fairs. This second privilege was especially important, since it constituted the single legitimate breach in the theoretical principle of monopoly which had been upheld by Madrid ever since the empire's creation two centuries before. All commerce to and from the American possessions was legally reserved to Spanish ships and to the subjects of the Spanish crown. During the sixteenth and much of the seventeenth centuries all fleets for the New World left from Seville; in 1717 this monopoly was formally transferred to Cadiz. By the first half of the eighteenth century a combination of external pressure and changing internal circumstances were weakening the monopoly, but it long remained the basis of Spain's official attitude to trade with her American empire.

The problem was that both the *asiento* and the annual ship were an open invitation to expand illicit commerce with the large and profitable market of Spanish America, which British merchants were both anxious and well-positioned to penetrate. The agents of the South Sea Company had exploited their legal right to trade to carry on a far more extensive commerce with Spain's colonial subjects than was permitted under the Utrecht settlement. The 'annual ship' came to be used as a floating warehouse, constantly filled and refilled by other ships sent out to the Caribbean. More important, and on a larger scale, was the blatant, direct contraband trade conducted by Britain and her own colonies in the American hemisphere, particularly the merchants in Jamaica and in the North American settlements. The Spanish colonists, starved of manufactured goods from Spain and unable to dispose of all their own produce there, welcomed these interlopers or smugglers, who often included Dutch traders from Curaçao. Madrid, however, was determined to uphold the theoretical monopoly, since the plans to revive Spanish power under the first Bourbon King all assumed that the empire's still-considerable resources could be exploited to restore Spain to a leading role within Europe.

Spain and her colonial governors sought continually to suppress the contraband trade. They were also unreconciled to British commercial privileges, always viewed as a temporary breach of the monopoly, which would be restored when the *asiento* lapsed in 1744. Faced by vast expanses of sea to patrol and lacking sufficient royal ships, even with the naval build-up which was in progress, Spain had recourse to the notorious *guarda costas*, who stopped and searched any foreign vessels found in or near Spanish–American waters. These coastguards were heavily armed patrol vessels, which had first been established by Patiño in 1722 and began to operate three years later. They were a government initiative and theoretically under strict Spanish control. Side-by-side with the *guarda costas*, however, there came to be an increasing number of unofficial vessels who preyed on foreign shipping and were little more than privateers operating in peacetime under licences issued by the cash-strapped Spanish authorities who were unable to finance an official customs service. Based mainly on the Caribbean islands and depending on their prizes to survive, they attacked British ships trading legitimately with Jamaica as well as the smugglers, and they often maltreated captured crews, sometimes in horrific ways.

The first Spanish offensive against British shipping began in 1726 and continued until 1731. In the same way that the distinction between the officially-sanctioned *guarda costas* and the independent privateers was difficult to draw, so the line separating legitimate commerce from smuggling was frequently blurred or simply ignored. The outcome was a rising number of seizures – in which legal searches could not easily be separated from piratical depredations – with ships arrested, their cargoes confiscated and their crews imprisoned. These years saw a significant number of violent Spanish outrages against innocent and not-so-innocent British traders. Best remembered was the severing of the ear of the unfortunate merchant Captain Robert Jenkins off Havana in 1731 by the commander of a *guarda costa*. His misfortune would later be commemorated in the name sometimes given to the conflict of 1739–48: the 'War of Jenkins' Ear'. Yet at the time these attacks caused surprisingly little concern to Britain's merchant community, while the level of popular agitation was also significantly lower than it would become in the later 1730s. The traders viewed the seizures as a kind of protection cost which could be shrugged off, both because of the considerable profits to be made from Spanish American trade and because the scale of the losses was relatively insignificant: a government-sponsored pamphlet, published in the year fighting began, calculated them at a mere 2.5 per cent of Britain's total commerce with the region.

Legal and diplomatic remedies could be pursued, but Spanish colonial justice was notoriously slow-moving and arbitrary, and before long the protests of the British merchants were being taken up by their own government with Madrid. In any case relations were not lacking in other sources of friction during the generation after Utrecht, with Spain's enduring resentment at British commercial privileges and possession of Gibraltar and Minorca. The establishment of the British colony of Georgia in 1732 added a new issue in the shape of a dispute over its boundary and whether it infringed Spanish colonial territory: Madrid ruled over neighbouring Florida. Within the established framework of relations, clashes over Spanish seizures had not seemed especially important, and certainly not a threat to peace, during the later 1720s and early 1730s. There was no steady deterioration extending over a decade and culminating in war. By the middle of the decade, however, there was growing discontent among Britain's merchants over Madrid's failure (as it was seen) to provide compensation for the ships and cargoes seized. It was accompanied by a desire to destroy completely the Spanish trading monopoly, in which large cracks were already apparent.

The second wave of seizures and depredations began in 1736 and continued for two years. Twelve ships were taken in 1737 alone, as Spain's colonial governors made a determined effort to shut out British traders. This time a sharp deterioration in diplomacy was soon evident which eventually led to war in autumn 1739. It was not a conflict which either government positively sought. Indeed, both Madrid and London demonstrated considerable moderation and willingness to compromise during the diplomatic exchanges which preceded the fighting. Spain, even after Patiño's efforts to improve the navy and overhaul the colonial defences and administration, was aware of the vulnerability of her ramshackle and far-flung empire to a British attack. Her rulers were in any case anxious to conciliate London in the interests of their European aims. During the War of the Polish Succession Philip V and Elisabeth Farnese had been absorbed in finding Italian thrones for their two sons. Their resentment at the way Fleury had dictated peace after 1735, ignoring Spanish interests, led the King and Queen to try to court London. Madrid's moderation and realism, however, was accompanied by a determination to defend the colonial monopoly and to prevent further British economic penetration. On certain key issues Spain was unyielding, and this was one source of war. Madrid also resented the periodic firmness of British representations and, in particular, the intransigent tone adopted by the South Sea Company, which was independent of ministerial control and adopted an unyielding approach which exacerbated relations. Such attitudes limited the scope for compromise and ensured diplomatic efforts to negotiate a settlement would fail.

The public clamour in England also inhibited a peaceful resolution. Sir Robert Walpole was even more conciliatory than Madrid. Peace was his overriding aim, as throughout his ministry. Yet by the later 1730s he was more vulnerable to challenges from within his own cabinet and to pressure from the public at large. The senior Secretary of State, responsible for Britain's foreign policy towards Spain and France, was the ambitious Duke of Newcastle, who craved fuller authority than Walpole allowed him. Scenting his leader's increasing vulnerability, Newcastle clothed his own bid for power in a plea for a vigorous defence of British interests, and at times he was supported by George II, who exercised real influence over policy. Such attitudes created obstacles in the way of the negotiated settlement which Walpole wanted. It was even more true of the significant extra-parliamentary agitation over the issue.

In autumn 1737 the merchants, illicit and legitimate, of London in particular, but also the leading provincial ports of Bristol, Liverpool, Glasgow and Jamaica (the 'West India interest') began a furious campaign for government action, and this increased in intensity during the next two years. They were backed by jingoist public opinion, demanding commercial imperialism, while the parliamentary opposition saw a fine opportunity to attack Walpole and his pacific policies. In this campaign, examples of Spanish outrages, real and imaginary, during the first offensive against British shipping after 1726, were dusted down and used to inflame popular opinion. Demands for justice for British traders and an end to Spanish searches developed into agitation for a commercial and colonial war. At a time of stagnation and decline in British commerce the simple mercantilist belief that Britain's survival demanded that she grab as much as possible of a fixed amount of world trade was widely influential. That fighting would inevitably destroy the very profitable British trade with Metropolitan Spain was ignored, probably because it was dominated by Catholics and Jews. There were also some demands, as yet far less strident, for war with France as well and claims that she was Britain's real enemy and rival in the Americas. There were those who pointed out that French commerce, unlike British, was forging ahead, particularly in the West Indies. In fact, although few grasped it at the time, what was really at stake was control of the whole Caribbean trading area, British, Spanish and French – as the future would demonstrate. The plantations developed on the West Indian islands and parts of the South and North American mainland during the late seventeenth and early eighteenth centuries had created a vast storehouse for tropical products – sugar, rum, tobacco, cotton, timber and dyes – and a demand for West African slaves and European manufactured goods.

The clamour of the opposition and of the merchants raised the political temperature and there were increasing demands for war. Walpole, who knew a conflict would force up the Land Tax and undermine his position in parliament, pleaded for moderation. In 1738 and the early months of 1739 he tried to reach agreement over the trade question and the subsidiary problems of the border between Georgia and Spanish Florida and the British claims to cut the logwood needed for producing vegetable dyes on the Honduras coast. The dyes were essential in the manufacture of woollen goods in Britain, and there had been English settlements around the Bay of Honduras and in Yucatan since the second half of the seventeenth century. These communities had flourished, beginning to trade illegally with the nearby Spanish colonies and erecting fortifications, both of which were resented in Madrid.

Spain also wanted to compromise, though not at the price of sacrificing her commercial monopoly. The agreement patched up in January 1739, the Convention of the Pardo, stood little chance of acceptance by the British public. Concentrating on compensation for vessels lost, it ignored the Spanish practice of searching legitimate shipping and evaded the crucial issue: Madrid's intention to go on suppressing smuggling. It was wrecked first by the independence and intransigence of the South Sea Company, which now refused to contribute its share of the settlement, and then by the Spanish ministry itself which declared it would not pay agreed compensation to British traders. Walpole finally had to yield to the clamour from outside and even from within his own government: war was decided on at the latest by July, when Vice-Admiral Edward Vernon was sent to attack Spanish possessions in the New World, and formally declared in October 1739. It was widely viewed as a war purely for commercial gain: at the declaration, stocks rose.

Sooner or later France would inevitably become involved. Although at first Fleury had characteristically urged moderation on Spain, his policy was now moving towards commercial and colonial conflict with Britain. During 1739 the two branches of the Bourbon family had joined more closely together by the marriage of Louis XV's daughter to Don Philip, the younger son of Philip V and Elisabeth Farnese. But Fleury had more practical motives: British victory and tough peace terms might damage French trade with Cadiz and probably threaten her valuable sugar islands of Martinique, Guadeloupe and Haiti. Within Europe, Britain was diplomatically isolated, whereas France was in a strong position after the treaties of Vienna (1735–38) and Belgrade (1739). In 1740, therefore, Fleury sent

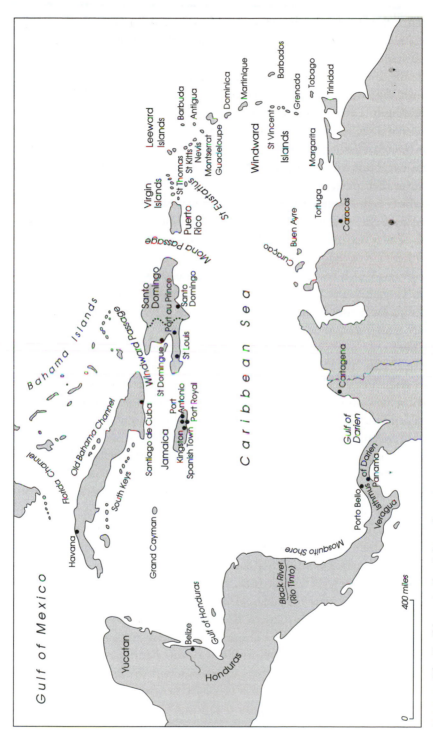

MAP 1 *The Caribbean in the eighteenth century*

Source: M.S. Anderson, *The War of the Austrian Succession, 1740–1748* (Pearson Education Limited, 1995), p. 236

a French fleet to the Caribbean with orders to assist a Spanish attack on Jamaica. This action implied an early outbreak of war between France and Britain.

In the event, the French squadron achieved very little. The Anglo-Spanish War was quickly overshadowed and enveloped by the outbreak of fighting in Europe from December 1740, but it is doubtful if it would have been decisive in any case. Spain's navy and her colonial defences had both been strengthened and successfully resisted British attacks, with the single exception of Vernon's initial raid on Porto Bello. Spanish privateers, for their part, inflicted considerable losses on British merchant shipping. Britain still retained a lead in naval power over the combined Bourbon fleets, and this increased during the 1740s due to substantial Spanish losses, but it was not decisive. The logistical difficulties of operations on the other side of the Atlantic were both novel and considerable, while the expeditions which reached the Caribbean were devastated by tropical diseases. Though Walpole's ministry made an impressive administrative effort, sending a large squadron to the New World in 1740, dreams of a decisive naval victory were soon revealed to be illusions.

There was also a degree of indecision in the British government's strategic thinking. Ministers could not decide whether to destroy Spanish trade and shipping or seize colonies, and their uncertainty was strengthened by their appreciation that France's clear intention was to intervene sooner or later. British operations against Caribbean and South American ports between 1739 and 1743 achieved little. In the first winter of the war Vernon spectacularly captured and briefly held Porto Bello, which was poorly defended and completely surprised by the attack, but two years later his attempt to seize Cartagena ended in failure, as did his subsequent operations against Cuba and Panama. When what was left of the British expeditionary force sent out to the Caribbean sailed for home in October 1742, its single territorial trophy was a small island in Honduras Bay. Until the peace in 1748, further action was limited to raids on shipping and attempts to cut off Spain from her colonies. Distance, climate and disease proved the main obstacles, but the Spaniards also put up a spirited defence. Britain's one consolation was that France's expedition of 1740 ended in disaster and returned home in the following year. This failure, together with the momentous events on the continent in 1740–41, destroyed Fleury's plans for active cooperation with Spain outside Europe. By autumn 1742 the Anglo-Spanish war had merged into the wider European conflict over the Habsburg inheritance.

Prussia's seizure of Silesia, 1740–1742

The War of the Austrian Succession was a loosely-related and indecisive series of struggles involving all the leading European states with the partial exception of Russia. Though extending overseas to the Caribbean, North America and India, the fighting took place mainly in central Europe, the Italian peninsula and, latterly, the Southern Netherlands. Fought between two loose and periodically changing alliances, it was as much a series of diplomatic manoeuvres as military operations and was principally notable for Prussia's emergence as a leading state. The war settled little, and the eventual peace settlement in 1748 was widely seen as a truce, which it proved to be.

The struggle's very name underlined the continuing importance of dynastic factors in international relations. In October 1740 the Emperor Charles VI, the last male Habsburg, died suddenly and unexpectedly. It was widely expected that his death would not lead to war or to the break-up of his territories, in contrast to what had happened when Charles II of Spain died in 1700. The succession of his elder daughter, Maria Theresa, appeared secure. All the leading European and German states, except Bavaria, had guaranteed the Pragmatic Sanction and, more importantly, Maria Theresa enjoyed the goodwill of the major powers. Although the Russian Empress Anna had died three days before Charles, the regency for the child Ivan VI was pro-Austrian. In France Fleury wanted to avoid continental war and concentrate on supporting Spain overseas. Since 1735 he had worked to reduce Austria to a friendly dependency and had no intention of challenging Maria Theresa's succession in the Habsburg territories. He hoped, however, to see Charles Albert of Bavaria elected emperor rather than Maria Theresa's husband, Francis Stephen: France's influence in Germany would increase, since Munich was an established French client, and Francis Stephen might be deterred from trying to recover Lorraine. Although Spain looked for further gains in the Italian peninsula, and both Bavaria and Saxony had claims to the Habsburg succession through marriages to the daughters of Emperor Joseph I, these second-rank states were not really dangerous without French support.

Though domestically Maria Theresa's succession went unchallenged, it was an unpromising inheritance. She ruled over a collection of provinces which still lacked any real administrative unity, while the army, the one integrating force besides the Church and the court in Vienna, had been shattered and demoralised by Charles's last calamitous wars. The effective strength of the field army stood at a mere 30,000 men – garrison troops brought the total to 70,000 – and could only be increased and improved by radical internal reform. Though long Charles VI's designated successor, the 23-year-old Maria Theresa had been totally unprepared for her new role and was politically inexperienced; her husband had few obvious political or military talents; her ministers were mostly old, timid and incompetent; she had no decent generals and her treasury was empty.

In December 1740 – less than two months after she came to the throne – the blue-coated troops of the King of Prussia crossed into Silesia, the most northerly province of the Habsburg Monarchy, and began the War of the Austrian Succession. The invasion was a complete surprise to Maria Theresa and to Europe. Prussia had no serious claims to any of her possessions and had not been a traditional enemy. Under Frederick William I (1713–40), the large Prussian army, the King's unpredictability and flirtations with Peter the Great and the Hanoverian George I of Britain, had occasionally annoyed Vienna, but Prussia's ruler inspired neither fear nor respect. In the international pecking order, Brandenburg–Prussia ranked only marginally above Bavaria or Saxony. The Hohenzollern monarchy had had little impact on the relations of the major states before 1740. Frederick William's only gain from the Great Northern War had been the important port of Stettin at the mouth of the Oder and its surrounds, which conferred direct access to the Baltic. He had spent his final years trying unsuccessfully to persuade the European powers to recognise his succession rights to the small Rhineland territories of Jülich-Berg which adjoined his duchy of Cleves. After 1726 he had loyally supported the Austro-Russian alliance in Poland and the Empire. Yet in 1738 Charles VI had shown his contempt for him by agreeing with France and the Maritime Powers to exclude Prussia from the Jülich–Berg succession. Deeply wounded, Frederick William turned to France, and in 1739 Fleury promised support over Berg: by separating Prussia from Austria, French dominance over both powers and, more widely, in Germany would be guaranteed.

Prussia's emergence as a leading European state during the middle decades of the eighteenth century was to be both dramatic and unexpected. When Frederick the Great came to the throne, Brandenburg–Prussia played an important political role only within the Holy Roman Empire and northern Europe. The Hohenzollern possessions, known as the Kingdom of Prussia, were exposed and scattered across half the continent, from the enclaves of Cleves, Mark and Ravensberg in Westphalia, through the heartlands of Brandenburg, Magdeburg and Pomerania in central Germany, astride the rivers Elbe and Oder, to distant East Prussia. The resulting problems of self-defence against hostile neighbours were considerable: the eastern border of East Prussia lay around 1,200 kilometres from the westernmost possessions in the Rhineland, a particularly great distance in an era when communications were slow and unreliable. All the leading European states faced wide-ranging and dispersed political commitments, as a consequence of their territorial extent. What made Prussia's position unique was not merely her wide-ranging involvement and the fragmentation of her possessions but her very limited resources.

Prussia always lacked the demographic and economic strength to compete with the established powers on anything approaching an equal footing. In 1740 her population was around 2.25 million; by the time of Frederick the Great's death in 1786 and due largely to his important territorial acquisitions, it had climbed to some 5.8 million. The population density was low by European and even German standards, and all the other leading continental states were far stronger demographically. Economic resources were in equally short supply. With the exception of the Westphalian territories, with their mixed and relatively prosperous agrarian economies and higher level of urbanisation, the Hohenzollern lands were poor and backward, and contained little rural industry. Subsistence agriculture, with small surpluses, mostly prevailed throughout the central provinces of Brandenburg and Pomerania. Contemporaries styled Brandenburg 'the sandbox of the Holy Roman Empire', so wretched was its soil. East Prussia, separated until 1772 from the Hohenzollern heartlands by more than 500 kilometres of Polish territory, was little better, if at all. Her commercial economy also provided an unpromising foundation for her enhanced international role. Grain and grain-based products were exported from East Prussia and, to a lesser extent, from the central provinces. Commercial activity, however, was at a low ebb, and largely driven by the demands of the state, while poor internal communications meant that the major continental trade routes bypassed the Prussian territories. The urban sector was similarly underdeveloped, at least by western European and even western German standards.

The very limited available resources, along with her strategic vulnerability, were always serious obstacles to Prussia ever securely establishing herself as a leading European power. Yet Frederick also inherited considerable assets when he succeeded his father on 31 May 1740. Principal among these was an army unusually large for a country of its size and population. Successive Hohenzollern rulers, aware of the vulnerability of their possessions, had built up a large military force for self-defence.

Its creation had shaped internal developments since the Great Elector's accession in 1640, and during Frederick William I's reign it ordinarily consumed around 70 per cent of the Crown's annual peacetime revenue. In 1740 it was some 80,000 strong, impressive on the barrack square but untested in combat. With the exception of some inconclusive operations in the Rhineland in 1734, during the War of the Polish Succession, the Prussian army had not fired a shot in anger since the siege of Stralsund in 1715. Its last important victory had been gained as long ago as 1675, though Hohenzollern contingents had fought impressively in the Allied armies during the War of the Spanish Succession.

This powerful force was supported, and to a considerable degree made possible, by a system of territorial recruitment finalised as recently as 1733, the celebrated Cantonal System. It imposed near-universal male conscription which fell principally on the peasantry, who received basic training and were then returned to their villages as a permanently-trained reserve. This enabled the need for a powerful military force for defence to be reconciled with the reality of Prussian poverty and contributed significantly to Prussia's rise. An officer cadre was provided by the territorial nobility: under Frederick William I, the Junkers, as the nobles came to be known, had come to dominate the military commands and, to a lesser extent, the civil administration. He also bequeathed to his son a war-chest of eight million talers in gold coin, stored in sacks in the basement of the royal palace. Finally, Frederick inherited a widely-admired administrative system, the centrepiece of which was the General Directory, established in 1723. Within the limitations upon all eighteenth-century governments, this was relatively successful in extracting the men, money and agrarian produce needed to support the army and pay the state's other expenses. It squeezed seven million talers annually from the poor and largely agrarian country. With the benefit of hindsight, it can be seen that the administrative and military foundations laid by 1740, together with the degree of social integration achieved under Frederick William I, would provide a secure basis for Prussia's eighteenth-century emergence. Yet in the estimation of most contemporaries these advantages were insufficient to overcome Prussia's territorial exposure and inherent poverty.

Frederick William I died a few months before Maria Theresa's accession. His son initially seemed likely to be even less of a threat to the European order than his father. Frederick the Great enjoyed a good deal of sympathy outside Prussia because of the oppressive upbringing he had received. Charles VI had interceded to save his life and had lent and given him money, as had his relative on the British throne. A philosopher who had published the *Antimachiavell* shortly before his accession, a poet and musician, friend of Voltaire and French culture, Frederick was expected to relax and humanise the brutal, militarised Prussian state. Yet the intellectual dilettante was in reality a callous, cynical, determined proponent of *Realpolitik* – whatever the contrary arguments set out in the *Antimachiavell*. He believed the logic of his father's administrative reforms and model army was territorial expansion, without which the Hohenzollern state would be incomplete. In this way Prussia's poverty and fragmentation could be overcome and the state be transformed into one capable of taking the political initiative, rather than being at the mercy of events. Desire for revenge on Austria for the shabby treatment of his father over his claims to Berg was a far less important influence on the young King.

Frederick would hardly have contemplated military action without the opportunity provided by Charles VI's death which itself became a motive. The accession of a young woman when Austria's finances and army were in chaos presented him with the chance to seize the rich province of Silesia. Bordering Brandenburg to the south-east, Silesia formed a natural extension higher up the Oder. Moreover, prudence suggested Prussia should seize it before the Elector-King of Saxony–Poland, Augustus III, did so. By seizing the land bridge between Saxony and Poland Frederick weakened both and made them possible victims for future Prussian expansion. The invasion, moreover, marked a clear breach with the dynastic motives which had traditionally been uppermost in international relations, but now gave way to considerations of power. Although Prussia had some vague claims to small areas of Silesia, dynasticism played no part in Frederick's policies and he only presented them for form's sake. He sardonically congratulated his foreign minister, Heinrich von Podewils, for concocting a legal justification for the attack: 'Splendid, that's the work of an excellent charlatan!' The King's view of international morality was that the ruler should unashamedly further the interests of his own state. In May 1741 he was to write: 'If we can gain something by being honest, we will be it, and if we have to deceive, we will be cheats.'

Yet the King was also impelled by motives a young ruler of an earlier age would have understood. He later confessed: 'My youth, hot-headedness, thirst for glory . . . the satisfaction of seeing my name in the gazettes and then in history carried me away.' In early June 1740, during the first weeks of his own reign, the King had downgraded the role of the *Kabinettsministerium* in foreign policy, which became his sole responsibility. The decision to invade Silesia was Frederick's alone, and was opposed by his leading advisers who believed it was too risky and also at

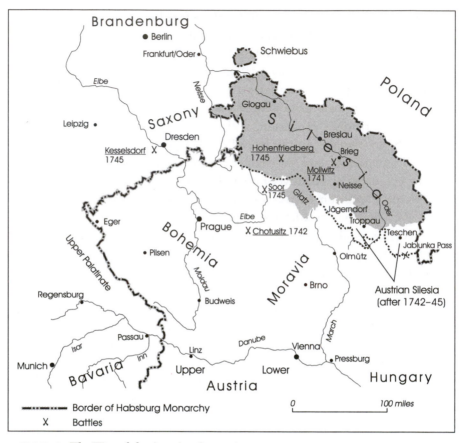

MAP 2 *The War of the Austrian Succession*

Source: M. Hochedlinger, *Austria's Wars of Emergence, 1683–1797*
(Pearson Education Limited, 2003), p. 247

variance with the established traditions of Prussian policy. Yet while the King was prepared to take risks and to fight for what he wanted, he was not a militarist and believed Prussia's standing army and full treasury only permitted him to wage short wars for limited territorial objectives. It was possible that he might gain Silesia without a fight, and he had no intention of provoking a partition of Austria or a general conflict. He counted on the passivity of the other powers and hoped Maria Theresa would yield. The regency in Russia would be wary of helping her Habsburg ally actively, and Frederick believed it could be bought off with 'a mule laden with gold'. Above all, Fleury's clear intention to help Spain at sea meant that probably neither France nor Britain would stand by Maria Theresa and might even bid for Prussian support.

After overrunning Silesia in December 1740 and January 1741, Frederick offered to purchase the province, but Maria Theresa contemptuously refused. Pride and obstinacy played a part, but clearly the cession of any of her lands would call into question the validity of the Pragmatic Sanction and encourage other claims on her inheritance. Moreover, it was easy enough for the King to seize an isolated province in the depths of winter but a different matter to keep it. Maria Theresa also expected the other powers would denounce him. At Versailles Louis XV declared that 'the King of Prussia is a fool', while Fleury called him 'a dishonest man and a cheat'. Unfortunately, others at the French court drew different conclusions, especially when Frederick won his first and decidedly fortuitous victory over the Austrians at Mollwitz in April 1741, a success gained by the impressive and disciplined Prussian infantry after the King fled the battlefield following initial setbacks.

Prussia's victory was primarily important in the wider European context. Though several states were prepared to claim parts of Maria Theresa's inheritance, none did so directly until Frederick's invasion and military triumph revealed the extent of Habsburg vulnerability. His actions encouraged others: Charles Albert of Bavaria claimed Bohemia and Austria, while Philip V of Spain demanded Tuscany (ruled by Francis Stephen) and Parma for Don Philip. The impact at the French court was especially decisive. Fleury found himself faced by a military faction of younger bellicose aristocrats, led by the ambitious comte de Belle-Isle, who wanted to be rid of him and his cautious policies. This grouping had gained in strength and coherence during the later 1730s, and Frederick's invasion of Silesia had enabled it to push aside the veteran first minister, whose grip on power was less secure. The marshal-duc de Belle-Isle, as he now became, was a veteran of Louis XIV's wars. He was supported by a group of courtiers who believed that warfare was the nobility's principal *métier* and that it should be directed against Austria, France's traditional enemy. This grouping received some sympathy from Louis XV, who was becoming impatient to free himself from the octogenarian Cardinal. Gradually Fleury lost ground and abandoned plans to concentrate on a maritime war with Britain. He had to accept French policy returning to the seventeenth-century tradition of territorial expansion at Habsburg expense. In fact no better opportunity to destroy Austria completely had ever presented itself.

This was the view championed by Belle-Isle, who by spring 1741 was at Frankfurt and acting in effect as France's foreign minister. He aimed to win the Imperial election for Charles Albert, his own relative by marriage, and to create a coalition to break up Austria: the Southern Netherlands should go to France, most of Silesia to Prussia, Bohemia, Upper Austria and the Tyrol to Bavaria, and the Italian lands to Sardinia and the Spanish princes. A new political order was to be created, with the Habsburgs' traditional ascendancy in central Europe replaced by three enlarged French satellites. To Prussia and Bavaria was added Saxony, whose elector was to receive Moravia (with the dignity of King), Upper Silesia and part of Lower Austria. In May, Belle-Isle gave France's blessing to the Spanish–Bavarian alliance of Nymphenburg, and a few weeks later he concluded French alliances with Bavaria and Prussia. Believing he could use both these states as pawns, he promised to pay subsidies and commit French auxiliary troops to the war in central Europe. French subsidies – exactly like those grudgingly provided by their British counterpart – paid only a fraction of the recipient's military costs. They were an important source of ready cash for smaller or more backward states, and could be used to secure loans. Subsidy payments were given by major states to their clients and were an instrument of political subordination. France's ambitious and wide-ranging diplomacy was supported by impressive military preparations, personally supervised by the energetic and all-powerful Belle-Isle during a brief return to the French court in summer 1741 and swept along on a tide of enthusiasm for a war to destroy Austrian power once and for all. The immediate objective was an invasion of the Habsburg Monarchy.

Belle-Isle's diplomacy had created a wide-ranging alliance which would eventually contain Saxony and the northern Italian kingdom of Sardinia. France also tried to neutralise Russia by encouraging a Swedish attack across the Finnish border in August 1741 (see below, p. 70). In the autumn Spanish soldiers landed in Italy, while French, Bavarian and Prussian troops, as well as those of another predator, Augustus of

Saxony–Poland, attacked Maria Theresa's Austrian and Bohemian territories. The fiction was maintained that France was not at war with the Habsburgs but merely acting as an auxiliary of Charles Albert. By the end of 1741 Belle-Isle was in Prague at the head of a Franco-Bavarian force, and both Bohemia and Upper Austria were occupied. Charles Albert had himself crowned Archduke of Austria at Linz and King of Bohemia at Prague, and then in January 1742 he was elected Emperor Charles VII, the first non-Habsburg for three centuries. He was clearly a French puppet: both the Empire as an institution and the Imperial title, which had retained much of its prestige through its association with the Habsburgs, had been debased, perhaps irreparably. His success was facilitated by the widespread neutrality of the smaller German states, most of whom abstained from supporting either the Habsburgs or Charles Albert himself. Belle-Isle appeared to have achieved French mastery of central Europe and to have gone far beyond Louis XIV's wildest dreams. France's decisive military intervention, rather than Prussia's initial attack, had brought Maria Theresa close to total defeat by the winter of 1741–42.

Austria none the less survived. This was because of divisions among her enemies and Maria Theresa's stubborn courage. Deserted by many Austro-Bohemian nobles and clergy, she turned to Hungary and threw herself on the chivalry of the kingdom's rebellious and independent nobility. After wringing constitutional guarantees from her, they raised a force of 20,000, most irregular cavalry, which saw her through the crucial winter of 1741–42. This support and her coronation as Queen of Hungary restored her credibility in Austria and abroad. Equally important was Frederick II's desertion of his allies by a short armistice with Maria Theresa in October 1741 and a more durable peace through the treaty of Breslau (Wroclaw) in June 1742, confirmed the following month in a second treaty at Berlin. This was bought by the cession of most of Silesia, which was all Prussia's King wanted from the war. It was a bitter humiliation for Austria and her ruler: a leading adviser declared that the settlement was the second edition of Belgrade, the disastrous peace with the Ottoman Empire three years before (see above, p. 21). Maria Theresa had no intention of making this permanent, but realised she had to concentrate on the French and Bavarians in Austria and Bohemia as they threatened her very survival. The armistices had been the work of British mediation and the Queen could not resist London's demands.

The outbreak of fighting on the continent in 1740–41 had radically altered Britain's situation. Fleury's plans to assist Spain overseas were abandoned and only revived in 1744, when a formal Anglo-French war was declared. The Spaniards also concentrated on grabbing what they could in Italy. Yet the British failed to take advantage of this in the New World and were drawn themselves into the European struggle. Walpole's attempts to preserve neutrality, as a decade before during the War of the Polish Succession, proved impossible. It was clear to the other ministers and to George II that Austria's existence was at stake and that her destruction would raise the power of France and her German satellites to a level which would threaten Hanover and ultimately Britain herself. They insisted London honour its guarantee of the Pragmatic Sanction and found Maria Theresa's cause popular in parliament. In June 1741 an alliance promised British subsidies and 12,000 troops. The money was paid and British diplomacy tried to improve Austria's military situation, however bitter the pill for Maria Theresa, by arranging the successive armistices with Prussia. But the troops hired from Denmark and Hesse-Casel were never sent. This was because when George II visited Hanover in summer 1741, he became so scared of a French attack that he insisted they remain to defend his electorate. He even signed a convention with Louis XV to neutralise Hanover, promised to vote for Charles Albert as emperor and actually did so the following January. For the first time since the accession of the Hanoverians, the danger emerged of France's seizing the electorate and using it as a lever against Britain: this threat was to be a constant factor in Anglo-French relations over the next generation.

British policy towards the continental war became more decisive in February 1742 when Walpole fell. For the next two years, control of foreign policy in the patched-up Whig administration lay with Carteret. Though political opportunism had made him a fiery protagonist of the trade war with Spain, he was essentially a Whig of the old school, who thought in continental terms, feared French ascendancy and wanted to revive the Grand Alliance which had proved so successful against Louis XIV: London should build a coalition and supply it with cash and troops. French hegemony would be destroyed, Britain would regain her position as arbiter of Europe and achieve supremacy overseas. It was vital, therefore, to preserve Austria since she was needed to help check France. But Carteret was also determined to have Maria Theresa come to terms with Prussia so that Austria could concentrate on France. The latter inevitably led to uneasy relations between London and Vienna. Carteret encountered similar difficulties with his ministerial colleagues and parliament because he was determined to please the King by defending Hanover, seeing it as an essential element in an anti-French system. Indeed, the effect of his policies was to coopt the Electorate into the struggle with France.

Austria's recovery, 1742–1744

The war turned dramatically in favour of the Anglo-Austrian partners in 1742, when Carteret persuaded first the Prussians and then the Saxons to make peace with Maria Theresa. Frederick had no qualms in deserting his allies and ending Prussia's First Silesian War (1740–42) in July. Having gained Silesia, he had no interest in furthering Franco-Bavarian ambitions, especially as he lacked the resources for a long struggle and needed peace to overhaul his army, the shortcomings of which had been evident during the fighting, and to replenish his war chest, substantially depleted by eighteen months' campaigning. Prussia's withdrawal enabled Maria Theresa to expel the French and Bavarians from Upper Austria and Bohemia, and even to occupy Charles VII's Electorate of Bavaria. Frederick's action was an especially serious matter for France, whose foreign minister acidly commented that the Prussian King was 'not perfidious by halves'. Belle-Isle's star was already waning fast, and by summer 1742 French reliance upon Prussia as the military arm of the anti-Austrian coalition had wrecked Louis XV's position. It now seemed possible for Austria and Britain to concentrate against France, although neither was officially at war with Louis XV. Maria Theresa wanted to continue to fight both to punish her enemies and to secure compensation for Silesia in Bavaria or in Alsace–Lorraine. Carteret had the less tangible aim of humbling France. The French, who were soon to be freed from Fleury's remaining passive influence by his death in January 1743, intended to reassert their influence in Germany and restore their puppet, Charles VII.

Carteret's dreams of repeating the victories of the Spanish Succession War were illusory. These had depended heavily on wholehearted support from the Dutch and German states including Prussia. Now the Republic insisted on neutrality, and the lack of enthusiasm among the German rulers, despite British subsidies, meant that Carteret's neo-Grand Alliance was a pale shadow of William III and Queen Anne. In June 1743 George II in person led the so-called 'Pragmatic Army' of German mercenaries, paid for by Britain, to a surprise victory over the French at Dettingen near Frankfurt. Although he forced French troops to withdraw from Germany, this battle proved to be no new Blenheim, Marlborough's great victory over Louis XIV's army in 1704. The Elector-King was too nervous of following it up with an attack on France in case Prussia re-entered the war and invaded Hanover. Nonetheless, French power had been removed from Germany and Carteret was determined to expel her Bourbon allies from Italy as well. In September he forced Austria, under the threat of cutting off the subsidies which her army needed to survive, to sign the treaty of Worms with Charles Emmanuel of Sardinia. The latter, following the traditions of his house, used the Habsburg–Bourbon struggle to extract promises from Maria Theresa of more of Milan as well as Piacenza. In return, with British cash and Austrian troops, he agreed to cooperate against France, King Charles of Naples and the Spanish forces in Italy. By the end of 1743, therefore, through British subsidies and bullying Austria into concessions she found distasteful, Carteret had managed to destroy France's predominant position in central Europe created by Belle-Isle in 1741. However, the anti-French grouping did not have the muscle to force Louis XV to accept this by invading French territory. In creating his alliances Carteret had largely ignored non-European factors and did not seriously try to destroy France and Spain at sea or in the colonies, where Britain stood the best chance of success. He did not realise, any more than most government or opposition politicians, with the possible exceptions of Bedford and William Pitt the Elder, that ultimately control of the world's trade was at stake.

Recent failures forced the French to make a long-overdue reappraisal of their policies in 1743. Louis XV was now clearly engaged in full-scale war with Britain and Austria, although formally at peace with both. The King lacked coherent objectives of his own except to increase his personal prestige and further Bourbon family interests, but he had been battered by conflicting ministerial advice. Eventually he decided, largely in self-defence, to concentrate on those areas where France had been most successful in the past and which would directly threaten Austria and Britain: Italy, the Rhineland and the Southern Netherlands. The kind of bold stroke undertaken by Belle-Isle had become a thing of the past. By this point France appears to have abandoned any idea of territorial gains for herself, though Louis XV sought them for his favourite daughter who was now married to Don Philip, the younger son of Philip V and Farnese. In October 1743 he signed a close dynastic alliance with the Spanish King at Fontainebleau (the Second Family Compact), formulating a policy mainly for his Bourbon relatives' benefit. France and Spain should cooperate in Italy to conquer Milan, Parma and Piacenza from Austria for Louis's son-in-law; the two powers would renew their joint action against Britain overseas, abandoned in 1741; and France would help Spain regain Gibraltar and Minorca and cancel the British commercial concessions. In spring 1744, war was at last declared against Britain (March) and Austria (April). Franco-Spanish forces invaded Italy, but met with little success against Austria and Sardinia. An attempt to invade Britain to restore the Stuarts was abandoned when a storm dispersed the French fleet. However, the French invasion of the Austrian Netherlands under Marshal Saxe, a natural child of Augustus II of Saxony–Poland, was highly successful.

A widening conflict, 1744–1748

Saxe's campaign was aided, and allied attempts to counter it along the Rhine undermined, when Frederick the Great re-entered the struggle. He invaded Bohemia in August 1744 to begin Prussia's Second Silesian War (1744–45). Ever since his withdrawal in summer 1742 the King had kept a close watch on the fighting's progress. He had been alarmed by the treaty of Worms, which had guaranteed the Pragmatic Sanction without any reference to his gain of Silesia. Thereafter, Frederick had tentatively embarked upon a *rapprochement* with France. It was Maria Theresa's recovery, however, her occupation of Bavaria and the alliance concluded with her previous enemy, Saxony, in December 1743, which pushed him into a new campaign to weaken Austria and secure further guarantees for Silesia. He feared that if the Habsburg recovery continued, Maria Theresa might in time attack him to regain the lost province. With his finances restored and an army now 140,000 strong, he soon took Prague and forced the Austrians to evacuate Bavaria. During the final months of 1744, however, Frederick was forced to retreat from Bohemia in circumstances which were close to a military disaster.

Prussia's renewed intervention was a serious blow to Carteret's anti-French policy: the Austrians once more had to face a war on two fronts, although the French had no intention of sending another army into central Europe. Carteret was also disappointed that the Dutch Republic, despite the French invasion of the Austrian Netherlands, still refused to enter the war. At home, his political position was crumbling. His ministerial colleagues, Henry Pelham, Pelham's brother Newcastle, and the great jurist and influential politician the Earl of Hardwicke, envied his close relations with George II and resented the burden of guiding his costly and unpopular subsidy policy through parliament. It was easy to claim that the British-financed 'Pragmatic Army' in Germany was defending Hanover and Austria rather than British interests: in the House of Commons Pitt called Carteret the 'Hanoverian troop-minister'. Yet it is difficult to see what else could have been done. George II was determined to defend his Electorate and, with only a small army of her own, Britain had to contain France through foreign alliances and troops, which were expensive. The imperialist war against Spain, and public enthusiasm for it, had fizzled out after the failures in the Caribbean. Nonetheless, in December 1744 Carteret was forced to resign. Newcastle assumed overall responsibility for foreign policy, while Henry Pelham, who became leader of the ministry, was at the Treasury.

The Pelhamite administration confronted much the same problems as Carteret and adopted very similar solutions. They showed no more appreciation of Britain's imperial interests, and they continued to view the war largely in terms of Europe, its balance of power, and the need to maintain a coalition against France. However, they were helped in making the struggle appear more necessary and intelligible to the public by the direction of the French war effort from 1744. Saxe's advances in Flanders brought home the French danger in a form not apparent since the days of Louis XIV, while France's support for the Stuart Pretender reopened the question of Britain's Protestant succession. The French decision to cooperate with Spain in the desultory war at sea revived the struggle between Britain and France for overseas supremacy which had been anticipated in 1740–41. The importance of this for contemporaries should not be exaggerated. Since Fleury's death, French ministers had no more real grasp of the importance of the contest for empire than those in Britain. On both sides of the Channel the overseas struggle was undertaken hesitantly and with the minimum of resources. Nonetheless, the clash of Anglo-French interests was now more direct and apparent, and it provided the main reason for the continuation of the War of the Austrian Succession beyond 1745.

In that year the struggle within Germany came to an end. In January the Emperor Charles VII died and Bavarian pretensions with him. An Austro-Bavarian peace was quickly signed at Füssen in April, restoring the electorate to the Wittelsbach family, and soon afterwards Maria Theresa's husband was elected emperor as Francis I. Throughout that year the British tried to persuade the new Empress to come to terms with Prussia, using the argument that France was her main enemy. Maria Theresa obstinately refused, declaring on one occasion she would 'rather give away my chemise and petticoat than Silesia'. But a series of impressive Prussian victories, at Hohenfriedberg (June 1745), Soor (September) and Kesselsdorf (December), culminating in the occupation of Austria's ally, Saxony, reinforced by a British threat to cut off the vital subsidies, forced her to agree to peace. Frederick himself desperately wanted this too. Though these successes over the Austrians had established his own military reputation and that of his army, the King was anxious to rebuild his forces and refill his war chest. He feared that the Russians, free from war with the Swedes since 1743 (see below, p. 70) and with Elizabeth securely established as Empress, would attack him to rescue her client Augustus of Saxony–Poland. He knew he could expect little help from France and none from Bavaria. On Christmas Day 1745, Austria and Prussia therefore concluded the peace of Dresden, where Frederick once more received guarantees for his possession of Silesia. The treaty, coming after the peace with Bavaria, effectively settled the question of the Austrian succession. The war itself now became essentially a conflict between the Bourbon powers and the Austro-British alliance for and against French hegemony in western and central Europe.

The Austrians now showed more enthusiasm for fighting France. Their only hope for compensation for Silesia lay outside Germany, and in 1746 Maria Theresa concentrated all her forces in Italy, the Netherlands and along the Rhine. The British had grown desperate for this help because of the extent of French victories in 1745. Bourbon troops had won successes in northern Italy but above all in the Austrian Netherlands, where Marshal Saxe had made remarkable gains for France. His impressive victory at Fontenoy over the Anglo-Austrian army in May 1745 was followed by the occupation of most of the country. This was facilitated by the withdrawal of the British regiments and those Dutch troops protecting the Barrier to suppress a Jacobite rebellion in Britain. In July 1745, the Young Pretender, Charles Edward, landed in Scotland and began the 'Forty-five adventure, the greatest challenge to the Hanoverian dynasty since its accession in 1714. Although it failed and Jacobitism died with it, the confidence of the British establishment was badly shaken and London's vulnerability had been clearly demonstrated by an invasion which only turned back at Derby. Fortunately, its naval power ensured the French could not dispatch direct military help, but the rebellion and French conquests in the Austrian Netherlands convinced the Pelhamite government and public opinion that the war was now one for Britain's survival, and that Louis XV had to be humbled.

The immediacy of the French threat made it more difficult than ever to consider the possibility of harming France seriously outside Europe. When the Anglo-French naval conflict broke out in earnest in 1745, the British fleets concentrated on protecting the British Isles, attacking the French in the Mediterranean, and, where possible, disrupting France's international trade, especially that with the West Indies. Neither government took much interest in the skirmishes between their North American colonists or the agents of their East India companies on the Indian subcontinent. However, in 1745, a largely colonial force, backed by the Royal Navy, captured Cape

Breton Island with its massive fortress of Louisbourg controlling the St Lawrence seaway, which was the gateway into French Canada. In Britain, public opinion immediately seized on the victory, after a series of reverses, and Louisbourg's retention was endowed with great symbolic importance.

If national survival had become the purpose of the war in Britain, what had it become for the French now that Bavarian and Prussian desertion had ruined their ambitions for control of Germany? Despite her success, it is difficult to know what France wanted, apart from a vague yearning for hegemony. In Italy Louis wished to continue the close co-operation he had achieved with Philip V and to further the dynastic ambitions of Don Philip, the Spanish King's son and Louis's son-in-law. But quarrels with Madrid over the details of the territorial settlement made it impossible for the Bourbons to capitalise on their military victories and Sardinia's willingness for peace. As to the Southern Netherlands, there were suggestions from some French ministers that their forces should be withdrawn and the area permanently neutralised, so as to reassure the Dutch and turn them against Britain. Louis, however, without any apparent intention of formal annexation, preferred to follow Saxe's advice to achieve complete military conquest, and the bulk of French forces operated there until the end of the war.

The Peace of Aix-la-Chapelle, 1748

During the War of the Austrian Succession, as in other eighteenth-century conflicts, diplomacy had continued side-by-side with the military and naval operations. The celebrated indecisiveness of warfare before the French Revolution was apparent to contemporaries, and meant that campaigns and battles aimed only to create a marginal advantage, which could then be turned into a clear-cut political success by skilful negotiation. Fighting was accompanied by a series of unofficial and semi-official diplomatic initiatives, designed to probe the opposition's ability and will to continue to fight and, in its final stages, by more formal discussions in peace congresses, which began at Breda in autumn 1746 and took two years to complete. The extent to which the Austrian Succession struggle became an Anglo-French conflict, particularly after 1744, was reflected in the peace negotiations, which were dominated by the two leading western powers. These also revealed a second characteristic of eighteenth-century wars: the tendency for the initial sources of conflict to be overtaken by other issues, as the fighting threw up new problems to be resolved. In the peace negotiations of 1746–48 the original Anglo-Spanish disputes played little part, while the question of the Austrian Succession had been resolved by 1745. Instead, the details of the Italian settlement consumed most time and caused most friction.

The settlement with Prussia in 1745 did not mean the end of Austria's war. The direction and, before long, the success of French military expansion obliged Vienna to defend its own possessions in Italy and in the Netherlands. Although the Austrian government increasingly considered the latter a financial burden, its loss would have been a further blow to Habsburg prestige and Vienna expected the Maritime Powers to defend the region. By contrast, Italy offered the possibility of territorial compensation for Silesia and the greater part of Austria's army was now deployed in the peninsula. By late 1746 her forces and those of Sardinia, both heavily subsidised by Britain, had expelled most of the quarrelling Bourbon troops from the north. Maria Theresa had become convinced that the Monarchy needed peace to carry out wide-ranging internal reforms. The Austrians, moreover, felt they were becoming British mercenaries in an Anglo-French war. The decision for war or peace did in fact largely rest with the two western powers, as the paymasters of Austria and Spain.

By 1746, Louis XV personally wanted a settlement despite difficulties over satisfying his Spanish relatives and Saxe's argument that once all the Austrian Netherlands were conquered, France could dictate terms. British intransigence, however, wrecked indirect French moves for peace. The first formal attempt to end the fighting, the congress which met at Breda in 1746–47, also broke up without any agreement. While Pelham wanted an end to the war because of the financial burden, Newcastle, George II and his influential second son, the duke of Cumberland, insisted on fighting until France had been humbled. The conquest of Louisbourg and its popularity in Britain, Cumberland's final defeat of the Jacobites at Culloden in April 1746, success in Italy and the death of Spain's Philip V in that July, led them to ignore the deteriorating situation in the Netherlands. They had high hopes that Philip's son by his first wife, Ferdinand VI (1746–59), might conclude a separate peace. The new Spanish King had a pro-British, Portuguese wife and was known to hate his stepmother, Elisabeth Farnese, and her children. The Anglo-Spanish commercial disputes which had led to the war of 1739 remained unresolved, however, and neither side had gained the upper hand in the fighting which followed, while Ferdinand personally wanted a principality in Italy for his half-brother Don Philip, in order to remove him from Spain.

The military conflict meanwhile appeared to be turning in France's favour. In September 1746 Madras fell to the French East India Company.

This was the sole event of significance in some small-scale fighting in the sub-continent. More importantly, the French advance in the Low Countries could not be staunched. Saxe captured many of the Barrier fortresses and won two more impressive victories at Rocoux (October 1746) and Laufeldt (July 1747), which gave France control over the Austrian Netherlands. By 1747 his army had reached the Dutch border. In April, France declared war on the Republic, which, despite the involvement of its Barrier fortress troops in the fighting, had hitherto struggled to uphold its neutrality. The resulting panic in Holland led to a revolution, the overthrow of the pacific Regent oligarchic regime, in power since 1702, and the restoration of the stadtholderate under William IV (1747-50).

Newcastle, who shared the misconception of other eighteenth-century British ministers about the enduring strength of the Dutch, deluded himself into believing they would now join in a new Grand Alliance. But the Republic was no longer a real force in international relations, its vitality sapped by economic decline. William IV was no William III, and the Dutch, whatever their régime, desperately wanted peace and a return to neutrality. It soon became clear that substantial British financial support would be essential if it were to play any part in the fighting. When the great fortress of Bergen-op-Zoom fell to Saxe in September 1747, even the most bellicose British leaders concluded that only an early settlement could save the Republic from being overrun. Maria Theresa would send her troops only to Italy and was suspected of spending British subsidies on building her palace of Schönbrunn. Although Britain had signed an agreement with Russia in 1747 for troops to be sent to the Republic the following year, the full cost would fall on London, which was already paying £1.7 million in foreign subsidies in 1747. This was in addition to £6 million spent on her own army and navy. Britain's Austrian Succession War was at least as expensive as that of the Spanish Succession had been. It was eventually to cost £43 million, of which £30 million was added to the National Debt. With the Land Tax at 4s in the pound, alarmists in the government raised the spectre of national bankruptcy. Early in 1748, therefore, serious peace talks between the Maritime Powers and France began at Aix-la Chapelle (Aachen).

Saxe's spectacular victories should have given France a strong bargaining position, but Louis XV and the country as a whole, which had suffered a food crisis in 1747, were as anxious for peace as the British. There were also straws in the wind for what was to happen in the next war, but they were signs which the British in their scramble for peace failed to grasp. During 1747 the French finance minister, Machault, had pleaded for an end to the fighting because the financial system was collapsing. The cause, besides its inbuilt weaknesses, was the dramatic decline in customs receipts as French foreign trade dried up. Initially the maritime war had hardly affected French commerce: Canada was bottled up, but contact was maintained with the West Indies, while neutral Dutch ships still entered French ports. By 1747, however, British naval victories, and an effective blockade of the French coast, radically altered the situation. The Newfoundland fisheries were cut off and there were justified anxieties that the priceless sugar islands might fall into British hands. In contrast, British commerce, which had declined after 1739, was now recovering and perhaps even expanding, as the navy secured increasing control over trade routes. Versailles assumed Britain could continue the war indefinitely at sea despite her defeats on land. The occupation of the Austrian Netherlands and the conquest of the Dutch Republic hardly seemed grounds for prolonging a struggle which was crippling France's economy.

In their haste for peace neither France nor Britain took advantage of their strength in different spheres to prolong the negotiations. It was particularly surprising that the considerable military advantage secured by Saxe for France was not reflected in the actual terms of the settlement. Although Louis wished to satisfy Don Philip, he wanted nothing for himself. An overriding concern about the financial situation and need to raise the British blockade made him agree to return the Austrian Netherlands without compensation. Britain exhibited a similar desire for peace and felt the preliminaries, signed at the very end of April 1748, had saved her from ruin. Austria, who had tried in vain to interest the French in separate negotiations, Spain and Sardinia all had to fall in line with their paymasters and the definitive treaty of Aix-la-Chapelle was signed in October 1748.

The Anglo-French settlement was based upon the return of all conquests: the Southern Netherlands were restored to Austria and the Dutch allowed back as impotent custodians of the Barrier fortresses. France's withdrawal from this region was matched by Britain's return of Louisbourg. London also recovered Madras, while the French once again expelled the Stuarts, guaranteed the Protestant succession and agreed to destroy Dunkirk's sea defences, renewing commitments given in the Utrecht settlement. As both states wished to cultivate him, Frederick's possession of Silesia was guaranteed in the final treaty. A similar guarantee was given to Maria Theresa for her remaining lands and her husband was confirmed in his possession of Tuscany, but she had to cede Parma and Piacenza to Don Philip and yet more of Milan to Sardinia. Once again the main territorial changes in a European settlement had applied to the Italian peninsula where the Bourbon dynasty was gaining ground, though this was the last occasion before the French Revolutionary Wars when this was to be so.

The peace of Aix-la-Chapelle ignored the disputes which had caused the Anglo-Spanish War in 1739. Both governments had been reticent in the negotiations as they wished to conciliate each other. Britain believed that Ferdinand VI's accession presented a clear opportunity to disrupt the Family Compact signed in 1743, and her diplomacy pursued a *rapprochement* with Spain. Their rivalry in any case had been dwarfed by that which had now erupted between Britain and France and which had been by no means resolved: the Anglo-French antagonism which had re-emerged during the 1740s would continue down to 1815 and even beyond. The outcome of this struggle was vital to the economic development of both powers. If Britain had not ultimately succeeded in holding on to and expanding her overseas markets, particularly in the New World, her great economic advance during the eighteenth century would have been severely reduced. Yet British ministers were slow to realise the economic significance of the mid-century conflicts at a period when colonial trade was more important ideologically than commercially. Public opinion, some members of parliament, government agents in the colonies and the colonists themselves were more aware of exactly what was at stake. Ministers similarly failed to grasp the extent of British success and French desperation in the naval struggle at the close of the Austrian Succession War. The Pelhamite ministry's priorities remained London's traditional concerns: the containment of France in Europe, the defence of the British Isles and strategically sensitive areas on the continent, principally the Low Countries, Hanover, the Italian peninsula and, to a lesser extent, Portugal. Trade and colonisation could be left to individual initiative. The exchange of Louisbourg for the Austrian Netherlands underlined that British ministers saw the settlement from a Eurocentric perspective. Certainly they had grounds enough to worry about Britain's future role in Europe, given France's military successes and the disarray of the alliances employed by London to contain her. The Dutch had proved useless, while the relationship with Austria had become increasingly strained. Something new would have to be worked out to replace or complement the moribund Grand Alliance to defend Britain, the Netherlands and Hanover.

France's position was equally paradoxical. Saxe's military victories had eclipsed those of Frederick the Great, while the anti-French coalition had achieved none of the success of its predecessors and had been close to collapse when the fighting ended. At Aix-la-Chapelle an Austrian diplomat had declared: 'France has achieved her great aim, the humiliation of the house of Austria.' The serious territorial losses suffered by the Habsburg Monarchy seemed to confirm this. Yet France herself secured no tangible territorial gains and few obvious political benefits from the fighting, and puzzled Parisians coined the phrase, 'bête comme la paix' – 'stupid as the peace'. What had begun as a bid for European hegemony in the style of Louis XIV had proved beyond French resources, while even the later more modest attempt at expansion had had to be abandoned because of the collapse of trade and finances. France's foreign policy objectives needed to be re-examined, particularly as her own alliances with Spain and Prussia were unstable. With decisive leadership and realistic goals Louis XV's monarchy could look forward to future success. Although less overwhelming than in the late seventeenth century, France was still Europe's leading military power and had the potential to match Britain overseas.

For Austria the peace was little short of humiliating. Although Maria Theresa's succession had been confirmed and the bulk of her possessions preserved, the fighting had led to losses in Italy as well as Silesia. Desperation for subsidies had reduced the Empress to a position of dependence upon London. On being told the peace terms by the British minister in Vienna, she had exclaimed: 'Why am I always to be excluded from transacting my own business?' Austria therefore needed to regain control of her own policies, if she were to act as a major state. Even more importantly, the domestic foundations of Habsburg power had to be rebuilt. The Austrian Succession conflict had confirmed the Monarchy's military and financial weakness, earlier apparent during the unsuccessful wars of the 1730s. To achieve recovery, a thoroughgoing reform of the army and of the administration and finances in Austria and Bohemia was undertaken in the late 1740s and early 1750s. Copying the reforms of government which had proved so effective in Frederick William I's Prussia, Maria Theresa's ministers tried to transform her diverse possessions into a more centralised and stronger state. Externally, the aims of the new Austria were to be concentrated on recovering Silesia and regaining a dominant position in Germany. Vienna's interests in the Austrian Netherlands and even in the Italian peninsula were now far less important than revenge upon the Prussian upstart. The differences with Spain and even with France were to fade into the background. Although Maria Theresa's family had regained the Imperial crown and the accompanying prestige, the traditional 'German mission' of defending the Rhine barrier against France and regaining lands lost to her, was to be far less important in the future.

The principal beneficiary of the war had not even been represented at Aix-la-Chapelle, though the final settlement guaranteed the annexation of Silesia. By this conquest Frederick the Great increased Prussia's resources and population by almost half. He spent the years after the peace of Dresden (1745) trying to assimilate the new province and expanding his army and revenues. The army was his principal asset, and soon became the model for other European forces. Ultimately, possession of Silesia and Frederick's own survival rested on these soldiers, whose reputation had been established by Prussia's victories in the Second Silesian War of 1744–45. International treaties might guarantee his conquest to him, but it could be snatched away just as cynically as he had seized it: his annexation had now set the pattern for international morality. Frederick himself judged the European situation was not ripe for further Prussian expansion; he also laboured under the disadvantage that no one really trusted him.

The King had gained Silesia by exploiting the wider continental struggle and allowing other states to bear the brunt of the fighting. The War of the Austrian Succession had lasted for eight years, yet Prussia had been at war for less than half this time, around three years. Convinced of his state's strategic vulnerability and believing that scarce resources forced him to fight what he termed 'short, lively wars', the King had pursued an opportunistic and single-minded strategy which gained him a rich new province but at the price of a well-deserved and enduring reputation for faithlessness where international agreements were concerned. The three occasions on which he had deserted the anti-Austrian coalition would come back to haunt him in the years ahead. Neighbours such as Hanover and Saxony were alarmed by the new potential of the Prussian military state. The extent to which its revenues and resources were devoted to the single objective of supporting a formidable army, now some 140,000 strong, caused especial anxiety: Prussia's army had increased by three-quarters since his accession, less than a decade before.

Prussia's striking gain was unusual in the eighteenth century, since territory – and a substantial province at that – had been seized from one of the established powers, rather than a second-rank or declining state, and its annexation undoubtedly increased her political standing. Yet it is important not to exaggerate what Frederick had accomplished by 1748. He had gained territory and prestige for his state, and renown for himself and his army, but he had not made Prussia a leading power. That would not be accomplished until the Seven Years War had been fought and drawn. Silesia was a considerable addition, particularly for the impover-ished Hohenzollern monarchy. Though economic motives had not played any part in the invasion, the new province's importance came to be primarily commercial. In 1739 – the final year of Habsburg rule – it had paid one-quarter of the direct taxation collected by Vienna from the Hereditary Lands (the Austrian duchies and the Kingdom of Bohemia), which underlined its prosperity and economic importance. Populous and with a strong agrarian economy, it brought the King one million new subjects, including a substantial Protestant minority who welcomed the Prussians as liberators. Silesia's Roman Catholic majority, however, were unreconciled to rule from Berlin and constituted a potential Habsburg Fifth Column. The river Oder which ran through Silesia and then Brand-enburg to the Baltic was now a potentially important commercial artery. The thriving Silesian linen industry was crucial to Prussia's backward economy while, with state support, woollen production would now develop impressively. Within a decade the new province was providing no less than 45 per cent of total Prussian exports. It thus brought what the Hohenzollern monarchy had hitherto lacked: a manufacturing region.

At the time, however, it posed problems for the government in Berlin. The new province had to be integrated into Prussia's administrative system and this proved a difficult and protracted process, while its fortifications had to be improved. Its acquisition increased the already extended borders which had to be defended, while the wedge it inserted into Saxony–Poland strengthened that state's enmity towards its Hohenzollern neigh-bour. Above all Austria was unreconciled to its loss, which compromised Habsburg security and military strategy. Prussian possession of Silesia meant that the invasion route from its foothills across the Bohemian plain to Vienna lay open, with only Moravia as a defensive barrier behind which Austrian forces could organise. From his Silesian redoubt Frederick could and did invade Bohemia at will, as he would during the Seven Years War. Silesia's strategic and economic benefits, however, were less signifi-cant than its symbolic importance. Prussia had become Austria's near-equal in the Empire where, by the 1750s, Frederick was able to block Habsburg initiatives in imperial institutions and in this way complicate management of the Empire, as well as a major force in European diplo-macy. The future of Germany, however, should not be seen solely in terms of Austro-Prussian rivalry. France still had plenty of scope, if she wanted, to follow her traditional policy of trying to make the German states, including Prussia herself, her satellites. Britain was also involved in

Imperial politics because of Hanover which had to be protected from French retaliation or Prussian expansion and because the allies she needed against France were likely to come from there. Finally, German affairs were of increasing concern to Russia.

Russia had remained in the wings throughout the fighting, at times apparently about to intervene on the Austro-British side but then drawing back because of her domestic troubles. Her expansionism and solidarity with Vienna, so evident in the 1730s, had collapsed amidst the political upheavals following Anna's death in 1740. In 1741 a Swedish attack on Russia, launched by the pro-French Hat party, had coincided with the successful coup against the child Emperor Ivan VI by Peter the Great's daughter, Elizabeth, who had Franco-Swedish support. Once on the throne, however, the new Empress had turned against her foreign friends and at the Treaty of Åbo (1743) the Swedes, after a disastrous and ill-considered war, were forced to yield more of Finland to act as a protective shield around St Petersburg. The peace settlements of 1721 and 1743 effectively partitioned Stockholm's eastern Baltic salient and, throughout the eighteenth century, there was to be a permanent military confrontation along the Russo-Swedish border there. Under the influence of her chancellor, A.P. Bestuzhev-Riumin, Elizabeth now moved gradually to a pro-Austrian and British stance. Although Frederick II had not challenged Russian control over Poland, his temporary occupation of Augustus III's Saxon electorate (1745) was deeply resented. Prussia's emergence as a strong power in north Germany threatened Russia's control of the eastern Baltic and would prove a barrier to further expansion westwards, while East Prussia appeared a menacing salient when viewed from St Petersburg and not the exposed target it appeared from Berlin.

In 1746 Russia renewed her alliance with Austria, first concluded in 1726, and this now acquired a decidedly anti-Prussian tone. Vienna feared further aggression by Frederick. While promising each other mutual assistance against attack from any power in the future, Elizabeth also agreed, in a secret article, to help Maria Theresa regain Silesia if Prussia attacked either Saxony or Austria. This 'Alliance of the Two Empresses' formed the basis of a growing determination by both powers to destroy Frederick himself. It was complemented in Bestuzhev's system by an alliance concluded with Britain in December 1747, one which George II's Hanoverian ministers had actively promoted to protect the electorate from possible Prussian attack. In 1747, however, the main purpose in British eyes was to use Russia as a convenient source of mercenaries to save the Dutch from France, and the following January 30,000 Russians had set out for the Republic in return for a £500,000 subsidy. The march of the Russians was an added incentive for France to make peace. This episode, however, underlined that the major continental battlefields were still out of range of Russia's forces. In 1748 the Russian corps had made a leisurely progress westwards. The army's established logistical problems meant that it covered only two to three miles a day, and rested up every third day. It had only reached Poland when peace was signed. Exactly the same thing had happened a decade before in 1735, when another Russian army had lumbered westward but arrived too late to play any part in the War of the Polish Succession. While Russia's potential was clear to contemporaries, her slow emergence as a continental military power delayed her political arrival. Her importance, however, was increasing. The threat of Russia in the background had made both Prussia and France uneasy during the war: now with Elizabeth securely established in power, Russia was to play a far more telling, and often decisive, role in Europe.

CHAPTER 3

The Diplomatic Revolution and the origins of the Seven Years War, 1748–1756

Europe enjoyed less than a decade of peace after the settlement of Aix-la-Chapelle before being plunged into another general conflict, the Seven Years War: the last war before the French Revolution to involve all the leading states. The peace was little more than a truce between Britain and France, particularly in the colonies, while in a similar way Austria was unreconciled to Prussia's gain of Silesia and immediately began internal reforms and diplomatic preparations for an eventual war to recover the province. Yet the new conflict was more than a continuation of the earlier one, especially with the intervention of Russia. The European system was becoming one of five major states with competing interests. No power dominated as France had in the 1730s or Britain in the years after Utrecht. The rise of Prussia and the re-entry of Russia as a major protagonist gave greater prominence to central and east European issues, and much of the diplomatic initiative after 1748 was to be taken by Austria and Russia. On the other hand, the Dutch Republic and Spain had now clearly ceased to be leading states and were to show a justifiable passivity.

The War of the Austrian Succession had witnessed the Republic's eclipse as a European power. It had been dragged unwillingly into the conflict in 1744–45 through its residual treaty obligations, legacies of the earlier struggle against Louis XIV. The fighting which followed had revealed the Republic's powerlessness, as Barrier fortresses fell like ninepins to French troops, who occupied the Austrian Netherlands and eventually invaded

Dutch territory. Efforts to re-establish the 'Barrier' system after the peace settlement, especially during detailed negotiations in 1753–54, only revealed its collapse. Austria was preoccupied with the struggle with Prussia and had abandoned her historic opposition to France, as Newcastle would discover at this period. The loss of the Republic's military and diplomatic shield contributed to the drift and uncertainty evident in Dutch policy, a mood which was further strengthened by the unambiguous evidence of economic decline. Though the court faction who ruled during the minority (1751–66) of the child-stadtholder William V favoured the traditional cooperation with Britain, such an approach now had little to commend it and was widely unpopular. The prevailing view within the Republic was to concentrate on its commercial and financial interests and ignore European quarrels. The Dutch army and navy were too decayed to contemplate war, while it was clear that neither of the traditional allies, Britain and Austria, could defend the Southern Netherlands. Badly shaken by Saxe's victories, the Republic now had little choice but to conciliate France.

The Dutch attitude resembled that of the new Spanish King. Ferdinand VI was uninterested in foreign affairs; his minister, Carvajal, intended to use *détentes* with Portugal, Britain and Austria to give Spain the chance to concentrate on her domestic and colonial economy and become independent of both France and Britain. These altered priorities were facilitated by a broader change in Spanish objectives apparent by the end of the Austrian Succession War. The Aix-la-Chapelle settlement conferred upon Farnese's second son, Don Philip, the Italian territories of Parma, Piacenza and Guastalla. The realisation of a long-standing dynastic aim brought to an end Madrid's preoccupation with the Italian peninsula, which four years later was put into political cold storage by the Austro-Spanish Treaty of Aranjuez (June 1752). An early symptom of the Habsburg–Bourbon *rapprochement* which was under way and would culminate in the 'Diplomatic Revolution' of 1756 (see below, pp. 81–92), this agreement stabilised and neutralised Italy and reduced French influence south of the Alps. Spain and Austria recognised each other's spheres of influence: Vienna was to be dominant in the north, where Milan was ruled directly and Tuscany was the personal possession of Maria Theresa's husband, the Emperor Francis Stephen. Spain controlled the Kingdom of Naples and Sicily where Charles VII ('Don Carlos') had ruled since 1738, while Don Philip's appanage was to be an outpost of Bourbon influence further north.

The agreement at Aranjuez guaranteed the territorial *status quo* in the peninsula and provided for reciprocal military assistance to defend it. The treaty was then imposed upon the various Italian states, who were unable to resist this Austro-Spanish security system for Italy. Its value was seen four years later when a new war broke out in Europe. The Seven Years War was the first general continental conflict since the early seventeenth century which did not extend to the peninsula. It was to be four decades after the Treaty of Aranjuez before war returned to Italy, during the struggle against the French Revolution. During this period Spain's principal concern was to be rivalry with Britain overseas, the importance of which had been signalled during the 1730s and 1740s. Yet at first the foreign minister Carvajal worked for a compromise with London. No more was said about Minorca and Gibraltar, and he hoped that the withdrawal of the *guarda-costas* and buying out the South Sea Company's rights to the final four years of the *asiento* for £100,000 in 1750, together with confirmation of trading concessions with metropolitan Spain, would persuade the British to end their smuggling with Spanish America. These hopes were to be imperfectly realised, but they contributed to a period of improved relations. Spain stood aloof from a growing Anglo-French confrontation after 1748.

The unofficial Anglo-French War in America, 1748–1755

Rivalry between Britain and France had been notably revived by the fighting during the 1740s. It is conventional to describe the Anglo-French competition and frequent warfare between 1689 and 1815 as the Second 'Hundred Years War', a renewal of the extended struggle during the later Middle Ages. Yet it would in some ways be more accurate to talk of a 'Seventy Years War' extending from 1744 to 1815, so continuous was the rivalry during these decades and so extensive and frequent the periods of open warfare. Anglo-French tension continued and was apparent to all after the settlement at Aix-la-Chapelle, seen by both states as precarious. War would formally be renewed only in 1755–56. From the early 1750s, however, an undeclared colonial conflict was in progress, and London and Versailles were both unable to exert the degree of control over events outside Europe which they wished. George II's ministers also had to contend with a volatile public opinion and parliamentary opposition, as they formulated a policy towards France, viewed more than ever as Britain's natural enemy.

While both states were prepared for confrontation and even unofficial warfare overseas, neither sought a general war in Europe. Both wished for peace, to attend to the financial legacies of the recent fighting. This was particularly so in France, where Louis XV's ministers were divided and government continued to drift without firm direction. Maurepas and, after 1754, Machault strove to rebuild the navy and so reduce Britain's lead at sea, which had grown during the War of the Austrian Succession. Their aim was to more than double the number of French battleships and frigates, and by 1756 these efforts had been successful, an achievement which was magnified by a simultaneous standstill in British constructions. Spain's navy grew even more impressively at this period, though the fact that the Family Compact was in abeyance during Ferdinand VI's reign meant that this revival was not of immediate significance. These efforts did not mean that either Bourbon power sought an early resumption of hostilities. Madrid was pacific and anglophile: one reason for Newcastle's wish to avoid a general war with France was his desire not to imperil the *rapprochement* with Spain which was in progress. France was preoccupied by domestic problems because of the revival of the Jansenist religious controversy and quarrels between the Crown and the privileged orders over taxation. The loss of almost half the French merchant fleet in the last conflict swayed such public opinion as there was to be non-imperialist and convinced that peace was desirable.

In London the Pelhamite ministry showed more unity of purpose and had a secure majority in parliament, but it was equally pacific. While Newcastle controlled foreign policy, the dominant influence until 1754 was his brother Henry Pelham at the Treasury. In the Walpole tradition Pelham believed war hampered trade, and he also wanted to keep the Land Tax low and avoid increasing the National Debt. Consequently, expenditure on the navy and army was cut, and he and parliament firmly opposed additional foreign subsidies. Like Walpole before him, he would have preferred to ignore Europe, but London could no longer afford to remain as detached from continental issues as during the 1730s. While the threat to the Hanoverian dynasty itself was now over, Britain remained directly involved because of the overt rivalry with France and the potential French threats to the Southern Netherlands and to George II's Electorate, which was also menaced by Versailles' ally Prussia. The year after Aix-la-Chapelle, Newcastle had described the French as 'the absolute Masters of Europe'. His active diplomacy (see below, p. 84ff) was designed to weaken this dominance and to protect these British interests from future French aggression. Throughout the inter-war period British assumptions about France's opposition within Europe were reflected in decisions taken over North America. The growing confrontation there in turn strengthened Anglo-French rivalry on the continent.

Outside Europe, British and French interests clashed in India, the Caribbean, West Africa and North America. Although rivalry in the other areas contributed to the increasing tension, only North America was to be a major cause of the Seven Years War. The volume of trade with the entire Far East was very small: the monopolistic English East India Company only sent out a score of ships every year. Yet it consisted primarily of luxury goods , and so its value was very high. The Far East, nevertheless, was viewed as less important than the American hemisphere, both in London and at Versailles. The clashes which developed in southern India between the agents of the English and French companies after 1749 were discouraged from Europe, as neither government considered vital interests to be at stake. Both governments viewed the Caribbean islands as the most important overseas interest. Hundreds of ships sailed back and forth across the Atlantic every year, while a fifth of France's entire external trade was with the West Indies. Although it made mercantilist sense to seize one another's islands and plantations, both governments showed themselves keen to avoid a clash. Conflict in the Caribbean required a willingness to commit their navies, and before 1755 neither was prepared to do so. While control of the West Indies would be the most valuable prize in any future war, it was not itself a motive for the renewed fighting.

In North America, by contrast, a direct but localised confrontation between the respective colonists escalated after 1753–54 into open conflict between the two governments and then into a full-scale war. The North American 'Seven Years War' was in reality a nine-year-long conflict. Its roots lay in the pattern of European settlement, with the 13 British colonies with their agrarian and commercial economies located along North America's eastern coastline. These far-flung settlements were hemmed in by Spain's outpost in Florida and especially France's in Louisiana and Canada: French possessions were strung out along the waterways of the St Lawrence, the Great Lakes and the Mississippi. Until the mid-eighteenth century, friction had been contained by the smallness of colonial populations and the vast areas available for settlement. By 1748, however, the rival colonies were coming into contact and tension increased. The population of the British settlements had leapt sevenfold over the past half-century to some two million, creating considerable demographic pressure within the existing colonies. Hungry for new land to settle, the colonists pressed relentlessly westwards and northwards: through the Allegheny Mountains towards the Great Lakes, through the Appalachians into the Upper Ohio Valley, and into Maine, the no-man's-land between New England and French Acadia. In each case British expansion collided with France's established colonial interests while, in the south, Spanish Florida stood in the way of a similar push from Georgia. The dynamism of Britain's empire by mid-century appeared to threaten the very existence of its French and Spanish rivals.

Although there were probably only 60,000 Europeans in French Canada and even fewer in the newer colony of Louisiana, they were more rigidly controlled by their governors than their British counterparts who were much more independent of London's control. After 1748 the latter were working to link together the two colonies with a chain of fortresses and alliances with native Indian tribes to stem the westward tide of the British. A *cordon sanitaire* was to be created, extending northwards from the Mississippi as far as Lake Erie. The French had clear advantages in the struggle with Britain's colonists which came to a head during the 1750s. The Indians preferred to cooperate with the French Canadians, who were largely trappers and hunters, rather than with the British who wanted their land to settle and farm. France had an efficient and centralised military organisation, unlike the squabbling British colonists, and Louis XV's government was willing to send out significant numbers of regular troops. Versailles recognised that Canada's population was too small to defend itself, and that a large garrison was needed, because in wartime the British navy could always cut off the supply of reinforcements. Although Canada, with its skins and furs, was of marginal economic value compared with the Newfoundland fishing banks or the tropical agriculture of Louisiana and the West Indies, Versailles looked on the defence of its oldest colony as a matter of national prestige and was determined not to leave the settlers in the lurch. Nonetheless, although France's agents in Canada were pursuing a forward policy and the number of French troops there was being steadily increased, Louis XV himself continued to try to conciliate London. Britain's naval supremacy made France's position very precarious, and to the eve of formal hostilities Versailles put up with continual provocation in order to avoid outright war.

Though the economic importance of American colonies for Britain was less than their ideological significance, it was still considerable. The southern settlements exported semi-tropical goods such as tobacco and cotton, while the north was seen as an alternative to the Baltic for the prized naval stores. Both regions absorbed British exports and supplied the West Indies with essentials. Nonetheless, George II's ministers flinched from open war over America, though frequently they adopted a firm stance over individual problems and were perfectly prepared to see fighting between the rival groups of settlers. It was really despite themselves – because of the lack of a consistent and properly thought-out central policy and weak control over their colonists – that they became drawn into a struggle which led to formal Anglo-French hostilities. Unlike in India, neither government could simply instruct its trading company to stop fighting. In North America large groups of British and French were directly involved in what they believed was a life-and-death struggle. Once the British colonists came to blows with what proved a far more formidable French military power, the Pelhamite government could not abandon them, subject as it was to pressure from within parliament and the country at large.

The impermanent nature of the recent peace settlement was most evident in the American hemisphere. French fears had been heightened by the recent fighting, which had seen not merely the capture of Louisbourg by an army of colonial volunteers backed by a small British fleet, but also a raid upon Montreal. France's governors believed that the British settlements now threatened the very survival of the French colonies. They therefore took a series of actions, beginning in the spring of 1749, to restrict British expansion. These were reported to London, where they confirmed established assumptions about French hostility and stiffened Britain's own resistance. Until 1753 the Anglo-French confrontation focussed upon Nova Scotia. In the first year of peace, Britain had drawn up plans to colonise more effectively the peninsula and mainland of Acadia, threatening France's position there and inevitably provoking reprisals. Relations were further soured by the establishment of a British base at Halifax in the same year. The counterpart of the great French base of Louisbourg, it gave Britain a stronger presence in Nova Scotia. The resulting tension wrecked extended negotiations by French and British representatives to settle the Canadian boundary, which had been provided for at Aix-la-Chapelle. Newcastle and the influential Earl of Halifax, at the Board of Trade, were fully informed of what they saw as French provocations, which they were prepared to meet with force of their own. At this point, both Britain and France believed that a colonial confrontation, even if violent, would not lead to a general war and this pushed up the political temperature between 1749 and 1753.

During these years, British and French colonists were also clashing, albeit less violently, in the back-country of Virginia, Pennsylvania and

New York. In summer 1753 the focus of tension came to be the northern-most reaches of the Ohio Valley. The French governor, determined to block further British migration westwards and so retain France's control over the region, sent a force to the Ohio region. This produced skirmishes with settlers from Virginia in which the French and their Indian allies scored easy victories. These successes were consolidated by the establishment in 1754 of Fort Duquesne (near modern Pittsburgh), at the junction of the Monongahela and Allegheny rivers. This became the focal point of French power in the Ohio Valley and the final link in a chain of forts which seemed to guarantee France's control. These events suggested that only regular British troops could challenge the French and deny them control of all the territory stretching south as far as Georgia and Louisiana. The British government, no more imperialist than its French counterpart, remained committed to peace and retrenchment, and at this point would not commit regulars to North America. Since 1750 the Board of Trade had been collecting information about colonial boundaries, in the process establishing what was viewed by ministers as a very strong British claim to the Ohio Valley. London's response to the French expedition was provocative: in late summer 1753, Newcastle, convinced France could be intimidated, authorised colonial forces to go on the offensive along the entire western frontier. This action produced French reprisals and further increased tension.

In March 1754 the resolutely pacific Henry Pelham died. Newcastle, who retained control of foreign policy, became leader of the ministry. By now the duke was convinced that the scale of French aggression in North America demanded a violent British response. Two events in summer 1754 strengthened this view. France was more pacific than ever after Rouillé was appointed foreign minister, while French influence in Madrid had been destroyed when Ricardo Wall became Spain's leading minister. The opportunity for limited aggression in North America, which might simultaneously preserve Anglo-French peace in Europe, was obvious and Newcastle decided to ship regular forces across the Atlantic. George II would not agree to this, though he favoured a firmer line against France. The duke therefore sought the support of the King's favourite son, Cumberland, and the commander-in-chief duly persuaded his father to commit British regulars to North America.

During the second half of 1754, Newcastle progressively lost control over the British response, which became more aggressive than he intended and which he rightly feared would provoke in turn large-scale French retaliation. Ambitious rising politicians such as Pitt and Henry Fox, the

Secretary-at-War, had been arguing that concrete help should be sent to the colonists and a tougher line adopted against France. Though political opportunism was involved, there was also a genuine awareness of the real issues of trade and empire, together with a concern that France's greater natural resources and home population would prove decisive unless London took immediate advantage of its naval supremacy. Cumberland and his ally Fox now controlled the British response and Newcastle's own political weakness prevented him overturning a course of action which he feared would lead to a new war first in America and then Europe, as it soon did.

Early in 1755, 10,000 British regulars under Braddock were shipped across the Atlantic with orders to seize French forts in the Ohio Valley and to attack Nova Scotia. It had been intended that this force should sail in secret, but Fox's action in announcing its departure ensured that it came to the attention of the French government. France responded by trying to augment their Canadian garrison. By early 1755 the scope for a negotiated settlement was fast disappearing, as positions became entrenched. Fearing that the French with a standing army many times that of Britain would soon achieve complete military superiority, the Newcastle government ordered Admiral Boscawen and his squadron to prevent ships carrying French reinforcements from entering the St Lawrence. George II's government seemed to have hoped for a brief colonial war in which Canada would be blockaded, Braddock would capture the Ohio forts and Louis XV's monarchy would be forced to accept a diplomatic settlement. Unfortunately, most of the French troop ships gave Boscawen the slip in June 1755, while the next month Braddock's force was wiped out near Fort Duquesne. Versailles still wanted to compromise: its efforts at naval rebuilding had enjoyed considerable success, though without the support of a Spanish fleet the French navy remained inferior to its British counterpart. But the ministry in London kept up the pressure because of the inevitable demands from public opinion and its parliamentary critics. To intimidate France by ruining her overseas trade, Newcastle ordered the seizure of French merchantmen when it became evident in the summer that Boscawen had failed.

It is clear in hindsight that these seizures were a decisive point in France's outlook. During the first half of the eighteenth century French hostility towards Britain had been far less than British animosity towards her rival. The events of 1755–56 transformed this situation and made England France's principal enemy. The seizure of French ships without a formal declaration of war produced an upsurge of anti-British feeling, which was encouraged by ministerial propaganda, and this proved enduring. The mid-1750s was the point at which hostility towards Britain became the dominant element in French foreign policy. Versailles' immediate reaction, however, was moderate. Although as many as 300 ships had been captured by the end of 1755, the French did not retaliate but asked for compensation. Britain refused and formally declared war in May 1756, to the delight of the colonists and the war party in London. Almost to the eve of formal hostilities, Newcastle had hoped to avert a general war and to limit fighting to North America. At crucial points, however, events had moved beyond the duke's control. In spring 1756 Britain and France found themselves involved in a world-wide struggle which both governments had sought to avert, though their own policies had contributed to its outbreak.

The origins of the Diplomatic Revolution, 1748–1756

In the mid-1750s the traditional pattern of European diplomacy, the rivalry between France and the House of Habsburg which had shaped international relations since the close of the fifteenth century, was suddenly overthrown. A *rapprochement* between Versailles and Vienna produced a firm and enduring alliance which would only be formally ended by the outbreak of war between Austria and Revolutionary France in 1792. Though the 'reversal of alliances' in 1756 had been anticipated by numerous initiatives to improve Franco-Austrian relations, such as that pursued by Fleury during the later 1730s, the actual treaty which resulted from essentially short-term developments. The rapid deterioration in Anglo-French relations in 1755 was the catalyst for a major realignment of the European states and a war crisis on the continent. This was possible because of established differences among these powers, particularly the implacable hatred of Austria and Russia for Prussia. These enmities, together with Britain's continuing search for European allies, transformed the alliance system, which had survived the Austrian Succession War in a tattered form, into an essentially different one. It was aided by the increase under way in the number of leading states, with the enhanced importance of Prussia and Russia, increasing possible diplomatic permutations. This change was sufficiently radical to have been called the 'Diplomatic Revolution' by contemporaries, and this designation is the label given by historians to the rapid shift in European alliances in 1755–6.

In the making of this revolution France played a largely passive role and in the process the threat of French hegemony, still a real menace in the 1730s and 1740s, became one which really worried only the British. Peace was the clear aim of Louis XV and his mistress Madame de Pompadour, who exerted considerable influence upon policy-making, even after her physical relationship with the King had ended, and acted for much of the 1750s as an unofficial 'first minister'. Yet they placed their confidence in no particular individual so that in practice French diplomacy lacked direction. Their most important alliance of recent years, the Family Compact with Spain, had collapsed. The alliance with Prussia survived rather tenuously, Berlin instead of Munich becoming the focus of French influence in Germany. Contacts were also maintained with other German states, the Scandinavian and Ottoman courts, but no conscious attempt was made to weld these diverse relationships into a strong pro-French bloc, which could be used against Austria or Britain to preserve peace or facilitate French expansion.

Louis himself devoted a surprising amount of time to diplomacy, directing his own 'king's secret' (*secret du roi*), which bypassed the secretary of state for foreign affairs and official channels. Secret diplomacy conducted by the ruler had been a recurrent theme from the Regent Orléans's time. To some extent this was an effect of the increasing importance of ministers and the decline in that of the monarch in the formulation of policy since the final years of Louis XIV's reign. In Louis XV's case its precise origins went back to 1743, when he started to discuss foreign policy privately with his cousin, Prince Conti, pursuing an established aristocratic family strategy directed towards securing the elective Polish throne. The French king hoped to have him chosen as Poland's next ruler, and secretly instructed French diplomats to further this. By 1752 his ambassador at Warsaw, the comte de Broglie, was at the centre of a web of correspondence between Louis and those of his diplomats who had been admitted to this private network. By now the aims of the 'king's secret' had gone beyond Conti's candidature to resurrecting the seventeenth-century eastern barrier of Sweden, Poland and the Ottoman Empire to check Russia as well as Austria. Its aims were not incompatible with France's real interests, given Russia's links with Austria and Britain since 1746. It might therefore have been more sensible to pursue this policy openly and vigorously. Instead, France abdicated her diplomatic leadership of Europe, confined herself to royal subterfuge and had to respond to initiatives from elsewhere.

France's principal ally, Prussia, also played a passive role. A great part of Frederick the Great's energy was absorbed by internal consolidation after 1748. Though he had acquired East Friesland (to which Prussia had dynastic claims) in 1744, securing thereby the significant North Sea port of Emden (occupied since the 1680s), the King still thought about further expansion, which he recognised would be difficult and potentially dangerous. Potential targets were identified in his first Political Testament, finalised in 1752, as Mecklenburg, Saxony and Polish Prussia, but he recognised he would have to wait for another chaotic situation like that of 1740 and this would probably not arise until the next reign. As he was very well aware, his widely scattered territories made Frederick highly vulnerable to attack, while he believed that his success in annexing Silesia had put all his neighbours on their guard. Faced with the permanent hostility of Austria and the growing hatred of the Russian Empress Elizabeth, he needed both the security of the connection with France and of his own army ready to strike fast and hard: by 1756 he would have over 140,000 men backed by almost 20 million talers in his war chest. Largely isolated, widely distrusted by the other powers and with a fragmentary, under-funded and poorly informed diplomatic service, Frederick would pursue military rather than political initiatives. The diplomatic lead in Europe after the Peace of Aix-la-Chapelle was to be taken by the Austrian, Russian and British allies.

Maria Theresa's military and administrative reforms had superficially impressive results: by 1756 she had approaching 200,000 men under arms, and for the first time the Monarchy's financial and military dependence on other states seemed to have been substantially reduced. Only events would show, however, whether the army would live up to expectations and how well Austria could support it. While the reforms were being carried through, peace was essential, and the time clearly had come to reappraise Habsburg external policies after the bitter experience of the last war. An attempt to rethink diplomatic objectives was made at famous meetings of the privy council or conference in March and April 1749. The decisive role in these was played by a young Moravian nobleman, Count Wenzel Anton von Kaunitz, who was to be largely responsible for Austria's foreign policy over the next half-century.

A typical product of the eighteenth-century Enlightenment, Kaunitz tried to approach diplomacy as an exact science, patiently calculating every move and its effects (see below, pp. 118–19). Though a very junior member of the conference, which agreed at these meetings that Prussia had now become a greater menace than even France and the Ottoman Empire, he enjoyed the decisive support of Maria Theresa. There was widespread agreement with Kaunitz's own description of Frederick as their 'greatest, most dangerous and most irreconcilable enemy' and his insistence that the recovery of Silesia should be their principal objective. Other advisers, however, were less sanguine that France's hostility could be ended. Fearing a further French attack and nervous of French strength, they concluded the old association with the Maritime Powers had to be retained despite its drawbacks. Kaunitz accepted they had to keep London friendly, or at least neutral, but argued that the British would never provide effective assistance against Frederick and claimed they were neither the 'guardian of the dynasty' nor Austria's 'natural ally', which only Russia could be because of their common enmity towards the Ottoman Empire and now Prussia. He therefore suggested the Habsburgs should base their policies on Russian friendship and try to accommodate with France, weaning her away from Frederick. Louis XV's neutrality and even his active alliance against Prussia should be bought by territory in the Southern Netherlands or Italy for his son-in-law, Don Philip, the new Duke of Parma.

This bold plan offered Maria Theresa the means to recover Silesia, and an attack on Prussia to regain the lost province remained Vienna's ultimate objective. But as her immediate concern had to be peace, she decided for the present to hold to the alliance with Britain as well as with Russia: to renounce the former prematurely would leave Austria dangerously isolated and deprive her of the subsidies she and Russia would need if war came. Nonetheless, Maria Theresa was willing to test out Kaunitz's ideas and, despite her husband Francis Stephen's hostility towards France because of his loss of Lorraine, she tried to appease Louis XV and sent Kaunitz himself to Versailles as minister in 1750. Here he soon discovered the King's liking for secret diplomacy and desire for peace, but his mission produced no immediate alliance: the Court and most ministers shared the traditional antipathy towards the Habsburgs and wanted to retain the link with Prussia. When he was recalled to direct the Empress's foreign policy as Chancellor from 1753, he accepted he would have to shelve his plan and be patient, although he seems to have become rather pessimistic about it. Two years later, however, his patience was rewarded, because the worsening relations between Britain and France in America and the obvious danger of war from 1755 facilitated a dramatic change in the existing alliance systems.

The real, but unwitting, instigator of the upheaval was not Kaunitz who wanted it, but the duke of Newcastle, who did not. Much against his will, Newcastle, whose interests lay in Europe, not outside, was being dragged into a colonial conflict with France (see above, pp. 76–81). Although he did not want war with her, he believed it was inevitable, and in the years after Aix-la-Chapelle he worked continuously to find continental allies against France and Prussia. He realised Britain's vulnerability to a direct French attack – the success of the Young Pretender in 1745 demonstrated what a regular French force might do – and the need to defend the Austrian Netherlands and Hanover, where Britain had direct interests. Both areas could be occupied by France and held hostage to force the return of any gains made in a colonial war. Although the Southern Netherlands were clearly the most vulnerable and important because of their proximity, Hanover was not without economic or strategic value. However, the main factor here was George II's personal interest. The King and his Hanoverian ministers feared a Prussian as much as a French attack, either for Frederick's own gain or to help his ally, France. They were convinced that only Russian power could restrain him, and from 1748 they had urged Newcastle to pay Elizabeth to station forces near Prussia's borders to intimidate Frederick. But St Petersburg's price was too high, and while Henry Pelham lived it would not be paid. Given the financial constraints on Newcastle's policy, and Prussia's hostility to tentative British approaches and clear preference for friendship with France, he had to look for most of the period after 1748 towards the powers where tradition and common interest could be expected to have most appeal, that is to the 'Old System' of the Dutch and Austria, reinforced by some German states and, perhaps, Russia. This, in any case, fitted in with the duke's own preferences.

Unfortunately the 'Old System' was almost played out. Newcastle underestimated the extent of Dutch decline, and was blind to the Republic's desperate wish for neutrality. Similarly, he had no idea that Maria Theresa was feeling her way towards abandoning the British alliance, and he tried to buttress this link in a rather ham-fisted way from 1749 by efforts to bribe the German electors to elect her son Joseph as King of the Romans, allowing him automatically to become emperor at his father's death. Newcastle hoped at the same time to recruit the electors for a coalition against France and Prussia. But by 1752 he had to abandon the initiative because Pelham refused to meet the soaring costs.

Maria Theresa herself had not liked the scheme as it smacked of outside interference in the Empire, and there was justifiable scepticism in Vienna about its prospects of success. When Kaunitz became foreign minister he was willing to maintain good relations with Britain, believing that continuing friendship was of some value. But he was determined this must not obstruct a future agreement with France. He also intended that the connection with London should cater for Austria's needs against Prussia rather than Britain's against France: Vienna would no longer serve essentially British interests by defending the Low Countries and acting as a diversion in the struggle against French power. However, he shared George II and his Hanoverians' concern over the Prussian threat to the electorate, and he tacitly cooperated with them in pressing Newcastle to try once more for a subsidy treaty with Russia to curb Frederick and to protect Hanover and Austria from Prussia and France. But the Russians continued to ask too much, and these negotiations dragged on inconclusively from 1753 to 1755.

The relations between the powers began to assume more definite shape in 1755, ending the period of indecision since 1748. The fighting in North America, and the imminent outbreak of war between Britain and France which it portended, forced the other powers to decide what they would do. Having resolved to act firmly in America by the dispatch of Braddock and Boscawen (see above, pp. 80–1), the British were desperate for guaranteed continental support in case France compensated for her weakness at sea by invading the Southern Netherlands and Hanover, or by asking Prussia to attack the latter for her. Both areas might be used as bargaining counters or even bases for invading Britain herself.

London's appeals to Vienna faced Kaunitz with both a dangerous situation and an unexpected opportunity. Austria might all too easily be drawn into a war to protect Britain and revert to the subordinate relationship of the 1740s. The Chancellor's plans for a shake-up of the European alliance systems and a coalition to attack Frederick would be stillborn. He therefore refused even to defend Austria's own possession of the Southern Netherlands, insisting it was an Anglo-Dutch problem – as it was – and urged Britain to make arrangements herself to protect it and Hanover through subsidy treaties with the German states and Russia. At the same time he was determined Austria herself should not go to war with France who posed no threat to her now, but instead should pursue a *rapprochement* with Louis XV and try eventually to persuade him to cooperate against Prussia. However, while Louis could be expected to welcome accommodation and the neutralisation of Austria, he would be even less likely than Britain to countenance or help an attack on Prussia to regain Silesia. Kaunitz had set himself an apparently impossible task, but he was convinced it was essential. Although he could depend on St Petersburg's support, since Elizabeth was growing increasingly hostile to Frederick, he felt French help and, specifically, subsidies to Russia would also be necessary to destroy Prussia.

In the Habsburg conference in June 1755 Kaunitz proposed a cautious approach, so as not to frighten off France, by first offering her Vienna's neutrality during the coming Anglo-French War. Austria should then try to persuade Louis XV to conclude an alliance with her, Russia and the other Bourbon monarchies. The proposal was to be larded with offers to support Conti's election in Poland, the cession of Luxemburg (at this period part of the Austrian Netherlands) to Don Philip in exchange for Parma and agreement to France's garrisoning Ostend and Nieuport during war with Britain. Silesia was not yet to be mentioned. By late August 1755 Kaunitz could instruct the young Austrian minister in Versailles, Starhemberg, to exploit Louis's weakness for secret diplomacy by trying an unofficial approach through Madame de Pompadour, whom the Chancellor had cultivated during his own embassy.

Louis responded: he was personally attracted to agreement with the other major Catholic power and admired Maria Theresa. At the same time he disliked Protestant Prussia's agnostic ruler, who had personally affronted him by assuming he was his equal and by ill-advised jests about his mistress. A simple *rapprochement* would bring France clear advantages: the permanent threat from the Habsburgs in the Netherlands, Germany and Italy would be lifted and Britain robbed of her traditional ally and the cornerstone of all the previous anti-Bourbon coalitions. Agreement seemed to offer what Louis wanted most: peace in Europe. Even so, Starhemberg's talks during the autumn with a protégé of Madame de Pompadour, the Abbé de Bernis (soon to be France's foreign minister), achieved little. Louis was probably too timid to push for agreement against the known anti-Austrian feelings of almost all his ministers, who had been kept out of the negotiations. Moreover, there was an understandable nervousness about falling between two stools and offending Frederick just as an Anglo-French war seemed about to break out. But for miscalculations by Britain and Prussia, the Franco-Austrian *rapprochement* might never have taken place.

By summer 1755 it was clear to British ministers that Austria would neither defend her own Southern Netherlands nor help London against France. All attempts to recruit a sizeable mercenary army from the German states had also failed. Unaware of Starhemberg's talks, Newcastle expected Austria would eventually return to the fold but realised he had to take other immediate measures. He pursued vigorously the subsidy negotiations with Russia and, for the first time, began a serious attempt to gain

Frederick. Both powers responded, especially Russia, whose importance in the background to the Seven Years War was crucial. Bestuzhev, the Empress Elizabeth's chancellor, intended both to destroy Prussia and contain France. Already enjoying close relations with Austria, he wanted to conclude a full alliance with Britain. He saw her value essentially as a provider of subsidies and as a state sharing the same hostility he felt towards France as well as towards Prussia. In fact, Russo-French relations had been very poor since Aix-la-Chapelle, when Louis had insisted on excluding Russia from the peace negotiations. Formal diplomatic relations had been broken off shortly after the treaty was signed and were not to be restored until 1756, while their respective ministers had competed at Stockholm, Warsaw and Constantinople. One purpose of the 'king's secret', according to its director Broglie, was to push Russia back 'into her vast wastes'. Yet there was a pro-French party in the St Petersburg court led by Bestuzhev's rival, the vice-chancellor M.L. Vorontsov, while the Empress had some sympathy towards France. What all parties at St Petersburg agreed on was hostility towards Prussia.

Elizabeth herself had been nettled by reports of Frederick's tactless jokes about her weakness for strong drink and strong men. Bestuzhev was driven by hatred for Prussia: he believed she had inherited the role played by Sweden during the seventeenth century and, backed by French power, was barring Russia from her rightful position of hegemony in northern and eastern Europe. He wanted to partition Prussia with Austrian and Saxon–Polish help and reduce the rump state to the Russian client she had been under Peter the Great. Silesia would be returned to Austria and East Prussia ceded to Poland, who would give Russia Courland together with all lands east of the Dvina and Dnieper. Though St Petersburg's aims fitted in well with Kaunitz's own plans, until 1755 he had tried to restrain Bestuzhev. The Chancellor did not yet regard Russia as a leading state, and believed foreign subsidies would be necessary if she were to become part of an anti-Prussian coalition. Aware of the financial weakness of both Austria and Russia, he was convinced they must first secure French help, or at least neutrality. As a second best they would have to be sure of British assistance. Bestuzhev, with his established fear of France, preferred the latter and until 1755 had hoped for British money to maintain a permanent force for use against Prussia.

By that summer, however, Bestuzhev's hopes appeared to have been realised. A harassed British government, faced by the prospect of the colonial and naval struggle spreading to Europe and feeling abandoned by Austria, accepted it must pay what Newcastle called Russia's 'very monstrous' price. In September 1755 a convention was agreed – it was never in fact ratified and was therefore inoperative – promising mutual help in case of attack and providing for an annual British subsidy of £100,000 for the upkeep of 50,000 troops and 50 Russian galleys in Livonia. If these forces were actually deployed to help George II, a further £400,000 a year would be paid. Bestuzhev was to receive £10,000 for himself: a bribe to facilitate the signature of the agreement which highlighted contemporary assumptions about the venality of the Russian court. But while he intended the agreement to be the first step towards attacking Prussia, the British considered it in purely defensive terms: if France or Prussia attacked Hanover, the Russians would come to the electorate's aid.

The British not only intended that their convention with Russia should deter the Prussian King from attacking Hanover but also, equally importantly, that it should frighten him into concluding a settlement with them. During the summer of 1755 Newcastle had become convinced the latter was essential because of Austria's refusal to help: agreement with Frederick would safeguard Hanover and Germany and might allow Britain to prevent the war with France spreading to Europe. It would also make it unnecessary to activate the additional and expensive clause of the Anglo-Russian convention, one which was bound to evoke strong criticism from those in parliament who opposed foreign subsidies, especially those paid in peacetime. This reasoning of course ignored Russia's designs against Prussia and assumed, as usual, that European politics could be shaped purely to suit Britain's requirements.

Frederick responded to the Anglo-Russian agreement precisely as Newcastle had hoped. Throughout the early 1750s the King had considered friendship with France essential and natural. Believing that permanent Bourbon–Habsburg rivalry meant he could always depend on her and that the French alliance would always be there for the taking, he had written in his first *Political Testament* in 1752: 'Silesia and Lorraine are two sisters, Prussia having married the elder and France the younger. This marriage forces them to pursue the same policy.' Consequently, he had never seriously considered agreement with London and, in fact, relations with George II had been very bad, exacerbated by a series of minor, but acrimonious, disputes. The Hanoverian Elector-King had often seemed a greater threat to Frederick in the Empire than Austria, and for his part George and his electoral ministers were openly hostile. Yet, fundamentally, the differences between Britain and Prussia amounted to little more than their association with the main enemies of the other, with Austria and Russia and with France.

By mid-1755 Frederick began to reconsider his outlook as he saw Britain and France clashing ever more violently in the colonies. He feared being involved in renewed fighting for France's sake and not his own. At the same time, he had no doubt that Austria and Russia – together with Saxony, which was now effectively their satellite – were determined to attack him as soon as they could. While confident against Austria and convinced that a *rapprochement* between Vienna and Versailles was impossible, he was haunted by the menace of Russia and her limitless manpower which had not been deployed against him in the previous war. It also appeared that the British in their search for continental allies were being forced into subsidising his enemies. Even if Austria and Russia did not attack him, there was the danger France would drag him into her war with Britain and then into a wider conflict with Britain's Austro-Russian friends. He would have to bear the brunt of the fighting against the latter while France concentrated on her own borders and overseas. All Frederick's fears seemed to be borne out by Britain's negotiations in St Petersburg and the agreement concluded in September 1755. Newcastle had already offered him a possible escape route, however, by opening simultaneous negotiations with him.

Although the rise of Prussia offered Britain a viable alternative to Austria as an ally against France, Newcastle still wanted to maintain the traditional relationship with Vienna and even hoped eventually to recon-cile Berlin to it. The British proposed an Anglo-Prussian convention to neutralise Germany: this would safeguard Hanover by removing the direct threat from Prussia and France and might help to preserve peace on the continent. For his part, Frederick was receptive, as the British proposal offered him a way of weakening the hostile coalition gathering round him. He was also convinced that the Russians in their greed for British gold would follow any lead from London and would abandon their hostility towards him at Newcastle's bidding: he greatly exaggerated both the venality of the Russian court and the influence of British diplo-macy there. The Austrians would in this way be rendered isolated and powerless. At the same time, Prussia's King hoped, and may even have convinced himself, that the French would not be offended by the Conven-tion of Westminster since, by neutralising only Germany, it left Louis XV free to concentrate on either the Southern Netherlands or overseas. Consequently, Britain and Prussia signed the Convention of Westminster on 16 January 1756. Here they agreed in a very vague formula – far short of the obligations created by a conventional treaty of alliance – not to attack one another and to prevent foreign troops entering Germany: the intention was that this would deter a French attack on Hanover and a Russian one on Prussia. Frederick – in an attempt to please Louis XV – had insisted the Southern Netherlands be specifically excluded and thereby left it open for France to undertake a war on the continent at a point where it would still directly threaten the British Isles.

The agreement was a makeshift arrangement to neutralise Germany and avert the war there which both parties feared, and not a conventional treaty providing for mutual assistance. Neither expected it to have the consequences it did. George II himself considered it just another convention to safeguard his electorate, similar to those made with Prussia in the previous war. Newcastle, preoccupied by the French threat and blind to the strength and importance of Austro-Prussian hostility, deluded himself into believing Frederick could soon be drawn into a wide-ranging system with Austria and Russia to contain France. He even told the Austrians that they were now safe enough in Germany to send troops to defend the Southern Netherlands. Inevitably this cut no ice in Vienna, where the Convention of Westminster was seen as another betrayal which undermined its own plans against Prussia. In the event, Austria's own objectives were to be furthered by its impact both in France and Russia in a way that could not have been predicted.

Frederick's bland assumption, or hope, that the French would not take offence was quickly and painfully disappointed. Versailles was enraged: the parvenu Prussian King, who had deserted France three times in the last war, was once again showing his bad faith by abandoning her when a conflict with Britain was breaking out and even appearing to dictate to Louis XV where he could wage hostilities by neutralising Germany. On 4 February 1756, the French council, without even considering the advantages of a neutralised Germany – where France did not in any case want to fight – angrily decided not to renew the Prussian alliance, due to expire in the spring. As France was now effectively isolated in Europe the secret, and so far fruitless, talks with the Austrians were taken up seriously and openly by Versailles. In Kaunitz's subsequent words, the Anglo-Prussian convention 'was the decisive event in the salvation of Austria'. Yet the Chancellor proceeded warily: he had no intention of becoming involved in the Anglo-French War and also realised France might be frightened off if he suggested military cooperation against Prussia. Louis XV wanted to punish Frederick publicly and saw the immediate advantages of a treaty with Vienna, however, and on 1 May 1756 France and Austria signed the First Treaty of Versailles. This agreement contained two separate parts. The first was a neutrality convention for Germany, modelled on that signed at Westminster by Britain and Prussia three months earlier. The second was a treaty of defensive alliance, by which Louis XV and Maria Theresa promised each other 24,000 men in case of aggression. Although the Anglo-French War, which was finally officially declared in the same month, was specifically excluded, Maria Theresa promised her neutrality to help Louis actively if an ally of Britain attacked France.

The Franco-Austrian treaty constituted the real 'Diplomatic Revolution': it ended the centuries-old enmity between the French and Austrian ruling families and announced their breach with their former allies. As it stood, the alliance served French interests well and was similar to the *rapprochement* desired by Fleury in the 1730s, since the other Bourbon powers – Spain, Naples and Parma – were to be invited to join. It had an immediate effect at The Hague, where it reinforced Dutch determination to keep out of the Anglo-French conflict. On 14 June, in return for a Dutch promise of neutrality in the war with Britain, Louis XV himself promised not to invade the Austrian Netherlands. This was the first occasion on which the Republic had formally declared itself neutral in a European war. The Austro-French alliance had therefore destroyed the Anglo-Dutch as well as the Anglo-Austrian legs of the 'Old System'. France seemed sure of continental peace and of being able to concentrate her resources overseas. The spectacular success of her navy in seizing Minorca from Britain in June 1756 appeared to promise a far more evenly-matched maritime conflict than before. France therefore had every reason to congratulate herself over the new alliance, and not for one moment did Louis and his ministers fear that its mutual assistance clauses would be invoked: Frederick would surely not dare attack Austria and risk war with the French monarchy.

The origins of the continental Seven Years War

The Diplomatic Revolution had been driven forward by war in two separate ways. In the longer perspective, Kaunitz's attempts to secure a French alliance were the foundation of Austria's plans to attack Prussia and seize back Silesia: from 1748–49 Habsburg policy aimed ultimately to wage an offensive war against Frederick. In the short term, the realignment had been propelled forward by the open Anglo-French fighting in 1755–56 and by Newcastle's response to this. These considerations, together with the fact that the continental Seven Years War began less than four months after the signature of the First Treaty of Versailles, might encourage the conclusion that it was a direct and even inevitable consequence of the

Diplomatic Revolution. While superficially attractive, such a view is mistaken. The Austro-French alliance may have made the continental war more likely and it certainly provided the basis for the anti-Prussian coalition after 1756. It did not, however, make the Seven Years War inevitable. The First Treaty of Versailles was a serious matter for Frederick, since it completed the encirclement of Prussia, now isolated and facing three powerful enemies. The King had been determined to preserve peace, believing that a new conflict could only imperil his possession of Silesia. Since 1745, and to some extent from as early as 1742, Prussia's foreign policy had been conservative and pacific in tone, while the accompanying military build-up was driven by considerations of self-defence. The First Treaty of Versailles, moreover, was a simple defensive alliance which required Prussian aggression to make it operative. Kaunitz had been unable to secure the offensive agreement which his planned war demanded.

The alliance certainly brought the Austrians immediate tangible gains. At a stroke the historic threat from France in Italy and Germany as well as through her connection with the Ottoman Empire had been removed, while the recent Franco-Prussian alliance, which had come close to ruining the Monarchy in the last war, had been severed. Moreover, the French had promised support if Frederick attacked Austria. Kaunitz was therefore some way towards his ultimate goal of a powerful European coalition against Prussia. During the coming months, however, Versailles resisted entreaties to join an anti-Prussian coalition with Austria and Russia, despite an offer of the Southern Netherlands for Don Philip of Parma if Maria Theresa regained Silesia. While Louis himself might have agreed, his ministers still hoped to balance between the two German powers and so preserve continental peace, while concentrating on the struggle beyond Europe against Britain. Kaunitz, however, was prepared to be patient and, in reality, had little alternative to waiting upon events. He seems to have hoped Prussia's King would blunder and allow Vienna to secure the more far-reaching alliance with France, essential if the planned war of revenge were to take place. His minister at Versailles, Starhemberg, wrote: 'We shall succeed sooner or later in our great scheme and perhaps the King of Prussia himself will be our most effective helper.' Frederick's anxieties and actions were in fact to do Austria's work for her.

The Prussian King had badly miscalculated on the impact of his agreement with Britain, not only on France but also on Russia. The news of the Convention of Westminster produced as much anger in St Petersburg as at Versailles: Britain had betrayed Russia by associating with her chief enemy and intended victim. Russia's own recent convention with Britain was now as good as dead: Elizabeth had no intention of letting George II hire her troops to use against any state except Prussia. As the Empress was also ready to restore relations with France, the influence of the pro-British Bestuzhev sharply declined. His enemy, the equally anti-Prussian and pro-Austrian but also pro-French Vorontsov, now came to the fore. In March 1756 a special Russian Imperial Council was set up to plan and execute war against Prussia with Austrian, and possibly French, help. The army, nominally 330,000 strong, though only a fraction of this total was available for a European war, began to mobilise and the Austrians were encouraged to mobilise as well. But Kaunitz applied the brakes, for the identical reason as before: the two powers' financial weakness made French subsidies and the support of a third army against Frederick essential and, as yet, they did not have France's active support. During summer 1756 he managed to persuade Elizabeth to postpone attacking Prussia until the next year.

Frederick only slowly realised that this attack was to be delayed. During the spring and summer, Russian troops had massed in the Baltic provinces, while in July Austrian troops had also been concentrated in Bohemia, to prevent a Prussian surprise attack and possibly to goad Frederick into one. His agreement with London in mid-January 1756 had produced an alarming, and by the standards of eighteenth-century diplomacy, extremely fast-moving sequence of events which he could never have anticipated and over which he could exert no control: he had lost his treaty with France, Russian hostility had been increased and his only friend was Britain, a non-continental power, with whom he had concluded no formal alliance. The encirclement he had long feared now appeared a reality, and there was no obvious way out of the predicament Prussia faced. Over him loomed the threat of an Austro-Russian attack, which France seemed willing to condone, although not, as yet, to help. His diplomatic efforts had rebounded on him and only desperate measures seemed to offer a chance of escape. Henceforth military considerations came uppermost in his mind.

By as early as mid-June, Prussia's King was convinced he would be attacked by Austria and Russia in the spring of the following year, and he therefore decided to strike first, hoping to secure a military advantage. Frederick himself was probably psychologically incapable of riding out the crisis patiently and instead preferred to act. Nonetheless, he waited until late August before pouring his troops into Saxony, which he considered an Austro-Russian dependency and a probable base for an attack on him as well as the key to Bohemia. The eighteenth-century Electorate was a relatively wealthy and powerful neighbour which Prussia's King feared might be used as an advanced bridgehead for an attack. In his 1752 *Political Testament* he had revealingly described it as a dagger pointing at Brandenburg's heart. Supplies could be moved rapidly down the river Elbe, which flowed through the Electorate before bisecting Hohenzollern territory. He went on to advocate occupying it at the beginning of any hostilities, and this he now proceeded to do. The delay until late summer meant that neither Russia nor France could help Saxony or Austria that year. Rapid Prussian victories might well break up the coalition against him and actively discourage France from honouring her defensive alliance with Austria. In fact, however, his action was to push Louis XV solidly behind Maria Theresa, particularly as the French King's son was married to a Saxon princess. France would probably not have made this decisive break with her past but for Frederick's invasion of Saxony. Together with the other continental states, the French court was outraged by this latest instance of Prussian aggression.

The invasion enlarged the coalition against Prussia by ensuring France would participate, a step which Kaunitz had felt essential for guaranteed success and one which he himself had failed to achieve. On the other hand, the Austro-Russian union was already in existence and would have attacked Frederick sooner or later with or without French help. War at some date was inevitable. The invasion of Saxony was a gamble which could have ruined Prussia, but it was one Frederick had to take if the new Hohenzollern state with its control of Silesia were to survive. The more he delayed, the greater the danger his enemies would come close together and complete their military plans. He had to use his advantages, a full treasury and an army permanently ready for action, to their maximum effect in a short war. His enemies had to be robbed of the chance to match his forces and involve him in a prolonged struggle. In the event they were to achieve both.

CHAPTER 4

The Seven Years War, 1756–1763

The fighting after 1756 extended overseas to an extent that the Austrian Succession struggle had never done, and for this reason has a strong claim to be viewed as the first truly world war. It was in reality two separate conflicts: the first in Germany and central Europe between Prussia and a coalition headed by Austria, France and Russia, and the second overseas between Britain and France, latterly assisted by Spain. The two wars were united principally by France's involvement in both, though as the fighting progressed this link became increasingly fragile. Both struggles were to prove politically decisive, albeit in different ways. The struggle in Europe established Prussia and Russia as great powers, while, overseas, Britain won an overwhelming victory and secured maritime and colonial dominance by 1763. The principal loser in each war was France, whose standing as the leading continental state was destroyed for a generation and would only be restored by the armies of the French Revolution.

Prussia's struggle for survival

The European war had a clear-cut beginning which its colonial counterpart lacked. On 29 August 1756 Frederick the Great led his troops across the border into Saxony. The King's decision had been a victory for military over diplomatic considerations, and from this perspective the invasion was a considerable success. The Saxon forces were surrounded and forced to surrender (October) and the Elector of Saxony was permitted to retire to his Polish Kingdom, where he remained until the conclusion of the fighting. The officers in the Saxon army were allowed to go into exile with their ruler and his court. The rank-and-file, however, was incorporated into Prussian regiments, though most of these unwilling recruits subsequently deserted. Austria's attempted counter-attack was then repulsed, confirming Frederick in his disdainful view of Habsburg military power. Saxony was treated as a Prussian province throughout the war and may even have suffered more than Frederick's own possessions, with permanent and heavy taxation and forcible recruitment for the Prussian army, along with relentless campaigning across its defenceless territories. One estimate is that it contributed around one third of the total cost of Prussia's Seven Years War. In the short term, the invasion removed the considerable strategic threat of an Austrian attack mounted from Saxon territory: the Prussian capital, Berlin, was less than 100 kilometres from the frontier.

The immediate political repercussions were far less favourable for Prussia. Though ostensibly neutral, the Electorate was firmly in the political orbit of France, Austria and Russia. The heir to the French throne was married to a Saxon princess, there were important links between Dresden and Vienna, while Augustus III was a Russian client, by virtue of his possession of the Polish throne and St Petersburg's protectorate over that country. This was why Frederick's attack was much less successful from a diplomatic perspective, since it completed the anti-Prussian coalition Kaunitz had not yet managed to create. Russo-French enmity had previously been one of Frederick's most important securities; the Prussian invasion of Saxony now gave the two states a common interest and inaugurated a temporary political partnership. In the autumn of 1756, the most important component in Kaunitz's intended coalition was his defensive alliance with France (First Treaty of Versailles, 1 May 1756). Frederick's aggression against Saxony and Austria not only brought France into the struggle, as Versailles chose to view Prussia's actions as a *casus belli*; it was also used by the Chancellor to complete the anti-Prussian coalition. In January 1757 Russia acceded to the First Treaty of Versailles and the following month concluded a new, offensive alliance with Austria against Prussia. Kaunitz's skilful diplomacy then produced a Franco-Austrian offensive alliance, the Second Treaty of Versailles (1 May 1757). This decisive agreement committed substantial French military and financial resources to the defeat of Prussia, and so transformed Versailles' role in the early stages of the continental war. There was, however, no separate Russo-French alliance: Russia was united to France only through their respective treaties with Austria, and this was to prove a significant weakness in Kaunitz's coalition. The anti-Prussian league was completed by the adherence of Sweden (March 1757) and by the dispatch of soldiers from the Holy Roman Empire to fight against Prussia.

The military and economic resources of his enemies were considerable, and Frederick appeared to be facing quite impossible odds. At first diplomatically isolated, the King was militarily encircled, while his far-flung territories were highly vulnerable to attack and there was a lack of defensible frontiers. In 1756 the strength of Prussia's army was around 143,000 men; Austria alone had some 156,000 under arms, a total which approached 200,000 during the campaigns of 1757–61, France at least 100,000 and Russia as many as 172,000 in her field army. Kaunitz was never able, however, to use the apparently massive superiority of the anti-Prussian coalition to fashion a decisive victory, which was in any case difficult to achieve during a century of 'limited' warfare. Eighteenth-century wars between leading states tended to produce marginal victories and small-scale political and territorial gains. Prussia's decisive acquisition of Silesia in the 1740s had been highly unusual. The kind of comprehensive victory needed to prise the province from Frederick's hands was always improbable given the structural constraints upon eighteenth-century warfare, and it was made more unlikely by the shortcomings evident in the allied war effort.

The explanation for this failure is also to be found in the nature of the coalition, irresistible on paper but seriously weakened in practice by the absence of a common purpose. All the allies agreed that Prussia must be defeated, but France was different in not wishing to see her political influence destroyed through a partition of her territories, which the others anticipated. Sweden's contribution to the war-effort was especially feeble. In 1757 Stockholm had joined the coalition with dreams of recovering the rest of Western Pomerania and so restoring its vanished influence in northern Europe. But the state finances quickly collapsed under the strain of funding a war, the commanders in Germany were obliged to borrow on their own private credit to pay for provisions and even wages, and Sweden's forces only undertook some desultory manoeuvring in Western Pomerania. The mainly Catholic princes of the Empire made a more significant military contribution, particularly in the early years of the struggle when they provided between 20,000 and 30,000 men each year to the Imperial forces which campaigned against Prussia. Sweden's political value was far greater than her negligible military role. She was – along with France, now also an Austrian ally – the guarantor of the Westphalian settlement in the Empire. The presence of these two states in the coalition enabled Austria to portray the struggle as a police action against Prussia for breaking imperial law, and this was to be of significant propaganda value.

The main burden of the fighting fell on the three principals, Austria, Russia and France; but at different times their efforts were blunted by other factors. The basic problem was that the partners each saw the war in a different light, and no amount of diplomacy could disguise this fundamental weakness. For Austria the war was, and always remained, a struggle to regain Silesia, and her military operations concentrated on the slow reconquest of this province. It was to be pursued through the established eighteenth-century approach of cautious advances conducted with due regard for lines of communication, a war of position, sieges and occasional battles. The traditionally cautious nature of Habsburg military planning made the kind of swift, decisive stroke needed to defeat Frederick all but impossible. For St Petersburg, the Seven Years War came to be primarily a war of territorial expansion in the eastern Baltic. The Russian military machine was, traditionally, cumbersome and slow-moving, and this drawback was exacerbated by the considerable distances between the army's bases and the battlefields of central Europe. During the Seven Years War the client state of Poland came to be used as a forward military base, but this merely reduced, rather than removed, the fundamental problem of distance. Russian forces retired each winter to Polish territory in order to recuperate and were forced to advance again each spring. The Russian army reached the theatre-of-operations later and later in the campaigning season as the struggle progressed: by 1761 it was mid-August before it arrived to join up with the forces of its Austrian ally.

Its operations were also hamstrung by deficiencies in the supply system and by the shortcomings of her senior commanders, who were frequently changed – only one of them commanded for more than a single campaign. Though Russian armies secured notable successes over their Prussian counterparts, they could never turn these into a complete victory. The ill-health of the Empress Elizabeth came to be an ever greater problem. Since her successor, the Grand Duke Peter (the future Peter III) was fanatically pro-Prussian, it was assumed that his accession would bring about an immediate reversal of Russian foreign policy. Consequently, Elizabeth's periodic and serious illnesses inevitably weakened St Petersburg's war effort by encouraging the Empress's commanders in their innate caution. France, for her part, increasingly regarded the struggle with Britain as more important. Though her political and military commitment to the continental war was considerable in its initial stages, her expectation of an early Prussian defeat proved unfounded, while the steady accumulation of French reverses in Germany and overseas reduced enthusiasm at the French court for the European struggle.

The difficulties which resulted from the divergent aims and faltering enthusiasm of the principals in the anti-Prussian coalition were increased by the inevitable tensions of wartime cooperation. The Diplomatic Revolution had made temporary partners out of old and sometimes bitter enemies. It was particularly true in the case of France and Russia who were now obliged to sink their established rivalry in eastern Europe in the cause of defeating Prussia. Their *rapprochement*, predictably, was imperfectly achieved. France was hostile to the march of the Empress Elizabeth's troops across Poland and to the enhanced control of the country which resulted yet, while official diplomacy eventually accepted nothing could be done to prevent this, the King's *secret* continued its traditional opposition towards Russia. This was resented in St Petersburg, though the futile activities of Louis XV's private diplomacy could not prevent the disintegration of the French position in Poland during the fighting, particularly after the duc de Choiseul entered office at the end of 1758. The success of France and Russia in suppressing their established rivalry in the cause of defeating Prussia was incomplete, and their partnership disintegrated amidst mutual recrimination in 1761.

The tensions within the Franco-Russian alliance were particularly acute, but wartime cooperation between Russia and Austria was also marked by friction and open distrust. The Franco-Austrian alliance was the most stable and proved to be the most enduring of the new alignments which emerged in 1756–57, yet even here there were repeated and severe disagreements, particularly over military strategy and finance. There was also an absence of any mortal danger which might have cemented the allies together, since Prussia appeared to lack the material resources to destroy even one of its major enemies, far less all three. These basic antagonisms within the coalition were never satisfactorily reconciled and the alliance's military failures inevitably strengthened them. Further tension arose from the problems inherent in coalition warfare, which was a novel experience for all the allies. Military cooperation between Vienna, Versailles and St Petersburg was incomplete, and no coordinated strategy was pursued with the consistency needed to defeat Prussia. Each state instead expected its partners to commit their resources to its own distinct objective and was resentful when this did not happen.

These basic weaknesses were highlighted and exacerbated by the early successes of the Prussian army. Frederick's response in 1757 to the serious situation he faced, as yet without any British help, while the anti-Prussian coalition was taking shape (see above, p. 97), was to go on to the offensive against the Austrians. He won a bloody victory at Prague (6 May), where Prussian losses were greater than Austrian, and then suffered an equally costly defeat at Kolin (18 June), in a battle which forced the King to acknowledge the progress which the Habsburg army had made since the last war. Simultaneously, the Russians advanced towards isolated East Prussia, the source of the Hohenzollern royal title but cut off from the dynasty's heartlands by over 500 kilometres of Polish territory. Two months after Kolin, Russian forces inflicted a second serious defeat upon the Prussians at Gross Jägersdorf (30 August).

The autumn of 1757 was the first crisis of the Seven Years War for Frederick: the Austrians forced him back into Saxony, the Russians invaded East Prussia and the French advanced on his western flank, having earlier forced the surrender of the Hanoverian army under Cumberland, sent to protect George II's electorate from France (Convention of Klosterseven, September 1757). This desperate situation in the first year of the fighting forced the King to reformulate his approach to the fighting. He now abandoned the outlying Hohenzollern possessions: those in Westphalia were under French and Austrian occupation from the first full campaign of the struggle, while East Prussia was occupied by the Russians in January 1758 and was to remain so until the final stages of the war. Instead he concentrated upon his compact central position, adopted a strategy of interior lines and fought the war in Brandenburg, Saxony, Pomerania, Silesia and Bohemia. To this extent Prussia's encirclement became advantageous strategically. The King pursued a war of mobility, striking first against one foe and then the next, trying to prevent his enemies combining their armies and thereby exploiting their considerable numerical superiority. This strategic approach was in the end to be successful. It was initially seen to spectacular effect in the closing months of 1757 when Frederick retrieved a desperate situation first by routing the Franco-Imperialist forces at Rossbach (5 November) and then, after a forced march, winning a remarkable victory over a much larger and more formidable Austrian army at Leuthen (5 December). These two victories ensured Prussia escaped the swift defeat which had seemed likely in autumn 1757.

In the wider perspective, Rossbach was the war's most decisive battle because of its enormous repercussions within France. Louis XV's monarchy was Europe's leading military power, a status seemingly confirmed by Saxe's victories in the last war, and had not expected such a shattering reverse, particularly at the hands of an upstart such as Prussia and in a battle in which it enjoyed a numerical superiority of two to one and, initially, a superior strategic position. The defeat undermined France's

MAP 3 *The Seven Years War in Central Europe*
Source: M. Hochedlinger, *Austria's Wars of Emergence, 1683–1797*
(Pearson Education Limited, 2003), p. 340

military power for a generation and seriously weakened the confidence of her generals and statesmen. The shortcomings which, to a few perceptive observers, had been evident for several decades now became obvious. The German campaigns demonstrated the extent to which France's army, imprisoned in its own past achievements, had become an outmoded military machine. Defective leadership, both at high command and battalion level, frequent changes in strategic plans and in the commanders charged with implementing them, inadequate logistical support, the lack of reliable intelligence, an artillery arm which was numerous but with an obsolete preference for large field pieces, above all acute financial problems: these and other weaknesses were all starkly highlighted. The decline since the age of Louis XIV, temporarily camouflaged by Saxe's successes, was now evident to contemporaries both within France and throughout Europe.

Rossbach also revealed the impossibility of supporting two wars simultaneously, even with France's large resources. One purpose of the First Treaty of Versailles had been to enable her to concentrate on the overseas struggle, which was coming to be seen as the priority. Frederick's invasion of Saxony had made this impossible, and in 1757 considerable French resources were committed to the continental war, with the aim of bringing about Prussia's early defeat. In the immediate aftermath of Rossbach, Versailles seriously considered a unilateral peace with Prussia. When it became clear that this could not be secured, France's commitment to the continental war was scaled down, being formally reduced by the Third Treaty of Versailles (March 1759) to the level prescribed in the initial Franco-Austrian alliance signed in May 1756. Thereafter, French troops fought principally, and indecisively, in Westphalia against the so-called 'Army of Observation', a polyglot force financed by London to support Prussia. This treaty was concluded by Choiseul, who had become foreign minister in December 1758 and was determined to concentrate resources against Britain.

France's weakened position and changed priorities proved to be crucial during the second half of the European war. Even the subsidies to Austria which Louis XV's monarchy was committed to pay under the terms of the first treaty of Versailles could not be met on time, due to the French state's own financial problems. Prussia's desperate struggle was reduced in scale, becoming primarily a war against Austria and, increasingly, Russia. The stalemate on the Westphalian front, together with the ineffectual Swedish military effort, significantly reduced the menace of encirclement which Frederick the Great had faced in 1756–58. Yet Prussia's situation from 1759 onwards was still serious and eventually became quite desperate. Frederick's victories at Rossbach and Leuthen also had a considerable impact on the other belligerents. Above all, they encouraged Britain to repudiate the Convention of Klosterseven and to provide effective support for Prussia's struggle for survival (see below, p. 112). Austria's defeat at Leuthen had the predictable effect of reinforcing the traditional Habsburg preference for securing strong defensive positions and for manoeuvre rather than battle. Vienna, under her leading commander, the notably cautious Field-Marshal Daun, henceforth aimed at exhausting Prussia's resources rather than defeating Frederick outright, a surprisingly defensive approach given her wish to reconquer Silesia.

Though the Austrians were to win an impressive victory over Frederick at Hochkirch (14 October 1758), the main burden of the campaigns of 1758–59 was borne by the Russians who fought a bloody draw with the Prussian forces at Zorndorf (August 1758) and, in the campaign of summer 1759, inflicted serious defeats at Kay (Paltzig) and Kunersdorf. These successes were never followed up, in part because of the failure of the Habsburgs to provide further necessary military assistance. Frederick described his own survival in the aftermath of the shattering defeat at Kunersdorf, as the 'miracle of the House of Brandenburg' and, given the prostrate condition of his army and of the Hohenzollern state, there was much to be said for his verdict. As French resolve continued to weaken, Austria was increasingly forced to depend upon her Russian ally. However, the Empress Elizabeth's designs on East Prussia (which she intended to exchange for Polish Courland) were deeply suspect in Vienna, which had no wish to see any strengthening of Russian power in central and eastern Europe. The aim of Austria's Seven Years War was to destroy one political rival, not to facilitate the emergence of another. Austro-Russian military cooperation therefore was never wholehearted, and Frederick was able to struggle on. Yet his resources were reduced each year, his position grew increasingly desperate and his central task of preventing the Austrians and Russians uniting their forces became more difficult with every campaign. By the end of 1759, however, a military stalemate had emerged which saved Prussia from extinction, while Frederick retained his knack of winning the important battles – as in the second half of 1760, when he retrieved an apparently lost position by decisively defeating the Austrians first at Liegnitz (15 August) and then at Torgau (3 November).

These two reverses ended Habsburg hopes of recovering Silesia. The Austrian government, in spite of the administrative reforms of 1749, was quite unable to raise the men and, more especially, the money to defeat Prussia. This contrasted with the ability of the Prussian administration to scrape together the human and financial resources to continue the struggle. Austria henceforth sought peace, and in 1761 reduced the size of her army, though the fighting continued, and set about the further internal reforms shown essential. Vienna had contributed to its own failure. The military performance of its armies, and especially the infantry and artillery, had improved notably since the 1740s, but not sufficiently to eclipse their Prussian adversaries. Against that, Prussia's cavalry had itself improved significantly since the Austrian Succession struggle, giving Frederick's forces a decisive advantage in the 'little war', and the Austrian horse was further handicapped by continuing problems over the supply of remounts. And, while Austrian troops had fought bravely, earning Frederick the Great's respect, Habsburg generalship was at best mediocre. The lack of reliable subordinates upon whom Austrian commanders could depend was a further problem: this was exacerbated by a purge of the officer corps in 1759–60 to deal with the widespread dishonesty which had been uncovered. The French alliance had failed to produce the expected contribution to the war-effort, while Russia was too much of a rival ever to be a comfortable ally: the vital military cooperation of the two states was always beset by suspicion and distrust.

Austria, however, fought on, unwilling and probably unable to conclude a unilateral peace with Prussia. The Russian Empress remained determined to eliminate the Prussian state as a political rival, and this prolonged the war for a further two years. Although Frederick's position remained critical, he was never faced by the major attack which might have proved decisive, and he was finally saved by Elizabeth's death at the very beginning of January 1762. The reversal of Russian policy which had long seemed imminent now took effect. The new ruler, Peter III, withdrew from the war and signed a peace treaty with Prussia (May 1762); Sweden followed suit in the same month; and, before long, a Russo-Prussian treaty was being negotiated, with the aim of securing for the Emperor his claimed right to Schleswig by a war against Denmark. This adventure was cynically backed by Frederick the Great, already searching for a Russian alliance on which to base his post-war foreign policy. Peter III in his turn was swept from the throne (July 1762) by a palace coup engineered by his formidable wife, who skilfully exploited the widespread resentment which his policies had aroused and became Empress as Catherine II (1762–96). But Russia's new ruler, though she refused to ratify the alliance negotiated with Prussia, remained neutral for the rest of the war and concentrated on securing her own position on the throne. During the second half of 1762 Frederick was therefore able to concentrate entirely on the Austrians, who suffered further defeats at Burkersdorf (July) and Freiberg (October) and were soon happy enough to conclude the peace of Hubertusburg (15 February 1763) on the basis of the *status quo ante bellum*. This had seemed improbable for much of the war, not least to the Prussian King himself. Despite his conviction – evident in his policy during the War of the Austrian Succession – that limited resources and strategic exposure demanded short, decisive campaigns, he found his state trapped in a struggle of attrition and endurance, yet still managed to survive. Frederick himself likened the conflict to a tightrope walk, but by 1763 he had reached the end of this high wire in safety.

Prussia's survival seemed to many contemporaries to border on the miraculous, and certainly there was real heroism in the resistance of Frederick and his soldiers. The King's own contribution was immense: his inventive strategy, his powers of leadership and his obstinate refusal to admit defeat sustained Prussia in the darkest periods of the Seven Years War. It was also significant that Frederick himself commanded a combination of military, diplomatic, political and administrative authority. This contrasted sharply with the divided counsels which prevailed in Vienna and St Petersburg: Austrian and Russian commanders had their strategy dictated to them, and at times had to consult their political masters before making major operational decisions. In Vienna both Kaunitz and Maria Theresa came to play important roles in the day-to-day running of the war. The resilience of Prussia's soldiers and the remarkable ability of her administrative system somehow to raise sufficient taxation, recruits and munitions to keep the war going were scarcely less important, and it was aided by the sense of Prussian patriotism which was deliberately and successfully encouraged by the monarchy. Its superior military recruitment proved especially important. Though the quality of troops declined sharply during the second half of the war, the Cantonal System proved more able to provide replacement soldiers than Austria's distinctly haphazard methods of recruitment. Russia's immense population and brutal though inefficient system of conscription alone provided more soldiers than were available to Frederick, and her generals used this manpower to buy victories at the cost of horrific casualties, as the war became a life-and-death struggle between Prussia and her powerful rival in north-eastern Europe. The 'miracle of the House of Brandenburg' was also aided by British support (see below, p. 107) and by the brutal Hohenzollern exploitation of occupied Saxony.

In the final analysis, only the Empress Elizabeth's death at the very beginning of 1762 may have saved Prussia from defeat and the threat of destruction. Yet Frederick's own contribution to his state's survival had been decisive. His strategy of attrition (known in German as *Ermattungstrategie*), striking first against one opponent and then against another, with the aim of preventing his numerically-superior enemies from uniting their armies and attempting the decisive blow he feared, was in the end successful. Along the way, however, Prussia's King lost as many battles as he won: his towering military reputation and that of his army after the Seven Years War reflected more the fact of his survival against overwhelming odds than an unbroken record of battlefield successes. That survival was also due, in considerable measure, to the weakness and divisions within the opposing coalition. The alliances which fought the Seven Years War were tenuous and uncertain, reflecting the considerable shock to the established political order provided by the Diplomatic Revolution of 1756, and this was reflected in the military performance of the opposing coalition.

Anglo-Prussian relations during the Seven Years War were similarly troubled, and the partnership ended acrimoniously in 1762. It had never been more than a marriage of political convenience, despite all the high-flown rhetoric lavished upon it in the House of Commons and the popular support for a Protestant ally. The Convention of Westminster was in no sense an Anglo-Prussian alliance, and, in the early part of the war, British ministers were uncertain whether to support Frederick. But after William Pitt took control in mid-1757 London's commitment to the Prussian cause increased significantly, the Convention of Klosterseven was renounced, and an annual subsidy agreement (the only formal bond between the two states during the war) was concluded in April 1758 and renewed in the subsequent three years. Though no alliance was ever signed, Britain was Prussia's political partner and contributed significantly to her survival. The annual subsidy of £670,000 from 1758–61, more significant assistance in the shape of a British-financed 'Army of Observation' in western Germany, whose operations protected Frederick's flank for much of the war, and the imperceptible psychological support that came from the knowledge that Prussia was not fighting alone, were all provided by this link. Anglo-Prussian relations, however, remained harmonious only for the central years of the war, when their mutual dependence and the magic name of Pitt were sufficient to paper over their divergent interests. The 'breach' of 1762, when cooperation between the two states broke down completely and acrimoniously, was significant chiefly for Frederick's enduring conviction that he had been 'deserted', and demonstrated that the two powers no longer needed each other. London's support for Prussia had always been opportunistic, a way of protecting Hanover without appearing to do so and thereby incurring hostility within Britain, and also of tying down French resources on the continent. Britain's spectacular victories overseas during the Seven Years War ultimately made the link with Prussia redundant.

The Anglo-Bourbon War

The Anglo-French struggle was the latest and, as it proved, decisive round in their established rivalry for colonies and commerce. It had a significant continental dimension, and considerable numbers of British troops were sent to Germany. But, unlike earlier wars, it was fought mainly outside Europe. The struggle began badly for Britain, as unexpected and disconcerting defeats exposed a lack of leadership, and revealed the need for effective direction of the war-effort. The first two campaigns saw a series of reverses: the capture of Britain's Mediterranean base of Minorca in June 1756, after the failure of a British naval expedition to relieve the garrison which led to the court-martial and execution of its commander Vice-Admiral the Hon. John Byng; the French victory in Germany at Hastenbeck (26 July 1757) and the humiliating surrender of Cumberland's army which followed at Klosterseven (September: see above, p. 101); and the failure in autumn 1757 of the first combined operation, which unsuccessfully attacked the French naval base of Rochefort. In North America, the French captured the important trading post of Fort Oswego on Lake Ontario in 1756, and in the next year seized Fort William Henry in the strategically-vital Hudson valley, while in the Indian sub-continent they took Calcutta. These reverses in turn contributed to the instability of British politics: from April until the end of June 1757 Britain lacked a government, as her politicians struggled for the upper hand against a background of a war going badly. It was the second half of that year before the Pitt–Newcastle coalition, which ultimately won the war, was sufficiently secure to give its full attention to the struggle with France.

This ministry – like Britain's war effort – was to be dominated by William Pitt the Elder. Pitt's single-minded aim was to destroy French power and he reinforced this by considerable administrative energy and complete self-confidence. He was not, however, able to dictate to his fellow ministers. In the first place his own ill-health – even at this point he was a frequent victim of gout – militated against any such dominance. Eighteenth-century British constitutional practice also remained fluid, and government was far removed from the later model of a unified cabinet dominated by a prime minister. Instead, it consisted of a series of powerful departmental ministers formally responsible only to the King, who remained closely involved in day-to-day policy-making. But, as Secretary of State for the Southern Department, Pitt occupied a key office in the war-effort, since he handled all colonial issues and relations with France and Spain. He gave direction and impetus to Britain's campaigning and, by the force of his own personality, he secured a degree of dominance over his colleagues. Yet Newcastle at the Treasury, Lord Anson at the Admiralty and Sir John Ligonier as commander-in-chief contributed significantly to the winning of the Seven Years War.

Pitt entered office because Newcastle needed him as leader in the House of Commons, and his parliamentary mastery was to contribute to Britain's eventual victory. The sophisticated system of public credit which had evolved since the 1690s and which was the basis of her impressive financial power ultimately depended upon the backing of parliament, which the 'Great Commoner' was able to secure. Particularly in the early campaigns, Pitt persuaded the Commons that the war could be won and was therefore worth funding through additional borrowing. Britain's resilient public finances enabled fleets to sail and armies to campaign. Newcastle, the ministry's nominal leader, also played an important role. As First Lord of the Treasury, he supervised the day-to-day workings of Britain's finances which were able to cope with both a virtual doubling of the national debt during the Seven Years War and an annual level of expenditure twice that of the 1740s. This strength was in sharp contrast to France's difficulties, which were exacerbated by Louis XV's decision to pay for the fighting through further massive borrowing, rather than by increased direct taxation: credit provided around 60 per cent of the total cost. The French King believed that his subjects were already overtaxed and recognised that any further increases would have involved confronting the whole matrix of privilege and fiscal exemption which dominated society and politics. His decision inhibited France's performance in the war. In the short term, France's army and navy – like her allies – did not receive the sums promised and essential for winning the struggle. In the longer perspective, the Seven Years War further weakened France's financial system and was a principal source of the problems which would bring about the Bourbon monarchy's collapse in 1789. The contrasting financial strength of the two states did much to determine the outcome. In two other respects, the fighting demonstrated Britain's superior resources. Her expanding population reduced manpower problems, while her naval strength ensured that trade and the revenues which accrued continued during the fighting.

In both areas France was to experience real difficulties. Her commerce was to suffer particularly at the hands of British privateers. French defeats in Germany, however, were always more important to the overall outcome of the struggle.

If financial and economic strength underpinned Britain's eventual victory, naval power was even more decisive. Pitt was here the beneficiary of a strategic revolution during the 1740s. In the previous Anglo-Bourbon war, Britain's navy had learned to operate for extended periods outside Europe and had acquired an infrastructure of local bases and shore facilities there to support this global projection of sea power. Spain, alone of her enemies, possessed a naval base in the American hemisphere, at Havana, but her fleet remained far inferior and, in any case, she only entered the struggle in 1762 (see below, p. 114). The British ability to campaign in American and Indian waters, together with a superior fleet and experience of successful operations outside Europe, combined to produce an impressive series of victories. Yet the Channel and, more generally, European waters were always the main focus of British naval deployments. The Seven Years War saw the consummation of an earlier strategic initiative, going back to the Spanish Succession war, which was to be equally decisive. This was the so-called Western Squadron, based at Plymouth and, latterly, Torbay, which was only perfected after 1755–56. By stationing a fleet in the Western Approaches, to the west of the Channel, Britain was able to protect its own commerce and to bottle up its French rival in its main bases along France's Atlantic coastline, as it did throughout much of the Seven Years War. Its principal, and unavoidable, drawback was that it could do nothing against France's major Mediterranean naval base at Toulon, and French squadrons operating from there inflicted significant damage upon British strategy in the initial phase of the Seven Years War, as in all eighteenth-century conflicts.

These new advantages consolidated Britain's established superiority in the essential foundations of sea power, possessing a larger merchant navy, better shore facilities, an adequate and regular supply of naval stores, more trained seamen, a recruitment system which operated more efficiently, superior leadership and favourable geography. The decisive benefit which these cumulatively conferred was evident during the Seven Years War, when France's manning and dockyards problems were particularly serious. Though her fleet had been built up since 1748, it was still far smaller than its British rival. During the years 1755–58 French naval strategy, recognising this inferiority, sought to avoid large-scale confrontation with Britain. Instead, it secured some minor strategic gains by concentrating resources against British weak points. At this period the main French fleet did not put to sea, unable or perhaps simply unwilling to escape Britain's blockade of its Atlantic and Mediterranean ports and risk direct conflict.

This acceptance of British naval supremacy, as much a matter of poor French morale as material deficiencies, was strategically decisive because it made possible Britain's victories overseas. France's inability to send supplies and reinforcements left her colonies exposed to attack by British forces, whose superiority in numbers and resources quickly produced an impressive series of victories. In 1758–59 Choiseul, newly installed in office, briefly adopted a more aggressive naval strategy. It was linked to his projected invasion of Britain, to be accomplished with the support of English Jacobites, a threat designed to force London to retain even more ships in home waters and so weaken its naval effort overseas. But when the French fleet put to sea in force in 1759, Britain's mastery was immediately confirmed by decisive victories off Lagos (July) and in Quiberon Bay (November), which removed any fear of invasion. Thereafter British superiority was complete, and indeed the French navy came close to disintegration during the final years of the war, when funding for the fleet was cut by half.

One source of Britain's dominance was that – in contrast to the wars of 1739–48 and 1778–83 – France did not receive Spanish naval support until the conflict's outcome was clear. The combined Bourbon navies were a threat to British maritime ascendancy in a way that the individual French or Spanish fleet could never be. Until the closing stages of the Seven Years War, however, Madrid remained neutral. This neutrality and the good relations upon which it rested were actively pursued by London and especially by Pitt as Southern Secretary. Anglo-Spanish diplomacy had improved significantly during Ferdinand VI's reign (see above, p. 75). It was not that sources of tension were lacking: on the contrary, the permanent sore of Gibraltar, Spain's demands to be admitted to the Newfoundland Fisheries and the activities of British logwood cutters in Honduras all caused friction. The outbreak of the Anglo-French war added the problem of neutral rights, as Madrid protested at seizures of its shipping. Relations had deteriorated after 1756–57, and it took all the skill of Britain's experienced and emollient ambassador Sir Benjamin Keene to prevent a formal breach in relations. London's desire to keep Spain neutral was apparent in a remarkable offer to hand back Gibraltar in return for a formal alliance. Though this initiative failed, the influence of Keene and of the Anglophile leading minister Wall was sufficient to preserve Madrid's neutrality, especially important during the early years of the fighting.

Financial and naval power, together with Spain's neutrality, all contributed to Britain's decisive victory over France. The years 1758–62 saw
spectacular British successes overseas: French colonial power in North
America and India was all but destroyed; in West Africa and even the
Caribbean it was severely undermined. That victory, however, was not
the result of a deliberate, articulated strategic vision so much as of successful improvisation from one campaign to the next and of vastly superior resources. A unified approach was impossible, given the global nature
of the struggle and the uncertainties of tides and winds. In any case Pitt
was a novice when he entered office and tended to improvise as he went
along. British strategy was in no sense novel, incorporating as it did the
Admiralty's experience of previous eighteenth-century wars with France,
and pragmatically refining and developing these insights. London's overall approach came to be essentially that of defeating France overseas while
keeping her involved in the European war. This was more evident in
retrospect than it was at the time. Though Pitt – finally accepting the
continentalist orthodoxy – famously declared that 'America had been
conquered in Germany', his remark was an oversimplification and, arguably, a distortion. America was conquered in America between 1758 and
1760. It was defended in Westphalia: as both Frederick the Great and
Choiseul noted at the time.

Britain's strategy thus successfully exploited the basic French weakness: even the apparently greater resources at Louis XV's disposal were
not sufficient for France to participate in a continental war against Prussia
and simultaneously fight Britain overseas. Despite this, France remained
committed to the European struggle, albeit on a much reduced scale after
the campaign of 1758, and Pitt sought to prolong and strengthen Prussian
resistance by the annual subsidy and, more significantly, by the British-
financed 'Army of Observation' in Germany. British aid to Prussia also
served the vital purpose of protecting Hanover. An original element in
Pitt's strategy was a series of amphibious 'hit-and-run' attacks against the
French coastline. Though the initial sortie against Rochefort had been a
failure, the summer of 1758 saw successful operations against France's
Atlantic coastline, culminating in the destruction of the port of Cherbourg.
These contributed to the retention in western France of units which could
have been employed in Germany or even overseas. Although Britain's
commitment to the European war was always small in financial and
material terms, strategically it was decisive since it enabled resources to
be concentrated on the colonial struggle to an extent that was impossible for France. British regular troops were shipped across the Atlantic
in unprecedented numbers, while Pitt's energy secured a novel degree of

cooperation against the French between Britain's colonies. At the height of the war there were 30,000 British troops in North America – more than had been sent to the Low Countries in 1742–45, and far more than were deployed in Germany (18,000) after 1756. It was the first major campaign fought by British regulars outside Europe.

This massive effort was the foundation of a series of important victories. Britain's gains were particularly striking in Canada, where French resistance had already been weakened by a serious quarrel between the military commander and the civilian governor, and by near-famine conditions. The British blockade was far from complete, but it did prevent essential food supplies from France reaching the troops in North America. In 1758–60 Britain's objective was the conquest of Canada, which was achieved in stages. The important base of Louisbourg, on Cape Breton island in the Gulf of St Lawrence, was captured in July 1758, and Fort Duquesne (renamed Pittsburgh) in December. In the following year Quebec was taken, after Major-General James Wolfe's dramatic scaling of the Plains of Abraham (September 1759). The British conquest of Canada was completed by the seizure of Montreal in September 1760. French trading posts in West Africa (notably in Senegal and on the island of Gorée) were captured during 1758 in an attempt to disrupt the supply of slaves for the French plantations in the Caribbean. Between 1759 and 1762 a series of successful combined operations destroyed France's position in the West Indies, with the capture of Guadeloupe, Martinique and the 'neutral' islands (Dominica, St Lucia, St Vincent and Tobago had been declared neutral and not to be settled by the peace of Utrecht in 1713).

In India, the situation was complicated by the existence of a confused, triangular struggle for influence between the English East India Company, its French counterpart and the native princes, but the final outcome was substantially the same. The Anglo-French struggle in the sub-continent was prosecuted at sea, as both states committed small numbers of warships, as well as on land. In 1757 Britain and her East India Company gained the upper hand, recapturing Calcutta (January) and seizing Chandernagore (March). Later the same year, Clive's somewhat fortuitous and small-scale victory at Plassey (23 June 1757) gave Britain, or rather her East India Company, control of Bengal, while subsequent successes at Wandiwash (January 1760) and Pondicherry (January 1761) weakened the French position on the Carnatic coast in the south-east. By the end of the war British power in India was securely established.

By 1760 Britain had comprehensively won the Anglo-French Seven Years War. The extent of her victory was remarkable. As British gains mounted up in the *annus mirabilis* of 1759, the English man-of-letters,

Horace Walpole, famously remarked that so numerous were the successes, the church bells were worn out ringing for victories. Britain's triumph was the product of superior sea power and financial resources, better admirals and generals, and experience of previous successful wars against France. Pitt was an energetic and, more importantly, a lucky war leader, rather than a strategist of genius. His reputation, at the time and since, owes much to the skilful way he was careful to exploit the successes and ring the bells of victory: his greatness rested upon his undoubted abilities as a propagandist.

Spain's entry into the Seven Years War at the very beginning of 1762 enabled further additions to be made to this catalogue of British triumphs. Pitt had by this time resigned, in October 1761, ostensibly due to his failure to obtain the support of his ministerial colleagues for a pre-emptive declaration of war against Spain and an attack on the returning treasure fleet, but more fundamentally because of disagreements over the war-effort in Germany. His strategy continued to be employed, however, and, almost inevitably, to bring further triumphs. Madrid had remained neutral for much of the struggle, despite its alarm at the tide of British successes, which appeared to be destroying the colonial equilibrium established by the peace of Utrecht in 1713 and confirmed in 1748, and its annoyance at wartime disputes with London over neutral trade. The accession in August 1759 of the implacably anti-British Charles III (1759–88) undermined this neutrality, a development encouraged by French diplomacy. London had initially attached particular importance to Spain's neutral stance but, as British victories mounted up, it came to view this as less important. Charles III had earlier been King of Naples and Sicily. During the War of the Austrian Succession he had been forced, by the threat of a British naval bombardment of his capital, to withdraw from the struggle, an episode which created an enduring hostility towards Britain. In 1753, after some personal royal diplomacy, he had signed a secret agreement with Louis XV by which, in return for France's support for the territorial ambitions of his younger brother Don Philip, he agreed to sign a French alliance when he became King of Spain. Observers in Madrid were in any case alarmed by the significant French defeats, which portended a growth of British power in the American hemisphere and a more serious and direct challenge to Spain's own imperial position.

Charles III's desire to defend the existing colonial balance of power was evident in a significant Spanish naval build-up during his early years on the throne. Considerable reinforcements were sent to Havana, particularly during 1761: by the time war broke out, Spain's Caribbean naval establishment was six times as strong as under Ferdinand VI. The number of ships under construction also increased, though these efforts were weakened by Spain's endemic manning problems, which limited the number of vessels put into commission. Simultaneously, Madrid adopted a tougher diplomatic stance over the logwood cutters. But Britain, buoyed by victories, was now indifferent to Spanish protests and relations quickly deteriorated. At the same time, formal Franco-Spanish alliance negotiations began, and a treaty was signed in August 1761. The Third Family Compact was an offensive and defensive alliance directed against Britain. With the exception of a few years during the early 1770s, it was to be the foundation of Spain's international outlook until the French Revolution. More immediately it brought Madrid into the Seven Years War in January 1762 as France's ally, when Britain anticipated a Spanish declaration of war with one of her own. Intervention was a disastrous miscalculation on Charles III's part. Madrid entered at an inopportune moment, with Britain victorious and France prostrate, while Spanish resources were wholly inadequate to fight alone against such a powerful enemy.

Spain's naval and military inferiority was clear at once. Britain's successful and well-tried formula of combined operations, together with the important element of surprise, enabled her in 1762 to capture Havana, the focal point of Madrid's empire in the Caribbean, at high cost; while an improvised, poorly-equipped attack mounted from India surprisingly succeeded in taking Manila in the Philippines. Within Europe, Spain attempted to invade Britain's traditional ally Portugal, but its failure demonstrated the poor state of Charles III's army. The war of 1762–63 revealed the disparity in power between Britain and Spain, and Madrid made no difficulty about acceding to the peace concluded between Britain and France.

Anglo-French peace negotiations had been conducted intermittently since 1759, but had broken down because of Pitt's Carthaginian terms and apparent lust for new conquests. By 1760–61 war-weariness was increasing in Britain, aroused by the seemingly high cost of the victories and focussed on the commitment to the fighting in Germany. The accession of a new king, George III, in October 1760 and the advent of his minister-favourite the Earl of Bute in the following year, both critics of the continental war and intent on courting popularity by giving the nation the peace it craved, provided a fresh impetus to a settlement. The resignation of Pitt in October 1761 removed a major obstacle. Anglo-French peace negotiations in that year had failed, and it took complex and prolonged discussions in 1762–63 to end the fighting. During these, Choiseul's skilful diplomacy, together with Britain's war-weariness, limited Bourbon losses. The final settlement was more generous to France and Spain than the prevailing military situation might have suggested.

The terms of the Peace of Paris (signed on 10 February 1763) were far less severe than Pitt would have imposed, but still underlined the scale of Britain's victory. France was totally excluded from the mainland of North America, retaining only a precarious foothold in the Newfoundland fisheries through her continued possession of the islands of St Pierre and Miquelon, while her position in India was effectively destroyed; only in the West Indies did the French avoid substantial territorial losses. Minorca, captured by the French at the beginning of the war, was also regained by Britain. London's gains from Spain were limited to Florida, and the French compensated Charles III by ceding Louisiana to him. The acquisition of this former French colony was a very mixed blessing for Spain, since with it came a further extended and exposed frontier to be defended against British encroachments. More than ever, Spain was now in the front line against British imperial expansion in the American hemisphere. In other respects, too, the Peace of Paris was a setback for Madrid, underlining the serious defeat it had suffered. Though Havana and Manila were returned, the settlement obliged Spain to renounce all hope of access to the Newfoundland Fisheries and to accept the presence of British logwood cutters in Honduras.

The Seven Years War had thus established British maritime and colonial dominance at the expense of her Bourbon rivals and especially France. After 1763 Britain was clearly Europe's leading commercial and imperial power. Within Europe, by contrast, no such clear-cut result was evident and no territory changed hands in the peace of Hubertusburg. Yet the political consequences of the continental war were even more momentous. Prussia's survival and Russia's military victories established these two states as great powers. France, by contrast, had been defeated in both struggles and experienced an international eclipse which would last until the 1790s. Her decline was symbolised by her absence from the negotiations which ended the continental conflict. The treaty of Hubertusburg was the first peace settlement involving German issues for over a century in which France had not been involved. It appeared as if her established role, created by the Peace of Westphalia in 1648, of guarantor of the Imperial constitution and upholder of the German *status quo*, was being abandoned. This was symptomatic of France's wider political decline, which in some ways was the most important consequence of the Seven Years War.

CHAPTER 5

The eighteenth-century international system

A system of Great Powers

The rise of Prussia and Russia, and the decline of France, were dimensions of a more fundamental change during the middle decades of the eighteenth century. This was not simply a matter of the system's expansion eastwards or the accompanying increase in leading states from three to five, important as both were. These developments were part of a wider transformation which created the international order which would, in its essentials, survive until the First World War. The establishment of the term 'great powers' and the widespread acceptance of the ideas it embodied were quite central, as theoretical approaches merged with actual political developments.

These changes had their roots in a more exact notion of power. The strength and relative standing of states had always been assessed. Such calculations, however, had hitherto been rather general. A monarchy's size, population, wealth and military might had been seen as indices of its potential, while success had been measured in terms of battles won and territories conquered. During the first half of the eighteenth century a more modern and precise concept of international power had come to be developed. This had been particularly evident in central Europe, where the later seventeenth and eighteenth centuries had seen the emergence of the theory of Cameralism. It rested on the assumption that the government could pursue policies which would enhance the country's economic well-being and thus its own revenue, and was one foundation of the new notion of power. This also depended upon the simultaneous emergence of the distinctively German science of political geography, based upon the collection of statistics (*Staatenkunde*). By assembling more accurate quantitative information, this facilitated precise calculations of relative potential and actual strength. During the 1750s this approach was elaborated by two celebrated Cameralist writers, Jakob Friedrich von Bielfeld and Johann Heinrich Gottlieb von Justi, both of whom owed a significant intellectual debt to Montesquieu, whose *Spirit of the Laws* – the key work of the European Enlightenment – had been published in 1748.

Bielfeld and Justi, like the earlier writers upon whom they drew, emphasised to novel extent that economics were quite central to calculations of power. Such measurements could now be made more precisely, and statistics assembled on demographic, economic and geographical resources. Such assessments were not purely quantitative but possessed a qualitative dimension. The scale and efficiency of a country's government, the extent to which natural economic resources could be drawn upon, even the moral condition of a ruler's subjects, were all significant components in a state's potential strength. Such power was, above all, relative to that of its rivals. This approach had an immediate and considerable impact upon practical statecraft. These ideas were quickly incorporated into the syllabuses of universities in Germany and Austria at which administrators and ministers were increasingly educated, and in this way came indirectly to influence foreign policy and domestic government. They incorporated the notion that a state's international standing ultimately rested upon its internal strength and coherence, and contributed to the widespread domestic reforms attempted during the generation after the destructive Seven Years War.

These ideas blended with Natural Law theories and Enlightenment doctrines to produce a new approach to international relations. The two most important statesmen of the middle and later eighteenth century, Kaunitz and Frederick the Great, were influenced by these doctrines, as was one of the King's principal advisers, Ewald Friedrich Graf von Hertzberg, subsequently influential during the reign of Frederick William II (1786–97). These notions were one important source of Kaunitz's distinctive approach to diplomacy, his celebrated 'Political Algebra', with its roots in Cartesianism. This was a more precise analytical mode of conducting foreign policy. It calculated the relative political power of individual states in mathematical terms, and employed these calculations to predict the policies of allies and rivals. The Chancellor's approach had its origins in his own education, which had given especial prominence to the mathematical deductive reasoning of Christian Wolff, whose influence had been reinforced by the young Kaunitz's extended period of study at the

University of Leipzig. It was set out in numerous state papers over his long career and influenced his conduct of actual negotiations, though the theory was not always as rigorously practised as Kaunitz imagined. His way of viewing international relations was shared by Frederick the Great, though, characteristically, Prussia's King allowed more for the element of chance.

The way in which a state's standing within the international hierarchy was coming to be assessed both with greater precision and relative to that of its rivals was crucial for the emergence of the notion of the 'great powers' during the third quarter of the eighteenth century. A 'great power' was simply a state which could be seen to be much stronger than its lesser rivals, whom it therefore dominated. The phrase 'great powers', which normally occurs in the plural form, appears to originate during the middle decades of the century and was clearly established by the 1760s and 1770s. It can be found, for example, in the section devoted to foreign policy in Frederick the Great's second *Political Testament* of 1768, while six years later the Russian foreign minister Nikita Panin produced a particularly comprehensive analysis of the phenomenon. This had two linked dimensions. A clearly-defined group of states – by the 1770s there were five – were recognised to be superior in resources and therefore power to the other members of the international system. Collectively, these large countries dominated European politics through their combined strength, and regulated entrance to the international élite. The great power system was rather like a British gentleman's club, with admission controlled by the existing members. If the established great powers began to treat another state as one of their number, that country *ipso facto* became a great power. This was essentially how Prussia and Russia joined the ranks during the Seven Years War.

By the 1770s, the idea that five powers collectively dominated European politics and were able to impose themselves on the other members of the international system was becoming established. The concept of the 'Pentarchy', like the associated notion of the great powers, was not, as is often argued, a product of the Napoleonic era, but belongs to the third quarter of the eighteenth century. The fault lines between western and eastern Europe during the generation after the Seven Years War (Chapters 6–8) impeded the immediate emergence of a European-wide system and partially disguised the leadership of the great powers. Until the 1790s the two leading western powers, Britain and France, with their stronger commercial economics and overseas priorities which set them apart from the three eastern monarchies, inhabited a largely separate political universe from Russia, Prussia and Austria. The noted revival of French military power and the territorial imperialism which it made possible after 1792, together began to reunify the diplomatic worlds of west and east, and this paved the way for the emergence of a single system of five great powers during the Napoleonic era (Chapters 9–11).

The leadership of the great powers was linked to a second mid-eighteenth century development: the much-diminished role of minor states. It was both a question of the changing nature of the international system, and of their own diminished military and financial power. Traditionally, states of the second rank, countries such as Bavaria, Saxony or Denmark, had played a subordinate and usually regional but still significant role within the European system. Some had prospered territorially by skilfully exploiting the dominant rivalries, especially the north Italian kingdom of Sardinia. This had been facilitated by the bipolar nature of the international system for much of the early modern period, with France ranged against the Habsburgs. Minor states had attached themselves to one side or another in this struggle and their support had been valued and sometimes rewarded by the principal adversaries. In the major wars of 1689–1714, Louis XIV had been grateful for Bavaria's alliance, particularly since the Wittelsbach Electorate at this period retained a respectable army, though this subsequently declined as the problems of Bavarian public finances mounted. By the mid-eighteenth century, the role of lesser states was becoming much less, within what was now a multi-polar system.

During the War of the Austrian Succession four second-rank powers – Bavaria, Saxony, Sardinia and, at the very end, the Dutch Republic – had been involved in the fighting. The Wittelsbach Elector, indeed, had briefly become Holy Roman Emperor, the leading secular ruler in Europe. The struggles of the 1740s, however, were to be the last occasion in which minor states played a significant part, before the upheavals of the Revolutionary and Napoleonic era. Only Sweden – in a notably desultory fashion – and, at the very end, Spain – briefly and unsuccessfully – fought in the Seven Years War, which was waged more exclusively between leading states than any previous conflict: a clear indication that the great powers now called the tune. Indeed, during the fighting after 1756, both the Dutch Republic and Denmark formally declared themselves neutral and sought to benefit from their established dominance of Europe's carrying trade.

Copenhagen had adopted such a stance after the ending of the Great Northern War and benefitted economically from her neutrality in all the continent's eighteenth-century conflicts. During its middle decades Danish foreign policy was in the very capable hands of J.H.E. von Bernstorff, a member of a prominent North German family who had entered Denmark's service in the early 1730s and rose to become foreign minister from 1751. Bernstorff's approach was shaped by his own dislike of war, on religious and philosophical grounds. He tried to chart an independent course, as far as was possible for a small state with a very weak army, although with a navy of respectable size, particularly in a Baltic context. Bernstorff's efforts were undermined by Denmark's fundamental weakness, and were further compromised by the complex problem of Holstein, which during the 1760s forced Copenhagen into dependence upon Russia (see below, pp. 153–4).

Denmark's experience mirrored that of all minor powers. It exactly paralleled Sardinia, whose ability to pursue an independent line was removed first by the Austro-Spanish *rapprochement* at Aranjuez in 1752 and, even more decisively, by the Diplomatic Revolution four years later (see above, p. 73). In a similar way the Franco-Austrian alliance, during the generation after 1756, also removed from the minor German rulers any opportunity to play off Versailles against Vienna, and so destroyed a fundamental feature of central European politics since 1648. The experiences of Munich, Dresden, Copenhagen and Turin underlined how completely the five great powers now dominated the international system and treated their second-rank counterparts as satellites: as Denmark and, in a different way, Poland were of St Petersburg, or Spain was to be of France, throughout the generation after the Seven Years War. Only by banding together under the leadership of a great power could minor states now exert real, if regional, influence, as the 'League of Princes' (*Fürstenbund*) would demonstrate in the mid-1780s (see below, pp. 184–5).

In all these ways, the third quarter of the eighteenth century was decisive for the modern great power system. Side-by-side with these new directions, however, there were important continuities. The practice of international relations had evolved gradually over generations and even centuries. Foremost among such continuities was the practice of diplomacy itself. International relations were conducted through a diplomatic network which overlapped but did not exactly coincide with the states system and had developed notably during the century before 1740.

The diplomatic network

Diplomacy, in its widest sense, is almost as old as human history. The sending of representatives had been familiar to the ancient and medieval worlds. Resident embassies and continuous political relations – the fundamental characteristics of the modern European states system – had only really begun around 1500. In the second half of the fifteenth century the Italian city-states had started to appoint permanent ambassadors, and during the next hundred years resident missions spread beyond Italy, until this network included most courts in western and central Europe. These embassies promoted closer contacts and provided information, and were one dimension of the monarchical and administrative states emerging at this time. But this trend towards resident embassies throughout Europe was neither linear nor unbroken. The later sixteenth and the first half of the seventeenth centuries saw a hiatus due to the problems caused by Protestant embassies in Catholic countries and vice versa during a period of frequent and widespread religious conflicts and near-continuous warfare. The next decisive stage had come about during the long personal rule of Louis XIV (1661–1715).

A network of embassies and minor missions, linking all the major capitals and many smaller courts as well, had been established. Louis XIV took the lead, and the other states, especially the Maritime Powers, quickly followed him, largely to counter the French. Louis XIV's France, however, did not merely complete the institutional framework of resident diplomacy: it also established the diplomatic traditions and practices of the next two centuries. The greater bureaucratisation apparent in French government extended into the world of diplomacy. While France's diplomatic service was always the most regulated and hierarchical, other states soon acquired more formal, although often different, machinery for formulating policy and conducting negotiations. Until 1815, and even beyond, French diplomacy provided the model for the rest of Europe. This was the consequence of France's military and political dominance, the resources available for her own diplomatic service and for foreign subsidies, and the consequent successes secured by French diplomats. By the early eighteenth century, permanent embassies and continuous diplomacy were established across most of Europe, and there were to be relatively few changes before the Congress of Vienna.

The most obvious consequence was the gradual replacement of Latin by French as the main language of diplomacy. Though this had begun in the mid-seventeenth century, it was only in the peace negotiations in 1713–14 that the Habsburgs first agreed to the use of French in formal agreements. The treaty of Rastatt had been the first to be drawn up entirely in that language. Thereafter, French rapidly became the first language of all diplomats. It was not only employed in international treaties, but also between diplomats and in negotiations, and increasingly in formal correspondence between foreign ministers and their ambassadors. French was the official language of Prussian diplomacy from June 1740 onwards, while in the second half of the eighteenth century Austrian diplomats frequently preferred it to German. It was employed during the same period by Danish diplomats and their superiors in Copenhagen, except for matters concerning the Holy Roman Empire which were transacted in German, and had been the language of Sardinian diplomacy from the Peace of Utrecht onwards. The principal exception was south-eastern and Mediterranean Europe, the area under Ottoman sway which stretched from Constantinople to the Maghreb. There a form of pidgin Italian, known as the *lingua franca*, remained the language of diplomacy and of official international documents at least down to 1830. Broader cultural questions were involved here. The position of French as the diplomatic language simply reflected its dominance, during the eighteenth century and beyond, as the principal language of monarchical and aristocratic society. Its growing use was quite deliberate. Since a diplomat would have to employ it in any negotiations, as well as on social occasions, there was felt to be an obvious benefit in drawing up his instructions and requiring him to report in French. It would sharpen his linguistic skills and might enhance official control over an envoy, who would be expected to follow his instructions to the letter.

The predominance of French contributed to the emergence of diplomatic corps in Europe's capitals. In 1738 Antoine Pecquet, a French foreign office functionary and the author of a widely-used manual of diplomacy, had declared that the ambassadors, envoys and representatives of lesser rank constituted a kind of 'independent society' bound together by a 'community of privileges'. Diplomats sent to one particular country were increasingly conscious that they did form a distinct community, united by several important common interests and possessing a corporate identity. In particular, they recognised that any attack on the rights of one ambassador was an affront to the entire diplomatic corps. By the second half of the seventeenth century it had already become widely accepted that the immunity of a diplomat and his household was necessary to ensure continuous relations between states. The only significant exception was at Constantinople where, until the nineteenth century, a foreign envoy was always likely to be arrested and imprisoned in the Castle of the Seven Towers on the declaration of hostilities between his own state and the Ottoman Empire. Everywhere else a diplomat could expect to be expelled or allowed to withdraw unmolested when war broke out. Napoleon's infringement of this principle was widely resented (see below, p. 304). By the mid-eighteenth century, diplomatic immunity, based on the concept of extra-territoriality, was securely established, though the precise extent of this inviolability was everywhere a matter of interpretation and dispute. Debts contracted by diplomats were the most frequent source of problems. In a similar way, it was now generally accepted that although correspondence sent by ordinary post might be opened and copied, couriers were inviolate. By this period incidents such as the blatant robbery of a French messenger, which had taken place in the Dutch Republic in 1684, had become very unusual. As couriers were expensive, diplomats tended to write the more secret parts of their dispatches in code, almost always numerical.

By the early eighteenth century, there was a generally recognised hierarchy both of states and of the level of diplomats exchanged. It was agreed that the European courts were not all equal in rank – irrespective of their political power. Rulers of Catholic states still allowed some measure of pre-eminence to the Pope, emperors outranked kings (this was why Peter the Great's adoption of the title of 'emperor' in 1721 had caused so many disputes and problems), while monarchies were superior to dukes, minor princes and republics: the Dutch had endless problems in securing due recognition, even from their allies. Beyond this narrow consensus lay endless quarrelling over precedence, which was important since it reflected a state's reputation. The eighteenth century paid considerable attention to 'the interest of regard', as the comte de Broglie styled it, while as late as 1812 the French representative in Naples fought a duel with his Russian counterpart over a matter of precedence, an action subsequently approved by his superiors in Paris.

A diplomat had to be permanently on his guard to ensure that his – and therefore his ruler's – honour was not insulted by being relegated to an inferior position at a dinner or other formal occasion. During the negotiation of a treaty, much time was often spent quarrelling about whether or not the 'alternative' was to be allowed. This was the provision that each signatory would sign a version of the agreement in which its name appeared first, in order to uphold the prized claim to equality. A serious and long-running dispute over the 'alternative' between the two imperial courts of Vienna and St Petersburg – a consequence of Peter the Great's adoption of the title of 'emperor' – ensured that the Austro-Russian alliance of 1781 took the unusual form of an exchange of private letters between the two rulers (see below, pp. 180–1). Questions of protocol were at the heart of eighteenth-century diplomacy. The explanation for this was set out by Nikita Panin, who declared that 'Etiquette strictly regulates forms of correspondence between states precisely because it serves as a measure of the mutual respect for each other's strength'.

In a similar way there was a recognised diplomatic hierarchy. It was accepted that only the major states had the right to send ambassadors, though this privilege seems to have been eroded during the eighteenth century. Envoys came next in importance to ambassadors: they were cheaper, they did not have to be nobles (though they usually were), and they were also a convenient way of side-stepping disputes over precedence, for an envoy was surrounded by less elaborate ceremonial. During this period the post of envoy became the most widely-used diplomatic rank. Ambassadors and envoys constituted the diplomatic élite and were clearly far above the lower strata of residents and secretaries of embassy, who often knew most about foreign courts, where they tended to serve for several years. During the eighteenth century this hierarchy was complicated by the increasing use of other ranks, in particular minister plenipotentiary, but the fundamental distinction remained.

By 1700 the major states all maintained reciprocal representation in peacetime: during war, or when relations became strained, diplomats were withdrawn or representation was limited to that of secretary of embassy. The two principal exceptions to permanent and resident embassies were Russia and the Ottoman Empire, and both came to be integrated into this network, in different degrees, during the eighteenth century. During the Great Northern War (1700–21) Russia had ended her previous isolation (see above, pp. 26–7). Her quest for allies and for European technology promoted closer links with the west, while Peter the Great's victories over Sweden gave his state a new-found European importance. Peter rapidly created a protean western-style diplomatic service with resident embassies in the major European capitals. These links, however, had been weakened after his death in 1725. Purely Russian factors contributed to this, above all the shortage of potential noble diplomats with a knowledge of Europe's languages and political customs, and St Petersburg's periodic isolationism. At least until mid-century, Russia remained on the diplomatic periphery. This was shown by most states sending representatives of a lower rank to the Russian court, where they encountered simple and fluid ceremonial. During Elizabeth's reign there was growing interest in etiquette, and information on foreign courts was assembled. It was only from the early 1760s, however, that Russia began to embrace fully the established diplomatic ceremonial and practices of other European states. This new concern was apparent in the evolution during Catherine II's reign of a Ceremonial Department within the Russian College of Foreign

Affairs, as the embryo foreign office was known (see below, p. 135). The Empress herself also sponsored Russian translations of French and German manuals on diplomacy and international law. Russia's full political emergence and admission to the ranks of the great powers under Catherine II involved a transformation of her political culture, which came to resemble that of the other leading states.

The other new member of the diplomatic network was the Ottoman Empire, though its entry occurred rather later and initially proved less complete. The Ottoman impact on early modern Europe had been considerable, yet it was not until the 1790s that its first embassies were established in European capitals. Until then the Porte had sent individual and temporary missions for specific purposes, such as the signature of a peace treaty (see above, pp. 34–5). The absence of resident embassies reflected a basic assumption of superiority: diplomacy was unnecessary since nothing was to be learned from the infidels who ought rather to appear as supplicants in Constantinople – Lord Macartney's mission to China in 1793 encountered the same reception. Many European states had maintained diplomats in the Ottoman capital, often for commercial reasons, though they operated under peculiarly difficult conditions.

During the century after the Peace of Carlowitz the Ottoman Empire was gradually drawn into closer contacts with Europe's leading states. Its integration was slowed by the enduring Muslim conviction of superiority over the infidels, but while this delayed change, it could not obstruct it altogether. Ottoman weakness contributed to growing European economic penetration of the empire, especially around the Black Sea and along the North African coastline, particularly at the western end of the Mediterranean. This in turn led to the dispatch of an increasing number of consuls. The capitulations which laid down their privileges had traditionally been dictated by the all-powerful Sultan, but by the eighteenth century the shift in political and economic power ensured that their terms were laid down by the European states. They imposed western assumptions and practices, such as the equality of all rulers, the need for strict reciprocity and the dictates of the law of nations, above all extra-territoriality. In this way the principles which underpinned the international system were imported into the Ottoman Empire through the capitulations. In practice, however, European representatives were prepared to compromise to secure their goals and recognised that local realities could oblige principles to be overlooked. One of the clearest illustrations was provided by the French consulate in Tunis, ruled by an Ottoman provincial governor (*bey*) under the loose overlordship of the Sultan. In an agreement signed in 1742, France's consul had to agree to kiss the hand of the *bey* and his designated successor during audiences, which all the other European representatives did; until then the French agent alone had been permitted to raise his hat and also to wear a sword on formal occasions. Such local compromises accompanied the wider Ottoman acceptance of reciprocal diplomacy.

It epitomised the way in which Europe's diplomatic practices were brought to Constantinople. Until the 1790s, Ottoman diplomatic missions, though much more numerous than in previous centuries, remained temporary in nature. The Empire's vulnerability ensured an expansion of European representation at the Porte during the eighteenth century and this, in turn, introduced Ottoman officials to the world of continental diplomacy. Military reverses eroded previous assumptions of superiority. It was apparent in the Ottoman Empire's acceptance of European mediation in most major peace treaties from 1699 onwards. The French had mediated at Carlowitz and again at Belgrade, while the Maritime Powers had done so at Passarowitz. Constantinople wished for such mediation to conclude the 1768–74 war with Russia, but the victorious Catherine II insisted on dictating terms (see below, pp. 167–8): as she would again do at the end of the 1787–92 conflict. Remarkably enough in 1745 the Porte itself attempted unsuccessfully to mediate the War of the Austrian Succession. This initiative, together with the willingness to employ mediation to settle its own wars, drew the Ottoman Empire further into the world of European diplomacy.

By the end of the eighteenth century, and in particular after the defeats in the wars of 1768–74 and 1787–92, the Ottoman Empire came to be involved in the European states system: as an increasing number of its own ruling élite recognised, it needed military and financial aid and political alliances, while its weakness made it increasingly the focus for the ambitions of the great powers. The Ottoman Empire signed its first European-style alliances with Sweden (1789) and Prussia (1791). An even sharper break with previous policies was the conclusion of a triangular alliance with Britain and Russia against France in 1799, which ended the Porte's diplomatic isolation (see below, pp. 292–3). The resulting integration, the need for greater knowledge of events in Europe and the desire of the reforming Sultan, Selim III (1789–1807), to modernise by learning from the west, produced in 1793 a formal decision to establish permanent embassies. The first was set up in London the same year, and during the next few years diplomats were also sent to Paris, Berlin and Vienna. The

Ottoman network of embassies was never extensive, however, and it was crippled by the absence of a modern foreign ministry to provide direction and also by the lack of a regular courier service: diplomats were forced to entrust their dispatches to the messengers of their European rivals, with a loss of confidentiality. By 1811 all four posts had been down-graded to the level of *chargé d'affaires* and a decade later they had disappeared. Selim III's initiative, however, did have important legacies. It endowed some Ottoman officials with knowledge of Europe and its languages, and prepared the way for the Empire's full incorporation into the diplomatic network during the nineteenth century.

The nature of diplomacy

Diplomacy during the *ancien régime* was largely a temporary employment for aristocrats and amateurs rather than a career for professionals. A leading nobleman, often with no previous diplomatic experience, would take an embassy in the same way as he would serve in the army or in government: it embodied the service he believed he owed to his monarch. By the early eighteenth century, resident diplomacy had acquired its aristocratic tone, which it would retain until the twentieth century. In the lower ranks of secretaries of embassy and residents, usually non-nobles, there is some evidence of growing careerism. But there were few professional diplomats among the ambassadors and envoys. These were drawn almost universally from the higher nobility and, occasionally, from leading churchmen, though the employment of clerics was becoming rare. This aristocratic dominance followed from the principle that ambassadors represented their sovereign; rulers therefore sent the men most capable of glorifying themselves. The employment of noblemen also reflected a general desire not to offend a recipient by sending a representative of a lower social standing. The principal exceptions were the Dutch Republic and Britain, whose distinct social structures were mirrored in their diplomats. Both employed noblemen, but some Dutch diplomats were members of the Regent oligarchy and many British ambassadors lacked aristocratic titles. Though it did contain some noblemen, the Russian diplomatic service was less of an aristocratic redoubt than most of its counterparts. In this, as in other respects, Prussia was also a significant exception. Her native nobility, the Junkers, aimed both by preference and by royal wish to follow a military career or even to secure a post in government. Few noblemen served in the Prussian diplomatic service, which contained much higher proportions of commoners and non-natives than in other states.

Leading aristocrats dominated the most important embassies – Rome (for Catholic states), Paris, Madrid, Vienna and London – but were reluctant to go to the more remote corners of Europe, such as Warsaw, St Petersburg and Constantinople. Aristocratic ambassadors frequently took merely one or two important missions and tended to occupy these posts only briefly. Few had any previous diplomatic experience, for their own social status was an effective barrier to accepting any of the lower-level appointments which would have conferred expertise. The inexperience of many ambassadors was in theory compensated for by the inclusion of more experienced diplomats in their retinues. Here again, however, the privileged world of the eighteenth century frustrated good intentions. An ambassador would usually select his own secretaries and other assistants, drawn from his family and friends, who were often inadequate. Though the size of embassies depended on the importance and formality of particular courts, a diplomat's retinue could be surprisingly large and extravagant. In Rome, for example, the Spanish and French ambassadors frequently had households numbering 100 or more, and one mid-eighteenth-century embassy from France contained 145 male personnel. Only a small part of the cost was borne by the diplomat's government. Ambassadors and envoys were everywhere expected to spend their own money in the service of their monarch and this reinforced the domination of major embassies by members of the high nobility.

The network of permanent embassies and the increased volume of negotiations inevitably raised the question of the training of ambassadors. The need for this was certainly recognised during the eighteenth century, but there were relatively few attempts to prepare young men for a career in diplomacy. The efforts made all sought to provide mainly practical training, either connected to foreign ministries or attached to embassies abroad. The most notable of these had been the *Académie politique* (the famous 'School for Ambassadors') founded by the French foreign minister, Torcy, in 1712. But it never recovered from its founder's political eclipse in October 1715, and had disappeared by 1721. Efforts to revive it in 1737 and again in 1770 were completely unsuccessful. The *Académie politique* was the most famous of a handful of similar schemes. The training of Papal diplomats at the Pontifical Ecclesiastical Academy began in 1701 and was more or less continuous thereafter, while the founding of the Regius chairs of Modern History at Oxford and Cambridge in 1724 was partly inspired by a wish to produce diplomatic recruits, though it failed to do so. Frederick the Great also founded a diplomatic nursery to produce Prussian secretaries and residents in 1747. A group of trainee diplomats was to be attached to the foreign ministry, but few recruits came forward and it collapsed within a decade. A later initiative during the mid-1770s to train future diplomats by sending them as secretaries to established Prussian missions also failed.

The Oriental Academy established in 1753 in Vienna and intended to train future diplomats for careers as consuls and ambassadors in south-eastern Europe was rather a specialised category. Its foundation was an early symptom of the Ottoman Empire's growing importance within the eighteenth-century diplomatic network. The curriculum emphasised the study of the difficult Turkish language which would enable an Austrian representative to negotiate directly with the Porte and not through a drago-man, while Ottoman laws, customs and methods of diplomacy were also studied. Among its earliest graduates was Franz Maria von Thugut, who served in Constantinople and rose to be Austria's foreign minister during the 1790s (see below, pp. 209, 269). Thugut's rise underlined that most foreign ministers were expected to have served as diplomats, receiving practical training in statecraft. The modern theoretical education acquired by his great predecessor and patron Kaunitz was highly unusual (see above, pp. 118–19), and the Chancellor took care to supplement this study by service as a diplomat to prepare himself for high office.

There were several efforts to train diplomats in eighteenth-century Russia. Peter the Great had found a chronic shortage of suitable person-nel, when he tried to create a western-style diplomatic service. He there-fore sent young Russian noblemen abroad to study, particularly western European languages. His reign had also seen two attempts to establish a training school modelled on the *Académie politique*, but both soon failed. These initiatives were revived under Empress Elizabeth by the noted legal scholar F.G. Strube de Piermont, though his plan also foundered. Instead, efforts continued to be made to attach young nobles to Russia's own embassies as a kind of diplomatic apprenticeship, to enable them to learn foreign languages and receive relevant training. In 1779 Catherine II sought to overcome a continuing shortage of diplomats by attaching one or two young men, at her own expense, to Russian embassies, while in 1797 Paul I laid down that 30 nobles should be trained by the College of Foreign Affairs. Napoleon also attempted to systematise the training of diplomats and did succeed in producing some improvement in their quality, particu-larly during his final years in power.

These various initiatives embodied the orthodoxy of the day concern-ing the necessary subjects a trainee diplomat should study. Diplomatic theorists and practical statesmen agreed that a knowledge of 'public law'

(later called international law), recent European history, particularly diplomatic history, and foreign languages, especially French, were essential:
this had been the curriculum at the *Académie politique* and was widely
copied, while the principal obligation on the new Regius Professors of
Modern History was the teaching of modern languages. The Prussian
official Bielfeld, whose *Institutions politiques*, published in 1760, contained a valuable guide to the workings of mid-eighteenth-century diplomacy, even identified the three key texts which a would-be ambassador
had to study intensively: these were Grotius, *De jure belli ac pacis*;
Pufendorf, *The Law of Nature and of Nations*; and Montesquieu, *The
Spirit of the Laws*.

The *Académie politique* and similar initiatives are primarily interesting
for the evidence they provide of the recognised shortcomings of established practice. They had little contemporary impact and, with the exceptions of the Oriental Academy and the Pontifical Ecclesiastical Academy,
all soon collapsed. The *ancien régime* consequently lacked professional
diplomatic corps, and these only emerged during the nineteenth century.
The explanation is twofold. In the first place, the aristocracy's near
monopoly over the higher posts militated against extensive training.
Secondly, there was little incentive to enter diplomacy when there was no
career structure, the top posts were reserved for the greatest noblemen,
and promotion was likely to be a matter of favour and patronage. Indeed,
it was a notoriously insecure and underpaid profession. Failure in a negotiation could wreck a career, while a diplomat could often be forgotten or
his position undermined while abroad. Not many people actually sought
a diplomatic career, regarding service abroad as an 'honourable exile', as
it was styled by the leading eighteenth-century French diplomatic theorist
François de Callières, to be exchanged for a suitable post at home as soon
as the opportunity offered. Pay and expenses were notoriously poor and
reimbursement frequently belated. It offered far worse prospects than
the readily-available posts in the expanding administrations of the continental states with their opportunities to supplement meagre salaries by
fees and perquisites. The quality of diplomats produced in this haphazard
way was variable and could be poor. At most, new envoys or ambassadors
might glance through some old dispatches bearing on relations with the
state to which they were being sent, though the elaborate instructions
which they received at the outset of a mission did something to make up
for these shortcomings.

The duties were relatively limited. Diplomacy was, essentially, a matter
of representing your own sovereign, and for this it was enough to be a

nobleman. Beyond this, the role of diplomats would obviously depend on whether rulers or ministers preferred to conduct negotiations in their own court with ambassadors accredited to it, or entrusted these to their own envoys abroad. The conduct of political discussions, though ostensibly the central purpose of diplomacy, in fact was relatively infrequent and unimportant. It occupied little of a diplomat's time, which was largely taken up by comparatively routine tasks. In any case, really important negotiations might often be handled by a special mission. The other duty of a diplomat, besides representing his monarch, defending his interests and those of his subjects (particularly merchants) was to provide information for the policy-makers at home. This filled up his regular dispatches to his superiors, by which his success or failure was judged. The young Clemens Wenzel Lothar, Graf von Metternich, setting off on his first diplomatic mission, was advised by an old chancery hand in Vienna to write frequently and at length if he wanted to rise in his superiors' esteem.

A diplomat was expected to gather as much information as he could about the state to which he was posted and, in particular, about its armed forces and public finances. The surviving files of correspondence contain substantial amounts of military and economic intelligence, sometimes secured in underhand ways. Napoleon, who had a low view of diplomats and diplomacy, declared: 'Ambassadors are, in the full meaning of the term, titled spies.' A generation earlier, Frederick the Great had pronounced a similar verdict when he declared ambassadors to be merely 'honest spies'. To be effective, however, it was essential for a diplomat to be accepted into the society of the court to which he was accredited. Much of an ambassador's time was spent on the social round of dinners, receptions, and all kinds of musical and theatrical entertainments at court and in the houses of ministers, aristocrats and fellow diplomats. By keeping his eyes and ears open he could obtain useful information to fill up his dispatches. Minor states, with a much smaller diplomatic infrastructure, also assembled information indirectly, through intermediaries such as merchants, financiers and publicists.

Another, less frequent, source of political intelligence was bribery or espionage. This is one reason for the widely-held but exaggerated view of the importance of 'secret diplomacy'. Since ambassadors and envoys frequently explained their own failures by extensive bribery by rivals, such excuses have too often been taken at face value. There is no doubt, however, that, at certain times and places, money was the principal basis of diplomacy. In Poland in the generation before partition, or in Sweden during the 'Age of Liberty' (1719–72), rival diplomats spent lavishly to build up a party in the intense domestic political struggles. Expenditure was usually on a much more modest scale, in the form of pensions or gratifications to courtiers or statesmen. Such gifts were an established feature of early modern diplomacy. They were not seen as corrupt, were frequently publicly acknowledged, and were intended not to influence a particular decision or to obtain information but to cultivate individuals already well-intentioned. Presents on the conclusion of a treaty were also expected as the norm, while at the beginning or the end of an embassy a diplomat could expect a gift from the ruler to whom he had been accredited. This might take the form of a painting or other *objet d'art*.

The wider importance of espionage has also been exaggerated. Every state maintained a secret office or *cabinet noir*, to intercept and copy the correspondence of its rivals. Skilled decipherers were available to crack the numerical codes employed. The French and British authorities were both very successful in intercepting and deciphering dispatches. The Austrian *cabinet noir* was also particularly energetic and wide-ranging in its activities, operating in Regensburg, Frankfurt-am-Main, Liège and Brussels as well as Vienna itself. It was claimed that it broke 15 ciphers of foreign diplomats during a single year (1780–81). Its operations certainly made life difficult for ambassadors in Vienna, though its efficiency could occasionally leave something to be desired. On one occasion the British minister Sir Robert Murray Keith had to protest formally that he sometimes received copies of dispatches from London while the originals were sent to Kaunitz! Most diplomats were aware that their dispatches were intercepted, often by postmasters in the countries through which these letters passed, and either avoided this by employing couriers during important negotiations or exploiting it by inserting misleading information into their reports. And while the eighteenth century was not lacking in spectacular coups – as when the entire correspondence of the British ambassador in Constantinople from 1770 to 1775 was betrayed to his French rival – the gains from espionage were very small compared to the cost and effort.

The rise of foreign offices

Eighteenth-century foreign policy was overwhelmingly monarchical, although Europe's rulers often delegated some initiative to a chief minister. The eighteenth century saw a notable revival of first ministers, the ancestors of the prime ministers of subsequent centuries, who were responsible to their rulers for external and internal policy: men such as Fleury, Choiseul and Vergennes in France, Kaunitz in the Habsburg Monarchy, and even Potemkin in Russia. These leading ministers were almost always primarily concerned with diplomacy because of its dominance. The precise mechanisms for the day-to-day formulation and control of foreign policy obviously varied from state to state, but the general tendency is clear: there was an evolution towards larger and more specialised departments, 'foreign offices' in all but name. Once again France had led the way. A much more elaborate foreign office had emerged during the second half of Louis XIV's reign, particularly under Jean Baptiste Colbert, marquis de Torcy, the King's last foreign minister (1698–1715). At Louis's assumption of real power in 1661, a single coach would have sufficed to transport the minister who controlled French foreign policy and his handful of assistants. By 1715 Torcy and his retinue would have needed 20 such coaches, so many specialised personnel (permanent officials, archivists, translators, cryptographers, clerks) had been added. The French foreign office remained supreme until the end of this period, its efficiency and good organisation providing a model for other states.

During these decades all the major states developed specialised departments with ministers primarily responsible for foreign affairs. This institutionalisation was both a reaction to advances in France, and a dimension of the wider administrative evolution; it also reflected the increased volume of diplomacy conducted. But it was not until the final quarter of the eighteenth century that this development was complete. Even then, the functional division of responsibility was usually imperfect. Many officials in the embryonic foreign ministries still spent much of their time transacting domestic business, while other departments of state retained some control over aspects of foreign affairs. Indeed, the Habsburg military council (*Hofkriegsrat*) handled diplomatic relations with Russia until 1742 and with the Ottoman Empire until 1753. France's foreign minister – like the other three secretaries of state – was responsible for the government of about one-quarter of the French provinces, while during his long ministry Kaunitz handled the administration of the outlying Habsburg territories of Milan and the Netherlands. These divided responsibilities underlined the slowness with which functional departments of state emerged. This was particularly so in Britain where, until 1782, the secretaries of state were responsible for both domestic and foreign policy.

The trend towards more specialised departments for diplomacy was unmistakable, however. In this, the remote state of Russia had led the attempt to catch up with France. Peter the Great's energetic external policies and his attempt to extend contacts with the West had resulted in the creation of a larger and more specialised foreign office. In 1719 the old *Posolskii Prikaz* ('Department of Embassies') was replaced by a College of Foreign Affairs. Its organisation and size, however, did not insulate it from the growing inefficiency of all Russian government during the generation after Peter's death. By mid-century, the College of Foreign Affairs had become slow-moving and cumbersome.

The foreign offices of France and Russia grew faster than those of any other state, but broadly similar developments took place elsewhere. The leading central European powers both acquired relatively sophisticated agencies. In Prussia, as part of Frederick William I's extensive administrative reorganisation, a Department of External Affairs (*Auswärtiges Amt*) had been set up in 1728; after 1733 it was known as the *Kabinettsministerium*. Its establishment did not mean that one official immediately became responsible for foreign policy, since it was organised on a collegial basis with responsibility shared between two, and sometimes three, individuals, as was characteristic of all Prussian government at this period. Unity of direction only began at the accession of a new monarch in 1740, when Frederick the Great sidelined the *Kabinettsministerium* and acted as his own foreign minister, personally conducting much of the correspondence and handling all important negotiations throughout his reign.

In the mid-eighteenth century Austria acquired one of the most modern and efficient foreign ministries in Europe. This came about in two stages. In 1742 the veteran adviser Johann Christoph von Bartenstein set up the State Chancellery (*Staatskanzlei*), which was to be responsible for 'foreign affairs and confidential dynastic matters'. Old practices persisted in the new institution, however, in a way which was typical of the eighteenth century. Bartenstein, for example, had continued to write the drafts of official papers himself. When Kaunitz entered office in 1753 the Chancellor, who had firm and novel views on the importance of modern administrative practices, carried out a wide-ranging reorganisation. This established a permanent staff of around a dozen clerks and servants to undertake necessary tasks such as copying and filing. The State Chancellery was divided into three separate departments, each responsible for clearly delineated areas of business and headed by a senior official, who was responsible to Kaunitz's deputy, Binder, who supervised the day-to-day running of the ministry. Such arrangements, with their clear administrative hierarchy and division of responsibilities, were still relatively unusual in the mid-eighteenth century. Their inspiration was the system of *premiers commis* in France's foreign office, with which Kaunitz had himself been familiar while ambassador to Louis XV's court (1750–52).

The French example also served as a model for developments in Turin and Madrid. In 1717, Victor Amadeus II had divided the secretaryship in two, creating for the first time a minister who was in charge of foreign policy. By mid-century, after further changes in 1742, Sardinia possessed a modern and professional foreign office, and two-thirds of its officials possessed legal training. Like many of its counterparts across Europe, it also acquired its own building, part of Turin's royal palace which had been extended during the 1730s. In Spain, French inspiration was even clearer, since the institutions and administrative practices of Louis XIV came south in the baggage of the first Bourbon King. A Secretariat of State for Foreign Affairs was established as early as 1714, though during Philip V's reign it merely administered policy rather than formulating it. After 1746, however, it slowly became more powerful and independent, and by Charles III's reign it had evolved into a specialised ministry of foreign affairs. A similar, if far less complete, trend was visible both in Poland and Sweden during the final quarter of the century.

Until 1782 the control of British diplomacy was divided on a geographical basis between two secretaries of state, respectively for the Southern and Northern Departments. Unified direction was then formally established with the creation of the office of foreign secretary. Yet the framework for the control of Britain's diplomacy always seemed elementary in comparison with the increasingly elaborate machinery existing in the major continental states. The British foreign office had under 20 permanent officials during the 1780s compared with over 70 in the French, and around 140 in the Russian College of Foreign Affairs a generation earlier. Even in the second-rank state of Sardinia, the foreign office contained almost 50 permanent staff. These new and enlarged foreign ministries gave greater precision to the conduct of national policies and to diplomacy as a whole. The officials assembled previous correspondence in a systematic way (in fact, many national archives began in the eighteenth century as departments of foreign offices), drew up treaty collections and compiled manuals of diplomacy and of international law.

Treaty collections were increasingly recognised as essential within a diplomatic system dominated by precedent and regulated by previous treaties of peace and alliance, and they were employed both in training future diplomats and during actual negotiations. The best known was the *Corps universel diplomatique du droit des gens* of the Dutchman, Jean Dumont de Carlscroon, which began publication in 1726 and eventually consisted of a dozen volumes. Most European states had begun to acquire such compendiums during or immediately after the age of Louis XIV. Russia's delayed entry into the international system was reflected in the fact that this was not undertaken until Catherine II's reign, when the leading role was played by G.F. Müller, the noted historiographer and secretary of the Russian Academy of Sciences. After almost two decades of pressure, Müller secured the Empress's approval in 1779 – significantly at exactly the point when St Petersburg's European influence was significantly enhanced by her mediation at Teschen (see below, p. 179) – for a collection of all Russian treaties and other international agreements. The first volumes appeared during the next four years, until his death in 1783 brought the project to a halt.

The nature of international rivalry

Foreign policy everywhere reflected the ambitions and concerns of Europe's rulers. Diplomacy was in the hands of a tiny élite, for only in Britain and the Dutch Republic could parliamentary or public opinion exert any influence on policy. The motives behind these monarchs' foreign policies were changing significantly in this period. In the sixteenth and seventeenth centuries, religion and dynastic interest had been the dominant issues. By 1648, however, religion was rapidly ceasing to be important and for the eighteenth-century great powers it was always a marginal consideration. It could be a useful propaganda weapon, as it was – improbably – for the disbeliever Frederick the Great, who was quick to proclaim the Seven Years War a religious struggle, with Protestant Prussia and Britain ranged against their Catholic foes. But, except within the Holy Roman Empire and in the struggles between the Muslim Ottoman Empire and its European Christian adversaries, religion was no longer central to international rivalry. The political decline of the Papacy, apparent in the diminished respect it received from the leading Catholic monarchies by this period, reflected this change. During the 1760s and 1770s successive Popes were bullied into suppressing the Society of Jesus, apparently against their wishes, by Spain and France.

The eighteenth century also saw some decline in purely dynastic motives behind foreign policy. Until the 1740s, the principal justification for territorial claims, at least in western Europe, tended to be dynastic rights, commemorated in the names of the major wars, such as that over the Austrian Succession. The personal wish or whim of a ruler remained important, since there were in practice few restraints on the monarch's actions, and reputation was always a significant dimension of international relations, but purely family considerations were less significant. Dynastic links remained important in relations between great powers and smaller states. The Romanovs, Russia's ruling family, sought to extend their influence within the Holy Roman Empire by intermarrying with minor rulers, above all Württemberg, a policy which flourished under Catherine the Great but had been started by Peter the Great. In this period nationalism was not a factor in relations between states. In a similar way it was only in the 1790s that ideological motives became significant, as members of the anti-French coalition aimed increasingly to reverse the political changes introduced by the Revolutionaries, which they regarded as a threat to their own security (see Chapter 9). And while, as a consequence of the new way in which state power was assessed (see above, pp. 117–19), economic factors were becoming more important, they were far from pre-eminent. Instead, eighteenth-century international relations were largely dominated by considerations of *raison d'état*.

The doctrine of *raison d'état* ('reason of state') was simply the argument of necessity as the basis for political conduct. Self-interest was – as it has always been – the dominant motive behind foreign policy. The consequence of the general acceptance of this doctrine was the competitive states system of the eighteenth century where, as one well-informed publicist wrote in 1760, 'In the end everything depends on power'. Force was an essential, if unspoken, element in international relations, underpinning the rivalry of the great powers. The effectiveness of a country's foreign policy was directly linked to the size and reputation of its permanent standing army and, in the case of the British state, its navy. 'The spirit of monarchy,' declared Montesquieu, 'is war and aggrandisement.' Rulers and statesmen strove to increase the wealth, and therefore the power, of their country and sought annexations to bring this about. International strength was everywhere measured in territorial extent and demographic and economic resources, which in turn determined revenue and the size of the army. Catherine II remarked in 1794, as Poland was finally being removed from the map of Europe, 'who gains nothing, loses'. The result was to make the eighteenth-century international system resemble the state of nature postulated by the seventeenth-century English political philosopher Thomas Hobbes, a competition of all against all, where violence was the only law.

The same self-interest, however, also provided a mechanism for restraining this atavistic struggle: the balance of power. This provided some stability within a states system dominated by a perpetual and frequently violent competition for supremacy. During its eighteenth-century heyday, the idea of the balance of power existed at a theoretical and practical level. There was widespread discussion among publicists and philosophers, particularly in Britain and France, about the desirability and practicality of a balance of power, which since the advent of Newtonian physics was increasingly viewed in mechanical terms. Rousseau, for example, saw it as a self-regulating mechanism for continuing harmony between states. The naïve optimism and frequent superficiality of much Enlightenment thinking was apparent in the frequent assumption that the balance of power would be a way of advancing the numerous plans for permanent peace produced at this time. But the argument, on the whole, went against the advocates of a balance of power. It proved very difficult to defend such a notoriously imprecise concept against intelligent sceptics such as J.H.G. von Justi, for whom it was only a chimera. In any case, the contemporary impact of such philosophical speculation on the practice of international relations was slight.

The maintenance of a balance of power was also the practical objective of many statesmen. The treaty of Utrecht (1713) had declared its purpose to be 'to confirm the peace and tranquillity of the Christian world through a just equilibrium of power (which is the best and most secure foundation of mutual friendship and lasting agreement in every quarter)'. This was the first occasion on which a peace settlement had referred quite so directly to the principle. In practice the balance of power meant simply that no one state, or alignment, should become preponderant; and that, if it did, the other European states would join together to curb it. The doctrine was both instinctive reaction and conscious policy, and, as such, was not new to the eighteenth century. It had originated in later-fifteenth-century Italy, as a means of preventing Venice from becoming dominant. In sixteenth- and seventeenth-century Europe, statesmen had thought more of localised balances than an overall balance of power, which only really began to establish itself after 1713–14, as Europe became a more unified political system. In the eighteenth century, these local balances, particularly in Italy, Germany, south-eastern Europe and around the Baltic, remained essential elements in a continent-wide equilibrium.

The new balance of power was difficult to uphold because of Europe's complex and competing rivalries. In the first place, throughout most of the early modern period there had been a simple equilibrium with only two major components: France had opposed the Habsburgs of Spain and Austria, while the second rank states joined one side or the other. But the eighteenth century saw the emergence of several more leading states: by 1763 Britain, Prussia and Russia had joined the established great powers of France and Austria. Secondly, the extension of Anglo-French rivalry overseas meant that, for the first time, the balance acquired an extra-European dimension. For both these reasons it became more difficult to uphold. Yet, at the same time, the near-equality of the great powers, with the exception of Britain on account of her immense colonial and commercial wealth, made the balance of power more important as a restraint. Any gain by one state was a matter of concern for all the others because of their near-equality. In this way the balance of power came to operate against the smaller, weaker states. If a state could not be prevented from making a territorial acquisition, the principle of equilibrium required that other states should secure equivalent gains. This idea was most clearly apparent in the three partitions of Poland at the end of the eighteenth century. As the author of *The Political State of Europe* (first published in 1750) wrote: 'The struggle for the balance of power is in effect, the struggle for power.'

Much of the thinking about the European states-system was static, a matter of habit and reflex assumptions more than constructive and forward-looking statesmanship. The minds of rulers and diplomats ran along familiar grooves; any variations in the established patterns were seen as unnatural and unwelcome. The fixed points of international relations were its well-established, permanent and seemingly ineradicable rivalries and enmities. Principal amongst these had long been the struggle between Habsburg and Bourbon which lasted until 1756, and the renewed hostility between Britain and France (usually aligned with Spain) which was continuous from the 1740s. Further east, rivalry between Austria and the Ottoman Empire, and the parallel antagonism between Russia and the Ottomans continued throughout this period. In the Baltic, Russo-Swedish and Swedish–Danish rivalries were deeply rooted, while, from the 1740s, the struggle between Austria and the rising power of Prussia, in Germany and in central Europe generally, became a permanent theme of continental politics.

The alliance of traditionally hostile states was certainly highly unusual. It was why contemporaries were so surprised by the treaty between such hereditary foes as France and Austria in 1756 that they styled it a 'Diplomatic Revolution'. Throughout much of this period the foreign policies of the European states were based not on traditional friendships, which were elusive, but on the established rivalries, and it proved difficult for any statesman to ignore them – as witness the obstacles to the attempted Anglo-French *rapprochement* in the early 1770s (see below, pp. 167, 220–2). Only in the wholly unusual circumstances of the wars of 1792–1815 between France and Europe (see Chapters 9, 10 and 11) did these

hostilities temporarily come to take second place, and even then, old antagonisms were for long a significant obstacle to effective cooperation against
the Revolution and Napoleon. The struggle against French power did
produce some unexpected if temporary alignments, such as the Anglo-
Spanish alliance during the War of the First Coalition and even, at the end
of the 1790s, a short-lived Russo-Ottoman *rapprochement*.

Alliances founded on these fixed rivalries proved most enduring: statesmen sought such alignments on the *ad hoc* basis that 'the enemy of my
enemy is my friend'. The most stable and enduring partnerships were
founded on shared hostility: towards the Ottoman Empire and then against
Prussia in the case of the Austro-Russian axis (1726–62, renewed in the
1780s) or against Britain in that of the third Bourbon Family Compact of
1761–90. Shared hostility towards France had been sufficient to keep the
intrinsically unstable alignment of Britain, Austria and the Dutch Republic
(the 'Old System' of alliance) together in three wars between 1689 and
1748. But some of the most perceptive and successful statesmen were
hostile to alliances as such, even if they were stable and enduring, believing that could create unwelcome obligations while simultaneously restricting freedom of manoeuvre. Frederick the Great, for instance, declared in
his *Political Testament* of 1752, drawn up to guide his successor: 'Policy
lies in profiting from favourable events, rather than in preparing them in
advance. This is why I advise you not to conclude treaties formed in
anticipation of uncertain events . . .'

The diplomacy of the *ancien régime* inevitably attracted the censure of
the Enlightenment. Some *philosophes* attacked its ruthlessness and selfish
competitiveness, and condemned the attention given by governments to
external affairs: what the nineteenth century would style the *Primat der
Aussenpolitik* ('primacy of foreign policy'), they believed, should give way
to a concentration on internal reform, together with an expansion of
international trade to increase general prosperity. Such idealism, however
admirable, had little contemporary impact. Vergennes, France's foreign
minister from 1774 to 1787, is widely believed to have been more influenced by the Enlightenment than any other statesman, but it is extremely
difficult to see precisely where the policies he pursued were indebted to
the *philosophes*. His much-vaunted refusal to seek further territorial
annexations can be more convincingly explained by France's weakness
and political decline since the Seven Years War. The early stages of the
Revolution saw reformers within the Assembly criticise the ineffectiveness
of French diplomacy during the final phase of the *ancien régime*, and take
up the *philosophe* critique of the old style diplomacy, even arguing 'France

should isolate herself from the political system of Europe'. Yet, within a few years, the Revolutionary leaders were pursuing a foreign policy more grasping and aggressive than anything the *ancien régime* had seen (see below, Chapter 9). One of the few statesmen to attempt the kind of foreign policy advocated by the *philosophes* had been the Marquis d'Argenson, who briefly and unsuccessfully controlled French foreign policy during the 1740s. And even he tacitly acknowledged the futility of idealism within a competitive great-power system of the kind which flourished in eighteenth-century Europe. 'A state,' he wrote in 1739, 'should always be at the ready, like a gentleman living among swashbucklers and quarrellers. Such are the nations of Europe, today more than ever; negotiations are only a continual struggle between men without principles, impudently aggressive and even greedy.'

CHAPTER 6

The transformation of the European System, 1763–1775

The division of continental and colonial issues evident in the two peace settlements of Hubertusburg and Paris lasted for the next three decades. Only in the 1790s, in response to the successful military imperialism of Revolutionary France, did international relations again begin to acquire a basic unity. Until then, the eastern powers and the western states existed almost in separate worlds, sealed off from each other. Britain concentrated on the maritime and colonial struggle with France and her ally, Spain (see Chapter 8), while Russia, Prussia and Austria were preoccupied with eastern Europe and exhibited an increasing appetite for territorial gains at the expense of their weaker and declining neighbours, Poland and the Ottoman Empire. Neither eastern powers nor western states exerted much sustained direct influence outside their own political sphere before the later 1780s. Russia's promotion of the Armed Neutrality of 1780–81, and her mediation with France of the Bavarian Succession War two years earlier were the main exceptions to this generalisation.

Such a separation had been apparent during the Seven Years War, two distinct conflicts held together by France's inability to break free completely from her initial commitment to the anti-Prussian coalition. Louis XV's monarchy long remained trapped between its growing desire to concentrate resources on the maritime struggle with Britain, and the continued involvement in continental affairs which geography and political tradition suggested was necessary. French foreign policy throughout the next two decades was dominated by hostility towards its British rival, which was primarily focussed beyond Europe. This restricted Versailles's European role, now reduced to maintaining peace and the *status quo*, and neutralising the continent in the next Anglo-Bourbon war. Together with Britain's effective withdrawal, this handed political leadership to the three eastern powers. By the mid-1770s, Russia and Prussia, allies since 1764, were in uneasy partnership with Austria, and collectively dominated Europe and especially its eastern half in a quite novel way. Hitherto, European diplomacy had revolved around France's rivalry with the Habsburgs and, more recently, with the British state. It was now dominated by the great military monarchies in the east.

The Great Powers after the Seven Years War

Defeated in Europe and the colonies, France had lost more than any other state by the fighting. The generation between 1763 and 1792 was the one extended period between the Peace of Westphalia and the Congress of Vienna when French power did not dominate international relations. France's substantial territorial cessions in the Peace of Paris emphasised the low point to which her prestige had sunk by 1763. Immediately after the peace settlement the duc de Praslin, Choiseul's cousin and political subordinate and foreign minister (1761–66), declared that her power was so reduced and her problems so considerable, that she might soon face relegation from the ranks of the great powers. While France's demographic and economic resources and compact strategic position were still impressive, the fighting had intensified severe financial and political problems. Her poor military performance surprised contemporaries, for whom she had long been Europe's leading power, and this decline was not speedily reversed. The next generation saw significant attempts at military reform, but it was to be the 1790s before the very different French armies of the Revolution again became formidable. Fundamental to this eclipse was financial weakness, exacerbated by the recent conflict. France largely paid for the war through further substantial borrowing, creating an enduring problem of public finance which was exacerbated by a series of credit crises. By the later 1760s the debt was estimated to be more than 2,000 million *livres*, six times the state's annual income. By that point, debt servicing consumed no less than 60 per cent of the government's yearly expenditure – double what it had been in 1753 – and was an important obstacle to future aggression. The financial problems militated against the reconstruction of the navy and, to a lesser extent, the army demanded by France's broader strategy.

It was only the most obvious legacy of the fighting. French prestige had been dented by defeat, while wartime cooperation with Russia, though acrimonious and short-lived, had involved abdicating the traditional role as friend and patron of Poland, Sweden and the Ottoman Empire. Attempts to restore the 'eastern barrier' after 1763 proved unsuccessful. France's political decline, together with the concentration on the struggle with Britain, reduced her impact on European diplomacy. The new strategy of neutralising the continent and fighting Britain overseas also fostered the belief that France was in decline. Though Versailles ostensibly pursued a European policy throughout this period, it was always one of weakness, since France could never support her objectives by force. The wartime alliance with Vienna survived until the Revolution, at least on paper. But it was undermined by Austria's participation in the first partition of Poland, a traditional French client. By the mid-1770s the alignment existed largely in name, though some revival would be apparent during the period (1774–87) when the comte de Vergennes was France's foreign minister. In the generation after the Seven Years War the Franco-Austrian treaty, with its defensive provisions, reflected both states' desire for peace. Until the early 1780s it was Austria's only available alliance, after the conclusion of the Prusso-Russian treaty in spring 1764 (see below, p. 151), and thus an insurance against diplomatic isolation. France always viewed her links with the Habsburgs as subordinate to the fundamental alliance with Spain (see below, pp. 214–15), but valued the peace and stability it brought. It was always challenged by the influential body of French opinion which favoured the Prussian alliance and by the growth of Austrophobia, which would be particularly evident by the 1780s.

France's disappearance as an effective continental power was at first less apparent than it appears in retrospect. European contemporaries, accustomed to her leadership, failed to recognise the transformation under way. French actions contributed to this myopia. The continuing if futile activities of the king's secret, Choiseul's short-lived and largely unsuccessful attempts to resume an anti-Russian policy by proxy after 1766, primarily by trying to incite the Ottoman Empire to declare war, and the seeming stability of the Franco-Austrian axis, all helped to perpetuate the notion that France remained active and influential in Europe. By the early 1770s, and the first partition of Poland, her withdrawal was becoming apparent. France was increasingly disregarded by the eastern powers as they recognised her decline. Here, the French monarchy's mounting domestic problems – with the *parlements*, over the Jesuits and the finances, increasingly the scandals at court – together with the accompanying publicity, contributed to her eclipse. Two successive French foreign ministers, the duc d'Aiguillon (1771–74) and Vergennes, aimed to recover this influence, but their efforts at first failed. Only in the 1780s, with the ending of the War of American Independence, did Louis XVI's monarchy once again attempt a significant European role, and by then her domestic problems were greater than ever (see below, pp. 236–7).

France's decline after the Seven Years War also contributed to London's minimal involvement in European politics before the mid-1780s. Superficially, Britain's virtual disappearance was surprising, coming as it did immediately after her most successful war ever. Yet eighteenth-century British foreign policy had interspersed bouts of involvement in continental diplomacy with periods of introspection and even insularity. The commanding position which her victories and her commercial wealth had secured for her by 1763 was not to be exploited during the next generation. Britain's isolation was not, initially, a matter of deliberate policy. It resulted from the failure of her own diplomacy, which for some time aimed to secure alliances. This search was largely a matter of habit and political tradition, but it now proved far less successful than in the past, and no major allies could be found. With the eclipse of the Dutch Republic, Britain looked to the eastern powers, whose refusal to conclude such treaties was a further symptom both of the fault lines running through European diplomacy and of their own growing political independence: no longer did the two leading western states control the international system. After the acrimonious dissolution of the wartime partnership in 1762, Britain's relations with Prussia were so bad that no alliance could be concluded for a quarter of a century. The one serious attempt, in 1766, was a fiasco. Approaches to Austria and especially Russia were more frequent during the generation after the Seven Years War, but proved no more successful. Only in the later 1780s did Britain emerge from this diplomatic isolation.

In fact, France's political decline had undermined the traditional basis of her rival's foreign policy: the exploitation of the Bourbon threat, whether real or imaginary, to the 'liberties of Europe' or 'the balance of power' to construct an alliance system to protect Britain's own security. Ministers in London were slow to appreciate this transformation and, in particular, to see that a price would now have to be paid, either a subsidy or an enhanced political commitment. Nor, apart from considerations of long-term security, did Britain appear to have much need of an ally before the later 1770s. Her problems in these years were internal and colonial: ministerial instability and the growth of urban radicalism at home, and the rising tide of opposition and, ultimately, rebellion in the American colonies. These deflected her own interest in Europe, and a continental alliance could do nothing to help solve them. Until the American revolt in the mid-1770s, British power remained substantially undiminished. Britain's prestige and political influence on the continent did decline, but less dramatically than those of France.

The severely-reduced role of the two leading western states after 1763 contributed to a novel international pattern. Although the territorial *status quo* in Europe had been restored by the peace of Hubertusburg, the Seven Years War had significantly modified the relative power and prestige of the belligerents, and this helped to produce new diplomatic alignments. In the first place, the struggle had made Prussia a great power. The successful seizure and defence of Silesia in the 1740s had elevated her to a position of equality with the Habsburgs in Germany. Frederick's survival, against overwhelming odds, in the Seven Years War raised his monarchy to the first rank of European states. Prussia was, along with Russia, one of the two leading continental powers after 1763. It was a position which rested on seemingly insecure foundations. Prussia was a small, territorially exposed and thinly-populated country, apparently lacking the material resources necessary for a great power; but, for the moment, the quality of her army, together with the leadership of her ruler, Frederick the Great, appeared to many contemporaries to compensate for these deficiencies. The almost total exhaustion of the Hohenzollern territories, which in effect prevented the King from playing the European role his victories had earned for him, was not generally evident to contemporaries, though it preoccupied Frederick himself. The King sought to protect Prussia's new-found pre-eminence by searching for an ally and by building his army up to new peaks of strength and effectiveness. He intended it should be an armed peace, with Prussia pursuing a strategy of military deterrence, able to mobilise her formidable army at the first sign of danger.

Russia was the other state to gain significantly. She had secured no territory – unusually for her eighteenth-century wars which mostly brought considerable conquests – but her prestige had been increased greatly by her successes over Frederick's armies, which were now seen as Europe's leading military force. Russia had been the dominant power in the coalition during the second half of the war (until her withdrawal in 1762) and this ensured that she was a permanent, and increasingly important, element in the European system after the Seven Years War. Her new status as a great power was magnified by the exhaustion of Prussia and Austria after 1763 and by France's political decline. No other state could challenge Catherine's dominant position in eastern Europe, though her own domestic preoccupations during the 1760s and 1770s at times weakened Russia's interest in continental politics. St Petersburg's position was considerably strengthened during the next generation by the continuation, albeit in a muted form, of Austria's fundamental rivalry with Prussia. Their antagonism ensured that, until the 1790s, the Russian ruler could always choose one of the two German powers as an ally. Russia's support would obviously be decisive in any renewed Austro-Prussian struggle, and the conclusion and retention of a Russian alliance was the principal aim of both Austria and Prussia.

The war had been a major disappointment for Vienna. The apparently overpowering coalition assembled by Kaunitz had failed to produce the anticipated victory, despite heavy sacrifices in men, money and material resources. Prussian possession of Silesia had to be accepted after 1763. In their hearts the Habsburgs could never renounce this valuable province, and in the years ahead the Chancellor produced a variety of ingenious, if improbable, plans for its recovery. In their heads, however, they knew that its reconquest was impossible in view of Austria's own weakness. Prussia's military survival had given Frederick the Great a personal ascendancy over his Habsburg adversaries, who believed he was invincible and were reluctant to fight him in the future. Formally, Prussia's King acknowledged imperial overlordship over the Hohenzollern territories within the Empire, and he also accepted that it was difficult for him to launch initiatives in imperial politics. Both Prussia and Austria wanted peace after 1763 and worked together to bring this about.

The new Emperor Joseph II, who took over on his father's death in 1765, deliberately sought to rebuild Habsburg influence. His efforts, however, met with considerable opposition and before long were abandoned. Tacitly, after 1763 Vienna was forced to accept Prussia's position of equality in the Empire, and in central Europe generally, while Russia's political advance during the Seven Years War would, in the longer term, prove an even greater source of concern. In another significant, if less important way, Austria's position had been weakened by the fighting. In an attempt to defeat Prussia – a German state whose ruler was an elector – Austria had allied with France, the hereditary enemy both of the Habsburgs and of the Empire. This action offended German 'patriotic' opinion and antagonised some of the German princes, particularly the Catholic rulers in southwest Germany, on whose loyalty and support Vienna had traditionally depended. Though their antipathy was restrained by a corresponding fear of Prussia and her warlike ruler, this sentiment was to be of some significance when the Habsburgs tried to acquire Bavaria (see Chapter 7).

Austria's relative international position was far weaker in 1763 than before the war. Her resources all but exhausted, her administration close to collapse, she may have lost as many as 300,000 men killed or seriously wounded during the fighting. The impact on public finances was even greater. The average annual cost of the Seven Years War was more than double the expenditure on the fighting of the 1740s. The state debt had increased by 150 per cent, from 113 million florins to almost 285 million florins, and, in the year peace was concluded, repayments consumed over 40 per cent of annual revenue. Financial exhaustion dictated an extended period of peace. By the closing stages of the war it had become apparent that further and wide-ranging domestic reforms were necessary, and these had been begun even before fighting ended. The conclusion of a Russo-Prussian alliance little more than a year after the fighting ended merely confirmed Vienna's predicament. The weakest of the three eastern states, Austria was immobilised by her own frailties and by the powerful Russo-Prussian alignment which she faced with only the faded power of France as an ally.

European diplomacy was unusually fluid and volatile after the Seven Years War. The alliances which had waged the struggle had been produced by an unexpected and even accidental realignment in 1756–57, and the fighting had done little to give permanence to the new alignments. Three of the wartime partnerships – those between Austria and Russia, France and Russia, and Britain and Prussia – had collapsed before peace was concluded. The Franco-Austrian alliance, characterised by friction and mutual disappointment during the war, survived into peacetime, partly because Vienna in particular lacked any obvious alternative. Only the Franco-Spanish alliance, signed in 1761, appeared to be securely based, and it was rooted in mutual dependence in the continuing rivalry with Britain overseas (see Chapter 8). The shock to the established political order which the Diplomatic Revolution had represented was still evident after 1763. The resulting uncertainty was intensified by a widespread hesitancy about new treaties, in case these led to further costly and destructive fighting similar to that produced by the last round of alliance diplomacy in 1756–57, and by the preoccupation with domestic reconstruction, which also demanded a period of peace.

The Seven Years War had two further legacies. It converted a system of three leading states organised around opposition to French power into one of five great powers, whose alignments were more complex and also less predictable. Secondly, the fighting had turned the political hierarchy upside-down. France, traditionally Europe's strongest power, now competed for third place with Austria, whose stock had also fallen sharply. The two leading continental powers were now Russia and Prussia, whose alliance would dominate European diplomacy for the next decade and more.

Russia, Prussia and the 'Northern System', 1764–1768

A clearer focus was given by the Polish crisis of 1763–64 and, in particular, by the Russo-Prussian treaty which it triggered. Poland had been ruled since 1697 by the Wettins, the Electoral House of Saxony, but real power belonged not to the elected monarch but to his Russian patron. Since the reign of Peter the Great, the Polish state had been a satellite of Russia, whose rulers enjoyed the formal status of protector of their western neighbour. The death of Augustus III of Saxony-Poland (ruler since 1733) in early October 1763 came at an inopportune moment. Catherine was only slowly consolidating her hold on the Russian throne and restoring order to government and the finances. As a woman, a foreigner – she was by origin a minor German princess – and an apparent usurper, her own position was, for some time, fragile. What contemporaries styled the 'Northern System' helped overcome that.

Russia's security dictated the continuation of her invisible empire in Poland and this, in turn, made the election of a pliable ruler essential. A third Saxon king might suggest the Polish throne was hereditary in the Wettin family and thereby weaken St Petersburg's control. This was appreciated by Catherine, who was determined to secure the throne for one of her former lovers, the Polish nobleman Stanislas Poniatowski, a junior member of the powerful Czartoryski aristocratic clan, known at the time as the 'Family'. The Empress, however, feared French and Austrian opposition and possible Ottoman intervention, and believed she needed foreign support to impose Poniatowski. In the previous election, Russia's partner had been Austria; now it turned out to be Prussia, with her formidable army to intimidate St Petersburg's opponents. One increasingly influential figure, Nikita Panin, favoured a Prussian alliance, but far more of the Empress's advisors supported revived links with the traditional ally, Austria. There was also widespread suspicion of treaties as such, since in the past such commitments had produced Russian subservience to other powers. Catherine was determined to uphold her Empire's political independence, which she believed had been compromised under her two immediate predecessors, Elizabeth and Peter III. At the same time, however, her fear of opposition over the Polish election was very real, while Peter III's quixotic foreign policy had isolated Russia. Frederick skilfully exploited this situation and, by pretending to be about to sign a treaty with the Ottoman Empire, forced a reluctant Catherine to conclude the alliance which the King believed essential for Prussia's future security.

The Russo-Prussian treaty of 11 April 1764, a defensive alliance which was to last in the first instance for eight years, was a considerable diplomatic triumph for Frederick who, as a contemporary had earlier commented, 'feared Russia more than he feared God'. This fear had always been central to his foreign policy. Russia's contribution to the Seven Years War and, in particular, the heavy defeats she had inflicted on Prussian armies reinforced this anxiety. Prussia's King certainly feared Russia far more than any other state after 1763 and he had therefore sought an alliance with St Petersburg since the closing stages of the war. Russia might have concluded such an alliance in any case, but would have dictated the terms. The 1764 treaty was concluded on a basis of equality. Though Russia secured Poniatowski's election as King without any serious fighting in the autumn of 1764, Frederick undoubtedly gained rather more from his alliance. It guaranteed Prussian security by effectively neutralising Austria, who could not contemplate fighting both Russia and Prussia, and thereby stabilised international relations in eastern Europe. To underline his political triumph, Frederick communicated the entire treaty including the secret articles to Vienna and not simply the summary which diplomatic custom would have required. In the longer perspective, the Russian alliance secured him a say in Poland's future and, in this way, an opening to pursue his latent territorial ambitions there.

It also left Frederick free to undertake vital internal reconstruction necessitated by the devastation of the Seven Years War. The Hohenzollern lands and especially the central provinces, which had borne the brunt of the fighting, had suffered considerable demographic and economic losses, and the overwhelming need for peace to facilitate recovery was a key element in Prussian foreign policy after 1763. Around 10 per cent of the population of four million died in the fighting, an especially serious loss for a country demographically by far the weakest of the great powers, while noble estates had been abandoned and agriculture interrupted. After the war, Prussia was simply too weak to risk another conflict, which would imperil her newly-acquired status as a great power. Recognising this, Frederick pursued a fundamentally pacific policy throughout the second half of his reign.

Prussia's preoccupation with domestic recovery mirrored the situation in the Habsburg lands, and to a lesser extent, in Russia. The fighting's legacies ensured that afterwards internal reform and reorganisation came to be the principal objective of all the participants, in keeping with the new notion of international power being rooted in domestic strength. After 1763 states acknowledged, perhaps fully for the first time, that such strength was a necessary basis for a successful external policy. The widespread reforms during the generation after the Seven Years War – the age of 'Enlightened Absolutism' – were, in the major European countries, motivated primarily by the desire to strengthen the state and, specifically, to finance the enlarged standing armies which were now universal. In the Habsburg Monarchy, for example, the significant and wide-ranging reforms during the second half of Maria Theresa's reign and the hectic decade of Joseph II's personal rule (1780–90) were essentially to improve the domestic basis of Austrian power, and this required an extended period of peace. The measures reflected the Cameralist doctrine that the best foundation for a strong state was a large and prosperous population able and willing to pay its taxes.

A similar pattern can be seen in Russia, where Catherine II needed initially to consolidate her own *régime*. These domestic priorities contributed to Russia's distinctive foreign policy during the early years of her reign, what to came be called the 'Northern System'. This was based on the shared belief of Catherine and Panin, the minister responsible for foreign policy after October 1763, that a long period of peace was necessary. During this the Russian administration, which had all but collapsed under the strains of the war, could be reconstructed and, in particular, the finances restored. Panin's projected system was defensive and underlined that St Petersburg had no immediate territorial ambitions: on the contrary, he, like the Empress, believed Russia already had land enough for her thinly-scattered population and fragmentary administrative system. It aimed, above all, to protect Russia's vulnerable western flank, particularly against the imagined wiles of French diplomacy, and to secure the glacis which was deemed essential. An exaggerated fear of France – and a corresponding hostility towards her – were the foundations of Panin's diplomatic outlook.

The 'Northern System' took shape largely in response to events first in Poland after Augustus III's death and then Sweden, which came to the forefront of Russian policy from late 1764, when the summoning of a diet (*riksdag*) by the bankrupt Swedish régime threatened political change in Stockholm. Russia feared an attack from Swedish Finland, which was dangerously close to St Petersburg. The permanent military confrontation along the Russo-Swedish border in Finland reinforced this anxiety. St Petersburg's policy was long conditioned by memories of the career of the warrior-king Charles XII: Russian observers always saw a connection between the restoration of absolutism in Stockholm and renewed Swedish aggression. In the confusing political and party strife of the 1760s, Russia therefore sought to maintain the Swedish Constitution of 1720, with its severe restrictions on monarchical authority and its elaborate system of checks and balances which made Sweden far less of a threat to her neighbours.

Russia's fear of French intrigues in eastern Europe, her need for security against Sweden and her desire to maintain the traditional protectorate over Poland were the immediate origins of the 'Northern System'. In the longer perspective, Panin's league was an adjustment of Russian foreign policy to the new pattern of European alliances created by the Diplomatic Revolution. This had allied France, Russia's traditional enemy, with Austria, her principal ally since 1726. The stability of the Franco-Austrian axis made it difficult for the Empress and Panin to continue the links with Vienna. The 'Northern System' was in conception to be a grandiose series of alliances: not only with Prussia but also with Denmark and Britain, while Sweden, Poland and Saxony were to be brought in as 'passive' members by pledging themselves to remain neutral in any future war in northern Europe. These alignments would neutralise northern and eastern Europe and so protect Russia's vulnerable and extended western frontier. In practice, however, the 'Northern System' was a much more limited affair; it was always more a matter of aspirations than of alliances.

A Russo-Danish alliance was signed in 1765 and strengthened by a second treaty two years later. These marked Denmark's move from a mildly pro-French neutrality into the political orbit of Russia for the next half-century. This decisive shift was brought about by the resolution of a complex dispute over the strategically-important territory of Holstein, to the south of the Danish mainland. It was one of two duchies; to its north lay Schleswig over which Denmark had first asserted control as long ago as 1460; it had been a Holstein fief since the later fourteenth century. Subsequent divisions, in 1482 and 1544, had fragmented both Holstein and Schleswig into 'royal' (Danish) and 'ducal' (Holstein) parts, while also strengthening the position of the local nobility. During the seventeenth century Copenhagen had periodically sought to annex the 'ducal' parts of both duchies.

The occupation of ducal Schleswig in 1713 was the latest attempt to annex it, though it had never secured international recognition. The senior branch of the House of Oldenburg ruled in Denmark, while cadet lines were established in the duchy of Holstein-Gottorp and in several smaller north German territories. Russia was involved through Peter the Great's eldest daughter, who had married a duke of Holstein-Gottorp. Their son and heir, Charles Peter Ulrich, had been summoned to St Petersburg shortly after Elizabeth became Empress and named heir also to the Russian throne, becoming the Grand Duke Peter. This dynastic imbroglio was further complicated in 1751 when Adolf Frederik, another member of the ducal house of Holstein-Gottorp, became King of Sweden. Though he had renounced his claim to Holstein, the Danes feared he might revive it if he strengthened the powers of the Swedish crown, as the court party now aimed to do.

Denmark sought to resolve the danger by promoting a complex territorial exchange. Its essence was that the Russian Grand Duke Peter would give up Holstein, which he was now ruling, and this would pass into Danish control. In return, a minor branch of the Holstein-Gottorp family would receive two small Danish principalities. These efforts were at first unsuccessful, but they were given a new urgency during the Seven Years War when it became clear that the Empress Elizabeth might soon die and that a regency for Russia's new ruler would be established directly to the south of Danish-controlled Schleswig. The threat became immediate when Peter III succeeded in Russia in early 1762. Before long the new Emperor had launched an attack on Denmark to enforce his own claim to Schleswig. Copenhagen possessed the strongest navy of any Baltic state, but lacked an army and soon faced advancing Russian forces threatening to overrun her territory. This invasion had been backed by Prussia, and only averted by Peter III's deposition and death in July (see above, p. 105). The threat to Denmark was obvious. It was resolved by J.H.E. von Bernstorff's patient and skilful diplomacy and by Panin's parallel wish to incorporate Copenhagen into the 'Northern System' and strengthen Russia's links with Denmark. This demanded a solution to the Holstein issue.

It was brought about by dangling the bait of the duchy's transfer to Danish sovereignty in return for a formal defensive alliance, signed in March 1765. Holstein's cession was then carried out in two stages. In 1767 a provisional agreement was concluded, and made permanent six years later. The nominal son of Peter III, and heir to the Russian throne, the Grand Duke Paul – who was almost certainly fathered by one of Catherine II's lovers – gave his consent in 1773, following his own majority. The duchy was now formally taken over by Denmark. The acquisition of Holstein strengthened Danish security and was a significant success for its diplomacy. Though by now Bernstorff had died, having been driven from office in 1770, the final settlement was a triumph for his policy. He had recognised more clearly than most contemporaries Russia's renewed advance during the Seven Years War and its implications, and had re-aligned Danish policy accordingly. Denmark's support against Sweden (where their aims coincided) and especially her navy were valued by Panin and Catherine, but it was always a very one-sided partnership. Though Bernstorff had sought political independence for his adopted homeland, the realities of power-politics forced it to become a satellite of St Petersburg. This underlined Russia's complete dominance in the Baltic and, more generally, highlighted the ascendancy of the great powers within the international system.

The other intended members of the 'Northern System' proved far more elusive. Britain's wealth and strength made her a far more desirable ally than Denmark, and during the next decade Panin and Catherine made considerable efforts to secure a political treaty. Britain, however, though she genuinely desired a Russian alliance to strengthen her own international position, would never agree either to the subsidy demanded as the price of its conclusion, or adopt the 'Turkish clause' in any political treaty. This was the provision that, in contrast to earlier agreements, Russian wars with the Ottoman Empire would now qualify for British support. London's refusal underlined its unwillingness to base relations on complete political equality, which Catherine and her leading minister, conscious of Russia's new enhanced status, were determined to secure. Yet this was far from the end of the matter. The two states were linked by mutually beneficial trade, reinforced by a new Commercial Treaty signed in 1766. Opposition to France, moreover, drove both Russian and British foreign policy, and this strong community of political interest by the later 1760s established an *entente* while simultaneously weakening St Petersburg's interest in a formal alliance. Why, as Panin asked the Empress, should Russia assume the obligations of an actual treaty when the existing *entente* already conferred many of the anticipated benefits? As long as British policy was anti-French – and there seemed every reason to believe it would be permanently – it would also be pro-Russian. Britain thus became a kind of honorary member of the 'Northern System', until her own insular policy undermined this. In time, Catherine and Panin came to doubt whether Britain would ever again be a real force in continental politics. The failure to secure a British treaty meant that the 'Northern System' always had a rather lopsided appearance, consisting as it did of alliances with one great power (Prussia) and one minor state (Denmark).

The 'Northern System' was also opposed by its leading member. Frederick the Great was determined that he should be Russia's only important ally, realising this would strengthen his own influence within it, and was fundamentally opposed to the extensive alliances envisaged by Panin. At the same time, however, the central importance of the Russian alliance for Prussia's own security inevitably restrained his opposition. The 'Northern System', though only partially realised – it was never more than a triangular alliance of Russia, Prussia and Denmark – nominally remained the basis of Russian diplomacy until the later 1770s and always had a certain utility. Its only weakness – and it was a serious flaw – was that it offered little protection against Russia's main enemy, the Ottoman Empire, against whom Austria was always a more attractive ally. It did much to stabilise international relations in the eastern half of the continent. Together with the Russo-Prussian alliance which was at its heart, it was an important restraint on Vienna's policy and in practice forced Kaunitz to continue his wartime partnership with France, which he was in any case inclined to do. There was no real alternative for the Habsburgs, now that their traditional links with Russia had been severed.

The 'Northern System' aimed to promote territorial stability. It therefore ran counter to, and was ultimately undermined by, the most obvious characteristic of continental diplomacy after the Seven Years War: the tendency of the major powers to expand at the expense of their weaker neighbours. This appetite for new territory was the corollary of their preoccupation with internal reform. Contemporaries assessed political power more precisely in terms of population and wealth. It followed that an increase in territory and, with it, subjects, would automatically strengthen a state. The resulting search for new territory was not confined to the great powers of eastern Europe. The Swedish King Gustav III (reigned 1771–92) dreamed all his life of conquering Norway, then ruled by the King of Denmark. France secured the expected reversion of the duchy of Lorraine, provided for by the Third Treaty of Vienna of 1738, on the death of Stanislas Leszczyński in 1766; and two years later Choiseul acquired the strategically important island of Corsica, in the western Mediterranean, by a thinly disguised purchase at a bargain price from the Republic of Genoa. The acquisitions by France, while undoubtedly important, were far less significant than the major territorial changes in eastern Europe during the generation after the Seven Years War. These took the form of forcible cessions of territory from Poland and the Ottoman Empire. Both had, by the second half of the eighteenth century, declined from their previous greatness; both presented an attractive target for their powerful and voracious neighbours; both lacked an effective central administration and financial and military strength, and each proved unable to resist successive encroachments.

The Russo-Ottoman War and the first partition of Poland, 1768–1775

The first victim was the Polish monarchy. The weakness and internal divisions of the faded power of Poland, whose elected king was effectively controlled by the magnates, had long suggested that it might become a victim of its powerful neighbours. Schemes to seize Polish territory went back to the seventeenth century and during Saxon rule (1697–1763) had become more numerous, as the kingdom's weakness and vulnerability became increasingly evident. The existence of the *liberum veto*, which theoretically enabled any member of the Diet to block legislation, the king's limited authority, together with the intervention of foreign powers, usually by support of the various factions which constituted Poland's political life, ensured this situation would be permanent. As a result, the fundamental administrative, financial and military reforms which many contemporaries recognised were essential could not be introduced. Internal weakness, however, did not make partition inevitable: it merely ensured that Poland's King could not resist the initial seizures carried out in 1772–73. The origins of the first partition are rather to be found in the wider pattern of continental diplomacy and specifically in the critical situation in south-eastern Europe by 1770, which was linked to the response of Poland's neighbours to events there since the Seven Years War.

The accession of Poniatowski seemed to have perpetuated Russian control over the country. St Petersburg's intention had been that the new King should be a puppet, but he proved more independent of its direction than anticipated. In particular, King Stanislas Augustus (as he now became) sought to introduce administrative, financial and military reforms to strengthen the Polish monarchy, and even to abolish the *veto*. Any such initiative was unwelcome to Russia, since the continuation of her invisible empire demanded a weak and divided Poland. To safeguard this protectorate the Empress now intervened directly, finding a convenient pretext in the Dissidents, Poland's numerous non-Catholic subjects both Protestant and Orthodox. This group amounted to some 10 per cent of the Kingdom's population and suffered real discrimination in a country with a strong Catholic tone to its public life. Poland's substantial Jewish community enjoyed religious toleration, but also suffered severe social and economic discrimination.

By acting as the defender of the religious freedom of the Dissidents, a cause in which she and Panin in any case believed, Catherine was able to frustrate Stanislas Augustus's efforts at reform. Increased numbers of

Russian troops were sent to supervise the Diet of 1767–68, which conferred extensive political and religious freedom upon the Dissidents, against the wishes of the fiercely Catholic majority. These privileges, together with the constitutional *status quo*, were then enshrined in the 'Perpetual Treaty' of March 1768 between Russia and Poland. This latest Russian intervention, however, provoked armed Polish resistance, Catholic and patriotic in nature, as Poland's nobility made use of its constitutional right to establish armed confederations to oppose St Petersburg's policy. With the formation in February 1768 of the Confederation of Bar in the extreme south of Poland, close to the Ottoman frontier, St Petersburg was faced by a serious guerrilla war and a corresponding fear that its opponents might secure French or Ottoman support.

Russia's growing dominance had been watched with considerable alarm at the Porte, since in any future war Polish military assistance might threaten the Sultan's province of Moldavia and, more generally, undermine Ottoman strategy, by forcing Constantinople to divide its own forces to deal with a Polish auxiliary army. Russian activities in the Crimea, an Ottoman vassal state to the north of the Black Sea, and Catherine's promises of assistance to some of the Empire's Orthodox subjects were also resented, but it was the situation in Poland which caused most alarm. The summer and early autumn of 1768 saw the growth of a war party, centred on the Sultan himself. French diplomacy was active in the Ottoman capital during these months, as Choiseul sought to incite a war as part of his strategy of opposing Russia by proxy, though whether it did any more than strengthen the growing Russophobia is doubtful. Matters came to a head in the autumn. The violation of Ottoman territory at Balta by Russian troops pursuing Polish Confederates provided a pretext, since Muslim lives and property had been lost. A more important reason for war was probably the news of the surrender of the important Confederate stronghold of Cracow in the previous August. This highlighted the scale of Russian successes in Poland and the resulting threat to the Ottoman Empire. On 6 October 1768 the Russian resident in Constantinople was imprisoned in the Castle of the Seven Towers, a symbolic action which in Ottoman eyes amounted to a formal declaration of war: the Porte still viewed diplomats as hostages for the good behaviour of their governments.

Russia was unprepared for this latest war. Until the very last moment it had been assumed that fighting could be averted by the traditional means of extensive bribery in Constantinople. Russian troops were heavily committed in Poland and this, together with innate Ottoman lethargy, delayed the first serious fighting until the late summer of 1769. The

Ottoman Empire still enjoyed some significant strategic advantages in its wars with its Russian rival. Control over the Khanate of the Crimea provided a sally-port into Russian territory, while the Sultan's dominance over the Black Sea eased the movement of supplies and reinforcements. In the war of 1768–74, however, these advantages were nullified by parallel political and administrative shortcomings. The Ottoman Empire had been at peace from 1739, and since then the military infrastructure which supplied and manned the Sultan's armies had disintegrated. Efforts to rebuild it in 1768–69 were only partially successful and, particularly during the early campaigns, the Ottoman Empire faced acute financial, provisioning and recruitment problems, exacerbated by poor leadership.

The distances across which Russian armies had to campaign always placed Catherine's forces at a strategic disadvantage. But once preparations for war were accomplished, Russia's clear advantage became apparent. Though her military performance in the Seven Years War had been uneven, this recent experience of fighting, together with the reforms commenced after 1763, ensured that Russia's administration coped far better with the pressures of war. Logistical problems were overcome more effectively, partly by Russian armies wintering in the Balkans and campaigning throughout the year, while the brutal recruitment system was efficient enough to keep up a steady flow of replacement soldiers south. Above all, Russia's political and military leadership was far superior, especially the impressive P.A. Rumiantsev, the real architect of victory in Catherine II's first Ottoman War. Russian armies made better use of their advantages in artillery and military intelligence, and eventually won an overwhelming victory.

In the campaigns of 1769–70 Russia initially encountered some effective Ottoman resistance, but her armies quickly began to carry all before them. In the first campaign, Khotin, the most northerly Ottoman outpost, and Bucharest were captured and the so-called Danubian principalities, the provinces of Moldavia and Wallachia, occupied. Russian successes in 1770 were even more striking. Ottoman armies were defeated at Falça (July) and Kartal (August); Russian forces advanced along the Danube; further east the Crimea was occupied; while the Sultan's fleet was destroyed at the battle of Chesmé – located in the channel between the island of Chios and the coast of Anatolia (July 1770). The victorious Russian squadron – with important aid from Britain, who refitted and repaired ships in her naval dockyards – had made the long and difficult voyage from the Baltic to the Mediterranean. This dramatic victory announced the arrival of Catherine II's Empire as a significant naval power, which would be consolidated during the remainder of her reign.

In the first two campaigns Russia secured a considerable advantage which she largely retained until the end of the war. From 1771, however, a military stalemate developed, and was strengthened by improvements in Ottoman organisation and leadership. The first two campaigns had largely been fought in Ottoman tributary provinces north of the river Danube and in the Crimea, which Russia had occupied by the war's mid-point. But the Ottoman forces still occupied an immensely strong defensive position south of the Danube and, from 1771, they were careful not to abandon this, now fighting a defensive war. The consequence was that Rumiantsev's forces could not make further gains, while Russia simultaneously became diverted to the situation in Poland and then around the Baltic.

The military struggle in south-eastern Europe shaped continental diplomacy at this time, as the extent of Ottoman defeats became clear. The scale of Russian successes was apparent in the continual reformulation of Catherine's terms for peace. By the closing months of 1770, her demands extended to freedom of navigation for Russian ships on the Black Sea (a traditional Russian aim), the independence of the Crimea, whose Tartar Khan had been an Ottoman vassal, the acquisition of considerable territory around the Sea of Azov, and control of Moldavia and Wallachia for 25 years as an indemnity for the war. The tide of Russian victories, moreover, suggested that the Empress might actually be able to impose these ambitious demands on a defeated Ottoman Empire, and this drew other powers to intervene.

Austria and Prussia were alarmed by the spectre of a considerable extension of Russian power in the Balkans and around the Black Sea, and by the parallel fear that the fighting might lead to an expanded war. These shared anxieties contributed to a limited Austro-Prussian *rapprochement* which emerged in 1769–70. It was advanced by two personal meetings between Joseph II and Frederick II, at Neisse (August 1769) and Neustadt (September 1770), the second also attended by Kaunitz who took the opportunity to give Prussia's King a political tutorial which both amused and irritated its recipient. The situation in south-eastern Europe had previously done much to bring Russia and Austria together; it was now beginning to drive them apart. Vienna, which at least since the Seven Years War had been concerned with the growth of Russian power and anxious to keep this at a distance, was further alarmed by the expansion of Russian influence into the lower Danube region, a traditional Habsburg sphere of influence, but was powerless to oppose this alone. Frederick was equally alarmed, since it would destroy the territorial balance in eastern

Europe and might undermine his own cherished alliance with St Petersburg. He was already becoming anxious that Russian expansion in the Balkans and the consequent opportunities for easy gains for the Habsburgs might eventually revive the Russo-Austrian alliance, which he always regarded as more natural than his own links with St Petersburg. More immediately, the victories gained were a serious threat to the existing European territorial, and therefore political, balance. Any acquisitions by one state, it was believed, required broadly equivalent gains for the others, if the balance of power were not to be overturned, and this was certainly one dimension of the diplomacy of these years. Yet while both Prussia and Austria wished to restrict Russia's gains from the Ottoman Empire, neither really wished to go to war for this purpose.

The danger that a general European conflict might be provoked by the fighting in south-eastern Europe appeared considerable. French diplomacy was active in Poland and at Constantinople, and the anti-Russian tone of Versailles's policy was fully apparent, though its impact was less so. Austria's opposition to Russian expansion was also clear. The obvious danger, as contemporaries saw it, was that one or other power would enter the war to support the beleaguered Ottoman Empire. This, in turn, would activate the two principal defensive alliances of the late 1760s, those between Russia and Prussia and between France and Austria, and in this way bring about a general European conflict. The danger was always more apparent than real: both Prussia and Austria were still recovering from the Seven Years War and wished peace to continue, while France wanted to avoid direct involvement in a continental war and, in any case, came to be drawn into a serious Anglo-Spanish confrontation over the Falkland Islands during the second half of 1770 (see below, p. 219). Yet the widespread fear of a broader conflict did affect diplomacy at this time. By 1770–71, moreover, it seemed that only a general European war could check the Russian advance into the Balkans. A series of efforts to mediate, first by Britain, still vainly pursuing a Russian alliance and believing a diplomatic initiative could advance this, and then by the Prusso-Austrian axis, failed during the first two years of the fighting. Though Constantinople welcomed such outside intervention, believing it might limit Ottoman losses, it was rejected completely by Catherine II, who was determined to impose her own peace terms militarily on a defeated enemy.

Frederick's ingenious solution to this impasse was to sponsor a three-power partition of Polish territory. He had long appreciated the potential strategic value of Polish Prussia and had advocated acquiring it in his three most important statements of policy: the so-called 'Natzmer Letter' of the early 1730s and the two *Political Testaments*, of 1752 and 1768. The Polish province would unite the central core of his lands with isolated East Prussia while, in a wider sense, the King was alert for any opportunity to make further territorial gains, which would increase the resources available to support Prussia's great power position. He also understood, however, that its acquisition would be difficult, while the cautious tone of his foreign policy inevitably reinforced his conviction that it would probably be for a future Prussian ruler. At this period he aimed primarily to exploit his Polish neighbour economically.

The precise origins of the scheme for a partition are unclear. A proposal which bears a striking similarity to the annexations in 1772 had earlier been put forward, ostensibly by a Danish diplomat, Count Lynar, but in fact by Frederick himself. But it had been rejected, after discussions with St Petersburg, as impracticable in early 1769. A year later, he tried to interest Vienna in the same scheme but, once again, secured no immediate response. The King's renewed belief in the possibility of partition resulted from a visit by his brother, Prince Henry, to Russia in 1770–71. Discussions at the Russian court revealed Catherine's potential appetite for Polish territory, shared by some of her advisers, though not initially by Panin. When he returned, Henry convinced his sceptical royal brother that partition was now practical. Frederick began to work on a broad diplomatic front, in an attempt to avert a general European war through the seizure of Polish territory in which Russia and Austria would also be involved, as Poland came to the forefront of continental diplomacy. His sponsorship of annexations was assisted by a significant shift within the Russo-Prussian alliance. By the later 1760s St Petersburg had gained the upper hand, as the Empress strengthened her position at home and abroad. The Ottoman war, together with Catherine's problems in Poland and, potentially, with Sweden, now allowed Prussia to recover the diplomatic initiative. Frederick's success in securing an eight-year extension of the alliance in the autumn of 1769 had been an early symptom of this shift. In 1771–72 he exploited Prussia's favourable position to push through partition.

This was to be agreed with Russia and then imposed upon Austria, whose reluctance was evident to the King. St Petersburg's support was secured relatively easily, though only after several months' patient diplomacy. The preservation of Poland's territorial integrity was an important dimension of Panin's 'Northern System', which remained the official basis of Russian foreign policy. But some military leaders had been pressing since the very beginning of Catherine's reign for a 'rectification' of the Russo-Polish frontier and, specifically, for the annexation of Polish Livonia on strategic grounds. This they believed had been made essential by the difficulties encountered in intervening militarily in central Europe during the Seven Years War. In 1767 Russian officials had begun to survey possible annexations in eastern Poland, underlining St Petersburg's latent appetite for Polish lands. Acceptance of the partition was facilitated by the continuing resistance in Poland, where the remnants of opposition to Russia were still waging a guerilla war, and by Catherine's anxieties at Austria's apparently bellicose stance.

The first half of 1771 had seen a significant if short-lived *rapprochement* between Vienna and Constantinople which culminated in the conclusion of a formal agreement in early July. On the Ottoman side this was motivated by a wish for outside support in the war with Russia, which was going very badly. Austrian aims were less clear cut. The initiative was the work of Kaunitz alone, who did not consult France, tacitly acknowledging the weakening of that alliance. He seems to have been prepared to go to war on the Sultan's side, in order to restrict Russian gains. Both Maria Theresa and Joseph II remained pacific, and though an Austro-Ottoman agreement was concluded in Constantinople, it was never ratified and was overtaken by events. Its main importance lay in its impact on Russia. Peaceful gains in Poland seemed preferable to the general European war which might result if Catherine tried to impose her massive demands on the defeated Ottoman Empire, which could be supported by Vienna and even its ally France. By October 1771 the Empress, ignoring Panin's reservations, signalled support for partition. In the following February, Russian and Prussian annexations from Poland had been set out in a formal treaty between the two courts.

Austrian acceptance proved rather more difficult to secure, as Frederick had anticipated, and Kaunitz revealed considerable ingenuity in his attempts to frustrate Prussian schemes. It was not that the Habsburgs lacked the appetite for new territories; on the contrary, the Austrian seizure and formal annexation of the Polish county of Zips and of three districts in the Tatra foothills in 1769–70 had revealed this. The initial occupation of Zips, an area on the Polish–Hungarian frontier which had been mortgaged by Hungary as long ago as 1412 and never repossessed by the Habsburgs, was carried out largely at Kaunitz's instigation early in 1769, in order both to prevent the warfare in Poland spilling over into Habsburg territory and to contain an outbreak of plague there. Frederick instituted a similar cordon on his border in the same year. But the formal annexation of Zips was the work of a military clique at the Habsburg court and, probably, Joseph II. It was actually opposed by Kaunitz who feared that it might provoke partition: as, indeed, it did. Vienna's action now provided the excuse for further and more important seizures from Poland.

The problem about partition, as far as the Chancellor was concerned, was that it would have benefitted not only Austria but Russia and, worse, Prussia as well. The Habsburgs desired a unilateral gain to compensate for the loss of Silesia and, at the same time, sought to prevent any further increase in Prussian power. But Vienna's political options narrowed sharply during 1771–72 and its policy was ultimately determined by the simple fact that the Habsburg Monarchy was not strong enough to fight a war to restrain Russian expansion in the Balkans. Nor, of course, could Austria watch while Prussia and Russia made substantial territorial gains, since this would further weaken her own relative position in central Europe, exactly as Frederick the Great had calculated would be the case, and so would ensure that all three eastern monarchies took land from Poland, which he believed essential if the partition were to succeed. Political logic finally convinced Kaunitz that Austria must, as the least of several considerable evils, participate in the proposed partition. He was eventually supported by Joseph II, who had been willing to annex Ottoman lands but was for long reluctant to see the Polish kingdom partitioned, preferring that it should survive intact as a buffer zone between Austria and Russia. Maria Theresa's stubborn opposition to the partition, believing it nothing short of a crime, was eventually overcome after an extended debate in January and February 1772, by the combined arguments and pressure of Kaunitz and Joseph II, and Vienna indicated to the other eastern powers her willingness to join in.

Kaunitz now sought to maximise Habsburg gains. The diplomatic initiative had passed decisively to Austria, for the other two eastern powers, having committed themselves by a convention signed in February 1772 to the seizure of Polish territory, needed her consent to complete the partition and to ensure its permanence. The Chancellor skilfully exploited this opportunity in the spring and early summer of that year to secure a significant increase in the Habsburg share. The precise annexations were then laid down in a series of conventions between the three eastern powers signed in St Petersburg on 5 August 1772. Russian bayonets and the threat of further seizures were sufficient to force the Polish Diet to ratify these arrangements (30 September 1773), though it would take several years, and much diplomatic manoeuvring, before the precise gains of each state were finalised.

The first partition deprived Poland of almost 30 per cent of her territory and 35 per cent of her population. The Habsburgs acquired 'Galicia' and

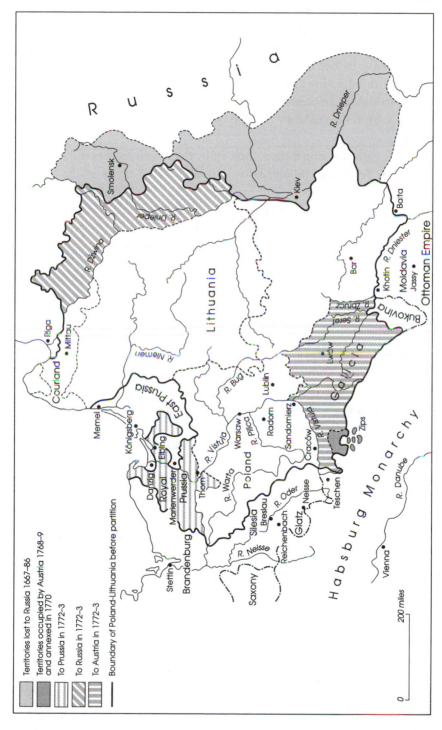

MAP 4 *The first partition of Poland*

Source: H.M. Scott, *The Emergence of the Eastern Powers, 1756–1775* (Cambridge University Press, 2001), p. 219

'Lodomeria', as they styled the new provinces. Russia made substantial gains in Polish Livonia and White Russia, while Frederick II secured the coveted prize of Polish (or 'Royal') Prussia which now became the Hohenzollern province of West Prussia. Austria acquired approximately 83,000 square kilometres of territory and some 2,650,000 inhabitants, while Russia's share amounted to 92,000 square kilometres and 1,300,000 inhabitants and Prussia's to 36,000 square kilometres and 580,000 inhabitants.

Prussia's gain was much more important than these figures might suggest. In fact, Frederick, though he was unable in 1772, or in the years immediately following, to extend his share to include Danzig and Thorn (Toruń), and thus secure complete control over Polish trade down the river Vistula, gained most. The acquisition of West Prussia provided a land bridge to East Prussia, creating for the first time a solid wedge of territory running from Brandenburg across north-east Germany to the eastern border of Hohenzollern territory. For the King, moreover, the partition was a considerable personal triumph: he had induced Russia and coerced Austria to accept his policy, and he had avoided the general war which he genuinely feared. Catherine had acquired the largest territorial share and strengthened her western frontier. But this was poor compensation for the ending of Russia's traditional undivided control over Poland, for the Empress had been forced to admit that first Prussia and now Austria should have a voice in the country's destiny. Vienna had, at first sight, made the most valuable gains, in terms of economic resources (Galicia contained important salt-mines) and a mainly Catholic population; but the first partition was in reality a further reverse for Austria, who probably gained least. Vienna's substantial territorial gains were little compensation for the visible decline in the power of France (still formally Austria's only ally), the renewed western advance of Russia and the further strengthening of Prussia and Frederick's personal prestige – developments which all seriously threatened the Habsburgs' position in Germany and in Europe generally.

The Polish partition had a considerable impact on the relations of the great powers. It revealed, in the first place, Britain's indifference to events in eastern Europe and France's declining interest and, more obviously, authority in continental affairs. The effective breakdown of the Austro–French alliance after Choiseul's fall in late 1770 contributed to the narrowing of Vienna's political options at this period while, in a wider sense, the diplomacy of the early 1770s made clear, perhaps fully for the first time, the political division of Europe into two separate and largely self-contained spheres. There is a sense in which a political partition of

Europe facilitated the territorial division of Poland. A recognition of this, and of the sharply reduced political importance of both western powers, lay behind a remarkable initiative by d'Aiguillon, who became France's foreign minister in summer 1771. He sounded out London about a possible alliance to confront the eastern powers and prevent the partition. But, though there was some interest in such a *rapprochement*, it foundered on Britain's established Francophobia, which was reinforced by an Anglo-French naval confrontation in the Baltic in spring 1773 (see below, pp. 221–2).

The first partition significantly affected subsequent relations between the three eastern powers. Though there was never a formal Triple Alliance, the annexations created an important common interest for the future. Partition affected their relations in a second way. At the time, it was a triumph for Frederick's diplomacy. In the longer perspective, however, it can be seen to have created a potential and serious threat to Prussia: it brought together Russia and Austria, whose separation the King had always regarded as the basis of his security, and so threatened the continuation of his fundamental alliance with Catherine II. Panin's 'Northern System' continued to be the official basis of St Petersburg's foreign policy, but the events of 1772 in Poland and in Sweden (where Gustav III had carried out a *coup d'état* in August restoring the monarch's authority) had been a severe and perhaps mortal blow to this alignment. Though the prejudices and the considerable political influence of Maria Theresa were powerful obstacles to any Austrian *rapprochement* with Russia, a political reconfiguration would become increasingly likely as the 1770s progressed.

The partition also highlighted the brutal acquisitiveness of continental diplomacy, an acquisitiveness sanctioned not merely by the new doctrines of power with their roots in Cameralist and Enlightened ideas, but also by contemporary thinking about the balance of power. By the later eighteenth century, there was general agreement that if one state was about to make territorial gains then the other great powers should join in and demand equal, or equivalent, shares, and this made the balance of power a threat to the smaller states. Poland had been deprived of one-third of her territory and remained an obvious target for her voracious neighbours, whose territorial ambitions were aroused, rather than satisfied, by their initial annexations.

Though its origins were to be found in a desire to limit Russian gains from the defeated Ottoman Empire, in practice the partition did very little to satisfy Catherine's territorial appetite. Even the considerable if unrealised threat of a war around the Baltic in the winter of 1772–73, in the aftermath of Gustav III's *coup*, did not seriously divert the Empress from this.

While the intensity of Austrian opposition did persuade Catherine to abandon her hopes of annexing Moldavia and Wallachia, she pursued her other war aims (see above, p. 160). Russia's victories in the early campaigns had revealed the extent of Ottoman decline and the consequent opportunity for expansion around the Black Sea. The scale of these ambitions brought about the collapse of extended Russo-Ottoman negotiations in 1772–73, in peace conferences first at Fokshany and then Bucharest.

Military operations were resumed in the spring of 1773. Russian troops crossed the Danube, winning several minor successes before they were checked and turned back in the early summer. Catherine was then distracted by the great peasant-Cossack rising led by Pugachev which broke out in the autumn. By the end of 1773 this had spread dangerously throughout eastern and south-eastern Russia and forced the government, which was forced to recall regular troops from the Ottoman front. But the Empress kept her nerve and, against the advice of many ministers, continued to insist on military victory over the Ottoman Empire and a dictated settlement, which proved easier to achieve than had seemed likely. There was considerable war-weariness in Constantinople, and a series of Russian victories when the fighting resumed in 1774, culminating in the near-destruction of the Sultan's army by Rumiantsev's troops, forced the Ottoman Empire to make peace.

The terms of the Treaty of Kutchuk-Kainardji, concluded on 21 July 1774 and signed in the victorious Russian commander's camp, reflected Russia's decisive military victory and secured most of her war aims. In the first place, Catherine made considerable territorial gains north of the Black Sea: the Kuban and Terek areas of the Caucasus, the strategically-important cessions of Kinburn and the fortresses of Kerch and Yenikale in the Crimea (which together controlled access into the Sea of Azov), along with important territory between the mouths of the Bug and the Dnieper. The port of Azov, ceded in 1739 on the proviso that it should remain unfortified, was now confirmed as Russian and the restriction removed.

The limited foothold on the northern littoral of the Black Sea which these acquisitions conferred was of considerable significance, but the annexations and the large war indemnity were to be less important in the longer perspective than Catherine's other gains. Her ships were granted freedom of navigation on the Black Sea (closed to non-Muslims since the late sixteenth century), and Russian merchant vessels could now pass freely through the Straits into the Mediterranean. The Empress was also permitted to build an Orthodox church in Constantinople. The further privilege of protecting this church 'and those who serve it' was ambiguous and would prove of immense significance, as a potential lever for Russian intervention in Ottoman internal affairs, during the nineteenth century. In 1774 Russia secured only the formal status of protector of the Sultan's Orthodox subjects in the provinces of Moldavia and Wallachia. Finally, the Tartar Khanate of the Crimea, a vassal of Constantinople since the mid-fifteenth century, was given an independence it did not want, with the Sultan retaining only his supremacy in religious matters. It was widely assumed that this would be a prelude to formal Russian annexation. Though these fears initially proved unfounded, for Catherine was not yet intent on annexing the Crimea, Russia's position in south-eastern Europe had been immensely strengthened by the gains at Kutchuk-Kainardji.

Within a year, the new-found Russian dominance had been demonstrated by the Austrian seizure of more land from the prostrate Ottoman Empire. During the second half of the Russo-Ottoman War both Kaunitz and the increasingly influential Co-Regent Joseph II, had exhibited real interest in annexing Ottoman territory. Any such gain could be unilateral and might reduce Austria's relative inferiority, confirmed by the partition. It would also block future Russian expansion into the region, which was already alarming Vienna. The obvious targets were Moldavia and Wallachia. The secret Austro-Ottoman agreement concluded in the summer of 1771 (see above, p. 163) had provided that the Habsburgs would secure territorial compensation in return for military and diplomatic assistance against Russia, though this agreement had been abrogated and no such aid had been forthcoming. This did not prevent Kaunitz, who was driving Austrian policy at this period, from claiming that Vienna was entitled to its territorial reward. In 1773 the Chancellor had unsuccessfully advocated purchasing Little Wallachia (the western part of the province, ruled by Austria between 1718 and 1739), but this was opposed by Joseph II.

The Emperor instead established the so-called Bukovina (as its new Austrian rulers styled it) as Vienna's target, an area in northern Moldavia he had identified as a desirable annexation during an extended tour of the region. It was a quadrilateral of territory of some 10,500 square kilometres wedged between Vienna's possession of Transylvania and its new acquisition of Polish Galicia. Though thinly populated (it contained only some 70,000 inhabitants) the Bukovina possessed considerable strategic value, since it would facilitate links between Habsburg lands and Austria's Polish gains, direct communications between which were all but impossible because the Carpathian Mountains lay between them, and would also be a valuable forward military base in any future fighting in south-eastern Europe. It would subsequently become an important agricultural region, though this was not fully appreciated at the time.

During the first half of 1774, Austria's wish to annex this territory was insinuated to Constantinople, which immediately made clear its resentment and opposition. The Chancellor then determined simply to seize the lands from the state which had been his intended ally only three years earlier. The Bukovina had been occupied by Russian troops throughout most of the recent fighting. When these regiments withdrew in late August 1774, after the settlement at Kutchuk-Kainardji, they were replaced by Habsburg units. During the following winter both Constantinople and Vienna mobilised their forces and sent troops to the region, suggesting a military confrontation. But the defeated Ottoman Empire was in no condition to renew fighting: as Kaunitz recognised, it could be bullied into acquiescence. By May 1775 a formal treaty to transfer the Bukovina to Austrian suzerainty had been concluded in Constantinople. The ceded province was then subjected to Vienna's direct military rule.

The episode possesses considerable wider significance. It extended the principles of *Realpolitik* which had underpinned the first partition into south-eastern Europe. The Austrian annexation involved the brutal seizure of land from a defeated state by a power which had recently pretended to be friendly and which had no serious historic claim to the region, though the argument was advanced that it should be part of Austria's gains from the first partition, since it had formerly been linked to Galicia. Less concern was shown with legal niceties than previously, as considerations of power politics came to the fore. Austria's annexation also highlighted the changing international alignments. The idea of a renewed Russo-Austrian alliance was gaining ground both in St Petersburg and in Vienna, as the weakness of the Ottoman Empire and, as a corollary, the potential for further territorial acquisitions became clear. Though distracted by the final stages of the Pugachev revolt, Catherine II's acceptance of Austria's actions constituted tacit support for Vienna's gain and was a portent of future developments. So too was the inability of the Prussian King to arouse any opposition in St Petersburg in 1774–75 to Austria's gain. On the contrary: Panin, the architect of the Prussian alliance, was already adjusting his policies to accommodate the new interest apparent in Russian governing circles in cooperation with Austria. In this perspective, the annexation of the Bukovina revealed the new alignments in St Petersburg which would soon transform Russian policy. In a wider sense, it was the last of a series of territorial changes which consummated the emergence of the eastern powers, and it underlined the transformation of the international system since 1763. Above all, it revealed Russia's dominant position in the eastern half of Europe, which would be further strengthened during the next two decades.

CHAPTER 7

Russian dominance in Eastern Europe, 1775–1795

The dramatic territorial changes of 1772–75 proved the catalyst for a major diplomatic realignment in eastern Europe, though it would be some years before it was carried through. Central to this was Russia's new power and ambitions. Catherine II's empire would dominate the political horizon for the next two decades and would make further vast gains, first from the Ottoman Empire and then Poland, which would actually cease to exist by 1795. During the 1770s, however, St Petersburg's pressing domestic problems delayed the adoption of more ambitious plans directed against her declining neighbour to the south. The impact upon the policies of the other two eastern powers was at first more evident.

Frederick the Great had always believed that a Russo-Austrian alignment was more natural than his own alliance with St Petersburg, and quickly concluded that the events of 1768–75 had made such an axis more likely. The Austro-Russian cooperation embodied in the first partition had united two states whose separation had been the basis of Prussian security. Though no alliance had been signed, Frederick believed that it had become possible and even probable. The evident weakness of the Ottoman Empire made it an inviting target for future Russian expansion, which he believed would be undertaken in alliance with Austria, as it had been previously. Fearing that he might soon lose his cherished alliance with Catherine, he sought during the 1770s to reopen the lines to London and Paris, disdained for a decade. But his efforts made little headway. They foundered on the political division of the continent into two self-contained spheres. Though Frederick's policies had contributed significantly to this trend, his own state was here a victim of it.

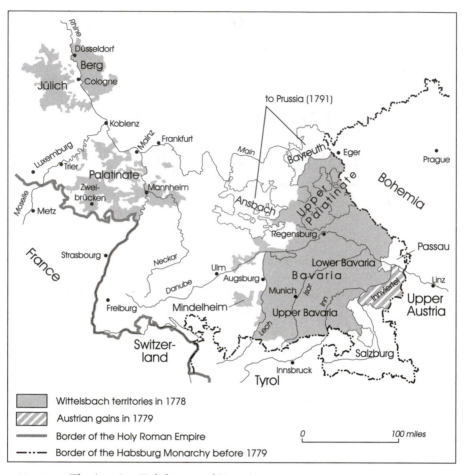

MAP 5 *The Austrian Habsburgs and Bavaria*

Source: M. Hochedlinger, *Austria's Wars of Emergence, 1683–1797*
(Pearson Education Limited, 2003), p. 365

Austrian foreign policy, which during the mid-1770s was largely directed by Kaunitz, was equally affected by Russia's westward advance. The Chancellor had long seen the utility of a Russian alliance, but recognised that the close links with France which guided his own policy effectively precluded this, given the extent of Russo-French rivalry. He also appreciated Russia's potential threat, and had always sought to keep her influence at a distance, by maintaining Poland as a buffer state and by excluding the Russians from the lower Danube region. Russia's recent gains challenged this established Austrian aim, particularly since her victories had been accomplished without the aid of a Habsburg army, in contrast to earlier wars. These unilateral annexations marked out Russia as a dynamic state whose potential appeared unlimited.

During the second half of the 1770s Kaunitz reconfigured Vienna's policy, aiming at a future *rapprochement*. He now believed that Russia, with her secure foothold on the northern shore of the Black Sea, could overthrow the Ottoman Empire by a direct attack on Constantinople. Underlying the Chancellor's attitude was his exaggerated fear of Russian potential. He hoped – exactly as Austria would do during the 1780s, after the conclusion of an alliance in 1781 – that political cooperation might provide leverage in St Petersburg to restrain the Empress's territorial appetite. If this proved impossible, Kaunitz was prepared to participate in any division of Ottoman territory, which he recognised might be inevitable. But Austria would have preferred to limit Ottoman territorial losses and so maintain it as a buffer against further Russian expansion. At this period the Chancellor was preparing for future contingencies by seeking to improve relations. He recognised that no treaty could be concluded both until the struggle for control of Russian foreign policy was resolved (see below, pp. 185–8) and, in all probability, until Maria Theresa died. During these years Habsburg attention instead came to be directed towards the acquisition of Bavarian territory.

Austrian attempts to acquire Bavaria, 1777–85

Habsburg participation in the first Polish partition had been belated and reluctant, since the principle of approximately equal gains upon which it rested was anathema to Vienna. After 1763, Austria had accepted that Silesia was part of Prussia, at least during Frederick the Great's lifetime, and that no further attempt could be made to recover it until he died. Maria Theresa and Kaunitz could never completely renounce the province, but instead concentrated on identifying potential 'equivalents' (which would have to be unilateral gains) to restore Habsburg leadership in Germany. The most obvious target was the medium-sized and once influential but now politically insignificant electorate of Bavaria, which was prosperous and fertile, and also attracted Vienna on strategic grounds, as it lay directly to the west of Austria (it bordered both Upper Austria and the Tyrol) and had served as the access for foreign invasions in 1703–4 and again in 1741–2. Possession of all or part of Bavaria would round out the Monarchy's frontier with Germany. The attraction was obvious, and since the end of the seventeenth century its acquisition had been period-ically entertained in Vienna. As the eighteenth century progressed, this had become linked with the idea of an exchange involving the Austrian Netherlands (obtained in 1713–14). Though these were populous and a significant source of revenue to the hard-pressed government in Vienna, they were seen as a distant distraction, particularly when Austria's foreign policy came to concentrate, from the 1740s onwards, on the struggle with Prussia.

Bavaria's acquisition had a new urgency after the Seven Years War due to the imminent extinction of the ruling Wittelsbach house. The Elector Max Joseph had no direct heirs, and his death would present Vienna with a very real opportunity. Indeed, it had been partly with this in mind that the future Joseph II had married, as his second wife, the Elector's sister, the hapless Maria Josepha, in an unsuccessful attempt to improve relations. When this marriage was under consideration Kaunitz had produced a memorandum on the Bavarian question. It pointed to the benefits of annexing all or part of the Electorate and also highlighted the legal and political obstacles. The situation was extremely complex: another Wittelsbach elector, Charles Theodore of the Palatinate, was heir to Max Joseph, but probably not to the whole of Bavaria. Vienna had considerable claims to areas under Wittelsbach control, both in Bavaria and in the lands of the other branch of the Wittelsbachs. Some of these claims, however, arose in respect of the Habsburg dynasty, while others could be made on behalf of the Emperor. The extreme complications and political drawbacks inherent in maintaining an Imperial role side-by-side with their position as rulers of the Habsburg Monarchy were very evident during the first attempt to annex Bavaria.

It was particularly so when the energetic and enterprising Joseph II succeeded his father in 1765. Kaunitz's memorandum, drawn up in the previous year, had underlined the opportunity presented by Bavaria. But he had concluded that, for the present, nothing could be done, and this remained his approach for a decade to come. Instead, momentum was provided by Joseph II, who was in any case drawn in through his position as Emperor and through the likely legal repercussions of the extinction of a ruling line in an electorate. By the later 1760s, he was urging Bavaria's acquisition, though as yet he found little support in Vienna. In 1772, acting on the recommendations of the Imperial Chancellery, he had even contemplated confiscating the Electorate as an imperial fief when its last Wittelsbach ruler should die. Though imperial fiefs had escheated to the emperor in the past, this was a historic right which does not seem to have been exercised since before 1648. In any case the idea was rejected as too risky by Kaunitz, who appreciated the problems of any attempt by the Emperor to annex lands within the Empire, and so imposed an 'Austrian' rather than an 'Imperial' policy. The Chancellor was certainly aware of Bavaria's potential value, but he also understood, far more clearly than Joseph, the obstacles to acquisition.

Max Joseph's increasing age, together with the growing influence of Joseph II, combined to make the issue more urgent by the mid-1770s, and the Elector's death (30 December 1777) brought the matter to a head. The designated successor was another Wittelsbach, Charles Theodore of the Palatinate. This also threatened Habsburg interests. The succession of a Palatine Wittelsbach in Munich would elevate the unified territory of Bavaria and the Palatinate to the status of third force within the Empire and so weaken Vienna's control over southern Germany. The Wittelsbachs were traditional rivals of the Habsburgs. It had been a Wittelsbach who had briefly been Emperor in 1742–45, and the resentment and fear occasioned by this episode were still influential in the Austrian capital. Charles Theodore's impending accession in Munich, however, also presented Vienna with an opportunity, since he had no direct heirs and, in any case, was at this point reluctant to leave his pleasant court at Mannheim. Charles Theodore had himself been brought up in Brussels (his mother was a member of the local aristocracy) and dreamed of reviving the fabled Kingdom of Burgundy, through the union of the Southern Netherlands to his own Palatine territories, with the simultaneous acquisition of a royal title. At this stage, Vienna was unconvinced of the value of such an exchange: the revenues of the Austrian Netherlands far exceeded the potential income of Bavaria, and the Habsburgs were still seeking to repair their public finances. The Austrians were careful, however, to disguise this lack of interest in their discussions with the Elector. The extended negotiations which followed Charles Theodore's approach to Vienna in 1776 produced an agreement, concluded immediately after Max Joseph's death. By this most of Lower Bavaria (the strategically important third of the

Electorate) was ceded to Austria, whose troops immediately occupied not merely the areas covered by this convention but also considerable additional lands. The agreement went on to suggest that Upper Bavaria would be ceded subsequently to Austria. Charles Theodore was under massive Austrian pressure during these discussions, and also continued to believe an exchange of the Southern Netherlands for the remainder of Bavaria would be concluded. This agreement appeared, superficially, a *coup*, but Austria's hopes were dashed by the serious international opposition which emerged in early 1778, when Habsburg isolation became very evident.

Austria's nominal ally, France, refused all assistance (even if Austria were attacked), on the grounds that Vienna was the real aggressor, and so not entitled to aid under the 1756 defensive alliance. The French foreign minister, Vergennes, was about to intervene on the side of the American colonists in their struggle with Britain (see below, pp. 223-5) – the Franco-American treaties were signed on 6 February 1778 – and had no intention of becoming involved in a parallel continental war, which London could exploit. He was, in any case, anxious to preserve the territorial equilibrium existing in central Europe after the Seven Years War, which would obviously be undermined by a unilateral Habsburg gain. There were, however, more deeply-rooted reasons for French opposition. Vergennes' attitudes had been formed during the very different political world which prevailed before the Diplomatic Revolution, when he had first served as a diplomat. Accustomed to seeing Vienna as a rival and enemy, he brought a notably critical view of Austria with him into office. The 1756 alliance would be supported, but only if it was in France's interest to do so, as securing Europe's neutralisation in any Anglo-French war clearly was. This approach was shared by the ministry's leader, Jean-Frédéric de Phélypeaux, comte de Maurepas – himself a relic of an earlier political age – and, for very different reasons, by the new King, Louis XVI, who had come to the throne in spring 1774 and who opposed Vienna's schemes despite the intrigues of his Austrian wife, Marie Antoinette.

Austria's involvement in the partition of Poland and subsequent seizure of the Bukovina had been sharply criticised by Vergennes as examples of the international lawlessness he so detested. Early in his ministry he had warned Vienna that no further annexations would be tolerated. When Joseph II, during a private visit to the French court in 1777–78, had hinted that France could annex part or all of the Southern Netherlands in return for accepting Austrian annexation of Bavaria, he secured no support at all. Though France's King was married to a Habsburg princess, this did not make French policy favourable to Austrian schemes. On the contrary, Vergennes took France's established role as guarantor of the peace of Westphalia very seriously and sought, now and in the mid-1780s, to defend the imperial *status quo*. French policy remained essentially traditional. The rights of the smaller states would be upheld by Versailles, which failed to provide the support upon which Vienna was counting.

Austria's principal and active opponent was Prussia's King. Frederick had a vested interest in preventing anything which would strengthen his rival, and he was able to exploit the latent opposition to the Habsburgs which Joseph II's actions had aroused within the Empire. Imperial politics and government were one of the relatively few areas where the restless new Emperor was permitted by Kaunitz and Maria Theresa to launch initiatives. Though Joseph had failed in attempts to modernise the Empire's legal and administrative structures, his efforts had aroused widespread fear. That the Emperor should himself seek to annex the whole or part of an electorate was against the spirit, if not the letter, of the imperial constitution.

This opposition was strengthened by the impact within Germany of the Polish partition. While there was never any serious prospect that the Empire would be similarly partitioned, the fear that the great powers might do this to the divided and vulnerable Empire was widespread. The Austro-French alliance had weakened Vienna's position in Germany from its inception, since it had been created to wage war on an Elector, and Joseph II's actions and, more important, presumed intentions aroused further opposition. Frederick the Great was too skilful a politician not to play the Imperial card. He managed to persuade Charles Theodore's own heir, Duke Charles Augustus of Zweibrücken, to protest formally to the Empire that *his* rights of succession in Bavaria had been violated by the Austro-Palatine agreement, and this protest was viewed sympathetically by many minor rulers, alarmed by the Emperor's policy. After some frenetic diplomacy during the first half of 1778, Austria found herself isolated, abandoned by France and opposed by many smaller Imperial states as well as by Prussia.

Frederick sought to frustrate Vienna's policy, and its diplomatic isolation provided the opportunity. By early May 1778, he knew France would not assist her nominal ally, while he himself remained allied to Russia. Though this alignment had come under pressure during the 1770s and an Austro-Russian *rapprochement* was becoming more likely, his alliance had formally been renewed for the second and final time in 1777, nominally for a further eight years. The contrast with the situation a decade before (see above, p. 161) was considerable, and, when Austria appeared determined to retain her acquisitions in Bavaria, the Prussian King invaded Bohemia (July 1778).

The conflict which followed, the War of the Bavarian Succession (1778–79), was the archetypal eighteenth-century war of position and manoeuvre, with each side raiding the other's territories in search of a strategic advantage which its diplomats could exploit. Neither Austria nor Prussia nor Saxony (who had her own claims on Bavarian territory and sent troops to join Prussia's army) really wanted to fight and managed to avoid actual battles. Both states had increased their military establishments since 1763, and armies of an unprecedented size were soon facing each other along the extended common frontier. In the war of position which followed, Frederick was eventually outmanoeuvred by his Austrian adversaries. The Prussian forces faced severe supply problems, and by the autumn had lost some 15 per cent of their manpower through desertion and disease. By contrast the Austrian army, though also suffering losses, performed rather better than in the Seven Years War. The main struggle of the rival armies was against disease and hunger, and this gave the conflict the sobriquet of the 'Potato War', because Prussian soldiers were reduced to digging up potatoes to survive. Their Austrian counterparts subsisted by picking plums as well.

Overtures for peace began in the same month as the military manoeuvring. Joseph, commanding in person for the first time, lost his nerve as soon as Prussian forces invaded Bohemia and appealed for more troops, asserting that Austria's situation was desperate. Though Maria Theresa had supported the Austrian seizure as long as it seemed likely to succeed, her innate pacifism, realistic awareness of Habsburg weakness and bitter memories of the destructive last war made her wish for peace at almost any price. She may have already been given *carte blanche* to negotiate by Joseph, and now initiated negotiations, sending a private diplomatic mission to Prussian headquarters. Marie Theresa's actions were endorsed by Kaunitz who was also anxious for an early settlement. These discussions dragged on inconclusively throughout the second half of 1778, complicated by Frederick's insistence, ultimately successful, that his claims to Ansbach and Bayreuth, two small territories in Southern Germany, must also be settled. He maintained pressure on his Russian ally which, until the autumn, was preoccupied with the Crimea but eventually had to promise to intervene unless there was an early settlement. Catherine II skilfully delayed intervening and so contributed to the military stalemate. This also enhanced her own diplomatic position and weakened her supposed Prussian ally. In November 1778 the belligerents formally accepted mediation by Russia and France, and in the following March a peace conference assembled at Teschen (Cieszyn) in Austrian Silesia.

The final settlement was quickly concluded under Russo-French mediation. Habsburg gains by the Peace of Teschen (May 1779) were far less than had seemed likely a year before, though still not negligible. They consisted of a small area – some 2,200 square kilometres with a population of 120,000 – in south-east Bavaria, the 'Innviertel' or 'Quarter of the Inn' as it came to be styled, which rounded out Upper Austria's western frontier. Even more important than Austria's limited territorial gain, however, was the political reverse suffered at Teschen. Frederick secured recognition of Prussian claims to Ansbach and Bayreuth, thereby establishing a potential Hohenzollern salient in southern Germany, hitherto a wholly Habsburg sphere of influence, when the present ruler died. Prussia occupied the territories in 1791, when the ruler abdicated. Frederick might have been outmanoeuvred on the battlefield, but he had won the diplomatic contest. Saxony secured a large indemnity for giving up her own claims on Bavaria. Russia, too, had gained notably by her mediation, securing both an enhanced and enduring European role and, under the terms of the peace of Teschen, the status of a guarantor of the constitution of the Empire.

This first attempt to acquire Bavaria proved a significant reverse for Vienna's policy. The Innviertel was certainly the single territorial gain made by the Habsburgs within the Empire during the reigns of Maria Theresa and Joseph II, but it came at a high price. The enormous cost of the military manoeuvring, as Austria fielded more troops than ever before, undid the recovery in public finances since 1763, while both Prussia and Russia made potentially significant political gains. Catherine II's prestige and influence were considerably boosted by the Peace of Teschen, which conferred upon Russia the status of guarantor of the Imperial constitution, which France and Sweden had enjoyed since 1648. St Petersburg's new role could only be exercised with the consent of the two established guarantors, and it conferred prestige rather than formal legal status, but it represented a further significant increase in Russian influence in central Europe. Vienna's inability to rely on the French alliance was also highlighted by the episode, and this would be important in the future.

The principal lesson which Joseph II drew from this political failure was the absolute necessity of a Russian alliance, for Catherine's influence was now dominant throughout central and eastern Europe. In 1778–79 the Empress, because she did not wish to see any change in the existing territorial balance in Germany which favoured Russia, had eventually given diplomatic backing to her Prussian ally, and this support had facilitated Frederick's vigorous opposition to Habsburg schemes. Catherine's joint mediation of the Peace of Teschen underlined Russia's new-found importance in German and European affairs. As Joseph II recognised, it would be necessary to destroy the Russo-Prussian alliance, which had neutralised Austria since the Seven Years War, before Vienna could pursue an active policy. For the moment this remained out of the question, though the Emperor's private visit to Russia in 1780 was designed to contribute to an eventual alliance. Maria Theresa retained final control over Habsburg diplomacy, as the recent settlement had underlined, and was opposed to any alliance with Catherine. Her death on 29 November 1780 gave Joseph complete control over Austrian policy and he immediately set out to ally with the Russian Empress.

Russia was, by this point, becoming increasingly committed to an expansionist policy in the Balkans (see below, pp. 187–9) and an Austrian alliance was attractive because of this; the long-lived Austro-Russian alignment after 1726 had been largely based on shared hostility towards the Ottoman Empire. The formal conclusion of a new treaty, however, proved difficult. The fundamental problem was Russia's imperial title, which was tenaciously defended by St Petersburg. Joseph, as Holy Roman Emperor, would not concede the equality of treatment and thus the 'alternative' which Catherine demanded, though Vienna would allow her the title of 'empress'. The resulting impasse meant that no formal treaty could be signed, and this explains the unusual form which the agreement eventually took. In May and June 1781, Joseph and Catherine exchanged private letters which laid down reciprocal obligations and amounted to a defensive alliance, aimed particularly at the event of an Ottoman attack on Russia. For the moment, the signatories intended that this should remain secret, though British diplomacy soon knew of it and by the autumn of 1781 when Panin, the architect of the 'Northern System', was exiled to his estates, Frederick the Great had concluded that a Russo-Austrian alignment existed.

The new agreement represented a reconfiguration of Vienna's foreign policy. During the later 1760s and early 1770s, Austria had been alarmed by Russian expansion in the Balkans and had tried unsuccessfully to restrict this, though by the end of Catherine's first Ottoman war Kaunitz saw the advantages of links with St Petersburg and was tentatively moving towards a *rapprochement*. Joseph now sanctioned further Russian expansion, hoping in return for the Empress's support for Vienna's future policy in Germany and, less certainly, his own ambitions in the south-east. The new alliance was always flawed, however. Each state intended it to serve different ends. For Joseph the treaty was ultimately directed against Prussia and also, covertly, against further Russian expansion, which he hoped to control through an alliance, while for Catherine the aim was essentially to use it to make further gains from the Ottoman Empire. The Russian alliance tacitly downgraded France's previous role in Austrian foreign policy, though the original treaty concluded in 1756 nominally remained in being for a further decade. After 1780, Joseph II took a more direct role in the formulation of foreign policy than his mother had ever done. He retained Kaunitz as foreign minister, in spite of periodic and some-times serious disagreements over policy. The Chancellor's long experi-ence and unrivalled knowledge of Europe were certainly valued by the Emperor. Kaunitz's own wish to hold on to office, and its rewards, enabled him to accept the reduced importance of the French system after Maria Theresa's death together with a diminution of his own influence and a need to discuss policy more fully than in the past. The most significant change in his outlook, apparent in the 1780s, was a growing willingness to contemplate war, caused principally by his appreciation that the ageing Frederick the Great would not live much longer and that Prussia would be far less formidable under his successor.

The early part of Joseph II's personal rule (1780–90) was dominated by his impetuous attempts at internal reform, and it was a few years before he again turned to the acquisition of Bavaria. A visit to the South-ern Netherlands during his first year on the throne weakened his interest in retaining the region. While its demographic and fiscal importance re-mained, the strategic arguments for an exchange became more influential in Vienna, particularly since it was believed that its cession would reduce dependence upon the French alliance. Towards the end of 1783, Joseph II finally committed himself to Catherine's forward policy in the Balkans, at the point when Russia formally annexed the Crimea (see below, p. 189). There were limits to his adventurism: he refused to join in a war in 1783–84 to partition the Ottoman Empire, as both Russia's ruler and his own Chancellor urged. In return for backing the Russian Empress, Joseph received a promise of support for his own ambitions towards Bavaria. Russia's new status, that of guarantor of the Imperial constitution, was believed in Vienna to make her support particularly valuable.

In April 1784 the Emperor began seriously to work to exchange the Austrian Netherlands for the remainder of Bavaria. Elector Charles Theodore, who had been ruling in Munich rather reluctantly since 1779, was now to be offered the royal title which he craved in order to persuade him to accept the scheme. Its realisation was complicated by Joseph II's initial attempt to include the Archbishopric of Salzburg in his plans. This substantial ecclesiastical territory was strategically significant, lying directly south of the Innviertel and south-west of Upper Austria. He hoped that its ruling Archbishop could also be transplanted to the Southern Netherlands, with his see based at Liège, and Salzburg exchanged for Limburg, Luxemburg or Namur. This too aroused opposition, and had been abandoned by the end of 1784. The obstacles to the main exchange were formidable, as soon became clear. The Elector's general agreement was soon obtained, but the actual implementation proved difficult, while his heir, Charles Augustus, the ruling duke of Zweibrücken, refused to give his consent, as did the latter's brother and heir.

The attitude of France, still Austria's ostensible ally, was crucial, both because of the proposed change on her northern frontier and because Versailles effectively controlled the Duke of Zweibrücken. Though Vergennes' views for long seemed ambivalent, he was always opposed to the transfer. His previous opposition to Austrian annexation of Bavaria, six years before, was strengthened by a specific objection to the exchange which was now proposed. Vergennes wanted the Habsburgs to continue ruling the distant Southern Netherlands, since he believed this would weaken Vienna and so increase French control over their alliance. Franco-Austrian relations were, in any case, rather acrimonious at this point, principally because of Joseph II's strenuous efforts to force the opening to international shipping of the river Scheldt, which flowed through the Southern Netherlands. This closure had been part of the Westphalian settlement in 1648, and had been renewed specifically in the Barrier Treaty in 1715. In 1782, however, the Emperor had unilaterally abrogated this agreement, expelling the Dutch garrisons and destroying all the Barrier fortresses with the exception of Antwerp and Luxemburg. He believed that if he could end the closure of the Scheldt it would revive the economic prosperity of the once-great trading city of Antwerp and thus the Austrian Netherlands, and hoped this might make the exchange more attractive to the Bavarian Elector. Joseph also resented the restriction upon his sovereignty implicit in the closure, which he deemed inappropriate for a great power.

Force majeure was used in an attempt to coerce the feeble Dutch Republic, which had itself been severely defeated in the Fourth Anglo-Dutch War (1780–84) and was further weakened by the growing party strife (see below, pp. 239–40). It proved a less one-sided dispute than might have been expected, however. The Republic responded with surprising vigour to Joseph II's bullying, firing on two Austrian ships which sought to sail up the Scheldt and securing diplomatic backing from Prussia and, crucially, decisive support from France. Vergennes, already opposed to Habsburg schemes, was also pursuing a Dutch alliance, which he viewed as integral to French diplomatic recovery after the War of American Independence (see below, pp. 239–40). When Joseph II broke off diplomatic relations with the Republic and war threatened (November 1784), France mobilised some regiments and intervened as an armed mediator. Negotiations proved extended, but the final settlement was set out in the Treaty of Fontainebleau (November 1785). Joseph II secured two minor frontier rectifications in his continuing border disputes with the Dutch, along with a substantial indemnity, around half of which was paid by France herself in order to safeguard the emerging alignment with the Republic. But the Scheldt remained closed to international trade, in its crucial upper reaches at least, and in that sense the Austrian initiative had been a failure.

Joseph II was no more successful where the exchange was concerned. He had sought to win French support for this more important scheme by concessions over the Scheldt. Versailles, however, feared the consequent strengthening of Habsburg power in Germany, and for this reason refused to sanction the scheme. This was crucial because of its impact upon the Duke of Zweibrücken, whose public rejection of the planned exchange in January 1785 signalled its failure. There was now considerable resistance within the Empire, both because of the Emperor's ambitious policies before 1780 and the new initiatives launched since the beginning of his personal rule. The election of his youngest brother, Max Franz, to the coadjutorship of both Cologne and Münster, two powerful and wealthy sees in western Germany, threatened a vast increase of Habsburg influence in that region when, in due course, he succeeded, and this was feared and resented. Joseph II's radical reforms and particularly his ecclesiastical changes inevitably aroused opposition within as conservative a political structure as the Empire, whose constitution protected established rights, however outmoded these might appear to a reforming Emperor.

His attempts to overhaul the Habsburg Monarchy's diocesan organisation caused particular resentment. This involved ending the control which archbishops and bishops in Germany exercised over parishes in the Austrian duchies. It appeared a direct attack on the *Reichskirche* ('Imperial Church'), itself part of the Empire's constitutional and political order. Despite Joseph II's expectations, moreover, Russia did not provide effective diplomatic support. On the contrary: the special envoy sent by Catherine II badly mishandled the ruling Duke of Zweibrücken. The mission inevitably strengthened the impression of two great powers seeking to coerce a minor German territorial ruler, and so further weakened Joseph II's standing within the Empire. Vienna's own diplomacy proved inept in 1784–85. The Emperor's impatient temperament was ill-suited to the delays inherent in any negotiation and the whole episode demonstrated his lack of finesse in foreign policy. The inability to appreciate the impact of his actions upon other states, crucial to diplomatic success, was Joseph's most obvious shortcoming in the international arena. He lacked the single-mindedness, clarity and sheer bravado that his idol Frederick the Great had demonstrated in 1740 in seizing Silesia. Only such a *coup*, planned in secret and ruthlessly executed, could have secured Bavaria for the Habsburgs. The delays and hesitations, together with the accompanying publicity, undermined and ultimately destroyed the Emperor's ambitious plans.

The Chancellor, Kaunitz, soon lost his initial enthusiasm for the scheme as the extent of the obstacles became clear. By spring 1785 even Joseph II was prepared to concede the exchange was quite impossible. It only remained for the aging Frederick the Great, alarmed by continuing but erroneous rumours of an imminent exchange and, more importantly, fearful of the diplomatic isolation which he faced because of the Russo-Austrian alliance, to form the *Fürstenbund* ('League of Princes') with Hanover and Saxony on 23 July 1785. This was the culmination of two developments. The first was the Prussian King's growing involvement since 1763 in imperial politics, as part of his wider strategy of safeguarding his international position. From the end of the 1770s, moreover, there had been separate discussion between several smaller German rulers – Anhalt-Dessau, Saxe-Weimar and Baden in particular – about political coopera-tion designed to revive the corporate, federal structure of the Empire against both Joseph II's and Prussia's ambitions.

This idea of a *Fürstenbund* was taken over by Frederick in 1783, who skilfully gathered support by playing on the fears and the sense of impotence of the smaller imperial territories. He was careful to speak the language of German patriotism in which the defence of the Empire's constitution was now expressed. But his successful advocacy of a 'League of Princes' distorted the original purpose, which had been resistance to both Austrian and Prussian encroachments. Instead, Frederick placed himself at the head of a grouping of smaller rulers, intending to resist the aggression of Joseph II. George III as Elector shared the widespread fear of the Emperor's ambitions and conducted an independent policy behind the backs of his British ministers, who were still pursuing the chimera of an alliance with Vienna. The *Fürstenbund* was subsequently joined by a dozen other minor German princes, and it proved a significant barrier to future Habsburg expansion within the Empire. The fact that the Archbishop–Elector of Mainz was one of its members underlined the complete reversal of Austria's fortunes. Traditionally a supporter of Vienna, Imperial Archchancellor and head of the Empire during any interregnum, the presence of this leading Catholic churchman within an alliance created by the unbelieving King of a Protestant state represented a new nadir for the Habsburgs. The wheel had come full circle. In 1740 the young Frederick had inaugurated his reign with a piece of unprovoked aggression which had thrown Germany and Europe into turmoil. The cautious elder statesman, as the King had self-consciously become, was now the sponsor of a union to preserve the territorial *status quo* within the Empire and to prop up an institution for which he had only contempt.

The failure of Austria's two attempts to acquire Bavaria was a significant diplomatic defeat. Considerable opposition and lasting unease, inside and outside Germany, had been aroused by Vienna's territorial ambitions, and its prestige was undoubtedly damaged. The prized Russian alliance had not delivered the anticipated political benefits. In 1784–85, as in 1778–79, St Petersburg had demonstrated a wish to uphold the political and territorial *status quo*, and so protect its own influence in the Empire. The alignment with France had done even less to advance Habsburg aims: after the second Bavarian episode, Joseph commented that to have 'a nominal ally who was a secret enemy was the worst of all possible worlds'. In a more general sense, the failure of his Bavarian projects once more underlined the near-impossibility of substantial unilateral gains of territory in the context of later eighteenth-century diplomacy. Prussia's opposition in 1778–79 was a particularly clear expression of the general unwillingness among the great powers to permit any one state to make a unilateral territorial gain. Only on the continent's south-eastern rim were such acquisitions possible. There, Ottoman weakness and Russia's relative strength and, perhaps more important, her considerable freedom of action, ensured that such gains could only be prevented by a full-scale European war.

Russian expansion in the Balkans, 1774–1792

Russia's sweeping gains by the Treaty of Kutchuk-Kainardji (see above, p. 168) inspired Ottoman fears that they would be the prelude to further ones, with the newly-independent Crimea as the obvious target. These anxieties at first proved unfounded, for Catherine II was not yet intent on annexing it, and in any case remained preoccupied with important internal reforms, especially of local government. The later 1770s were a

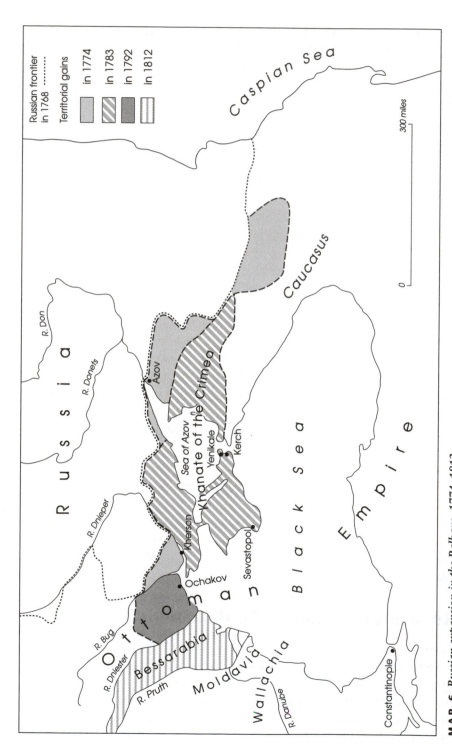

MAP 6 *Russian expansion in the Balkans, 1774–1812*

Source: D. McKay and H.M. Scott, *The Rise of The Great Powers, 1648–1815* (Longman Group Limited, 1983), p. 365

confused and essentially transitional period in Russian foreign policy. The earlier orientation embodied in the 'Northern System' had been compromised by the Russo-Ottoman War after 1768, and then effectively undermined by twin events in 1772. Poland's role as a buffer state in the 'Northern System' was diminished by the first partition, while Panin's league had been intended to prevent exactly the kind of *coup* carried out successfully by Sweden's Gustav III. In the event, however, the revived monarchy there proved incapable of mounting a serious threat, and the improvement in relations which followed the Swedish *coup* substantially reduced anxieties around the Baltic and so further weakened the 'Northern System'. Thereafter, Panin fought a losing battle to maintain his influence over Catherine and her foreign policy.

His principal rival was Prince Grigory Aleksandrovich Potemkin, whose star was rising in the mid-1770s and who would play the central role in the dramatic southern expansion during the second half of Catherine II's reign. The victories in the war of 1768–74 and the acquisitions at its conclusion were one source of Russia's enlarged territorial and political ambitions. The extent of Ottoman weakness and hence the scope for further annexations had not been appreciated. A much more direct cause was the enduring personal influence of Potemkin upon the Empress. The Prince was a larger-than-life figure. Born into the lesser nobility and in an environment which was as much Polish as Russian, he had risen through the Guards' Regiment and, unusually, studied at Moscow University. He had been on the fringes of the coup which installed Catherine in power, and thereafter a member of her Court. A dashing cavalry officer, he fought with distinction in the first Ottoman War. In February 1774 he became Catherine's lover, and retained the status of favourite for two years. Much more importantly, he probably married the Empress in secret at this period, and throughout the rest of his life exercised a dominant influence upon her as consort and minister. Potemkin was a man of immense energy and breathtaking political vision, and the real creator of Russia's new empire. His arguments – far more than Rumiantsev's victories – established the drive to the south, while his position as governor-general of the territories acquired in 1774 enabled his consciously imperial designs to be implemented.

Potemkin's continuing influence on the Empress and the undoubted appeal of his schemes to her imagination, proved stronger than Panin's reservations. What came to be known as the 'Greek Project' was the Prince's personal creation. It was a heady mixture of religious zeal, political opportunity and romantic imagination. Potemkin aimed at nothing less than the expulsion of the Ottoman Empire from Europe and its replacement by a restored Byzantine one, ruled by a Romanov, and less certainly at the creation of an independent principality in the Balkans for Potemkin himself. The notion was far from new: it was rooted in the doctrine of Moscow as the 'Third Rome' which had developed after the fall of Constantinople in 1453, based upon the fact that the Muscovite state was the sole Orthodox polity which had never been subject to Ottoman domination. The 'Greek Project' had a significant and often neglected religious dimension. The eighteenth century had seen a strengthening of the links between Russia and the Greek Orthodox communities of the Ottoman Empire, and these had been especially important after Catherine II's accession. Potemkin possessed a wide knowledge of Byzantine theology and history, and he employed these to win the Empress over to his ideas. By 1779, Catherine seems to have been convinced: her second grandson, born in April of that year, was christened 'Constantine'. The child was given a Greek nurse and taught the Greek language, and was clearly intended to be the ruler of a new Byzantine Empire, the creation of which was the central purpose of the rest of Potemkin's life. It must be doubted, however, whether the 'Greek Project' was ever formally the basis of Russian policy in south-eastern Europe, as distinct from a set of aspirations, and it is certainly the case that its realisation was far beyond the resources available to Catherine II's government. Yet the territorial ambitions to which it testified were real and Russia's desire for further expansion in the Balkans undoubted.

The essential first stage, as Potemkin ceaselessly argued, was the strategically-vital Crimea. Since the Treaty of Kutchuk-Kainardji, Russia's policy, dictated by the Prince, sought to maintain the Khanate as nominally independent but firmly under her control, and she had been prepared to intervene militarily to ensure a friendly *régime*. Russian treatment of the Crimea after 1774 was strongly reminiscent of that towards Poland during the 1760s. The problem was the Khanate's intense tribal rivalries and violent politics, which ensured that any solution which Russia sponsored would be temporary. Catherine's troops first established Sahin Giray as Khan, defeating a powerful rival, and then suppressed an uprising against him. The clear intention was that the new Khan would be a puppet, since he was believed to be both pro-Russian and malleable. The Ottoman Empire resented Russia's growing dominance over what had been the first entirely Muslim territory to be lost to the control of a Christian power. After the Treaty of Kutchuk-Kainardji a sizeable Muslim exile community from the Crimea became established in Constantinople, where they proved vociferous and, at times, influential, urging intervention against Russian control of the Khanate. They were opposed by the moderates, who emphasised the Ottoman Empire's weakness and the need for radical reform. The Treaty of Kutchuk-Kainardji had not been ratified by the Sultan, and efforts were made to renegotiate it over the next few years. The ostensible reason was the unstable situation in the Crimea, though, before long, events there would resolve the situation.

Sahin Giray's *régime* was narrowly based on the Nogay tribe (one of the Khanate's three dominant clans), and depended on continuing Russian support. Despite this, the Khan launched a wide-ranging reforming programme immediately after he secured control over the whole region in spring 1777. This provoked a further and widely-based rebellion which wrested control of both the Crimean peninsula and the Kuban region from their nominal ruler. Once more Russian troops attempted to buttress the Khan's authority. On this occasion, however, the moderates in Constantinople lost control of Ottoman policy, and in 1778 large-scale military and naval operations to recover the Khanate were launched. These failed, however, and underlined that the Empire's military and financial weakness inhibited effective action. The Porte was forced to acknowledge Russia's *de facto* control of the Crimea and Sahin Giray as its ruler by the Convention of Aynali Kavak, signed in early 1779. The Khan was now clearly a Russian puppet.

Open annexation and further expansion elsewhere in the south, however, required a reversal of Russian policy, in which Potemkin again played the central role. The Prussian alliance had to be replaced by an Austrian one, and, while Panin's own laziness and complacency facilitated this change, it only became possible once Joseph II began his personal rule (November 1780). The secret Russo-Austrian alliance concluded in May–June 1781 (see above, pp. 179–80) was essential for the emergence of an expansionist Russian policy in the Balkans. Until the early 1780s, Russia wanted the Crimea as a satellite. But this approach failed because of Sahin Giray's unwillingness to accept the role intended for him. The Khan's own ambitious and aggressive policy, and brutal treatment of his political opponents, produced a further rebellion, his own flight and then renewed Russian military intervention on his behalf. By the end of 1782 the Crimea had been effectively conquered by Russian troops under Potemkin, who convinced the Empress that outright annexation was essential. It was formally proclaimed on 19 April 1783. On this occasion, in contrast to the situation five years before, the Ottoman government accepted that war was impossible, and there was no alternative to accepting the Russian seizure.

The Sultan's only hope was international support, but this did not materialise. The value of the Russo-Austrian alliance concluded two years before now became evident, as Vienna's representative at the Porte backed his Russian counterpart in exchanges with Ottoman ministers. Russia's annexation of the Crimea was the most significant territorial change in south-eastern Europe during the generation after the Seven Years War, and it was widely recognised as a decisive gain, particularly in the context of Russo-Ottoman relations. Catherine II now possessed adequate naval bases and ports on the Black Sea and could launch a seaborne attack directly against Constantinople whenever she wished. Potemkin, who had earlier founded the naval base of Kherson, now established an even more important one at Sevastopol on the Crimean peninsula, to serve as the principal port for Russia's Black Sea fleet which he was energetically constructing.

The threat of further Russian expansion at the expense of the helpless Ottoman Empire was certainly appreciated by the other great powers in 1783–84, but international support for the Sultan was not forthcoming. Concerted diplomatic action would have been extremely difficult, given the fundamental antagonisms which divided Britain from France, and Austria from Prussia. No single power could provide effective support. Britain was not as yet sufficiently concerned at the extent of Russian expansion in south-eastern Europe, while the definitive treaty ending the War of American Independence was not signed until September 1783 and this effectively prevented her playing an active international role. It made Britain reject out of hand the French foreign minister Vergennes' tentative suggestion of cooperation against Russia. France, traditionally the friend of the Ottoman Empire, was most hostile to the annexation of the Crimea, but Catherine II's well-timed disclosure in the summer of 1783 of the existence of the previously secret Austro-Russian alliance, hitherto only suspected, intimidated Vergennes (who, in any case, doubted whether the Ottoman Empire was worth preserving) from action against Russia. This alignment also neutralised Frederick the Great. The Empress's bold use of her secret treaty with Joseph II effectively prevented any great-power opposition and was instrumental in securing international acceptance of a major and, of more importance, unilateral gain, which was accepted by the Ottoman Empire in a convention with Russia signed in January 1784.

The annexation of the Crimea gave new impetus to Russian expansion and produced considerable tension with Constantinople. Their interests clashed in the Danubian principalities and, more particularly, in the

Caucasus, where a fierce struggle for influence followed the territory of Georgia's acceptance of a Russian protectorate in 1783. By 1785–86 Russian troops had been deployed there to contest Ottoman influence in the most direct way. Russia's support for her consuls, whom the Sultan had been forced to admit to Ottoman territory in 1781, was also resented by the Porte. Catherine's apparently systematic exploitation of her recent acquisitions was seen as particularly menacing: the full incorporation of the Crimea into the Russian administrative system in the mid-1780s underlined its importance, while the creation of a Russian Black Sea fleet emphasised the vulnerability of Constantinople itself to attack by sea, since it was only one day's sailing from Sevastopol. The scale of Russia's ambitions, particularly after Potemkin was placed in sole control of policy towards the Ottoman Empire (October 1786), inevitably increased Ottoman resentment and desire for revenge. In the spring of 1787, Catherine's spectacular imperial progress down the Dnieper and through the Crimea, visiting the new Black Sea ports and the two naval bases, Kherson and Sevastopol, produced a new crop of alarming rumours about Russian intentions, while the presence in her suite of her ally, Joseph II, inevitably increased its anti-Ottoman appearance. The war party in Constantinople, gaining strength throughout the 1780s, now secured the upper hand, and hostilities were formally declared against Russia in August 1787.

Austria fought on Catherine II's side in the war of 1787–92. The Austro-Russian alliance of 1781 had not conferred the political advantages Vienna had anticipated. Russia had failed to provide effective diplomatic backing for Austria's second attempt to acquire Bavaria. Habsburg hopes that the alliance might also be a way of restraining Russian expansion had proved equally ill-founded. In 1782–84 Vienna eventually had to support the formal annexation of the Crimea, underlining that it was Russia's client as well as her ally. Throughout the decade Austria's efforts to restrain St Petersburg's appetite for more Ottoman lands had been ignored. Yet the alignment remained the foundation of Austrian policy.

Involvement in the Ottoman War, however, was not simply a matter of Joseph II's acknowledgement of an unavoidable obligation to an ally. It was also closely linked to Vienna's policy both towards Prussia and towards Russia. Kaunitz's traditional hostility to the latter had revived in the mid-1780s, intensified by Frederick the Great's success in creating the *Fürstenbund* (see above, p. 184). The Chancellor's dreams of revenge were encouraged by the increasingly poor health of the formidable Prussian King, who finally died in August 1786. The anticipated death had allowed Kaunitz – who, ironically, was a year older than Austria's great rival – to look forward to a war of revenge against the new, and far less formidable, ruler, the future Frederick William II. In any such conflict, Russian support would be essential. By contrast, Joseph II was interested in a *rapprochement* with the new Prussian King. The Chancellor had been anxious to prevent a Russo-Ottoman war, since this would distract Catherine II from Germany. Once the Ottoman Empire declared war, however, his view changed and became similar to that of Joseph II. The established anxieties of Emperor and Chancellor, that Russia would make further gains from the apparently helpless Ottoman Empire, were now stronger than ever. There was also the spectre of a future revival of the Prusso-Russian alliance which had only broken down in 1781, since Catherine's heir, the Grand Duke Paul, was known to be pro-Prussian, and this particularly concerned Joseph II. The Emperor was to be reassured by the renewal of the Austro-Russian alliance for a further eight years in 1789, underlining his own commitment to it.

During the next few years Austria's diplomatic outlook was to be further complicated by two new factors: the international decline and then collapse of her ally, France, and the new activism of her established rival, Prussia. By the later 1780s the problems of the French monarchy, increasing for a generation, had become acute. The political and financial crisis which preceded the outbreak of the Revolution in 1789 disabled France as a European power and her international role diminished still further as her domestic upheavals gathered pace. Prussia's trajectory was the reverse: the accession of Frederick William II (1786–97) saw the cautious policies which had characterised the second half of Frederick the Great's reign abandoned overnight. Boosted by successful military intervention in the Dutch Republic and the Triple Alliance involving Britain which it produced (see below, pp. 242–3), the new King and his influential foreign minister Hertzberg pursued a more active and ambitious foreign policy. They were concerned that the Austro-Russian war with the Ottoman Empire might worsen Prussia's relative position, and were therefore alert for opportunities for territorial gains of their own, which were expected to come from Poland. They were also prepared to mobilise the formidable Prussian army to threaten Austria, and to fish in troubled waters both in Poland and in the Habsburg Kingdom of Hungary, where support seems to have been given to Vienna's opponents.

The Ottoman declaration of war posed once again Austria's fundamental problem in the later eighteenth century: that of reconciling her need for Russia's support in Germany against Prussia with her fundamental opposition to further Russian expansion in south-eastern Europe.

Kaunitz eventually concluded that, both to uphold the alliance and in the hope of restricting Catherine's gains, Vienna had to help her. Joseph II, who retained the final decision, was unconvinced by such arguments. The Emperor would probably have preferred to remain at peace and, indeed, had vainly tried to restrain Russian aggression during his visit to the Crimea; yet he accepted that in practice Austria had little alternative to fighting alongside Russia. In September 1787, barely a month after the Sultan's declaration of war, Vienna acknowledged that, under the terms of the 1781 alliance, it would have to join Russia's war with the Ottoman Empire.

The Austrian declaration of war was delayed until 9 February 1788 in the hope that a surprise attack could capture Belgrade, which controlled the crossing of the Danube. Two attempts to do so were made before hostilities were formally declared, but both failed. Vienna's approach to the campaign of 1788, in which Joseph II commanded in person, blended military considerations with established political concerns. Though Austria fielded an army which rose to be more than a quarter of a million soldiers, a significant number were deployed to guard against a surprise Prussian attack, which was already concerning Vienna. The logistical problems of campaigning in the Balkans were also considerable: the harvest of 1787 had been poor, while a combination of bad roads and worse weather intensified the difficulties of supply. Disease was soon rife, reducing Austrian numerical strength. Habsburg strategy in 1788, moreover, was inhibited by fear of Vienna's adversaries. The fact that – unlike Russia, with a considerable expanse of steppe to act as a glacis – the Monarchy's heartlands, with their extended shared frontier, were vulnerable to Ottoman raids forced the Emperor, acting on Lacy's advice, to deploy a considerable proportion of the army as a thin cordon. This overextension, coupled with poor Austrian intelligence, enabled the Ottoman forces to break through in the middle of the summer and devastate the Banat of Temesvar. The Banat was a region on Hungary's southern frontier, recaptured in 1718 and actively repopulated during the eighteenth century, but highly vulnerable to Ottoman raiding. Vienna's approach, moreover, was also shaped by wider political concerns. There was significant distrust between the allies, and this was exacerbated by Russia's slow mobilisation and the failure of help expected by Vienna to arrive. Since Austria would only annex territory if Catherine did, the Habsburg army remained inactive for much of the campaign. In the autumn, however, Austria's own position was significantly improved by a careful advance, which established a strong strategic position for the future.

Russia's campaign was equally lacklustre until its final stages. As in 1768, St Petersburg was unprepared and the first full year of fighting was indecisive, though in December Potemkin captured Ochakov. This key fortress on the Black Sea, at the mouth of the river Bug, was St Petersburg's principal target in the war. It was the final stronghold in the Ottoman defence line which lay along the river Danube and the northern coast of the Black Sea, and its acquisition would secure control of the region west to the Dniester. Russia's war-effort, however, was complicated by Gustav III's declaration of war in July 1788, launching a struggle which would last until 1790.

The new conflict was unexpected, particularly in view of the improved relations since the mid-1770s (see above, p. 187). Gustav III dreamed all his life of emulating his great seventeenth-century predecessor, Gustav II Adolf, and of reviving the power of the Swedish monarchy at home and abroad. Yet in the tense aftermath of his *coup* in August 1772, the king had had to recognise Sweden's weakness compared to Russia. Thereafter he had begun essential military and naval reforms, which in the longer perspective would strengthen Sweden's armed forces. But the Russo-Danish alliance, further buttressed by the completion of the Holstein exchange in 1773 (see above, pp. 154–5), prevented the launching of any ambitious external schemes and, specifically, prevented Gustav III from attempting his long-meditated plan to seize Norway from the Danish monarchy.

During the later 1770s and early 1780s Gustav sought improved relations with Russia, partly to weaken the Russo-Danish alignment. These were fostered by his state visit to St Petersburg in 1777 and a further meeting six years later with Catherine in Finland. The improvement was welcomed by both sides: in Russia's case because a quiescent Baltic facilitated southern expansion, in Sweden's because it permitted essential reconstruction. By around 1784, however, Gustav III had concluded that the Russo-Danish axis was as strong as ever and that Sweden remained encircled. He therefore began to think of direct attacks first on Catherine II's empire at its weakest point, the Gulf of Finland, and then on Denmark. The King's changed attitude, together with a recognition of the opportunity presented by the Ottoman conflict, produced a declaration of war. He also hoped a short and successful war would strengthen his position within Sweden where aristocratic opposition was assuming significant proportions. It was the King's personal initiative, together with a few close advisers, and was opposed by many military and naval commanders, who recognised Sweden's relative weakness. By contrast, Gustav hoped to recover parts of Finland, and even areas of Livonia and Estonia.

Though his bold plan was not fully realised, any Swedish attack was a serious matter for Catherine II, since there were fewer Russian troops in the north, the naval defences had been neglected and St Petersburg itself appeared vulnerable. In the event, she was saved first by shortcomings in the Swedish campaign and then by the severe internal opposition to Gustav III which she herself had encouraged. The Swedish plan envisaged landing an army near St Petersburg and so taking pressure off the Finnish theatre-of-war, where Russia's military might could be decisive. Though Sweden's mobilisation was swift and well-coordinated, the inexperienced King underestimated the difficulties. Fatally, he failed to secure control over the Gulf of Finland by either defeating or blockading the Russian squadron which was preparing to sail to the Mediterranean. In mid-July the Swedish fleet withdrew after an engagement with its Russian counterpart, while the army's advance also had to be abandoned.

Sweden's war-effort was now paralysed by internal unrest. Gustav III's aristocratic opponents had been further enraged by the declaration of war, since the King had not consulted the *riksdag* as he was constitu-tionally obliged to do; simultaneously, a nascent separatist movement in Swedish Finland came to the fore. These two strands of opposition coalesced in the so-called League of Anjala which paralysed the Swedish army throughout the autumn of 1788. Though Gustav's political skill and populist instincts enabled him to overcome his domestic opponents, Stockholm's war effort was blunted. At the same time, Russia's ally Denmark declared war on Sweden (August 1788), but pressure from Prussia and, unofficially, from two British diplomats quickly restored peace. By spring 1789 the Swedish King was able to resume the war, with financial backing from the *riksdag*.

Catherine was now forced to give more attention to the Baltic, where Russia's position remained vulnerable despite her impressive naval build-up. Though Sweden's fleet was paralysed by a devastating typhoid epi-demic which killed up to 10,000 naval personnel, the Russian navy failed to exploit the resulting opportunity. A further year's fighting produced no clear-cut result. An overwhelming Swedish naval victory in the second battle of Svenskund (9 July 1790) was sufficient to induce Russia to offer a settlement, quickly accepted by Gustav III. In August 1790 peace was signed at Verela (Värälä) in Finland, restoring the territorial *status quo* of 1788. Catherine's increasing preoccupation with the Ottoman War and with Poland (see below, pp. 202–5) produced two significant Russian concessions to Sweden. St Petersburg recognised the constitution of 1772 and with it the enhanced powers of the monarchy, and implicitly undertook never again to interfere in Swedish domestic politics.

Gustav III's attack, though it distracted Russian attention, did not seriously affect Catherine's struggle with the Ottoman Empire. Though the campaign of 1789 would end triumphantly for the Russo-Austrian alliance, such an outcome seemed unlikely at the outset. Joseph II, discouraged by setbacks during the first years' fighting and by Russia's poor performance, dogged by his own ill-health which prevented him from campaigning personally, and alarmed by Prussian military preparations and Hungarian discontent, determined on peace. Though Kaunitz urged the continuation of the war, the Emperor (after consultation with Russia) had initiated indirect negotiations late in 1788. These were making some progress when the situation was transformed by the death of the Sultan Abdul Hamid I (who had ruled since 1774) on 6 April 1789. His nephew and successor, the bellicose Selim III (1789–1807), immediately renounced any thought of a negotiated settlement and, on a wave of popular enthusiasm, the Ottoman Empire renewed the war.

The campaign which followed saw sweeping gains for the Russian and Austrian forces, based on the stronger strategic position which each had secured by the end of the previous year's campaigning. On the Habsburg side, this was accomplished despite continuing supply problems and immense cost, and against a background of growing concern with events in France, with the beginning of the Revolution in the summer, and fear of an attack by Prussia, as Frederick William II contemplated exploiting his favourable international position. Potemkin's success in taking Ochakov in late 1788 forced Austria to adopt a much more aggressive strategy. Laudon assumed command in the summer and, urged on continually from Vienna by Joseph II, adopted a more dynamic strategy. The impact of Austrian military reforms during the previous two decades made the campaign very successful for the Habsburg forces, who adjusted to the different climate and geography of the Balkans. The Ottoman army also adopted more aggressive tactics and these proved catastrophic. It was shattered in two defeats at Fokshany (July) and Martineshti (September), and these opened the way for a series of spectacular allied successes: Belgrade, Akkerman, Bucharest and Bender were all captured during October and November 1789, while Austrian troops advanced into Moldavia and Wallachia. Neither the unrest in Hungary, nor the serious rebellion which broke out in the Austrian Netherlands in October, nor Prussia's growing diplomatic support for the Ottoman Empire (with whom a treaty was signed in early 1789 but never ratified) seemed major obstacles to a triumphant Austrian peace. The death of Joseph II in February 1790, however, produced a modified Habsburg policy, which was a response to Prussia's seemingly aggressive stance. The new Emperor was Leopold II (1790–92), hitherto ruler of the Italian Grand Duchy of Tuscany. Leopold's earlier career had established his credentials as an enlightened reformer and even as a critic of the competitive great power system, and he has sometimes been portrayed as the antithesis of his brother, Joseph II. In fact his foreign policy after he succeeded in Vienna continued the broad approach of his predecessor towards the Ottoman war, which in his final months Joseph II had become determined to end. In his conduct of foreign policy Leopold himself could be confused, duplicitous and prone to panic: as he did over relations with Prussia, which assumed far greater importance.

The early months of his reign were dominated by a military confrontation with Berlin along the extended common frontier, which was resolved by the Convention of Reichenbach (27 July 1790). It was an armistice which provided for the summoning of a general peace conference, and it marked Austria's effective withdrawal from the war. Kaunitz, whose influence had declined sharply during the new reign, denounced Reichenbach as a surrender, and Habsburg policy after 1790 was less anti-Prussian than hitherto. It was made possible by a parallel change in Berlin where Hertzberg, whose influence had been declining since the autumn of 1789, now lost control of Prussian policy, which became much less adventurous. The author of the agreement with Vienna was the pro-Austrian and pacifist Count Johann Rudolf von Bischoffwerder, a member of Frederick William II's immediate entourage, who personally carried out the secret negotiations which paved the way for the Convention of Reichenbach.

The settlement was welcomed in both capitals. Leopold's principal concern was to deal with the rebellion in the Austrian Netherlands and to confront the opposition in Hungary. He was also suspicious of Catherine's growing ascendancy in eastern Europe and his brief reign was to see Vienna's foreign policy adopt a more critical approach to relations with Russia, though the alliance was still recognised to be essential. For the moment, however, Leopold's principal aim was peace and, after lengthy and difficult negotiations, it was concluded at Sistova (August 1791), by which Austria returned most of her conquests to the Ottoman Empire. She retained small areas along the frontier and these improved the security of the Banat and Croatia. Austria's principal gain from the war of 1788–91, however, was political: the key Russian alliance had been retained and extended in duration, despite the vicissitudes of the previous few years.

The effective withdrawal of Austria and Sweden in the summer of 1790, together with the shift within Prussian policy, appeared to give Catherine a free hand in her struggle with the Ottoman Empire. Instead, the early months of 1791 saw a real if short-lived crisis, with the threat of a general European war which briefly concerned the Empress and Potemkin. It was produced by a British attempt, occasionally encouraged by Prussia, to prevent further Russian expansion. Since the early stages of the Russo-Ottoman War, the Triple Alliance of Britain, Prussia and the Dutch Republic, which had emerged in 1788 (see below, p. 243), had vainly tried to restrain St Petersburg and had given diplomatic support to the Ottoman Empire and Sweden. The impact of these posturings had hitherto been negligible, not least because London had been almost as suspicious of Prussia's ambitions as of Russia's threat to the European balance of power. But in the closing months of 1790 attitudes in London hardened significantly, and towards the end of that winter Britain moved decisively into the anti-Russian camp. The prime minister, William Pitt the Younger, sought to repeat his diplomatic brinkmanship, which had been so successful in defeating both France over the Dutch Republic in 1787 and Spain over Nootka Sound in 1790 (see below, pp. 239–42 and 246–50) and had encouraged overconfidence on the part of ministers in London.

The rapid deterioration in Anglo-Russian relations had commercial as well as political causes. The commercial treaty had lapsed in 1786. In the following year it was replaced by a Russo-French agreement, and this aroused resentment in London, where the idea of substituting Poland and the eastern regions of Prussia for Russia in the map of British trade was gaining ground. It was particularly attractive to Pitt, with his established interest in developing commerce. Ministers believed that eastern Europe could become a more satisfactory and even cheaper source of naval stores and other raw materials, and a market for British goods. This required that Russia should not consolidate her control, and specifically that she should not annex Ochakov from the Ottoman Empire. British ministers believed the fortress controlled the outlets of the Dniester and the Bug into the Black Sea, and was thus a key to Poland's trade.

Relations were also soured by political clashes, which went back to the Armed Neutrality of 1780 (see below, p. 230), which had seriously weakened British assumptions that Russia was a natural ally. Instead, there was increasing concern at Russia's dominance and fear that this would be reinforced by more gains from the Ottoman Empire. The Russophobe British envoy in Berlin, Joseph Ewart, who privately exerted considerable influence on Pitt and acted as a conduit for Prussia's urgings, encouraged Britain to oppose Russia outright. Ewart's role was to be crucial, particularly in the winter of 1790–91 when he returned to London and saw Pitt frequently. The rising star of the British diplomatic service, Ewart was young, ambitious, imaginative but fatally inexperienced. Married to a Prussian noblewoman, his links with Frederick William II's court were unusually close and his enthusiasm outran his discretion. In particular he established the seductive but erroneous notion that Ochakov, as he expressed it to Pitt in January 1791, was 'essential for enabling the Turks to maintain a defensive frontier against Russia'.

Ewart, supported by a group within the ministry, favoured using the Prussian alliance as the basis of a wider system to curb Russian expansion. Treaties with Sweden, Poland and the Ottoman Empire would enable London to take over the old French *barrière de l'est* to restrain Catherine. Pitt's 'federative system' of alliances was pursued in a diplomatic offensive, culminating in an ultimatum to Russia in late March 1791, drawn up after a cabinet meeting attended by Ewart. Unless Catherine would immediately agree not to annex Ochakov and the territory west to the Dniester, Russia would be attacked by British fleets in the Baltic and Black Sea, and by a Prussian army in Livonia. But the prime minister's bellicose stance was supported by a minority of ministers, while there was widespread press, parliamentary and public opposition which the Russian envoy skilfully orchestrated. Within a few days Pitt was forced to abandon his 'Russian armament', as his great political opponent and long-time admirer of Catherine II, Charles James Fox, inflicted real damage in the Commons. Though the government won the vote, its supporters were sceptical about whether British interests were involved at Ochakov and lukewarm about war, while ministers were also forced to admit that necessary naval preparations had not been set in motion. A further blow was the news from Berlin that the vacillating Frederick William II was no longer prepared to fight. By mid-April Pitt had abandoned any diplomatic confrontation. In the summer Britain and Prussia both acknowledged they could not limit Russian gains. The failure of Pitt's policy was total. Catherine and her advisers had briefly been concerned that a wider grouping of states might threaten her successes against the Sultan, but in the event the crisis was over before it had begun.

The episode possesses a symbolic importance, since it was the first time Britain adopted what would become her classic nineteenth-century stance as protector of the declining Ottoman Empire and would-be guarantor of its territorial integrity against Russian expansion. Yet Pitt's stance was based more upon traditional concerns with the balance of power, and it revealed the impossibility of securing support for a British policy not based on opposition to France. There was no enthusiasm for a war against Russia, still seen in some quarters as a 'natural ally', particularly over the distant and seemingly unimportant Ochakov, which most British ministers could not have located on a map. Only when the crisis was far advanced was detailed information sought on the geography of the northern Black Sea coastline, and this proved damaging to the British stance, since it revealed it was not essential for Ottoman defences. In fact Ochakov's importance was symbolic rather than real, its abandonment by Catherine II seen as an indication that her empire's growing power could be checked. The fortress's initial capture by Russian forces at the end of 1788 had aroused little interest, far less apprehension or opposition, in London. Pitt's failure also confirmed Britain's very limited influence in eastern Europe after the Seven Years War, and highlighted once more the continent's diplomatic fault lines.

Russia could now impose her own terms on the Ottoman Empire, since France, traditionally the friend of the Porte, was no longer a force in European politics, while by 1791 Prussia was intent on a *rapprochement* with Russia as a prelude to a further partition of Poland (see below, pp. 203–4). Peace, as usual, required military victory. The celebrated capture of Ismail, the strongest Ottoman fortress on the Danube (December) had been the sole success during the 1790 campaign, but the next year brought further significant Russian victories including a major naval success by Russia's Black Sea fleet at Varna, and these, together with the lack of diplomatic support especially from Prussia, forced Constantinople to accept a settlement. Military operations were suspended in August 1791 and, after extended negotiations, a settlement was signed early the next year. By the treaty of Jassy (9 January 1792), Russia acquired Ochakov and the lands between the Bug and the Dniester, which consolidated her grip on the northern shore of the Black Sea. The Porte was forced to recognise the Russian annexation of the Crimea and had to confirm the provisions of the treaty of Kutchuk-Kainardji. These gains were significant, but fell some way short of Catherine's initial expectations, for, as two decades earlier, there was a close link between the fighting and Poland's fate. Once again, the principal – though indirect – victim of the war's shifting fortunes was the Polish monarchy.

The destruction of Poland, 1772–1795

The first partition did not make Poland's final destruction inevitable; on the contrary, it served as a salutary shock and provided one impetus to significant educational and administrative reforms after 1772. Important legal reforms were planned, but could not be introduced because of noble opposition. These decades also saw a noted literary and artistic revival. Russia retained control over Poland, however, since the King and many magnates concluded that the only secure course was absolute submission to St Petersburg. In the 1770s and 1780s, although Stanislas Augustus continued to reign in Warsaw, the Russian ambassador, the emollient and politically-astute Otto Magnus von Stackelberg, ruled. The King depended financially and politically upon Stackelberg, whose authority was pro-consular, while the Permanent Council established after the first partition further restricted the ruler's authority. Russian rule was relatively benign and tolerable, largely because Catherine II was preoccupied elsewhere: in the 1770s with the Pugachev revolt, the final phase of the first Ottoman war, and the reform of provincial administration, in the 1780s with relations with the Ottoman Empire. These priorities induced her to lead Poland on a looser rein than during the 1760s and she even sanctioned a few modest reforms. It was symptomatic of the changing nature of her control that most Russian troops were withdrawn in 1780, sixteen years after they had entered Poland. Three years earlier Stackelberg had confidently reported that the country 'has become a sort of Russian province'.

There appeared little reason why Russia should contemplate further annexations. Her acquisitions in 1772 had strengthened the western frontier while her control of Poland remained intact. Catherine's appetite for new territories would be satisfied by Ottoman, not Polish, lands. Austria was equally uninterested: indeed, she would have been quite prepared to have given up those territories seized in 1772 for a satisfactory exchange. Vienna remained fundamentally opposed to any additional gains by Prussia and this ruled out further partition, given the prevailing assumptions about the need for approximately equal acquisitions for each of Poland's neighbours.

The principal threat to Polish territorial integrity after the first partition was always the Prussian state. Prussia had been disappointed in 1772 not to acquire the towns of Danzig and Thorn, which controlled the bulk of Poland's export trade down the Vistula. Frederick the Great had made considerable, though unsuccessful, efforts to annex these after the first partition. At the same time Prussia's ruler continued to exploit Poland economically, particularly through the notably one-sided Commercial Treaty imposed in 1775. He wanted to reduce his neighbour to an economic colony: its manufacturing was to be destroyed, so that it could become a captive market for Prussian goods, moreover, and also a convenient source of raw materials and customs revenues. Frederick felt the original partition had been incomplete in another way: the gains had been welcome, but had also left the western tip of Poland ('Great Poland'), a diamond of territory pointing directly at the heart of Brandenburg and separating Silesia from the new province of West Prussia. The Prussian monarchy's fundamental geopolitical problems had not been solved by the first partition, merely posed in a new form. For these reasons, the acquisition of Danzig, Thorn and at least part of Great Poland long attracted Prussia. While the cautious policy and diplomatic isolation which characterised Frederick the Great's final years militated against any territorial aggrandisement, with the accession of a new king, Frederick William II, in 1786, these ambitions came to the fore.

Hertzberg, foreign minister to Frederick the Great and then to his successor, had as early as 1778 advanced his own scheme for Prussia to acquire the desired territories through an exchange which was as ingenious as it was improbable. The 'Hertzberg Plan' had initially been put forward when Austria first attempted to acquire Bavaria (see above, p. 173ff) and it reflected this context. In return for being permitted to annex the latter, Vienna would return Galicia (gained in 1772) to Poland, which would then reward Prussia by ceding Danzig, Thorn and Great Poland. The scheme itself was unlikely to succeed given its complexity and the sacrifice it entailed for Poland, but the territorial aspirations it embodied were real and became an important dimension of Prussian policy after Frederick William II's accession. The 'Hertzberg Plan' was modified to take account of the outbreak of the Russo-Ottoman War in 1787. Austria was now to receive Ottoman territory rather than Bavaria, and Russia was also to make gains in the Balkans. While the plan failed and Hertzberg himself lost influence in 1789–90 (see above, p. 197), its basic objective – further, and peaceful, Prussian expansion at Poland's expense – remained unshaken, and Frederick William II was to prove more willing to fight for territorial gains during the next few years.

The origins of the second partition carried out in January 1793 lie in these Prussian ambitions and in the wider political impact of the fighting. Once again, Poland's fate was linked to events in the south-east, though the *dénouement* was rather different from 1771–72. Catherine II's

Involvement in a war against the Ottoman Empire, together with the Swedish attack the following year, inevitably distracted her from Poland. The reforms she had sanctioned there had been piecemeal and, in particular, Catherine would not allow any substantial increase in the Polish army. Russian control during the 1780s, though less obvious than immediately before the first partition, was still considerable and was felt to be humiliating by an increasing number of Poles. Catherine's renewed preoccupation with the Ottomans was seen by many increasingly patriotic members of the Polish political nation as an opportunity to throw off the Russian yoke. The meeting of the 'Great Diet' (the four-year Diet of 1788–91) overthrew the Russian protectorate. This period of patriotic enthusiasm and intense political debate, partially inspired by the Revolution in France, culminated in the celebrated constitution of 3 May 1791. It transformed Poland into a hereditary constitutional monarchy, provided for the restoration of the Saxon dynasty after the death of Stanislas Augustus, and abolished many of the domestic causes of Polish weakness, in particular the famous *liberum veto* and the right of confederation. The first steps were taken towards strengthening royal authority, and the Diet also adopted fiscal reforms to strengthen the monarchy's financial position and military potential.

These political changes were remarkable, but they ultimately depended on the attitudes of Poland's neighbours and, in particular, Russia. The Kingdom's new rulers recognised the necessity of international support and, in view of the Russo-Austrian alliance, they hoped above all for that of Prussia. Berlin's foreign policy under Frederick William II was puzzling, inconsistent, a prey to court faction; it was also calculated to deceive. The King aspired to play a decisive role on the European stage. He recognised the opportunity presented by the new Russo-Ottoman War and dreamed of leading a great alliance system. His position had been strengthened by the Triple Alliance of Prussia, Britain and the Dutch Republic signed in 1788 (see below, p. 243), though his influence within this alignment was less than that of Pitt. But until its collapse in 1791, after the crisis over Ochakov, Prussia worked within the framework of this alliance. Berlin's objective remained consistent: to acquire more Polish territory. But the means to achieve this were variable and even contradictory.

The two principal strategies were cooperation with the Poles against Russia, but also cooperation with Russia against Poland with the aim either of realising a modified version of the 'Hertzberg Plan' or bringing about a new partition. At times these two strategies were even pursued simultaneously, and this was the source of much of the confusion surrounding Prussian policy. During the Russo-Ottoman War the first of these strategies predominated. Catherine's Ottoman war, together with Sweden's attack in July 1788, created a situation favourable to Prussia. Ostensibly, Berlin's policy sought to encourage the growing Polish freedom from Russian control and to pose as Poland's friend, with the intention that Prussian influence should become dominant there. This was why Berlin offered Warsaw an alliance at the very beginning of the four-year Diet in 1788, and it was finally concluded on 29 March 1790, after considerable hesitation by Frederick William II. The agreement was a conventional defensive alliance containing a reciprocal guarantee of territories; it reflected the absence of any alternative foreign support for the Poles, who were always anti-Russian rather than pro-Prussian. But in 1791 this was reversed and Berlin henceforth cooperated closely with St Petersburg.

Poland's emancipation from Russian control between 1788 and 1791 had enraged Catherine. She was also alarmed by the measures passed by the four-year Diet and especially the Constitution of 3 May 1791, which seemed imitations of the Revolution in France, which she abhorred. The heightened ideological conflict of the 1790s led her to believe that she was combating Jacobinism in Warsaw. Any considerable strengthening of the Polish monarchy, which the reforms would have brought about, was in any case unacceptable to Catherine. During the Russo-Ottoman War she had to turn a blind eye to developments in Poland. But she remained determined to reassert Russian control, for an independent and strengthened neighbour would imperil her security in eastern Europe. This was why she ignored Austria's representations that she should accept the Constitution of 3 May 1791, which Kaunitz believed would strengthen the Polish barrier against Russia which Vienna still craved.

By the winter of 1791–92 France's neighbours were becoming more and more alarmed by the radical events in Paris and were moving towards intervention (see below, pp. 254–8). Catherine was able to exploit the growing European preoccupation with this to increase her own freedom of manoeuvre. She encouraged Austria and Prussia to concentrate on France; her own posturings against the Revolution were intended to leave her free to act in Poland. In the early 1790s these three states did become involved with the French Revolution; but for Russia it was always less important than Poland. This was usually the case for Prussia also, given Berlin's desire for Polish territory, though Frederick William II characteristically could not make up his mind and over-extended Prussia's scanty resources by pursuing an active policy in both eastern and western Europe.

For Austria, however, the situation in France increasingly took priority, particularly after the accession of Leopold II (see below, pp. 252–3). The new Emperor was always opposed to any further Prussian gains and therefore tried to uphold the *status quo* in Poland. He worked to convince Catherine II that the new situation there was compatible with both Russian and Austrian interests. The Emperor thus exercised a moderating influence on Russia, since Austria could not be safely ignored. But his death on 1 March 1792 removed this and also intensified Vienna's preoccupation with the French Revolution (see below, pp. 258–9). Within two months, his successor, Francis, was at war with France, and Austria turned decisively away from Poland.

The shift in Habsburg policy after Leopold's death helped to free Catherine for decisive action. This could only follow the conclusion of the Russo-Ottoman War which came about with the settlement at Jassy in January 1792 (see above, p. 200). In a similar way, the factional struggle at the Russian court following Potemkin's death (October 1791) was now resolved in favour of the group advocating military intervention in Poland. In the following spring Catherine set about restoring her authority in the traditional way. Russia's treaties of 1768 and 1775, guaranteeing the constitutional *status quo*, provided a convenient pretext. The Empress first sponsored a confederation of some Polish noblemen, drawn up in St Petersburg on 27 April 1792, but dated '14 May Targowica', to pretend it had arisen on Polish soil. Russian troops crossed into Poland on the night of 18–19 May under the pretext of supporting the confederation of Targowica. While these units were moving towards the Polish border, news arrived at the Russian court that France had declared war on Austria (20 April 1792), which in turn brought Prussia into the struggle against the Revolution. This further strengthened Catherine's position over Poland.

The Poles were largely unprepared for this latest Russian military intervention. Their leaders were now shown to have been politically naïve: in Poland it had been widely believed that Catherine would not risk antagonising Prussia and Austria, and would accept the new situation there much as she had, two decades earlier, accepted the *coup* in Sweden. This hope, and the expectation of Prussian support, were rapidly revealed as illusions. The ramshackle Polish army was no match for the more professional and much larger Russian forces, and in July 1792 Poland, in the person of the King, Stanislas Augustus, submitted to St Petersburg's control. The emigration of many Poles who had played prominent roles during the past few years underlined the scale of the defeat. Henceforth the decisive voice in Polish affairs would once again be that of Catherine II.

The Empress's precise intentions at this point are by no means clear. A return to the situation before 1788 would perhaps have suited her best; yet she was certainly not entirely opposed to a further partition and was obliged to take some account of the views of Prussia and, less certainly, Austria. The signature of defensive alliances with Vienna and Berlin (July–August 1792) further strengthened Catherine II's hand. The attitudes of the two German powers towards Poland in the second half of 1792 were somewhat different. Austria opposed any further partition, a stance which had inevitably been hardened by knowledge of the 'Hertzberg plan'. Ever since that spring, however, Frederick William II had looked towards more seizures from Poland. The unexpected resistance of the French armies to the Prusso-Austrian advance in the autumn (see below, p. 261) increased his wish for Polish territory, since it would compensate for the failures in the west. The King also wanted to prevent, if at all possible, the re-establishment of Russia's undivided control over Poland.

Francis's accession in early March 1792 produced a rapid reversal of Habsburg policy. By June, the new Emperor had agreed that Prussia and Russia could make additional gains in Poland provided Austria was allowed to carry through the exchange of the Austrian Netherlands for Bavaria. This was, of course, an old and deeply-cherished Habsburg plan; its failure in 1784–85 had not dampened Vienna's enthusiasm, and it had resurfaced periodically during the Ottoman War. At this point, however, its re-emergence was principally the work of the two subordinate ministers who now became responsible for Habsburg diplomacy, the influential court secretary Baron Anton von Spielmann and Count Karl Johann Philipp Cobenzl, who had been a close friend of Joseph II and held several major posts in Habsburg government. Both men had gained influence under Leopold as Kaunitz's influence ebbed away, and they now began to direct Austrian policy. There was considerable opposition at court to their initiative. Official policy, however, was now in the hands of two individuals who believed not merely that they could realise the Bavarian exchange but that cooperation with Berlin against the French Revolution could create an enduring Austro-Prussian alliance, which would free Vienna from its old dependence upon France and Russia. The anti-Prussian principles which had guided Habsburg policy for half a century were abandoned overnight. Kaunitz struggled unavailingly against the new approach, which was backed by the Emperor, and in the summer of 1792 the veteran Chancellor resigned.

In the autumn Poland's fate was decisively affected by events in western Europe and the war against Revolutionary France. The defeat at Valmy

(20 September 1792) and disastrous retreat (see below, p. 261) further increased Frederick William II's desire for Polish lands, to salve the wounds inflicted by the French armies. The allied failures also exacerbated Prusso-Austrian tension over Poland, since Berlin believed that Vienna had not provided sufficient support against France. The situation was brought to a head by Prussia's announcement in the final week of October that its price for continuing the war against the Revolution was an indemnity in the form of Polish territory. Habsburg policy at this critical juncture was hesitant and contradictory. Spielmann and Cobenzl remained committed to the Bavarian exchange, but their approach continued to encounter heavy opposition at court and was, in any case, effectively undermined by France's conquest of most of the Austrian Netherlands following her victory at Jemappes (6 November 1792). The dramatic successes of the French armies forced Vienna to accept that, for the foreseeable future, this war had to be its main priority, and Prussian support was believed essential to its success. Austria was therefore forced to accept Berlin's demands for Polish territory, though any gains for herself by an exchange involving the Netherlands were, for the moment, impossible.

Until now Catherine II had played a masterly waiting game, resisting Prussia's considerable pressure, since she herself was not yet committed to further partitions. Her final decision to force this through, which became apparent in mid-December 1792, reflected a wish to keep Prussia in the anti-French coalition and, especially, her growing anxiety at developments within Poland, where the pro-Russian Targowica *régime* was losing control. The formal justification advanced for the second partition was to combat the 'same spirit of insurrection and dangerous innovation' which had gained the upper hand in France and 'was ready to break out in the kingdom of Poland'. Catherine was genuinely alarmed by the spectre of Jacobinism in Warsaw, and in mid-December 1792 she announced her willingness to see Prussia occupy the territory Berlin was demanding and then set out her own terms. Their scale was breathtaking, and certainly amazed Frederick William II, but he had no intention of haggling over proposals which gave him all his own demands. After very brief negotiations, in sharp contrast to the prolonged exchanges over the first partition 20 years earlier, the formal Russo-Prussian partition treaty was signed in St Petersburg on 23 January 1793. Catherine effectively dictated it: Russia made vast acquisitions in eastern Poland, acquiring some 250,000 square kilometres, principally comprising the districts of Minsk, Podolia, the western Ukraine and eastern Volhynia with a population of over three million. These gains dwarfed those of Prussia, who secured only some

MAP 7 *The second and third partitions of Poland*

Source: M. Hochedlinger, *Austria's Wars of Emergence, 1683–1797*
(Pearson Education Limited, 2003), p. 422

58,000 square kilometres (Great Poland, together with the cities of Danzig, Thorn, Posen [Poznań] and Kalisz) with around one million new subjects, one-quarter of the territory and one-third of the population seized by Catherine II. Yet Vienna's political defeat was even more complete. Austria was not officially informed of the second partition until March 1793, and received only a vague and specious promise from the partitioning powers to assist in bringing about the Bavarian exchange at some future date and, perhaps, to secure some territorial compensation from France when the Revolution had been defeated. Austria had suffered a serious diplomatic reverse, a further shift against her in the political balance in eastern Europe.

Vienna's ministers were largely to blame. The initial mistake of Spielmann and Cobenzl in resurrecting the exchange project had been compounded by their dogged refusal to abandon it when circumstances changed dramatically and by the dilatoriness, timidity and indecision with which Habsburg policy had been conducted. The inexperience of the new Emperor Francis was also of considerable significance during these months. Its aftermath in Vienna was of enduring significance. The two ministers were relegated to very minor positions (27 March 1793) and replaced by Kaunitz's *protégé* Franz Maria Baron von Thugut, one of the first graduates of the Oriental Academy and an influential ambassador in Constantinople two decades earlier. Thugut brought a greater realism and a new sense of purpose to Austrian policy and restored its traditional anti-Prussian orientation, which the Second Partition appeared to have justified too late.

The second partition was an immense triumph for Russia. Prussia, though her share was far less, had made further significant gains. Poland, the helpless victim, had suffered a mortal blow in 1793, losing half her territory and people, and was now a rump of 212,000 square kilometres with a population of some four million. Polish resistance was strong and vocal, and it was only with considerable difficulty – and the help of Russian bribes and soldiers – that the ratification of the formal treaties of partition was forced through the Diet of Grodno in the summer and autumn of 1793. A further series of measures passed at this meeting dismantled the new regime of 3 May 1791 and restored the constitutional practices which had contributed so much to Poland's weakness, above all the elective monarchy and the *liberum veto*. Finally, a Russo-Polish 'treaty' of 16 October made her once again a Russian protectorate. Russian troops remained in Poland, while the Empress also supervised the Polish army and directed Warsaw's foreign policy.

In retrospect, the second partition was decisive; yet there was nothing inevitable about Poland's final extinction two years later. Immediately after 1793, the attitudes of her neighbours remained contradictory. Prussia clearly desired a further, final partition. Austria, equally clearly, was opposed to this, yet, at the same time, strongly resented her own exclusion from the second partition. Russia's attitude was ambiguous and perhaps undecided. Catherine II, who held the political initiative, may well have seen the necessity of a further partition as a final solution to the Polish question, for the situation created by the second partition was inherently unstable. The reimposition and, indeed, strengthening of Russian control intensified the mounting indignation and resentment within what was left of Poland. A general Polish insurrection against Russia and Prussia began on 24 March 1794. Its heroic leader, Tadeusz Kosciuszko, achieved a hard-won but symbolically important victory in a small-scale engagement at Raclawice (4 April 1794) and Warsaw evicted its Russian garrison. Within a few weeks the rebellion had spread to much of Poland's remaining territory but it was weakened by severe internal divisions (particularly the fundamental split between the conservatives and the radical 'Polish Jacobins') and it was bound to be defeated, given the infinitely superior resource of its enemies. Yet the makeshift Polish army caused Russia and Prussia considerable problems in the spring and summer of 1794, securing some successes. It was only the arrival of powerful Russian reinforcements which finally broke Polish resistance. The Russian victory at Maciejowice on 9 October, where Kosciuszko was wounded and captured, seriously weakened the rising. Three weeks later, Suvorov's forces stormed the Praga suburb of Warsaw, massacring the civilian population and frightening the capital into surrender. By the closing weeks of 1794 the Polish insurrection was over.

The origins of the third partition lie in the response of Prussia and, especially, Russia to this rising. The initial Polish successes had greatly alarmed Catherine II, who called on Berlin for military support. Frederick William II remained determined on a final partition and was therefore delighted to respond to her appeal. The entry of Prussian troops into Poland (May 1794) effectively decided the issue of partition for, as Russia recognised, Prussia was not going to evacuate this newly-occupied territory. St Petersburg soon acknowledged that a further partition was the logical solution, since it seemed unlikely that Poland could ever be pacified. Russia's success in suppressing the rebellion gave her the political initiative. Austria, resentful at her exclusion in 1793, had no intention of being excluded again and quickly announced her acceptance of a final partition. By the end of June 1794 the obliteration of Poland had been agreed by the eastern powers. Negotiations to determine the precise division continued throughout the year, while the Polish rising was being sup-pressed, and each state sought to pre-empt a final settlement by occupying as much territory as it could.

These negotiations were considerably more prolonged and complex than the two previous partitions. In the first place, Austria and Prussia were already on thoroughly bad terms, due to Vienna's resentment at its exclusion from the second partition. This tension also reflected the diffi-culties of their unsuccessful war against Revolutionary France, and Prussia's conviction that Austria had not played a full part in this struggle. A more fundamental difficulty was the fact that, for the first time, the borders of the partitioning powers were actually to meet; strategic considerations and, in particular, the question of 'natural' (or merely defensible) frontiers had to be taken into account. The negotiations between the three courts during the second half of 1794 ended in deadlock. Russia and Austria quickly agreed on their respective shares and hence on the need to restrain Prussia's territorial appetite: Catherine had now reversed the pattern evi-dent two years before. By favouring Austria and not Prussia, she hoped to deny Berlin the Vistula frontier it wanted. Frederick William II, however, remained intransigent; in particular, he refused to give up the city of Cracow (Kraków) and its surrounding region, long coveted by Austria but occupied in 1794 by Prussian troops. The Austrian and Russian shares were set out in a secret treaty directed against Berlin in January 1795. The impasse remained, however, and Frederick William II, fearing a war against the other two eastern powers, now withdrew from the coalition against France (Basel, April 1795: see below, p. 267).

The Prussian state was too weak to contemplate further fighting, and in August accepted the Russo-Austrian partition scheme when it was finally revealed to Berlin. The King was satisfied by some minor Austrian conces-sions, and Austro-Prussian and Prusso-Russian treaties were signed on 24 October 1795. The third partition had now been agreed. It remained only for further treaties signed on 5 December 1796 and 26 January 1797 to arrange the final details of the obliteration of Poland. By the third parti-tion, Russia acquired Courland, Lithuania, Podlesia and the western por-tion of Volhynia; Austria obtained Little Poland along with Lódz (Lublin) and Cracow; and Prussia took the remaining Polish territories, including Warsaw. In 1795 Russia's territorial gains were more than those of the others combined: 120,000 square kilometres to Prussia's share of 48,000 and Austria's 47,000. The relative population gains were much more equal: Russia secured 1.2 million new subjects, Prussia just over 1 million and Austria 1.5 million. Poland had disappeared; to underline this, the partitioning powers solemnly undertook never to use its name in the future. Stanislas Augustus was forced to abdicate, and lived out the final three years of his life as a political prisoner in Russia.

The three eastern powers all made vast territorial gains from the partitions of Poland (see map, p. 208), but these did not initially prove permanent. Within two decades Poland was to be first partially restored by Napoleon and then re-partitioned at the Congress of Vienna, when the bulk of what had formerly been Polish territory passed into Russian hands (see Chapters 11 and 12). The eighteenth-century partitions were quite unique and unprecedented. The third largest continental state had been removed from the map of Europe within a generation, and this inevitably produced a lively and continuing debate over the reasons for its extinction. The explanations advanced can be grouped under two principal headings: internal weakness and external pressure. The former have received considerable emphasis, and it is certainly clear that the weaknesses of the Polish monarchy were significant. Poland's development in the early modern period had not conformed to the general continental pattern. Instead of the absolute monarchy, centralised administration, strengthened fiscal system and powerful standing army which were familiar elsewhere, Poland had an elected monarchy largely at the mercy of the magnates, a weak central government with limited powers of taxation, lacked defensible frontiers and had a small and backward army. But this primarily explains the ease with which Poland was obliterated. The Holy Roman Empire underwent a broadly similar evolution during the early modern period and suffered from some of the same problems, but it was not partitioned and, indeed, never seriously threatened with that fate. The partitions of Poland were brought about by her powerful and ambitious neighbours. The real culprits were the three eastern monarchies, not the selfish magnates or the ineffectual if idealistic Stanislas Augustus Poniatowski. Poland also suffered from the absence of external support; the disappearance of France, a traditional friend of the Poles, from any active political role in eastern Europe after 1763 was significant. But it is by no means clear how either of the western powers could have resisted the successive seizures of Polish territory without a full-scale war, and even that might well have been unsuccessful. As the English man-of-letters Horace Walpole sardonically observed at the moment of the first partition, the British fleet could not easily sail to Warsaw.

Russia gained most from the vast territorial changes after the Seven Years War, and her relative position among the great powers increased accordingly. Her annexations from Poland were far greater, in lands and people, than those of either Austria or Prussia, reflecting her ascendancy over them. She also made immense and all-but-unilateral gains from the Ottoman Empire. By 1796, the year of Catherine II's death, Russia was securely established on the northern shore of the Black Sea and was poised for further attacks against an apparently defenceless Sultan. The foundation of the port of Odessa in 1794 had signified Russia's intention to exploit her fertile new southern territories and their considerable economic potential, particularly for grain to export to Southern Europe. Her intense and continuing pressure on Ottoman borderlands, at a time when Constantinople was already finding difficulty in controlling its outlying provinces, was the principal explanation for Russia's dramatic southern expansion.

The other European powers were quite unable to resist this. As a 'flanking power' (see above, p. 3), Russia long possessed an inviolability from attack and a consequent strategic freedom of action which her rivals envied. It was why Pitt's attempt to confront her over Ochakov was so futile. In a similar way the rivalry of Austria and Prussia worked to St Petersburg's advantage, for it prevented effective cooperation against Catherine and always gave her a choice of a German ally. This ability to exploit Austro-Prussian rivalry had been clear during the final two partitions of Poland, when Russia cooperated first with Berlin and then with Vienna, emerging with by far the largest share. Russia's decisive westward expansion was also aided by the fact that Anglo-French rivalry was largely conducted overseas, particularly until the 1780s. Her parallel emergence as the dominant power in eastern Europe and, perhaps, on the continent had been the principal development during the generation after the Seven Years War.

CHAPTER 8

The Anglo-Bourbon struggle overseas and in Europe, 1763–1788

Anglo-French relations after the Seven Years War, 1763–1774

Britain's victory in the Seven Years War, the latest round in the long Anglo-French duel for colonial and commercial dominance, had been unusually decisive. The Peace of Paris securely established her maritime and imperial supremacy and represented a serious and humiliating defeat for France. Only in the West Indies had she avoided large territorial cessions, which excluded her from the North American mainland and all but destroyed her position in India (see above, p. 116). An early attempt to recover these losses by a new war was widely expected. The peace settlement, far from easing tension, had increased it and constituted the main obstacle to future good relations. Throughout the next two decades, the principal aim of France, and of her ally Spain, was usually to undermine Britain's supremacy.

The existence of a solid Bourbon alliance after 1763 was itself novel. The accession of the French Bourbon family south of the Pyrenees at the beginning of the eighteenth century had not created permanent political unity. On the contrary, Franco-Spanish relations had periodically been acrimonious and, more frequently, distant. During Ferdinand VI's reign Madrid, with strong British encouragement, had been neutral. The accession of Charles III had been a turning-point. Spain's ruler was as hostile as his French cousin towards Britain (see above, p. 114). Two years after becoming Spanish king he duly signed a firm alliance in August 1761, which brought about Spain's ill-fated intervention in the closing stages of the Seven Years War. It was symptomatic of the dominance of colonial issues in Anglo-Bourbon relations that this Third Family Compact, unlike its predecessors of 1733 and 1743, was entirely a response to overseas, rather than European, rivalries.

Though Choiseul as foreign minister had carried out the detailed negotiations, the alliance had been at least as much the work of King Louis XV. He took a very dynastic view of international relations, believed he should support his cousin and may even be the source of the designation 'Family Compact'. Thereafter Choiseul, as he came to dominate the ministry from 1761 onwards, imposed a much more self-interested view of relations. His need for royal support to stay in office ensured he was careful to dress up French policy in the language of family solidarity. This rhetoric, however, did not fully conceal how far he intended to exploit Spain economically and strategically. The commercial opportunities her vast empire offered should be opened to French traders, who would enrich themselves and Louis XV's state. This had been France's aim ever since the Bourbons succeeded in Madrid. The Third Family Compact declared that French merchants should be placed on the same footing as their Spanish counterparts. Yet it was only in January 1768, after lengthy negotiations, during which Madrid limited concessions, that a formal agreement was signed. It was linked to a wider and quite deliberate shift within French policy, which under Choiseul aimed not at the possession of colonies of settlement but a more purely trading empire, to generate wealth but avoid the high cost of administration and defence. Spain's role would be to provide raw materials and a captive market for French manufactures.

Choiseul's strategic calculations were equally self-interested. He had been disillusioned by Spain's feeble performance in the war of 1762–63 and, thereafter, believed she had limited value as an ally. The Spanish fleet was a significant component in the all-important naval balance, and he ceaselessly urged its reconstruction. Yet he judged that Spain was now too weak to be an effective ally. Indeed, as Choiseul wrote late in 1764, she had become a dead body who could only play a role in a future war 'through her losses'. Two years later, he even declared that it would be better if Madrid kept out of any future conflict, as it would be a burden rather than a source of aid. Only if French defeats mounted up could Spain play a useful role: to provide a vulnerable colonial empire for Britain to attack, its exact role at the close of the Seven Years War when British expeditions had seized Havana and Manila. Though both had been returned, their loss had taken pressure off France in the final year and so aided Choiseul's skilful diplomacy during the peace negotiations which limited French losses.

France's own international position had been seriously weakened by her defeats during the war (see above, pp. 144–6) and this eclipse lasted for three decades. During these years, however, Spain was in all respects even weaker, with a crumbling system of colonial defence, a government urgently in need of reform and armed forces which were only slowly rebuilt. Her vulnerability, particularly in the American hemisphere, made her dependent upon France in the anticipated confrontation with Britain, significantly strengthened by her victories during the Seven Years War. This Spanish dependence was the real source of the Family Compact's stability. Indeed, during the first decade of peace many contemporaries judged Choiseul the leading minister of both Bourbon powers, believing he directed Spanish policy as well as French. An additional bond was with Spain's foreign minister, the marquis of Grimaldi, who had previously been ambassador in Paris and was a personal friend and close political confidant of Choiseul. The two men corresponded privately, and Grimaldi was usually content to follow the other's lead.

Spain's severe defeats in 1762–63 potentially threatened the alliance's stability, and France had ceded Louisiana west of the Mississippi to her in November 1762 as compensation for likely losses at the peace, which in the event amounted only to Florida, and also to persuade her to accept an early settlement. This cession also fitted in with France's wish to create an empire of trade, rather than of settlement. The Bourbon alliance was always an unequal, and at times an uneasy, partnership. Versailles' assumption of political leadership – however much it reflected the realities of power – was resented, as were France's systematic efforts to exploit Spain commercially. The precise strategy to be adopted against Britain also produced periodic disagreements. Each state – though agreed on hostility towards England – viewed the alliance differently. Spain's extensive and far-flung overseas empire was highly vulnerable to future British expansion and made her emphasise the defensive nature of the Family Compact. The French, however, at first wanted to use it offensively and intended Spain's armed forces to play a significant, if minor, part in the war of revenge against Britain for which Choiseul was preparing. Yet this substantial difference – which in any case changed over time – was blurred in practice because each needed the other's support, and this gave the partnership a remarkable permanency. For 30 years the Family Compact of 1761 remained a fixture in European politics, and it broke down only in 1790, in the crisis produced by the French Revolution.

Relations with the two Bourbon powers shaped British foreign policy, as throughout much of the century. Ministers assumed that this rivalry was permanent and probably ineradicable, that the peace restored in 1763 would be short-lived, and that clashes and perhaps war would soon be resumed. Britain and the Bourbon powers had been exhausted by the recent fighting: both London and Versailles were very concerned at the state of their finances, while Madrid contemplated an imperial structure visibly in decay. The financial and colonial problems created, or simply exposed, by the recent conflict were the first priority, and this meant that neither side wanted a rapid renewal of hostilities, ensuring a period of peace. But there was no expectation that it would last. Britain believed there was considerable evidence of continuing Bourbon enmity. The efforts by France and Spain to rebuild their navies caused particular concern, as did a series of small-scale colonial disputes immediately after 1763. The fact that Anglo-Bourbon rivalry was now focussed on the imperial sphere made sea power decisive. Throughout the next generation, relations between the three states were to be largely determined by their respective naval strengths.

The Seven Years War had demonstrated Britain's supremacy at sea, and initially this continued. The British fleet had reached a new peak in size and relative effectiveness during that conflict, while both Bourbon navies were in poor condition. Naval reconstruction was Choiseul's main aim, and he himself took the all-important naval portfolio from 1761 until 1766, handing over the foreign ministry to his cousin and political subordinate Praslin. Choiseul, however, retained overall control of French diplomacy and handled the all-important Spanish correspondence himself. He sought to rebuild the shattered French fleet, while simultaneously urging Spain to do the same. His efforts enjoyed some success, while Spanish naval reconstruction moved ahead impressively during the later 1760s and first half of the 1770s. The real challenge which Britain would face from the combined Bourbon fleets during the American War was largely produced by these building and repair programmes. In the short term, however, Bourbon naval reconstruction fell appreciably short of initial unrealistic targets. France and Spain lacked the men and *matériel* (especially the timber), the infrastructure and, above all, the money to rebuild their fleets as fast as Choiseul had first hoped, while Britain's superiority at sea – though weakened by economies and partial neglect – could not quickly be challenged. Recognising this and that there could be no early war of revenge, Choiseul abandoned the naval ministry in the spring of 1766, returning to the foreign office, where he concentrated on combatting Russian power in eastern Europe (see above, p. 145). Though naval reconstruction continued on both sides of the Pyrenees, in France it proceeded at a slower pace than had earlier been anticipated as reduced resources were committed to it.

Britain's continuing lead was known in some detail both in London and at Versailles. The enlarged importance of naval power within the overall framework of relations was apparent in the attention devoted to the gathering of intelligence on the rival fleets. France maintained a spy-ring in Britain, run from her embassy, and picked up scraps of information in many ways. It provided the basis of detailed tables, maintained by the French ministry, of British naval strength, together with the exact location of the ships. For her part, Britain secured naval intelligence both indirectly, through an agency run from the Dutch Republic, and directly through the reports of strategically-placed diplomats and of captains in both the merchant navy and the fighting fleet. The result was that each side knew with surprising accuracy the state of its opponent's naval power and thus its own relative position. Detailed knowledge of French and Spanish rebuilding confirmed British ministers in their assumptions of enduring Bourbon enmity, though it also revealed that they retained the advantage at sea. This made them more willing to use their naval supremacy in a series of disputes during the decade after 1763.

The Peace of Paris had left some minor problems to be resolved: the perennial issue of the fortifications at Dunkirk, the Canada Bills (a complex dispute over the extent of France's responsibility for loans made by British merchants to the former French *régime* there) and in particular the so-called Manila Ransom, allegedly due to Britain for not destroying the capital of the Philippines in the final stages of the conflict. None was likely to lead to a renewed war, but they provided a barometer of Anglo-Bourbon diplomacy. These disputes both contributed to and were exacerbated by the poor state of relations immediately after 1763, caused friction and bad feeling, consumed the time and filled the despatches of diplomats, but were in the end all settled by negotiation. The unpredictable clashes which arose at the imperial periphery between agents of the British state and the Bourbon monarchies were a much more serious threat to peace. Metropolitan governments were usually forced to respond to events, rather than being in control of their subordinates, and this led to several serious confrontations in Europe. Immediately after the Peace of Paris there were disputes over Turks Island, then the Gambia, and finally and most seriously (in 1766) the Falkland Islands, which were known in Spanish as the 'Malvinas'. Each had its origins in the actions of an enthusiastic subordinate probably exceeding the instructions, or at least the intentions, of his own government; each for a time threatened a wider conflict; and all were eventually resolved by Bourbon concessions produced by immediate British naval mobilisation. Choiseul recognised that the Bourbons' inferiority at sea forced them to accede to British pressure, and imposed this view upon Spain. Successive British governments, realising the potential for successful naval blackmail, used the threat of force rather than diplomacy to secure favourable settlements of each dispute.

The most serious of these clashes was that over the Falklands, and it was shelved rather than solved in 1766. Lying as they did in the South Atlantic, to the east of the Straits of Magellan, these islands were seen in London as strategically important – as a staging post – for any British attempt to break into the Eastern Pacific Ocean, which Madrid was determined to maintain as a Spanish *mare clausum*, a status which the Treaty of Utrecht appeared to uphold. Britain's attempt to exploit her gains at the Peace of Paris and to expand into the Pacific, where France nurtured similar ambitions, inevitably led to tension. At issue in 1766 had been the blockhouse established at Port Egmont on West Falkland by a British expedition, and in the later 1760s the Spanish government determined to remove this by force. Calculating that in any war France would have no alternative but to support Spain, Madrid evicted the small British garrison in the late spring of 1770. The arrival in Europe of news of this expulsion in the summer of that year set in motion a crisis. Spain refused to make the restitution demanded by London, and this brought open conflict closer than at any point since the Peace of Paris.

At first the dispute assumed a predictable form. Britain mobilised her fleet, the Bourbons followed suit, and the government in London then brought forward more ships of the line. The same mechanisms which had preserved peace since 1763 now seemed likely to lead to a war over Spain's actions in the distant South Atlantic. The dispute was intrinsically more serious in London's eyes than previous clashes: force had been used against the British flag. Fighting almost broke out in 1770–71 because of three factors which had not been present in earlier colonial disputes. Britain's response was handled by the then Southern Secretary, the Earl of Weymouth, who covertly adopted a much more hard-line approach than most of his colleagues and certainly than the king, George III, wanted. The earl was prepared to risk, and may even have hoped for, open conflict to advance his own political ambitions. Weymouth believed war might bring the Earl of Chatham (as Pitt had become in 1766) back to power and that he himself would dominate any ministry which replaced the government of Lord North, which had only taken office in January 1770. In the second place, Madrid was determined to expel British forces from West Falkland and to exploit the Family Compact to bring this about: the second Falklands crisis was, until its final stages, much more of a purely Anglo-Spanish dispute than previous clashes. Finally, in the critical last months of 1770, Choiseul – who in earlier disputes had advocated moderation and a negotiated settlement – accepted and perhaps encouraged the risk of war. This was because his own ministry was being undermined at the French court, and he believed that hostilities with Britain might be the only means to hold on to power.

In the end, peace was preserved by the fall of two foreign ministers. Choiseul was dismissed by the pacific Louis XV on Christmas Eve 1770, while Weymouth, increasingly opposed by his cabinet colleagues, had finally resigned two weeks earlier. Spain, deserted by France, backed down in the face of Britain's clear naval supremacy and a negotiated settlement was patched together. In January 1771, Charles III's government, while not renouncing its claim to the island, restored West Falkland to Britain and formally disavowed the Spanish captain whose action had provoked the crisis, receiving in return only vague British assurances to abandon the island in a few years' time. When the evacuation occurred, after three years of Spanish pressure, it was entirely due to a British desire to save money, rather than improve relations or honour a settlement. France's desertion of her ally created a period of tension with Madrid and weakened the Family Compact, which had been far stronger and more unified under Choiseul than during the decade after his fall.

His dismissal marked a turning-point in relations. Choiseul's hostility had been considerable and deep-rooted. Formal diplomatic contacts during his ministry had been tense and periodically acrimonious, and had been worsened by his striking success in annexing the Mediterranean island of Corsica. In 1768 the ailing Chatham administration, paralysed by its own divisions and facing severe unrest on the streets of London, could do nothing to prevent France securing the most important political and territorial gain of Choiseul's ministry. He was able to buy the island – at a bargain price – from its nominal ruler, the declining Italian Republic of Genoa, though French troops subsequently had to defeat a Corsican independence movement. This episode was the only occasion when France and Spain were not forced to back down by British naval superiority. Only Choiseul's recognition of Bourbon inferiority at sea had prevented him from launching a war of revenge. The early 1770s, however, saw a remarkable change. The fundamental causes of tension continued, but new personalities and political priorities in both capitals produced several years of comparative harmony unparalleled since the collapse of the Anglo-French *entente* in 1731.

The initiative came from France. The duc d'Aiguillon, who eventually became foreign minister in summer 1771, shared Louis XV's well-known love of peace and tried to conciliate. D'Aiguillon's desire for improved relations and distinctly pacific foreign policy were initially prompted by the preoccupation during the early 1770s with remedying the crown's debilitating financial weakness and solving the problems posed by any attempt to increase direct taxation, which would be opposed by the *parlements*, politically-powerful law courts in Paris and the provinces, and by the General Assembly of the Clergy. These priorities had their parallels in London where the North ministry, which gave much-needed stability after 1770, was similarly preoccupied with financial retrenchment and the American colonies. The resulting improvement in relations culminated in secret discussions for closer political cooperation and a possible alliance in 1772–73. After several hints from d'Aiguillon, they were eventually taken up by Lord Rochford (the Southern Secretary) with the encouragement – briefly – of George III and North.

D'Aiguillon based his initiative on a superficial but essentially correct analysis of the rapidly-decreasing influence of both France and Britain in Europe, apparent since the Seven Years War and especially clear in the early 1770s. The menacing turn of events in eastern Europe (see Chapter 6), where Russia seemed about to dictate peace to the Ottoman Empire and Poland was being partitioned with scant regard for the views of the western powers, was particularly irksome because of France's traditional influence at Constantinople and Warsaw. Discussions about Anglo-French political cooperation went on intermittently and secretly in 1772 and were briefly revived early in 1773, but ultimately to no avail. D'Aiguillon's proposal ran counter to the traditions and, more important, the prejudices of British policy, and its considerable political logic failed to overcome the growing official indifference to eastern Europe and the violent Francophobia of English parliamentary and public opinion. The proposal was partly destroyed by France's encouragement and support for Gustav III's *coup* in August 1772. Versailles' role in this was fully known to British ministers, through the interception of French diplomatic correspondence, and was sufficient to end any thought of a *rapprochement*. The failure of d'Aiguillon's approach did not lead to increased diplomatic tension after the early 1770s. On the contrary, the improved relations survived a brief but serious crisis in the spring of 1773, produced by

Britain's fear of a general war and consequent refusal to allow France to send a fleet to the Baltic to support Gustav III against Russia, and continued until the beginning of the American colonial rising. Lord North's government was increasingly preoccupied with the opposition in Britain's American colonies, and it was the outbreak of a rebellion there in 1775 which would lead to the next crisis in Anglo-Bourbon relations.

Britain, the Bourbon powers and American independence, 1775–1783

Britain's territorial gains in 1763 had created their own problems. The need to assimilate the new acquisitions, particularly in North America, and to govern and defend the enlarged empire, produced policies which conflicted with the growing desire of many colonists for increased freedom from metropolitan control. Separatist sentiment had been strengthened by the removal of the French threat in Canada during the Seven Years War, which had acted as a solvent of the Anglo-American relationship. The origins of the American revolt lie beyond the scope of this present study: suffice it to say that by spring 1775, colonial opposition had turned into open rebellion, and by the summer British ministers reluctantly concluded that America would have to be reconquered.

The logistical problems were immense. The theatre of war was 3,000 miles away, and troops not only had to be transported across the Atlantic but supplied and partly fed from Britain. From the outset, shipping was London's major concern. These difficulties were intensified by the nature of the struggle. The conventional military wisdom of hitting the opponent's political or military centre of gravity was little use against an enemy whose strength lay in its popular support, its irregular warfare and a country substantially hostile to Britain's forces, many of them German mercenaries. Victories in set battles would not in themselves defeat the American rebels, yet these still had to be pursued both in the hope that such victories might bring the Americans to negotiate and because the entire area could not be occupied. Instead Britain occupied key towns and coastal areas, partly in an attempt to cripple the colonial economy.

The very different parameters of the war in America soon became clear. In 1776 neither an overwhelming victory at Long Island (27 August) nor the capture of New York City proved decisive, while, in the following campaign, the victory at Brandywine Creek and the subsequent capture of the new American capital of Philadelphia (September) failed to produce the surrender likely after such losses in European warfare. London's task was also seriously complicated by the desire to avoid any action which might hinder a subsequent political settlement. There was also an exaggerated and enduring belief in the extent of loyalism, which had a similarly inhibiting effect upon military strategy. The ambivalence of British ministers, and of the commanders in the field, towards a war against fellow Englishmen was always a considerable obstacle to success. Yet these various barriers to British victory, substantial as they were, were almost overcome. In 1775–76, London made a considerable military effort in North America, believing an early and decisive victory would force the rebels to accept a settlement. The campaigns of 1776–77 saw significant British gains, and colonial resistance would probably have been defeated and a political settlement imposed at least temporarily, but for France's open intervention in 1778.

Even before the standard of rebellion was raised, colonial leaders had been seeking to expand their contacts with European states. They aimed to secure essential munitions and, by expanding their own trade, additional income for their struggle. Several countries had colonies in the Caribbean, and these along with Europe's own ports became the focus of American shipping, which increased in volume as the revolt became established. More and more, however, the colonists sought the financial and political support essential to success and sent agents to leading European capitals. Their principal target was Britain's old rival, France.

Since Louis XVI's accession in 1774, French policy had been in the capable hands of Vergennes, an experienced and perceptive career diplomat. He shared Choiseul's desire to humble Britain, whom he described shortly after entering office as a 'restless and greedy nation' which could well launch a surprise attack. Vergennes' career had coincided with the revival of Franco-British antagonism after the 1740s, and he always believed rivalry inevitable. His hostility was calculated, however: French policy throughout the War of American Independence sought to restore the colonial balance of power, which had been tilted so decisively towards Britain in 1763, and in this way facilitate a possible *détente* with London on French terms. Vergennes's policy combined elements from those of his predecessors. Choiseul's planned war was to be the prelude to the political cooperation sought by d'Aiguillon. He also intended, in accordance with the tenets of mercantilism, to weaken Britain's power by depriving her of the American colonies and the commercial and naval strength drawn from them. In this way, Vergennes hoped that France could recover her traditional influence in Europe, which was the ultimate aim of his policy.

American independence for him was always a means to an end. He was alarmed at the dominance of the three eastern powers and especially Russia. Vergennes had seen these developments at first hand as a diplomat in Constantinople and Stockholm, and his anti-Russian attitudes had been strengthened by membership of the 'King's secret' during Louis XV's reign. He viewed the first partition of Poland and Catherine II's massive gains in 1774 (see Chapter 6) as evidence of France's declining authority, which would not speedily be reversed, as well as highlighting a new lawlessness in international relations. British supremacy overseas was forcing France to spend too much on the navy and restrict the sums available for her army and for subsidies to other continental states – the means (Vergennes believed) by which Versailles's authority in Europe could best be restored. The considerable weakening of British power caused by the loss of the American colonies, and the resulting improvement in relations should, in due course, permit reduced expenditure on the French navy. Vergennes's model was Fleury, who had also aimed to make France secure through better relations with Britain. This curiously introspective analysis was flawed by its effectively ignoring the French crown's crippling financial weakness – France would have to spend substantially on a war intended to make possible future reductions in naval expenditure! – and also underestimated the actual dominance of Russia and Prussia in particular.

Vergennes had immediately recognised the opportunity presented by the American revolt, which itself became a motive for French intervention. By spring 1776, he had secured Louis XVI's consent to the principle of French assistance to the colonists. This decision effectively ended the efforts at internal reform and, in particular, financial retrenchment championed by Turgot, who had long cautioned that the fiscal system could not bear the costs of a war and resigned almost immediately. At first, however, French support was limited to providing the colonists covertly with money and arms. The King was pacific and reluctant to support a rebellion, and had to be coaxed into intervening openly. Political logic suggested that France should do so, but the condition of the French navy and the state of the Spanish alliance made it impossible. As throughout the period since 1763, the level of naval preparedness determined Bourbon policy. Expenditure had been reduced after Choiseul's fall in 1770 and the fleet had suffered accordingly. Louis XVI's accession was soon followed by the energetic Sartine becoming navy minister, while Versailles's commitment to the American cause from spring 1776 was accompanied by a considerable increase in naval expenditure, soon leading to a significant build-up of French naval power.

British ministers had, from the very outset, feared France might intervene, recognising that the revolt could provide a tempting opportunity for Louis XVI's monarchy to launch the long-anticipated war of revenge. Relations with France had recently improved, but these were now supplanted by the more familiar watchful concern, and particularly close attention was kept on the French navy. Initially, British ministers, preoccupied with the war in America, tried to maintain the existing good relations, and were prepared to turn a blind eye to the evident expansion of Franco-American trade. This continued until the second summer of the war, by when Sartine's naval build-up demonstrated France would probably intervene. London now returned to the strategy of naval blackmail and intimidation pursued so successfully between 1763 and 1773, and this contributed to a sharp deterioration in relations in 1776–77. France's blatant support for the colonists could not be reconciled with her declared neutrality. As the war spread to European waters, the use of French ports by American privateers produced a serious crisis in mid-1777. It was clear that hostilities could not be far off: in that summer a foreign diplomat in London described the two countries as being in a state of 'half war'. By the beginning of 1778 Vergennes was convinced that the navy was strong enough to fight, while the British surrender at Saratoga could be used to convince Louis XVI, who still hesitated. Throwing off the mask of neutrality, French ministers began negotiations with the American representatives in Paris, and on 6 February signed treaties of friendship, commerce and defensive alliance. This provoked an immediate breach in relations in March, when ambassadors were withdrawn. Britain and France were formally at war from July 1778, following naval clashes in the Channel.

A secondary reason for Vergennes's delay was his wish to have the support of Spain and her fleet, upon which French war-planning depended. The long-term success of Charles III's efforts at naval reconstruction had, by the mid-1770s, made the Spanish navy a significant factor in Anglo-Bourbon relations. From the outset, however, Madrid's policy towards the American revolt was ambivalent. Charles III remained hostile towards Britain, and his desire for revenge and, in particular, for the recovery of Gibraltar and possibly Minorca was strong. But Spain's attitude proved less predictable than France had anticipated. In the first place, she resented having had to follow repeatedly the dictates of French policy, most notably in the Falkland Islands dispute: particularly when she was then abandoned and forced into a humiliating surrender in January 1771 (see above, p. 22). The next few years had seen cooler, more distant relations.

Though the Family Compact was still the principal component in Spanish foreign policy, it was no longer the only one.

In the early 1770s, Spain had looked to the western Mediterranean and to relations with the Ottoman Empire's dependencies in North Africa. In mid-1775 an attack on Algiers (the lair of many of the Barbary pirates who still preyed on Spanish shipping) proved a disastrous failure, and this fiasco inevitably tempered Madrid's policy as a whole. During the early stages of the American revolt, moreover, Spain was preoccupied with relations with Portugal. Lengthy negotiations had failed to settle disputed colonial boundaries in South America and in 1776 Madrid had determined on force. The resulting small-scale colonial war with Portugal (1776–77) made her more reluctant to undertake additional commitments, since it had depleted the treasury. Above all, while France retained comparatively few possessions in the New World and had much greater freedom of action, Spain had an extensive colonial empire there. With her dominant presence around the Gulf of Mexico, she was still expanding in North America at this period, when Los Angeles was established. She therefore wished to confine any independent American Republic behind the Allegheny Mountains and so keep it out of the Mississippi valley, where Spanish interests were dominant. There was also significant antipathy towards the colonial rebellion as such. The fear that a successful revolt might produce rebellions against Spanish rule undoubtedly influenced Charles III's ministers, and this was a further important reason for the hesitant and limited support they provided Americans. From summer 1776 onwards, Spain was secretly providing a little financial support, but this long remained the limit of her assistance.

Vergennes intended to bring Spain openly into the war, but to do so he had both to overcome Madrid's coolness and to use the Family Compact as an offensive alliance, and this proved difficult. Spain had not been consulted over the French decision to intervene, and this was resented in Madrid, where it strengthened established anxieties. Vergennes believed that this omission prevented France from simply requesting aid under the Third Family Compact. Instead he set out to persuade Spain of the benefits of intervention, and this placed her at a considerable advantage during extended negotiations in 1778–79. The appointment of a new foreign minister, the conde de Floridablanca, in February 1777 gave Spain a leader who was more prepared to exploit the opportunity presented by the American rebellion, in contrast to Grimaldi, who was more cautious after France's earlier desertion of Spain in 1770–71. Madrid continued to be ambivalent, especially as France's refusal of aid during the brief war with Portugal aroused resentment and reawakened anxieties about the one-sided nature of the Bourbon alliance. Eventually Spain was won over by a mixture of her own ambitions and Vergennes's arguments, and the pressure of circumstances: her territories in the New World and ports in Europe were increasingly used by American traders and privateers. In April 1779 Charles III committed himself to the war by the Convention of Aranjuez. This considerably extended the scope of the Family Compact; it made Spain France's military ally, provided for a joint Bourbon strategy and prohibited either state from concluding peace until American independence was secured. It also set out the high price of Madrid's intervention: France was to aid the recovery of Minorca and Gibraltar and the acquisition of extensive lands in America, in particular the vast territory of Florida, with the ports of Mobile and Pensacola, together with the Bay of Honduras and the coast of Campeche on the Central American mainland. These war aims underlined that the real Spanish objective was to drive out British settlements around the Caribbean and so remove the principal colonial rival there.

The entry of France and Spain transformed Britain's struggle in America into a world war. The considerable problems of suppressing a distant colonial revolt were now dwarfed by those of fighting the Bourbons all over the globe, and doing so without a single continental ally to divert her enemies' resources to Europe. It completely reversed the situation during the Seven Years War – and, indeed, in Britain's eighteenth-century struggle with France generally – when her victories overseas had been made possible principally by the French having to divide their war effort. This reversal of the established pattern has usually been explained by Britain's inept diplomacy and, specifically, her failure to secure allies during the 1760s and 1770s. Though superficially this appears an attractive explanation, Britain did not lose the land war in America simply because she lacked an ally in Europe. That struggle was unsuccessful because of a complex series of military and logistical factors. An alliance could have provided useful assistance, such as military forces, and might have altered the war's strategic complexion, but no more than that.

In any case, Britain's isolation was caused by a fundamental shift in the international system over which she could exert surprisingly little influence. The dominance of the eastern powers, and especially of the Russo-Prussian alignment (see Chapter 6), left little scope for Britain, or France, in continental politics. Moreover, Britain's very success in her mid-century struggles with the Bourbons had actually weakened her own diplomacy. The French threat, real or imaginary, had previously been exploited by British ministers to construct an alliance system which tied France down in Europe while they concentrated on the struggle overseas. Britain's triumphs in the Seven Years War and the parallel decline of Louis XV's monarchy had finally undermined the credibility of this argument, since if anyone threatened Europe after 1763 it was Britain with her powerful navy, command of colonial trade and substantial empire overseas.

These obstacles were not apparent to British ministers, who continued to search for allies. Austria (in 1780–81) and Prussia (in 1778 and again in 1782) were unsuccessfully courted, while several approaches were made to Russia during the war. In 1778, as Anglo-French hostilities began, Catherine II was finally offered a subsidy – though ministers still insisted upon the 'Turkish clause' – and three years later the Empress was even promised the Mediterranean island of Minorca in return for an immediate treaty. These approaches were all unsuccessful, though there was considerable sympathy for the British cause at least in Vienna and St Petersburg. In part, the search for support was undermined by its timing. Britain was trying to conclude a treaty during wartime, and any ally would immediately become involved in the fighting. More fundamentally these failures underlined London's own political marginalisation. Britain, as Edmund Burke truly said, was now 'at the Circumference' of European politics. Continental diplomacy was dominated by the eastern powers, who during the American war were preoccupied with the Balkans and the War of the Bavarian Succession (see Chapter 7), and the obstacles to Britain securing an ally were insurmountable.

The Bourbon intervention inevitably reduced the importance for Britain of the war in North America. Burgoyne's surrender at Saratoga (October 1777) had boosted American morale, and French intervention transformed the war: what had been a struggle to avoid defeat by Britain became one to force London to accept a political settlement. In the succeeding campaigns the Americans made further progress, but the real focus of the fighting now lay elsewhere. Britain was more concerned with countering French threats to her interests world-wide and to attacking France's own remaining colonies, aims which made the Caribbean the crucial theatre of war. Inevitably British naval power became crucially overstretched and she was unable to blockade the enemy coastline as in previous wars. In autumn 1779 Britain even temporarily lost control of the Channel, but an attempted Franco-Spanish invasion was an immensely costly fiasco. French strategy at this point was surprisingly cautious and defensive, particularly after the failure of an initial attempt to give decisive naval support to the Americans. Intimidated by memories of previous British successes, France failed to take advantage of this favourable situation to exploit her enemy's over-extension and exposed position. French naval activity was largely concentrated on the West Indies, where in 1778–79 she captured the islands of Grenada, Dominica and St. Vincent. But these gains were far from decisive and must be set against the simultaneous collapse of French power in India and the failure to give effective support to land operations in America. Britain's difficulties, nevertheless, increased as the war progressed.

The entry of the Bourbons and the extension of hostilities to European waters inevitably highlighted the established problem of neutral trade. It had been in Britain's interest to establish a strict interpretation of the rights of neutrals in wartime, and her dominance at sea had enabled her to impose this during the wars of 1739–48 and especially 1756–63. During the latter, British prize courts had developed a doctrine designed to curb neutral traders, which came to be known as the 'rule of the war of 1756'. It held that commerce which was 'closed' – in other words, not open to outsiders during peacetime – could not be 'open', or permitted, after hostilities broke out. This struck directly at the opportunities for profitable trade, and it was naturally resisted by the neutrals. Although it had significant foundations in legal thought, it was driven by political considerations, its purpose being to contribute to an eventual British victory by weakening her enemies, denying them trade and income from the non-aligned commercial states. Superior naval power had enabled Britain to establish this ruling within international law, and this approach again guided her actions during the War of American Independence and once more inflamed relations with many of the neutrals.

From the very beginning, Britain had sought to close European ports and New World colonial harbours to American shipping and privateers. A diplomatic offensive against the neutral commercial powers enjoyed some success, though by its nature it was bound to be incomplete. Portugal, Denmark and Sweden were all cooperative and placed obstacles in the way of American trade with their possessions in the western hemisphere and in Europe. Though particular problems arose with the Dutch Republic – the leading neutral commercial power – these did not assume serious proportions until after 1778. Since the beginning of the fighting in America, ships from the other European countries had sought to evade the British prohibition on trade with the rebellious colonies. The capture of some of these vessels by British warships and privateers had inevitably produced considerable diplomatic tension. But it was only in summer

1778, with the outbreak of hostilities between Britain and France, that the issue of neutral rights came to a head.

France's need of naval stores, together with Vergennes's hope of isolating Britain, led French diplomacy to cultivate the neutrals by championing the liberal doctrine of 'free ships, free goods'. Some of the lesser European states, in particular Denmark and the Dutch Republic, possessed sizeable merchant fleets and protested strongly against British action in 1778–79. The leadership of the neutrals, however, came to be assumed by the somewhat unlikely figure of Catherine II. This was because the Empress sought enhanced international prestige and increasingly wished to mediate in European disputes, as she had recently done at Teschen (see above, p. 179); it also reflected Russia's wartime importance as the principal source of vital naval stores and the Empress's resentment at the seizure of Russian ships and goods by the belligerents. By February 1780 she had determined to lead a league of neutrals and to define and defend their rights: the two essential components in the Armed Neutrality, which emerged during the same year. It consisted of a series of conventions between Russia, Denmark, Sweden, Austria, Prussia, the Kingdom of the Two Sicilies and, eventually, the Dutch Republic (who joined in January 1781, the month after an Anglo-Dutch war was formally declared). The Armed Neutrality aimed at upholding the most liberal interpretation of neutral rights, that of 'free ships, free goods'. It was more anti-British in effect than in original intention, and aroused considerable resentment in London, doing much, in the longer term, to undermine the view of Russia as a 'natural ally'. At the time its actual impact was rather limited, though it did highlight Britain's isolation in a seemingly hostile Europe.

The question of neutral rights was also one major reason for the outbreak of hostilities between Britain and the Dutch at the end of 1780. A long period of cooperation against Louis XIV had made the two states traditional allies, and memories of this link influenced their policies long after changed circumstances had rendered it redundant. Both the political importance and the economic position of the Dutch had declined significantly during the eighteenth century, and the alliance had become very one-sided, with Britain clearly the dominant partner. At least from the Seven Years War onwards, the Republic's foreign policy – if its international posturings merit that name – had been one of passive neutrality, and this continued during the early stages of the American revolt.

After 1775 the Dutch Republic's stance was increasingly difficult to reconcile with London's expectations. From the very beginning it had been a major American target, particularly for munitions and especially the all-important gunpowder. The Dutch colonial empire in the western hemisphere, particularly the Caribbean islands of St Eustatius and Curaçao, was soon trading extensively with the rebels. Inconveniently from London's perspective, the relevant Anglo-Dutch treaty – that of 1674 – clearly established the liberal doctrine of 'free ships make free goods' and thereby permitted the Republic's merchants to trade with Britain's enemies during wartime. During the first three years of the struggle this produced some tension and rather more resentment. Dutch neutrality was inevitably viewed in London as pro-American, particularly when the Republic refused to provide the aid in troops and ships to which the British government claimed it was entitled under existing treaties. But it was the spread of the war to European waters, and the accompanying sharp increase in the number of Dutch ships seized by British warships and privateers, which led to a marked deterioration in relations and eventually to war. Britain's attack on Dutch shipping during 1778 immediately worsened relations, and this was exacerbated by the rough treatment of the Republic's ministers and even the Stadtholder, William V, by Britain's long-serving ambassador, the notably blunt Sir Joseph Yorke. By 1779–80 relations had been reduced to a very low ebb by the escalating maritime dispute.

Britain eventually declared war on 20 December 1780. The timing was determined by two British decisions. First, ministers became convinced that Dutch trade would be less of a problem if they were enemies rather than neutrals: this would deprive them of the protection of 'free ships'. By the autumn of 1780, the Republic's intention to accede to the Armed Neutrality was clear and with it the real threat (in British eyes) that its stance over neutral rights would secure Russia's formidable support. In the second place, Britain's declaration of war was linked to the Republic's domestic politics, where the feeble, though pro-British, Orangist *régime* of William V was under attack by the Patriots and had been seriously weakened. Britain was the traditional supporter of the stadtholderate, and continued this established approach in what were very changed political circumstances. During the final months of peace, ministers in London, particularly Stormont (in charge of foreign policy and encouraged and, in part, directed by Yorke) became convinced that war might actually revive the stadtholderate's authority, as it had done in 1672 and 1747. The extent of this British miscalculation was to be demonstrated by the fighting's domestic political repercussions (see below, pp. 239–42).

The Fourth Anglo-Dutch War (1780–84) proved a disaster for the Republic. Its navy, as ever a casualty of Dutch domestic politics, had been starved of funds and was in a wretched state, while its colonies in the

West Indies and Ceylon lay open to attack. Though they fought bravely, the Dutch suffered enormous losses, particularly initially of commercial shipping, while the British fleet mopped up Dutch colonies in the Caribbean and the Far East and expelled the Republic's merchants from the Indian subcontinent. French forces subsequently recovered two important losses (Trincomalee in Ceylon and St Eustatius) and occupied the colony at the Cape, but this merely underlined that the Republic was at the mercy of both its ally and its enemy, and had become powerless in international relations.

Dutch disasters, and the Fourth Anglo-Dutch War as a whole, were principally important for their impact on the Republic's internal politics, but the addition of another enemy, however weak, made Britain's naval predicament even worse. Indeed, Britain was largely saved from defeat by the evident shortcomings of the enemy coalition. Throughout, Spain was France's ally not the Americans' (with whom she quarrelled over the area west of the Mississippi) and she single-mindedly pursued her own interests. The successful Florida campaign of 1780–81 underlined the enduring potential of Spanish colonial power and, overall, Madrid's war-effort was moderately successful, though it further stretched its fiscal resources. The European war went less well for Spain. The island of Minorca was captured after a lengthy siege in 1781–82, but another extended siege begun in 1779 failed to secure the prized possession of Gibraltar.

By contrast, France's commitment to the American cause became more positive in 1781, when for the first time strategy was fully coordinated and produced dramatic results. The main French fleet now operated in North American waters, where it held off British reinforcements while the Americans forced the surrender of Yorktown (October 1781). This victory virtually ended the fighting on the mainland and made American independence a *fait accompli*, for British ministers now accepted that reconquest was impossible. Britain's fortunes were everywhere at a low ebb in 1781, but they revived in the final year of the fighting. Rodney's naval victory at the Saints (April 1782) put an end to a series of French conquests in the Caribbean and was the start of a significant British recovery in the final months of the war: a recovery reflected in the terms of peace. By 1782 all the belligerents were war-weary and financially exhausted, and recognised that a negotiated settlement was essential. Britain was prepared to recognise American independence, while the parlous state of French finances in particular demanded an immediate end to the fighting. Though funds could be scraped together for a campaign in 1783, it was believed that money could not be raised for a further year's fighting. It was also recognised at Versailles that Russian intervention in the Crimea (see above, pp. 189–90) and the formal annexation to which this led, demanded peace with Britain as a prelude to possible political cooperation.

The peace negotiations of 1782–83 were complex, reflecting the war's geographical extent and the number of participants and issues involved. Britain's enemies all had differing objectives, and the months of negotiation merely increased the incipient tensions among them. Spain's ambitions seriously delayed the negotiations. She still expected to recover Gibraltar, though her forces had failed to capture it, and also hoped for lands west of the Mississippi, although this obviously conflicted with American aspirations. The American representatives had, superficially, the simplest task: to secure formal recognition for their independence. But their position was weakened by their dependence on France, and their task was further complicated by the territorial ambitions which they attributed – not always correctly – to their Bourbon allies. Spain's appetite for further expansion on the North American mainland was real enough, but the belief that France hoped to annex Canada was wrong. Vergennes wanted Britain to keep it since this would strengthen France's future strategic position by forcing her rival to take account of North America, though this clashed with American ambitions in Canada. The negotiations, which began in autumn 1782, were dominated by Britain and France, who very quickly resolved the issues between themselves, reflecting their overriding need for peace. Vergennes's objectives remained unchanged: a new Franco-British balance as the prelude to a *détente* and even eventual political cooperation in Europe.

In 1782–83, moreover, British aims were identical. London now accepted the loss of the American colonies and wanted a settlement with its other enemies. The resignation of Lord North's administration (March 1782) had made this easier, as its replacement had not had to endure the defeats since 1775, and its own political survival depended on a rapid agreement. The leading spirit in this administration and in the peace negotiations was the Earl of Shelburne. Aided primarily by George III, Shelburne handled all the detailed discussions himself, often behind the backs of his colleagues, and personally negotiated the Anglo-French settlement. The final treaty constituted the one positive if flawed achievement of his career. Though he had held office during the 1760s, he had been in the political wilderness for over a decade when the vagaries of party strife brought him back into power in 1782, first in Rockingham's short-lived government and then from early July as leader of the ministry. The lieutenant and political heir of Chatham, Shelburne was widely distrusted and even more widely hated. To contemporaries he was the 'Jesuit of Berkeley Square'. In private Shelburne could be charming and entertaining, but in public he displayed an aloof sarcasm which alienated friend and foe alike. The ease with which he had discarded his earlier political ideas – the Chathamite Francophobe had become the advocate of political reconciliation with Versailles – together with a distinct evasiveness in personal relations intensified the general suspicion and dislike which he aroused. Yet he was a statesman of unusual vision and real originality, open to the ideas of the European Enlightenment and strongly influenced by *philosophe* ideas of trade liberalisation. He appreciated that peacemaking should be more than a negative surrender, though his ideas could be unrealistic and many had to be abandoned during the discussions. Shelburne demonstrated considerable tactical skill during the negotiations, while the relationship of trust he eventually established with Vergennes paved the way to the final settlement.

The crucial importance of American independence in the modern history of the western world has encouraged historians to conclude that the Anglo-American peace negotiations were most significant. In fact, with the passing of the Conway motion against 'offensive war' in America by the House of Commons at the very end of February 1782, independence had already been accepted in Britain. Shelburne's principal contribution was to dress up military and political necessity – the reconquest of the former colonists was recognised to be impossible – in the guise of magnanimous statesmanship. He dreamed of an Anglophone Atlantic political community being born of a future reconciliation, though this aim was soon revealed to be unrealistic at the end of a long, bitter and bloody civil war. He also hoped that the new American Republic would remain a British economic colony, providing raw materials together with a captive – and growing – market for Britain's nascent Industrial Revolution. He was therefore prepared to grant generous terms. Though Britain retained Canada, the Americans secured a more favourable north-western frontier than anticipated and no obstacles were placed in the way of future expansion westwards. They were also admitted to the Newfoundland Fisheries, and secured less unfavourable terms than they expected over two difficult issues: the Loyalists (those former colonists who had suffered losses due to their continued support for Britain) and the Americans' responsibility for debts to British subjects contracted before the war. The peace preliminaries signed in November 1782 were more generous than the Americans had anticipated, and certainly than their Bourbon allies had intended.

The Anglo-French peace was the most important part of the settlement for contemporaries. Shelburne's ideas once again went beyond the simple search for a negotiated settlement. Recognising that the dominance of the eastern powers had undermined the place in Europe not merely of Britain but of France as well, he set out to construct a treaty which laid the ground for reconciliation and future diplomatic cooperation. This was to be buttressed by a trade agreement, benefitting the economies of both Britain and France and eventually signed in 1786. France, close to bankruptcy, needed peace even more than Britain, while Vergennes fully shared Shelburne's anxieties about the eastern powers, and this eased the path to a settlement. The speed with which peace was negotiated, and the actual terms accepted by each party, were influenced by the revival of British fortunes during the final campaigns of the war. The chief obstacle was, predictably, the scale of Spanish demands. But Howe's relief of Gibraltar (mid-October 1782) eventually broke Madrid's stubbornness. The Spanish negotiator Aranda, under overwhelming French pressure, ignored his formal instructions and accepted terms which left the fortress in British hands. A peace, however, proved easier to secure than Anglo-French diplomatic cooperation. Close political understanding was a difficult and perhaps impossible goal at the end of an extended and highly destructive war. Shelburne himself was swept from power in early 1783, though the Fox-North ministry which succeeded him did endorse the terms he had secured and signed the definitive treaties.

The series of bilateral peace preliminaries between Britain and her enemies in 1782–83 were consolidated into a general settlement signed at Versailles on 3 September 1783. It brought about surprisingly few territorial changes. France acquired the unimportant West Indian island of Tobago, the Senegal River, the right to fortify Dunkirk and minor concessions in the Newfoundland fisheries and in India. Spain received Minorca and Florida together with vague promises that Britain would limit her wood-cutting settlements on the Honduras coast. Dutch intransigence, together with the Republic's cumbersome political structure, delayed the final settlement until May 1784. Britain sought to use the prolonged negotiations to disrupt the Franco-Dutch *rapprochement* under way and restore her own influence, and therefore limited her gains at the Republic's expense. The Dutch gave Britain the long-disputed trading station of Negapatam on the south coast of India, together with the potentially crucial right of navigation among the Indonesian islands, hitherto reserved to the Republic's own merchants. This was the first acknowledged breach in the strict commercial monopoly in the Dutch East Indian archipelago and was to be a fertile source of future disputes.

The principal beneficiary of this settlement was the new American Republic, whose independence was recognised by all the belligerents. Britain's prestige was severely damaged by the loss of the Thirteen Colonies, but her successes in the final campaigns together with French financial exhaustion meant her concessions to her European enemies were far less than had once seemed likely. To a surprising extent the Anglo-Bourbon peace of Versailles restored the situation created by the peace of Paris in 1763. Only in India was France's position really stronger, and then only marginally. Vergennes's strategy of undermining British power by depriving her of economic strength was also unsuccessful, since Britain's near-monopoly of trade with her former colonies survived American independence. Bourbon policy could be said to have failed in real terms. Though each had secured some territorial trophies, the price had been high and, in France's case, would prove to be fatal.

British recovery and French eclipse, 1783–1788

American independence was a triumph for the Bourbon powers, and certainly boosted France's international standing. Yet the costs had been enormous and severely weakened both Bourbon monarchies for the next decade. The war of 1779–83 saddled Spain's government with a recurring peacetime deficit, which the rigidity of the fiscal system did not help to resolve. Spain's substantial territorial gains hardly compensated for her increasing financial chaos, and her foreign policy remained feeble throughout the 1780s. Renewed preoccupation with the western Mediterranean brought further Spanish failures at Algiers, and in 1786 Madrid was forced to sue for peace.

On the other side of the Pyrenees, the established financial and political problems of the French crown now became acute. Louis XVI's government confronted a critical situation. At its heart lay the problem of borrowing and debt repayment. Before the Seven Years War slightly less than 30 per cent of the monarchy's annual income had been devoted to servicing the debt; by 1786 this figure had soared to almost 50 per cent, with an annual deficit in that year of over 100 million *livres*. In the aftermath of the American War, France borrowed even more extensively in peacetime to bridge this massive shortfall, primarily from the international capital market, and this worsened the fundamental weakness of royal finance. The slowing down of economic expansion from the 1770s had intensified these problems. Only increased taxation could ameliorate France's financial difficulties, and securing approval for this seemed unlikely given the widespread fiscal exemptions enjoyed by many of the better-off members of society and the ability of the *parlements* to defend these privileges and block radical reforms. By 1787, with the calling of the Assembly of Notables, the situation was sufficiently serious to remove France from the ranks of the great powers, at least temporarily. In that year it was estimated that no less than three-quarters of the annual budget was committed in some way to supporting France's failing position as a leading European state. In 1788 the foreign ministry was obliged to accept a 42 per cent cut in funding, and this did nothing to improve the effectiveness of French diplomacy. The main lesson of the war of 1778–83, for Vergennes, was that foreign policy had fiscal consequences, which he was now forced to confront directly.

France's problems during the 1780s were far wider. The death in 1781 of Maurepas, the veteran first minister, and the dismissal of the financial supremo Necker in the same year, had deprived the ministry of its earlier stability. The monarchy had lost much of its popularity and even legitimacy during the eighteenth century, and this process was accelerated by the court's scandals and the publicity which accompanied these. By the end of the American War, court and government were fissured by personal rivalries, and these increased during the early years of peace. Vergennes's poor health and preoccupation with domestic affairs, as he strove to establish his leadership of the ministry, contributed to the subdued tone of foreign policy, which aimed only to preserve peace and stability. Relations with Britain improved immediately after 1783. Vergennes's pacific aims coincided with London's wish for reform and retrenchment. Though a commercial treaty was signed in 1786, any prospect of a long-term realignment was wrecked by a new crisis the following year over the Dutch Republic, which made clear the extent of France's eclipse and Britain's parallel recovery.

The British revival was all the more surprising in view of the apparently desperate position London had faced by 1780–81. The recent war had seen Britain fighting France, Spain and her traditional friend and ally, the Dutch Republic, while the issue of neutral trade had united the continent against her in the Armed Neutrality. The loss of the American colonies, though not a serious blow to Britain's actual power, certainly lowered her standing in Europe. Defeat in America, however, had not altered the tenets of British diplomacy, which remained essentially a matter of automatic opposition to France and her ally, Spain. And in the early years of peace – despite the improved relations – there appeared ample evidence of Bourbon hostility. France continued to take what was viewed in London as an unhealthy interest in the prize British possession of India and was attempting to undermine the supremacy of the East India Company by the foundation of a new French company. In the mid-1780s there was significant British concern at the new and large-scale naval base at Cherbourg, intended to replace the existing harbour at Brest, which might (Britain feared) make it easier for the French to dominate the Channel. Its construction was abandoned, due to shortage of funds, in 1789, but not before it had caused significant friction. Though London sought better relations with Spain after 1783, in an attempt to disrupt the Family Compact, problems remained over the perennial problem of British logwood-cutters on the Honduran coast. There was little in the early years of peace to divert the anti-Bourbon grooves along which Britain's diplomacy traditionally ran.

The formal conduct of her foreign policy lay in the hands of the inexperienced and incompetent Marquis of Carmarthen, subsequently Duke of Leeds, nominally foreign secretary from 1783–91. (The system whereby diplomacy was controlled jointly by two secretaries of state had been superseded by the creation of the foreign secretaryship in 1782: see above, p. 136). Carmarthen was not a consistent, far less constructive influence upon British policy, though he was prone to ill-judged initiatives and periodically exaggerated issues. He was an extreme Francophobe and at times this became an obstacle to the good relations desired by the ministry as a whole. As a consequence, foreign policy came to be controlled by the prime minister, William Pitt the Younger, who took office in December 1783 at the age of 24.

Pitt's priorities were peace, reconstruction and commercial expansion, and he was particularly anxious not to incur the expense of a further war. Though the absence of a continental ally troubled some members of the cabinet, the prime minister was at first inclined to accept diplomatic isolation and concentrate upon internal recovery. His economies did not extend to the navy, which was substantially rebuilt during the next decade. Recognising the importance of naval power, Pitt ensured that money was available for the fleet, while Sir Charles Middleton, comptroller of the Navy Board (1778–90), provided the necessary administrative drive. Reforms in Britain's naval dockyards enabled more ships to be refitted and repaired, and by the early 1790s her fleet was in very good condition. Indeed, the period after 1783 saw a naval race, as Spain and France tried to match Britain's efforts and largely succeeded in doing so, contributing to the continuing diplomatic tensions. Despite the prevailing financial economies, the Spanish navy was successfully refitted and rebuilt during the 1780s – albeit on borrowing which could not be sustained – and it remained crucial to relations between the Bourbons and their British rival. The French naval build-up was equally impressive, despite the crown's overwhelming financial problems, but took several years to accomplish, and this facilitated Britain's recovery of the political initiative after 1783.

Pitt knew little of Europe and, until 1786, largely abstained from diplomacy, except for commercial negotiations, which were part of his wider aim of promoting economic recovery. Britain negotiated with eight European countries, though a treaty was concluded only with France. Throughout the eighteenth century Anglo-French trade had been relatively limited, but in the peace of Versailles both states had agreed to conclude a commercial treaty within two years and to appoint commissioners to negotiate this. It had been an imaginative initiative on Shelburne's part, and, after his fall, British ministers showed little enthusiasm for the project. Vergennes, however, was anxious to conclude a treaty, believing that an expansion of trade might alleviate the crisis in the French wine trade and, indirectly, improve the desperate state of French finances, as well as consolidating the recent improvement in diplomatic relations. France therefore proposed that commerce should be established on a reciprocal 'most-favoured nation' basis, and this suggestion was exploited by Britain when Pitt's ministry took up the project in earnest in 1785–86. William Eden was sent to Paris and skilfully negotiated favourable terms. The commercial agreement signed on 26 September 1786 (the Eden Treaty) abolished some tariffs between the two countries and lowered many others. But its effects were not what Louis XVI's ministers had anticipated. British manufactured goods flooded French markets, while French agricultural products failed to penetrate the British.

By the mid-1780s, France's financial weakness, together with a common preoccupation with internal reform, had made diplomacy unusually harmonious. But any thought that the old animosities were disappearing was removed by another crisis in 1787, this time over the Dutch Republic. The defeats during the Fourth Anglo-Dutch War of 1780–84 had highlighted the shortcomings of the Stadtholder, William V, and encouraged the urban patriciate to attack his *régime*. Though this strife between the Regent class and the House of Orange resembled previous political struggles, there was also a new and, very soon, decisive element: the Patriot movement. Whereas the Regents simply wanted to supplant the Orangists, the Patriots were 'democratic': they sought to extend participation in Dutch politics to those groups traditionally excluded, especially the lower middle class, and claimed that political authority was rooted in the sovereignty of the people. In the early 1780s the Patriot movement grew rapidly, acquiring considerable provincial support, a rudimentary party organisation and, through the 'Free Corps' militia, an apparent military potential. Their success was based on their ability to secure support from exactly those social groups which had hitherto supported the Orangists.

Though Regents and Patriots cooperated for some years, by 1785 this tactical alliance was becoming uneasy as the radical movement gained in strength and boldness. In the autumn the Patriots expelled William V from The Hague, the Dutch capital and centre of his power in Holland, and in 1786 they took control of Utrecht. Though the Orangists retained significant support in certain provinces, the feckless Stadtholder was incapable of providing decisive leadership. Frederick the Great had called him 'my booby of a nephew'. But this link with the Prussian royal family – itself the symbol of the Republic's move during the past generation from London's orbit into that of Berlin – was a major political asset. His wife, Princess Wilhelmina, was the niece of Frederick the Great and sister of Frederick William II who became Prussian king in August 1786, and this family connection proved decisive in the crisis of 1787.

By the later 1780s there was complete political deadlock in the Dutch Republic. The Patriots controlled three of the seven provinces, the Stadtholder two, and two were disputed. William V appeared helpless, even though the growing radicalism of the Patriots was producing a *rapprochement* between Regents and Orangists. The real saviour of the House of Orange was to be the British minister at The Hague, Sir James Harris, whose influence in the mid-1780s was increased because – unusually for a foreign diplomat – he knew the Dutch language. Traditionally France had backed the Regents, while British diplomacy had supported the stadtholderate and the House of Orange as London still did. One reason for the British declaration of war on the Republic at the very end of 1780 had been a wish to help restore the authority of the stadtholder (see above, p. 231). But Britain's support for William V in the mid-1780s owed most to the initiatives of the ruthless and resourceful Harris, with first Carmarthen and then Pitt following his lead. Britain's diplomat was resolutely anti-French and wrongly viewed the confused and localised political struggle in the Republic entirely in terms of France's intrigues. There appeared sufficient evidence to support his interpretation: the Patriots were now being supported by Versailles, and a Franco-Dutch treaty of friendship and alliance had been signed in November 1785 after Vergennes had successfully defused the Republic's serious dispute with Austria over the Scheldt (see above, p. 183). After its conclusion Harris moved onto the offensive against the growing French ascendancy, setting about organising the Orangists and so rescuing William V. His tactics were a mixture of skilful bribery and intimidation; he risked civil war and did much to bring about the crisis of 1787, for the Orangists' counter-attack contributed to the increasing extremism of the Patriots.

Harris could act ruthlessly partly because he was receiving more political and financial support from London as Pitt assumed greater control over policy, effectively superseding Carmarthen from late 1786. Largely under Harris's tutelage – the two met frequently in spring 1787, when the envoy returned to London – the initially more moderate prime minister recognised the French threat and provided money for the Orangists. Though Pitt did not want a war, he had no wish to see France dominate the Low Countries: a traditional British strategic concern, lying as it did on the other side of the 'Narrow Seas'. The American War had added a colonial dimension to the established support for the Republic. Dutch bases at the Cape, Ceylon and Sumatra had been important to France during the recent fighting, enabling her for the first time to operate a squadron effectively in the Indian Ocean, and this, together with impressive Dutch naval reconstruction, reinforced Britain's desire to keep it out of the French orbit. By early summer, the prime minister had moved steadily towards outright resistance to France, sharing Harris's conviction that Versailles was too weak to risk war. In fact, the diplomat, who suffered from the common British failing of viewing all developments solely in terms of Anglo-French rivalry, had exaggerated both the extent of France's commitment and actual control over her Dutch allies. His error became evident when the crisis finally broke in the summer of 1787 with the arrest of Princess Wilhelmina by the Patriots.

His sister's detention drove the previously indecisive Frederick William II to dispatch a series of ultimatums to the Patriots in the summer. Britain encouraged Prussia and sought to neutralise any French threat. The means adopted was the familiar one of naval blackmail: in September Pitt briefly mobilised a sizeable fleet. In fact, France was now trying to avoid a clash over the Dutch Republic, where her diplomacy was in disarray. She had been drawn to intervene principally by the enthusiasm of her agents there. France could not control the Patriot movement and was becoming alarmed at its radicalism. The fissures within the French ministry, until now confined to the related issues of the *parlements* and royal finance, spilled over into diplomacy in the Republic, as Vergennes' rivals sent their own, unofficial, diplomatic agents to the Dutch capital, where they pursued policies which were often far more radical than the foreign minister wished.

The result was that there were never fewer than two foreign policies operating there nominally in France's name, as the fierce ministerial and court rivalries of these years came to be fought out by proxy on the Republic's soil. Vergennes, his own health failing as his political authority ebbed away, could not impose a coherent policy and was as much the pawn of the Patriots as their master. Above all, French policy was determined, as it had been since 1783, by financial weakness: Versailles simply could not risk a new war, as Vergennes clearly recognised during the final six months of his life. On Vergennes' death in February 1787, Montmorin, who became foreign minister, briefly considered active support for the Patriots and war with Britain. But French weakness, together with a preoccupation with the Assembly of Notables, ruled this out and, once it was apparent that France would do nothing, Pitt left the field clear for Prussia's army to resolve the crisis.

Frederick William II finally decided to act on hearing (7 September 1787) of the Ottoman declaration of war on Russia (see above, p. 191). This removed any anxieties about Austrian intervention, for the King and Hertzberg concluded Joseph II would have to aid his Russian ally. In mid-September a Prussian force of 25,000 men invaded the Republic. Faced with real soldiers, the Patriot militia collapsed and, within a month, the Stadtholder's authority had been restored. Although the formal glory belonged to Frederick William II's troops, Pitt and Harris certainly contributed to the triumph and Britain harvested the main diplomatic benefits. The episode revealed both the utter impotence of the Dutch – the Republic was now treated like Poland or the Ottoman Empire – and the weakness and mounting internal problems of France, who had suffered a major reverse. By the autumn of 1787, events in the Republic seemed far less important to French ministers than their difficulties with the *parlement* of Paris.

The immediate result of William V's restoration was to worsen Anglo-French relations by forcing France to declare she would not intervene. Pitt, more confident after his success in 1787, now set about constructing an old style anti-French alliance, seeking treaties with the Dutch Republic and Prussia. He was encouraged in this by Joseph Ewart, the influential and youthful minister in Berlin (see above, p. 199). Negotiations with both states began immediately after the restoration of the Stadtholder, but proved more difficult and extended than anticipated. Pitt wanted an Anglo-Dutch treaty to consolidate the recent success over France, to settle colonial disputes in the Far East and to prevent Prussia's gaining too much influence at The Hague. Although the Dutch too were anxious for an alliance, progress was delayed by the British insistence on first resolving the colonial difficulties. Only when this condition was dropped could an agreement be concluded (April 1788). In the same month Prussia signed a similar defensive alliance with the Republic.

Discussions had also been in progress for an Anglo-Prussian agreement, but these proved difficult. This was because of Britain's suspicions about Prussia's wide-ranging ambitions in the Russo-Ottoman War (see above, p. 192). Pitt feared the threat to the territorial *status quo* and to the continental balance of power. He was therefore worried that an alliance with Berlin might drag Britain into a new war and destroy her financial recovery. He would have preferred a wider alliance with other powers, but overcame his reservations when it seemed (late May 1788) as if the volatile Prussian King might join France instead. As the treaty was partly intended to prevent such a Prusso-French alignment, Britain now acted. Harris negotiated directly and successfully with Frederick William II, who was visiting the Dutch Republic: an agreement was signed on 13 August. This completed the so-called Triple Alliance of 1788, which was in reality not a single treaty but a triangular series of defensive alliances between Britain, Prussia and the Dutch Republic.

The Triple Alliance, together with Britain's earlier success in the Dutch Republic, superficially marked her return to an active role in Europe after a quarter-century of effective isolation. The next few years saw increasing concern with the continent, as Pitt dreamed of restoring peace and stability through a British-dominated Triple Alliance. Yet the prime minister remained wary of Prussia's elaborate schemes; in 1788–91 he aimed primarily to contain the war in the Balkans and, if possible, maintain the existing territorial balance. Ultimately, this made British foreign policy anti-Russian, since it sought to preserve the Ottoman Empire and deny Catherine II further territorial gains. In 1791 Pitt even tried, briefly and completely unsuccessfully, to force Russia to give up Ochakov (see above, pp. 198–200). But this brief crisis only revealed Britain's limited influence, especially in eastern Europe. Her temporary anti-Russian role, moreover, was only possible because of France's virtual withdrawal from international affairs during the early phase of the French Revolution, which began in the summer of 1789.

CHAPTER 9

Europe and the French Revolution, 1789–1797

The initial impact of the Revolution

The outbreak of the French Revolution can be recognised, in retrospect, as one of the most decisive events in modern history. The prolonged warfare it unleashed was to prove a similar watershed in the development of the international system. By 1793, Europe was at war with the Revolution and this conflict was to continue, with only one real pause (in 1802–3), until France's final defeat in 1815. Yet this struggle did not immediately come to dominate European politics, whatever its longer-term significance. The destruction of Poland and the fate of the Ottoman Empire (see Chapter 7) remained important and, on occasions, overriding issues throughout the War of the First Coalition (1793–97). The political legacies of the previous generation – the barriers between eastern and western Europe and the rivalries among the three eastern powers – were also an obstacle to concerted opposition to France. By the second half of the 1790s, however, the Revolution had restored western and central Europe to the forefront of political calculations. Revolutionary France's military successes gradually ended the division of the continent into two largely distinct spheres, which had prevailed since the Seven Years War. Throughout the next generation French power, which revived spectacularly during the later 1790s and 1800s, once again became the central issue in international relations. In resolving it, Europe's leading states finally completed the modern great power system.

The quarter-century from 1789 to 1815 was to be of considerable significance for European diplomacy. Although there was continuity in its formal, institutional framework, there were several important innovations which did not become fully apparent until after the settlement at Vienna.

A need to coordinate the military struggle against France eventually produced closer cooperation between the great powers and, finally, the notion of permanent consultation and coordinated action. The famous 'Congress System' after 1815, with its implicit belief that statesmen should control and even shape events, rather than merely respond to them, had its origins in the long wars against France. The diplomacy of the Revolutionary and Napoleonic period, moreover, was always strongly influenced, and sometimes even determined, by changing military fortunes to an unprecedented extent. Months of patient negotiation could be undermined by one battle. Diplomacy in wartime posed particular problems and European governments only slowly adjusted to its new demands. Above all, international relations acquired a new, ideological dimension. The older dynastic and territorial motives behind foreign policy came to be supplemented, though never completely replaced, by the idea that the struggle between Europe and the French Revolution was one between conflicting views of society and political organisation. Increasingly, the European monarchies aimed not merely at the military defeat of France and the restoration of a territorial equilibrium – the conventional objectives of eighteenth-century warfare. They also sought to reverse the political changes which had taken place during the 1790s and to restore a more familiar, and therefore less menacing, régime in Paris. The Younger Pitt spoke for Europe when he declared in 1794 that he had 'no idea of any peace being secure, unless France return to a monarchical system'. Such ideological considerations, however, only gradually permeated international relations, for the Revolution did not at first arouse the hostility of most governments, and few contemporaries were initially aware of the momentous significance of events in Paris and the French provinces from the summer of 1789.

Initial reactions were far from unanimous. Particular responses were determined by local circumstances and by the proximity, or otherwise, to France. The attitude of Europe was a variable blend of individual and private enthusiasm, official hostility and simple indifference. Considerable enthusiasm was immediately apparent in intellectual circles, particularly in Germany, where many writers interpreted events in France as the birth of a new era. The generation of Kant, Herder, Wieland and even the more cautious Goethe and Schiller were initially united in welcoming the Revolution. Intellectuals in the Italian peninsula were equally enthusiastic. Similar support was to be found elsewhere in Europe. In England the existence of a movement for reform, particularly parliamentary reform, ensured that events in France at first received considerable popular support, while Charles James Fox, leader of the Whig opposition, famously apostrophised the fall of the Bastille as the greatest and best event in human history.

In official circles, the French Revolution was at first viewed mostly with indifference and only occasionally hostility. Governments throughout Europe were notably slow to appreciate the potentially subversive nature of political materials spreading from France. The one important state anxious from the very outset was Spain, where a determined attempt was made to isolate the Spanish people from any possible repercussions. As early as spring 1789 the official press in Madrid ceased to report events in France. The considerable French colony in the peninsula was kept under close surveillance; the periodical press was suspended in 1791, when troops tried to seal the border with France; and stringent efforts were made to prevent the circulation of any news from Revolutionary France. In several of the smaller German Rhineland territories, particularly Mainz and Trier, the early stages of the French Revolution produced similar concern to that in Madrid, and brought to a precipitate end attempts at enlightened reform. The presence of French *émigrés*, together with the Rhineland's proximity to France, strengthened this concern.

Initially, however, events in Paris were largely ignored by European governments. The period of internal confusion in France was widely seen as an opportunity for other states to benefit, as they usually did, from a rival's internal weakness. France's international collapse in the later 1780s (see above, pp. 236-7) encouraged this approach. Her effective disappearance as a European power allowed Britain a further triumph over Spain in 1790. In that spring a serious Anglo-Spanish dispute blew up and for six months another War of Jenkins' Ear appeared possible. The ostensible cause was a clash over Nootka Sound. Located on the west coast of what is now Vancouver Island, though it was then believed to be part of the mainland, the Sound was the finest natural harbour north of San Francisco. It had long been part of Spain's territorial sphere, but during the preceding quarter-century Madrid had been forced to defend its cherished colonial monopoly here against both Russian and British rivals. The seventeenth-century expansion of the Muscovite state into Siberia had carried Russian traders across the Bering Strait and into Alaska. The potential value of sea-otter pelts, and the thriving fur trade with China which developed from Russia's base in the Aleutian Islands, had established one rival in the North Pacific. In 1784, the Russians had set up a forward base on Kodiak Island (off Alaska) and had begun to push southwards, exploring the coastline.

Britain's growing involvement during the final decades of the eighteenth century proceeded both from the established interest in discovering

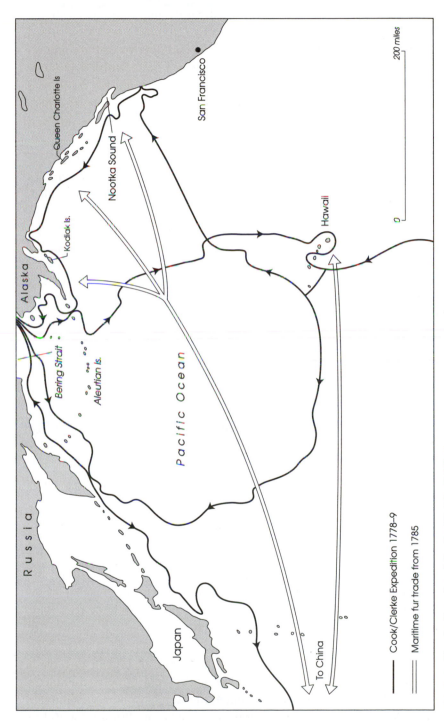

MAP 8 *Nootka Sound and the Pacific North-West*
Source: P.J. Marshall (ed.), *Oxford History of the British Empire: Vol 2 – The Eighteenth Century* (Oxford University Press, 2001), p. 569

a north-west passage to the Pacific and, more immediately, from the enhanced awareness of the region created by Captain James Cook's third and final voyage (1776–79), during which he had discovered the commercial potential of the fur trade. It had encouraged both British merchants searching for the fabulous profits to be gained from the fur trade, and Spanish counter-measures to secure their own exclusive sovereignty. These combined to produce a serious diplomatic crisis which lasted for much of 1790.

Once again, governments in Europe found themselves forced to react to events at the very periphery of empire, familiar from earlier clashes over the Falkland Islands (see above, pp. 219–20). In 1789 a Spanish squadron had been sent to secure the coastline northwards from San Francisco (the limit of Spain's settlements in California) and to establish a base in Nootka Sound. It had seized four British ships discovered in the Sound, detained their crews and destroyed a British trading post there. Although the episode was minor, far wider issues were involved. The spectacular growth of Britain's 'empire of trade' after 1783 had brought it into conflict with the decaying Spanish American empire. Indeed, sporadic British activities seemed part of a sustained attempt to break into the Pacific. Spain had already tacitly abandoned her claim to monopolise the region by accepting Russian settlements in Alaska, but it was determined to control the long coast between Spanish California and the Russian outpost. The real issue was not the incident at Nootka Sound, but Madrid's claim to a territorial monopoly in north-west America, which conflicted with tentative British attempts to open up the Pacific and to share in its fur trade and in the lucrative and fast-growing whaling activities.

When the first news reached Europe in late January 1790 both states hoped for a peaceful settlement; at this point it was believed that only one ship had been taken. But in the spring Britain's attitude stiffened when the full extent of the seizures, together with Spain's claim to justify them, became evident. The foreign secretary, Leeds, adopted an extremely bellicose stance which alarmed his cabinet colleagues, and, before long, the prime minister had once again assumed responsibility for Britain's response. This did not signal a more moderate approach on London's part. Pitt, who faced an election the next year, quickly recognised the opportunity for a diplomatic triumph. Charles IV, who had become King of Spain in 1788, was weak and inexperienced and might find it difficult to resist a British show of strength. The French Revolution had completed France's eclipse as a European power and disrupted the Family Compact, effectively isolating Spain. In the final stages of the confrontation, Pitt was careful to send two unofficial envoys to Paris to reassure the leaders of the Constituent (or 'National') Assembly that Britain did not intend to attack France.

The prime minister adopted a warlike posture which reflected both his growing confidence in foreign policy, and his wider interest in overseas expansion. He was supported by popular enthusiasm for war, particularly following the publication in May of an exaggerated account of events at Nootka by the owner of the British ships, John Meares, which inflamed the situation. Britain kept her fleet mobilised for six months from May until the dispute was settled, and Howe patrolled off France's Atlantic coast with a powerful squadron, to underline London's willingness to fight, while plans to attack the Spanish Caribbean were drawn up. The origins might lie in the remote north-west of America, but Britain intended that any war would be fought much nearer home. The Spanish government was left in no doubt that Britain was ready for full-scale hostilities unless her demands were met.

This was the dominant factor throughout this crisis. Though Spain had rebuilt her fleet impressively and mobilised a month before the British, she found it as difficult as ever to man these ships and, crucially, lacked the political will to fight. Her finances were in no condition for war, while she was unable to rally France to her side. A formal request for aid was made in mid-June, but the weakness of the French King's own position ensured it was not passed on to the Constituent Assembly for six weeks. Louis XVI would have liked to uphold the Family Compact and support Spain but, though the dispute raised considerable anti-British feeling in France, the whole issue became entangled and ultimately submerged in revolutionary politics. The Constituent Assembly challenged the King's right to declare war, and Madrid received no reply to its requests for help at critical points in summer 1790. By contrast, Britain was promised support from her Dutch and Prussian allies. Weak and isolated, Spain had to agree in late July to release the captured ships and to pay compensation. But this failed to satisfy the British prime minister, who sought trade and fishing rights together with the abandonment of Madrid's claim to exclusive sovereignty. Increasing Spanish disquiet at the radical events in Paris made it unwilling to accept French support, even when the Assembly voted in August to arm 45 ships of the line. The impact of this decision, which was an attempt to contribute to a peaceful settlement rather than to prepare for hostilities, was in any case considerably reduced by the foreign minister's assurances to London that it would be carried out very slowly and by the chaotic state of the French navy after 15 months of revolutionary upheaval.

The Spanish foreign minister, Floridablanca, once again had to give way to *force majeure* and concede London's demands. An Anglo-Spanish settlement, the so-called Nootka Sound Convention, was concluded at the end of October 1790. It brought Britain substantial gains: compensation for the seizures, which were restored, access to the coastline between Alaska and California, and Spanish acceptance that British whalers could fish in the Pacific. More importantly, however, it signalled the effective ending of Spain's claim to monopolise the trade and colonisation of the region, and made possible further British and foreign incursions, as London had always intended. Pitt's brutal diplomacy, based on continuing naval supremacy, had thus been successful. The wider significance of the dispute was its demonstration of France's international collapse and the opportunity for her rivals to benefit.

It had been evident for several years. Prussia's foreign minister had reacted to the Bastille's fall by hoping the confusion might undermine the Franco-Austrian alliance and so benefit Berlin. Two years earlier, in December 1787, Joseph II had predicted that severe domestic problems would prevent the French aiding the Ottoman Empire in its war with the Russo-Austrian alliance. As late as September 1791, Kaunitz, arguing against any thought of a war of intervention, had stated bluntly that 'The new constitution renders France far less dangerous than she was under the old *régime*'. He went on to declare that 'The alleged danger of the possible effects of the evil example of the French on the other peoples is nothing but a nightmare'. There was, in 1789–90 and even subsequently, little serious anxiety; the revolutionary potential and infectious nature of developments in Paris were simply not appreciated. Indeed, the disturbances in France initially seemed to many observers to be less serious than the contemporary upheavals in Poland, the Austrian Netherlands and Hungary. If any monarchy appeared in peril in 1789–90 it was that of the Austrian Habsburgs and not the French Bourbons.

In a similar way, though the danger of a general European war appeared considerable at this time, France would not be the occasion for such hostilities. Eastern Europe's complex rivalries appeared a much more likely source of a wider conflict. Russia was simultaneously fighting the Ottoman Empire (as was Austria) and Sweden (see Chapter 7). It was widely believed that Britain and her allies, the Dutch Republic and Prussia, might employ force to restrain Catherine's territorial ambitions against the defeated Ottoman Empire. France did not occupy a prominent place in the political calculations of the other states. For the moment, Europe's rulers had sufficient problems without giving more than passing attention to events in Paris. They did not, as yet, feel particularly hostile towards the new *régime* in France, which remained a monarchy, and welcomed the pacific foreign policy pursued by the Constituent Assembly during the first two years of the Revolution. Nor were they at this stage threatened by the kind of popular unrest within their own territories which might have aroused real anxiety about the dangers of revolutionary 'contagion' from France.

The French government, for its part, saw no real threat from Europe until the middle of 1791, though an exaggerated fear of foreign intervention was widespread and, at times, influential. It was, in any case, preoccupied with domestic affairs. The dramatic events which signalled the outbreak of the Revolution – the fall of the Bastille, the 'abolition of feudalism' on the night of 4 August 1789, the march to Versailles and the symbolic return of the monarch to his capital – were followed by a lengthy and less spectacular, though no less significant, period of political and constitutional change. A series of important reforms in local government, the detailed agrarian measures made essential by the declaration that the feudal *régime* in the countryside had been abolished, and important religious changes (particularly the Civil Constitution of the Clergy) occupied the early months and years of the Revolution. Measures such as these did not arouse much fear in the other European capitals, while revolutionary violence had not reached such proportions as to generate widespread alarm. Above all, there had been no direct challenge to the continued existence of France's monarchy nor any real threat to the royal family. But a significant shift in attitudes can be detected from mid-1791 onwards. The war which broke out in the spring of 1792 between France and the two German powers, Austria and Prussia, was to have a significant ideological dimension, and this would increase during the years which followed.

The origins of the War of 1792

The *émigrés*, from the very beginning of the Revolution, had been the one group who had consistently urged and attempted to organise armed intervention from abroad. Until the spring of 1792 there were, in practice, few restraints on leaving France and a considerable number of noblemen, churchmen and army officers had fled, either from anxiety about their own future, or revulsion at recent events, or both. The first important *émigré* was Louis XVI's brother, the comte d'Artois, who, along with two other princes of the blood, left immediately after the fall of the Bastille and took up residence, with the aristocrats who followed them, briefly in

Brussels and then more permanently in Turin. The *émigrés* organised themselves effectively, with a government-in-exile and, by early 1792, a dozen
diplomatic representatives in European capitals. Until the early months of
1791, the King of Sardinia's court was the centre of this activity. Leadership naturally devolved on Artois; political direction came to be provided
by the former controller-general of finance, Calonne, who had himself
gone into exile before the Revolution and came to Turin in late 1790.
The 'Turin Committee' was very active in 1789–90, planning to rescue
the King, plotting counter-revolutionary insurrections within France, and
seeking foreign financial and military assistance to restore monarchical
absolutism. Several European rulers – Catherine II, predictably enough,
Charles IV of Spain, even the impoverished Prussian King, Frederick
William II – provided funds, which enabled the movement to conduct
wide-ranging political activities and maintain a small army. But these rulers
had different priorities, baulked at providing large-scale military support
and were, at this stage, in no rush to restore royal absolutism in France.
The *émigrés* were singularly unsuccessful in their wider activities, and
their most obvious achievement was to alienate the King of Sardinia, who
ordered them to leave early in 1791.

They failed primarily because they could not secure the foreign military
assistance essential for success and, in particular, the support of the
Habsburgs, whose attitude in 1789–92 was decisive. Vienna had never
been especially sympathetic towards the *émigrés*. Joseph II had perempt-
orily cut short their stay in the Austrian Netherlands by ordering them
out of Brussels, while his successor after February 1790, Leopold II, was
initially little disposed to support the cause of counter-revolution. The
new Emperor was favourable to constitutional, even representative, government, as had been apparent during his rule in Tuscany, and he sympath-
ised with the early, moderate reforms. The acute internal problems which
Leopold faced on his accession were in any case his priority. Joseph II's
wide-ranging reforms had provoked considerable opposition throughout
the Monarchy and produced open insurrection in the Austrian Netherlands and near-rebellion in Hungary. There was also the unfinished
war against the Ottoman Empire, which was running into difficulties as
Prussia threatened military intervention. Leopold devoted his short reign
(1790–92) to dealing with this critical situation and generally making the
Josephinian reforms more acceptable. The Austrian Netherlands were
reoccupied by Habsburg troops; Hungarian resentment was skilfully
appeased by concessions, while Austria soon came to terms with Berlin
and withdrew from the conflict in the Balkans (see above, pp. 196–8).

These purely Habsburg problems strengthened his inclination to ignore the pleas of the *émigrés*.

There were, however, important reasons why Leopold might be drawn to intervene. As Emperor, he was constitutionally obliged to defend the territory and uphold the privileges of the German princes against the strident demands which the French were making along the Rhine. As the brother of France's Marie Antoinette, he received frequent pleas about the threat to the French royal family, though he had never been especially close to a sister he had not seen for a quarter of a century and at first he does not seem to have been greatly concerned. As the most obvious source of substantial military support, he was the target of incessant requests for assistance from the *émigrés*. Until summer 1791, however, Leopold revealed little interest in French affairs. In May he met Artois at Mantua where he proved unwilling to act against the new *régime* in Paris. His own pacific attitude, together with a wish to do nothing to imperil the position of the French royal family, made him reject all appeals for assistance.

This reluctance to contemplate war was only slowly undermined by the radical developments in France and the increasing personal danger to the royal family. Louis XVI, and especially Marie Antoinette, had, from the summer of 1790, pursued a series of international initiatives designed to restore royal authority. These intersected both with the activities of the *émigrés* and with the schemes for the royal family to flee France. The two central figures in this shadowy and confused private diplomacy were Breteuil and Fersen. The Baron de Breteuil had been a leading diplomat and minister before 1789, and in July of that year had been briefly first minister. During the early years of the Revolution he was to be indefatigable in the cause of the beleaguered royal family, acting as their leading minister in exile. That was even more true of the Swedish count Hans Axel von Fersen, agent of Gustav III and close friend – and probably lover – of Marie Antoinette.

Their efforts to secure international support became more urgent during the winter of 1790–91. Increasingly, however, the danger to the royal family was believed to inhibit any crusade to restore the authority of the French monarchy. It was one reason for the flight to Varennes (June 1791), which proved a crucial episode. From the very outset there had been various schemes for Louis XVI to flee France and to take command of an army of reconquest, but these had always foundered on the King's dim sense of duty and refusal to desert his post. Only in spring 1791 was such a plan finally sanctioned by Louis XVI, increasingly conscious that the Revolution would not simply run out of steam as he hoped and tormented by the approval he had been forced to give to the religious reforms. He now recognised that only foreign intervention could save his throne, and tried to bring this about by leaving France. The attempt was a fiasco, as its organisation fell apart. Once outside Paris the escape became a leisurely monarchical progress, and the royal party was ignominiously recaptured at Varennes and brought back to the capital under guard. Shortly afterwards the King was temporarily suspended from his functions, with the Constituent Assembly taking over full control of government, while the royal family was held under house arrest in the Tuileries.

The repercussions were considerable. There was widespread anxiety within France that foreign intervention was on hand, and military preparations were hastily begun. The apparent existence of an external threat to the Revolution was, henceforth, an increasingly important factor in French domestic politics. The unpopularity of France's Austrian alliance ever since its inception in 1756 and the parallel support for a treaty with Prussia had made Austrophobia widespread, and this sentiment flourished in the early years of the Revolution. It coalesced with an exaggerated view of the court's counter-revolutionary activities to produce the influential myth of the 'Austrian committee', a cabal in the Tuileries headed by the Habsburg Queen and intent on reversing the Revolution. There was sufficient circumstantial evidence to give plausibility to ideas of a super-conspiracy, and such notions flourished as the external threat increased. The Varennes episode, however, was of even greater importance outside France. A wave of sympathy for Louis XVI, indignation at his treatment and anxiety for his fate swept round Europe, and it was strengthened by Marie Antoinette's incessant intrigues and pleas for assistance.

In the immediate aftermath of the attempted flight, Leopold was moved to issue an appeal (the 'Padua Circular', July 1791) to his fellow rulers proposing a joint declaration to secure the release of the royal family. He assumed that France's new leaders could be intimidated by a display of monarchical solidarity. Though it was the first occasion he had come out publicly against the Revolution, the Emperor was not prepared to go any further than this kind of intimidation, and he never sought a war against France. Austria's finances were in no shape to support more fighting, after the recent Ottoman War, and in that summer a cut of 25,000 in the strength of the army was pushed through, underlining that military intervention was not intended. Yet, in retrospect, the summer of 1791 can be seen as decisive for the creation of the international constellation which would fight France. The failure of the flight to Varennes increased Vienna's anxieties about developments in France. This in turn heightened Austria's dependence upon Berlin, and so accelerated the *rapprochement* which was under way. It would strengthen during the next six months and by early 1792 produce a firm Prusso-Austrian alliance against the Revolution.

Leopold's fellow monarchs were no more united in their desire to intervene directly, though several gave subsidies to the *émigrés*. The Revolution's principal opponents at this stage were the rulers of Sweden and Russia. Gustav III fervently preached the doctrine of intervention against the 'Orang Outangs of Europe' and, alone of contemporary rulers, planned to attack France. Sweden's King was a personal friend of Artois' elder brother, the comte de Provence (the future Louis XVIII, who himself emigrated in the summer of 1791), and an inveterate foe of the Revolution. In June of that year, Gustav had travelled to Aix-la-Chapelle (Aachen), ostensibly to take the waters there, but in fact to meet the expected royal refugees who instead were captured at Varennes. But his resources were limited, his country close to bankrupt and Sweden too far away for him to act effectively on his own. He was, in any case, to be assassinated in March 1792.

Catherine II was undoubtedly as ill-disposed to the Revolution, encouraging Gustav III and Leopold II in 1791–92 to intervene in a royalist crusade which never materialised, and she took the opportunity to insult the French ambassador. Significantly – along with the Swedish King – she was the sole European ruler to favour a revival of France's power brought about by a full restoration of absolute monarchy, since she believed this would create a counterweight to Britain's dominance in western Europe. She never ceased to press the cause of the *émigrés* at Vienna and Berlin, and in 1793 she would lionise Artois when he visited. But her attention remained fixed on Poland and the Ottoman Empire and territorial acquisitions there. Britain appeared indifferent (see below, p. 263), while Austria wanted to keep France stable but weak, and believed that the existing constitutional monarchy would do this more effectively than a restored Bourbon absolutism. Only Prussia's Frederick William II consistently called for military intervention; yet he too wanted to annex Polish territory and was also unwilling to act unilaterally against France. There was, in mid-1791, little prospect of any concerted action against the Revolution, despite the growing hostility of individual governments. The burgeoning Austro-Prussian *rapprochement* (see above, pp. 254–5) now produced the declaration of Pillnitz (27 August 1791), a joint statement by the Emperor and the King of Prussia of their concern at the predicament of Louis XVI, and hope that united international action would be undertaken to extricate him. This was much less menacing than it appeared at first sight, however: it also stated that Austria and Prussia would do nothing unless and until they were joined by the other European states, which its authors knew was improbable. The declaration was in fact a discreet recipe for inaction by the major powers.

The agreement at Pillnitz nevertheless contributed to the mounting anxiety already apparent within France. Its threatening tone could only increase French fears that outside intervention was imminent. During the second half of 1791, moreover, war came to be seen by several French political factions as the means to achieve their objectives. In particular, the war party in the new Legislative Assembly, with significant support in the Jacobin Club and fervently led by J.P. Brissot, made significant progress during the winter of 1791–92, while King, court and aristocracy all saw open hostilities as a means to restore the traditional order. The decisive political development was the 'war of peoples against kings' which the Brissotins advocated from October onwards. Brissot was a demagogic orator of rare skill, and his campaign was aided by the location of the Assembly's debates, which took place in the Manège, a former riding school close to the Tuileries with space for several hundred enthusiastic spectators. Its deliberations assumed more the character of a political rally than of a measured debate. The fact that the Legislative Assembly, which had just come into existence (1 October 1791), was largely composed of inexperienced and, in many cases, more radical politicians exacerbated this problem: members of the former Constituent Assembly, which ceased to meet at the end of September, had excluded themselves from its successor, and this facilitated Brissot's aims.

He was far from alone in seeking to confound his enemies by fostering war. After mid-September, when the King was forced to take an oath to the new constitution, which in reality he rejected, Louis XVI and Marie Antoinette increased their efforts to secure international pressure and even military intervention. The Queen was especially active, and her appeals to Leopold were significant during the final months of peace. The Emperor was now more inclined to action than the veteran Chancellor Kaunitz, and began to heed his sister's entreaties. These pleas were reinforced from Berlin in particular, leading to the adoption of an Austrian strategy of intimidation which in turn strengthened French determination to resist: exactly the reverse of what was intended in Vienna. Within French politics, however, the court's private diplomacy was to be even more important, contributing to a more and more febrile political atmosphere.

The activities of the *émigrés* aroused particular alarm within France, an alarm which far exceeded the actual threat they posed. Their importance lay not in what they had actually achieved, which was little enough, but in what they symbolised and seemed capable of bringing about. The presence of Artois and Calonne at Pillnitz was what impressed observers in Paris, although their actual influence had been minimal. In a similar way, the concentration of *émigré* activity in the Rhineland and in particular at Coblenz, after the movement's expulsion from Turin, aroused considerable anxiety due to the proximity to French territory. The 'court in exile' at Coblenz was known to be in contact with counter-revolutionary forces within France. It was – in view of the Pillnitz declaration – wrongly believed to be capable of exerting considerable influence at the other European courts. It was subsidised by leading continental rulers and able to maintain a considerable army in the Rhineland (though this force began to disintegrate in the winter of 1791–92 as the money ran out).

During the winter of 1791–92 there was mounting tension, caused partly by French fears of an attack and partly by Austria's continuing conviction that France could be intimidated. These Habsburg threats inevitably helped to raise the political temperature in Paris. Although Leopold really intended to strengthen the moderates in French politics, he actually strengthened the radicals. In Vienna, as in Europe's other capitals, attitudes were changing. The political élite had long underestimated the potential threat of the revolution and its challenge to the old order. Yet it was becoming more difficult to ignore French breaches of international treaties and what were viewed as established legal rights. This was central to the disputes which flared up first over papal enclaves within France and then disputed areas on the eastern border.

Avignon and the Comtat Venaissin were two small territories in southern France which the Papacy had governed for five centuries. From the very beginning of the Revolution their inhabitants had been agitating for reunification to France, but their pleas were rejected out of hand in Rome and received little influential support in Paris. In summer 1790 they rose against the papal administrators and demanded reincorporation into the French state, citing the doctrine of popular sovereignty as a justification. It took some time – and significant fighting in the Comtat – to accomplish, since the *régime* in Paris recognised its combustible potential and adopted a moderate stance. The issue also became submerged in the wider and much more serious dispute over the Civil Constitution of the Clergy. In September 1791, however, the Constituent Assembly voted to incorporate the enclaves. The Austrian ambassador melodramatically described the decision as a declaration of war on the established monarchies. Although this was an exaggeration, he was correct to point to the threat represented by the assertion of national sovereignty to an international system based upon the sanctity of treaties as well as upon monarchical power.

The growing divide which this represented between the Revolution and Europe was even more evident in a second dispute which concerned the rights of the owners of fiefs in eastern France. Vienna's blustering support for the German princes who claimed that their rights in Alsace had been infringed caused even more resentment during the final months of peace. This complex dispute resulted from the ambiguity of the Peace of Westphalia (1648) over Alsace. Although it had ceded Habsburg possessions there to France, it had specifically guaranteed the feudal privileges of certain German princes. The obvious limitation upon French sovereignty had been explicitly confirmed by several later treaties. The problem was how far, if at all, these Imperial enclaves were affected by the declaration of 4 August 1789, which had abolished the feudal régime throughout France. The French government believed that Alsace was part of its territory and that national sovereignty enabled it to legislate there as it wished. The German princes, on the other had, believed that they were their property, and that their feudal privileges in Alsace were guaranteed by treaty and could not simply be swept away by the French government. They refused to accept the compensation offered and appealed to the Emperor, though most would have favoured a negotiated settlement of the dispute.

Leopold II was at first happy to exploit the opportunities for delay provided by the cumbersome machinery of the Empire. In July 1791, however, the Imperial Diet pronounced in favour of the princes' claim, and the Emperor was finally obliged to take up the matter with France in the following December. The high-handed tone of the resulting dispatch aroused resentment in Paris, as did the apparent protection now being given to the *émigrés* by two Rhineland ecclesiastical electors, the Archbishops of Mainz and Trier. France's protest was met with a statement by the Emperor that, while the *émigrés* should be dispersed, he would protect the Elector of Trier's territory if it was violated by French troops seeking out *émigrés*. The inflammatory language and provocative tone of these exchanges between December 1791 and March 1792 accurately reflected, and also contributed to, the hardening of attitudes both in Paris, where a new willingness for war was visible, and in Vienna; Berlin had long been willing and even anxious to fight. At the same time, however, these negotiations underlined Leopold's continuing conviction that France could be intimidated into concessions.

The sudden and unexpected death of the Emperor on 1 March 1792 preceded the outbreak of war, but did not contribute substantially to it.

From the very beginning Leopold II had resisted the arguments of the *émigrés* and of Frederick William II for an attack on France. His own desire for peace made him limit his policy to intimidation, and he had been more willing than most to view Louis XVI's restoration in September 1791 as satisfactory. During the winter of 1791–92, however, he had been forced to acknowledge that war was becoming more and more probable and that the scope for compromise was fast disappearing. Intimidation as a substitute for war had been replaced by intimidation as a prelude to war during the final months of Leopold's life. A defensive alliance with Prussia signed in February 1792 underlined his recognition that open fighting was unavoidable. His successor, Francis II, was a ruler of a very different stamp. A politically-immature 24-year-old, he was bellicose and impetuous where Leopold had been pacific and cautious, and prone to see matters in military terms. The young Emperor was, and would remain, stubborn, but also hesitant and insecure and, fatally, prone to be swayed by the last person to whom he had spoken. The new reign saw more belligerent spirits in the ascendancy and the final exclusion of the cautious old Chancellor, Kaunitz, who effectively retired, though nominally he was still consulted.

The firmer line in Habsburg policy evident during the final months of Leopold's life in turn increased French anxieties that intervention was on hand. A political change in Paris now made it possible for France to launch an attack. The energetic and ambitious Charles-François Dumouriez, a general before 1789 who found a career in the French Revolution, was swept to power as foreign minister on 15 March 1792. A long-time enemy of the Habsburgs, he advocated an aggressive war against them. During the preceding winter he had become an unofficial adviser to the Brissotins, whom he convinced he would lead France to victory over the Austrians and, equally erroneously, that Prussia would remain neutral in any such conflict. At this period the French foreign minister was Antoine De Lessart, who had replaced the exhausted Montmorin in November 1791 and was a noted moderate who favoured a political settlement with Vienna. In February 1792, however, the Brissotins set about trying to remove De Lessart and, a month later, they succeeded. Dumouriez's appointment made fighting inevitable, by ensuring that the government shared the Legislative Assembly's wish for war. The latest Habsburg ultimatum was rejected out of hand, and on 20 April 1792 France declared war on Austria and sent her forces into the nearby Austrian Netherlands. Both this invasion and a second advance north failed, precipitately ending Dumouriez's brief period as foreign minister (13 June 1792). But even before news of the French attack reached Vienna, the Habsburgs too had decided to fight. This was also the case in Berlin, underlining Frederick William II's wish for hostilities.

The war was not a matter of deliberate political calculation for France's enemies. Attitudes were as important as policies, while both sides misunderstood the impact of their own actions. For Austria and Prussia, the military operations were essentially a police action to restore order in France, similar to the Anglo-Prussian intervention against the Dutch Patriots in 1787 and to Vienna's restoration of her authority in the Austrian Netherlands by force three years later. The nomination of the Duke of Brunswick, a veteran who had served Frederick the Great and had earlier led the Dutch invasion force, to command the allied army underlined these expectations. In spring 1792 Habsburg officers disdainfully referred to the coming campaign as a 'stroll' (*Spaziergang*), while their Prussian counterparts spoke of a 'Promenade to Paris'. For France, however, it was the 'war of peoples against kings' which Brissot had been preaching ever since October 1791. The French certainly believed they would be assisted by the subject peoples of the Habsburgs.

The origins of the war therefore contained an undoubted ideological dimension. But the speed with which France's enemies produced their own established territorial objectives was firmly in the tradition of eighteenth-century limited warfare, underlining the Janus-faced nature of the struggle. By the autumn of 1790, two years before fighting was to begin in the West, Berlin was urging that the costs of any fighting should be defrayed by annexations. These territorial objectives also reflected the widespread belief that the war would be short and the revolutionaries would be no match for the disciplined armies sent against them. Anxiety at events in France was certainly becoming more widespread among other governments and it was fostered by the shrill pleas of the *émigrés*, but French domestic developments were not yet seen as an overwhelming threat to Europe's monarchies. It was the victories of the French armies in 1793–95, the annexations which followed and the aggressive attempts to export the Revolution which made the struggle the overriding international issue.

The War of the First Coalition, 1793–1797

French leaders had originally hoped to isolate Austria, but their vision of a war against the Emperor alone was soon shattered. Prussia declared war on 21 May 1792, as she was bound to do under the alliance concluded in February. France was soon threatened by separate attacks from the north,

north-east and south-east, where the King of Sardinia, another ideological opponent of the Revolution, also prepared to fight, though he did not yet take the field. Though the French régime had declared war, it was unprepared for the coming struggle. The enormous loss of noble officers, 60 per cent of whom had emigrated between 1789 and 1792, together with the collapse of discipline and general administrative breakdown, had brought the French army close to disintegration, and it put up little resistance in the initial fighting. Public finances were in disarray, while France was diplomatically isolated. Prussia, still widely if erroneously regarded as Europe's foremost military power, took the lead in the campaign of 1792. Her ruler was more intent on reversing the course of events in France, and more anxious for military glory and territorial gain, than the Emperor whose earlier bellicosity was modified as he came to appreciate Austria's weakness. The early months of the new reign saw a struggle for ascendancy in Vienna, and this weakened the war-effort.

In August 1792, the Prussian army, accompanied by contingents of *émigrés* (whose military value was negligible) and under Brunswick's command, invaded France and won some initial successes; but its advance was slowed by its own lethargy and the late summer rains and finally halted by defeat in a skirmish at Valmy (September). Initial optimism, apparent in the so-called 'Brunswick Manifesto' (July 1792) with its threat to punish the French people if Louis XVI and his Queen were harmed, was shattered by the military disaster which followed. It soon became clear that the Manifesto itself was a serious miscalculation. Drafted by *émigrés* and intended to intimidate, it instead stiffened French resistance. Less than half of the 42,000 Prussian soldiers who had invaded crossed back over the Rhine in the autumn, and half of this reduced force in turn was sick from eating unripe grapes as it passed through Champagne. Encouraged by their victory, the French launched a massive counter-attack, sweeping into the Rhineland and capturing Mainz, which controlled a passage across the Rhine. Further confidence and encouragement were provided by the significant victory which the French invading army secured over the Austrians at Jemappes (November 1792), a success which gave France effective control over most of the Austrian Netherlands.

These initial successes, and the further progress made in the Rhineland and in Italy during the winter of 1792–93, both contributed to, and were themselves sustained by, events in France which were taking a more radical direction. The constitutional monarchy created in the early years of the Revolution had not aroused widespread hatred or fear; but it was now bloodily destroyed. In the summer of 1792, in an atmosphere of imminent invasion and with a royalist coup expected at any moment, long-held suspicions about the court's counter-revolutionary intentions had crystallised, and in August Louis XVI was suspended from his functions as ruler. It was the first real success for the popular, radical movement, based on the Paris sections, which steadily gained ground during the following months. The overthrow of the monarchy was followed a few weeks later by the first large-scale act of revolutionary violence, the 'September Massacres', when many allegedly counter-revolutionary prisoners in the Parisian gaols were butchered, inaugurating a period of violent upheaval. Political leadership was now assumed by the National Convention which declared France a republic and tried and condemned the King. These events provided momentum to the war-effort, but did so at the price of emphasising the growing divide between the French government and the European monarchies.

It was the execution of Louis XVI in January 1793 in particular which focussed international anxiety about the new and very radical *régime* in Paris. The truly revolutionary nature of events there was evident, while it was becoming clear that this Revolution might also be exported. The announcement by the Convention that it would aid all peoples trying to imitate the French and overthrow their oppressors (the 'Fraternity and Assistance' decrees of November and December 1792) further raised the ideological temperature, while France's substantial territorial gains during the winter of 1792–93 (in particular the annexation of Nice and Savoy from Sardinia and the temporary incorporation of the former Austrian Netherlands) revealed the aggressive intentions of her new rulers. The opening of the River Scheldt, contrary to the provisions of international treaties and confirmed less than a decade before (see above, p. 183), in order to secure the support of the commercial interests of Antwerp, and the implied threat of a French attack on the Dutch Republic, was also resented, particularly in Britain. The doctrine of 'natural frontiers', propounded by the Convention, which asserted that France had a historic right to all the territory within the area bounded by the Alps, the Rhine and the Pyrenees, aroused further alarm. The treatment of Belgium, the former Austrian Netherlands, when it was occupied, underlined that French conquests would be exploited and revolutionised. By early 1793, the aggressive, expansionist, regicide rulers of France stood revealed as a challenge to the monarchical system of Europe, and by March the Convention had declared war on Britain, the Dutch Republic and Spain. A much wider conflict had become inevitable: the French declaration of war on Britain on 1 February 1793 merely anticipated identical British action.

Britain's entry represented a reversal of official policy and a considerable change in public attitudes since 1789. Initially the French Revolution had been welcomed, though this enthusiasm rested in part on a misunderstanding. Events in Paris were widely portrayed as the equivalent of 1688 in England, the beginnings of constitutional monarchy on the other side of the Channel. But the increasing radicalism in Paris diminished support in Britain, and quickly polarised opinion. Edmund Burke had soon denounced the Revolution as 'a wild attempt to methodise anarchy', most notably in his *Reflections on the Revolution in France*, published in November 1790, and his viewpoint found a growing number of adherents in Britain and throughout Europe: French, German, Italian and Spanish translations were immediately published and sold in significant numbers. Simultaneously, the radical supporters of the Revolution in Britain continued to make progress. By 1792, the strength of the popular societies, and their links with France, were beginning to concern the prime minister, Pitt, though loyalist agitation caused at least as much alarm as radical.

Official policy remained the strict neutrality adopted at the outbreak of the Revolution. The growth of hostility contributed to the beginning of fighting, but did not cause it. Ministers were long convinced that these upheavals would weaken France internationally, a view which had been encouraged by the clash over Nootka Sound (see above, pp. 246–50). In February 1792, two months before France declared war, Pitt had predicted that French weakness would give Britain 15 years of peace, and – confident of British naval supremacy – had made significant cuts in expenditure on the fleet. The prime minister knew his economic and financial reforms would be undermined by a new conflict. When the continental war began in April 1792, Britain had restated her established neutrality, and this approach survived the initial allied defeats in the summer and autumn. During the second half of 1792, however, Pitt became concerned at the more radical course taken by the Revolution, while the 'Fraternity and Assistance' decrees reinforced fears about French and domestic subversion. The food riots in parts of England during that autumn were misinterpreted by ministers as evidence of radical agitation. By mid-November 1792, when military and naval recruitment began, war was seen as unavoidable by the cabinet, which agreed it would fight for the Dutch Republic and so made little effort to lower Anglo-French tension. There was widespread revulsion in Britain at the trial of Louis XVI, and diplomatic relations were broken off when he was executed. The resulting diplomatic stalemate led to the hostilities being viewed both in

Paris and London as inevitable, exactly as had been the case when France went to war with Austria and Prussia in the spring.

The King's execution was not the main cause of the war for Pitt, however. As in 1787–88, the instability of the Low Countries was seen to threaten British security. He was particularly alarmed by the French victory at Jemappes and the easy conquest of the Austrian Netherlands which followed, because this menaced the Dutch Republic and challenged one permanent premise of British foreign policy: that the region should never be dominated by France. The subsequent reopening of the Scheldt increased his concern, although the closure of the river possessed a symbolic importance for British policy-makers which far exceeded its commercial significance. The French advance northwards had made war inevitable. In a wider sense, British ministers viewed the notable French military victories of late 1792 as evidence of the revival of France's power, which should be resisted. Yet whereas strategy was more important than ideology for Pitt, the foreign secretary Lord Grenville and the King, George III, along with several other ministers, were more concerned to combat the ideas of the Revolution.

It was symptomatic of the changing nature of this conflict that it was viewed as an economic as well as a military struggle. Britain immediately agreed with Russia to prevent the export of grain to France (25 March 1793, reinforced by a British Order in Council of 8 June 1793). This had occasionally been done in the past; but the rapid introduction of a blockade of foodstuffs indicated the total nature of the war, and this was underlined by Pitt's unsuccessful efforts to organise a complete commercial boycott of France in its early months. He was convinced that the French would find it difficult to sustain the struggle, given their serious financial and economic problems during the previous decade.

The achievements of France's new leaders in 1792–93 had been remarkable, yet this success rested on insecure foundations and, in particular, divisions among their enemies. Austria and Prussia had been disheartened by initial defeats, while Frederick William II was soon distracted by the Polish situation, combining with Russia to bring about the second partition in 1793 (see above, pp. 206–9). This renewed preoccupation with Poland and the slowness with which France's enemies banded together gave the revolutionaries a necessary breathing-space. The new rulers of France were confronted by dangerous internal problems throughout 1793: the civil war in the Vendée, where royalist sentiment would long remain strong, the federalist revolts in the summer and serious economic difficulties throughout the year. These difficulties, together with the renewed threat of foreign invasion, produced more radical measures, with the emergence of the war government of the Committee of Public Safety dominated by Maximilien Robespierre, the beginning of the reign of Terror (September), and the suspension of the republican constitution (October 1793). This new leadership, in the longer perspective, may be said to have saved the Revolution. In the short term, France owed its survival more to the failure of its opponents to deliver a properly co-ordinated attack.

The First Coalition was largely organised by Britain and took shape in the months following the outbreak of general European war (February–March 1793). Traditional suspicion of a standing army along with the need as an island power to maintain a strong navy had ensured that the British military establishment was very small, when compared to major continental states, and in the past the emergency of a war had usually been met by hiring mercenaries, principally in Germany. This was again done in 1793. A series of subsidy treaties was signed with minor German states: Baden, Hesse-Cassel, Hesse-Darmstadt, George III's own electorate of Hanover. This mobilisation of the German princes, who were largely unwilling, was forced by Austria and Prussia, and intensified rivalry between these two powers over access to the resources of the Empire. A British subsidy was also paid to the King of Sardinia to attack France. The other members of the First Coalition were Prussia, Austria, her dependency Tuscany, the Dutch Republic, Naples, Spain, Portugal and, on paper, Russia and the Papacy. London signed a bilateral treaty with each, though there was as yet no question of a British subsidy for the larger states. Britain, inspired by memories of the Grand Alliance in the wars against Louis XIV, made determined but unsuccessful efforts to transform bilateral treaties into one all-embracing alliance against France. The First Coalition was always a heterogeneous political partnership of states who, though recognising the need to defeat the Revolutionaries, were more concerned with the pursuit of their individual, and usually territorial, objectives at the expense of France or in eastern Europe.

The search for territory which had dominated the diplomacy of the eastern powers since the Seven Years War continued during the early stages of the struggle against the Revolution, and exerted an important if intermittent influence on it. Prussia, for example, simply could not support two separate armies on her limited resources and chaotic public finances, and was soon forced to choose between Poland and the war against France. By the spring of 1794 Berlin was receiving an annual British subsidy of £1.2 million, to keep fighting the Revolution. Frederick William II therefore left the Prussian contingents financed by London with the allied forces in the west and allowed operations there to falter, while moving the bulk of his army east, where Prussia completed the final destruction of Poland in 1795 (see Chapter 7).

The clearest illustration of the enduring political fault-lines was provided by Russia, whose membership of the First Coalition was always nominal. From the beginning, Catherine II had been alarmed by events in France and took measures to keep the Revolution out of Russia. She was particularly horrified by the execution of Louis XVI, immediately broke off diplomatic relations with Paris and thereafter provided some financial aid, and rather more advice, for the *émigrés*. This anxiety, however, did not divert her from her preoccupation with the Ottoman Empire and, in particular, Poland, and she ignored insistent pleas from both Vienna and London to provide active support in western Europe. Indeed, Catherine realised that this war was potentially very useful for her: Austrian and Prussian involvement increased Russian freedom of manoeuvre in Poland. Precisely the opposite calculation was made in Vienna and Berlin, where the dangers of leaving the Polish monarchy's fate entirely in Russia's hands were certainly appreciated. Poland ultimately did much to undermine the First Coalition. Above all, the second partition had destroyed the good relations between Austria and Prussia built up between 1790 and 1792, and the resulting friction weakened the military struggle against France. Prussia and Russia were preoccupied with securing their Polish gains and Austria, at first resentful of her exclusion from the second partition, was quick to join in the third partition of 1795. The price for the survival of the French Revolution was, in a very real sense, the destruction of the Polish state.

The continuing preoccupation with Poland also reflected a widespread assumption that the Revolution's defeat would be a relatively easy matter, particularly in view of the chaos within France and the apparently overwhelming forces against her. This encouraged each of the allies to formulate its own territorial objectives, and these came to be more vigorously pursued than the defeat of France. Coalition warfare was still a novelty and there was little appreciation of the need for coordinated military planning and regular political consultation. The result was that there was never an effective allied strategy. When the anticipated easy victories did not materialise, the members of the coalition lost heart and, in the case of Prussia and Austria, sought compensation in Poland; this concern had a parallel in Britain's desire to plunder colonies from France, inevitably diverting British attention from the continent.

France's weakness and urgent internal problems gave the coalition some easy, uncoordinated gains in the spring and summer of 1793. In particular, Austria's victory at Neerwinden weakened French control over the Southern Netherlands. These successes were not properly exploited, and the opportunity for an early, decisive victory was missed. The armies of the coalition, all but immobilised by a traditional concern with man-oeuvre and siege warfare, began to disintegrate at the first signs of serious French resistance in the autumn. The military performance of the First Coalition in 1793–95 reflected the belief of all the allies that they were fighting an old-style war. The new Jacobin leaders, having crushed inter-nal opposition and survived the crisis of that summer and autumn, moved on to the offensive with spectacular success. French armies carried almost all before them in the closing months of 1793 and, despite the fall of the Jacobins, in the years that followed. A series of victories in 1794 firmly established Revolutionary control over Belgium. The defeat at Fleurus (June 1794) signalled Austria's effective abandonment of the former South-ern Netherlands. Simultaneously, Vienna's financial problems sharply worsened, as the public debt and the annual deficit both spiralled. Other French armies advanced into the Rhineland, into Spain and against the King of Sardinia, seeking evidence of foreign support for the revolution but finding very little sign of this. The Dutch Republic was occupied, with surprising ease, in the winter of 1794–95, a British expeditionary force being evacuated with heavy losses. The Austrian and Prussian armies in the Rhineland were forced to retreat by the French onslaught. Before long, serious recriminations over these defeats were dividing the allies, and peace parties were emerging in the major capitals and the smaller states of the Empire.

Military defeat thus completed the destruction of the First Coalition, which by 1795 visibly fell apart, as individual states came to terms with France. The King of Prussia, discouraged by military failure and with his finances in ruins, concentrated even more on Poland. He withdrew from the coalition, concluding first an armistice (November 1794) and then a separate peace with France, by which he handed over all Prussian territ-ory on the left bank of the Rhine (Peace of Basel, April 1795). Unusually, Berlin negotiated not merely on its own behalf but for all the smaller North German states, who had been alienated by the way they had been forced into the struggle in 1793 (see above, p. 265) and were now swept into the Prussian orbit. The Peace of Basel also established a neutralised zone in northern Germany, which sought to disguise Prussia's abandon-ment of the allied coalition. The demarcation line established in 1795 followed very broadly the rivers Ems, Old Yssel and Rhine. Prussia and her north German clients promised to prevent military operations in this region against France, who undertook not to send her own armies there. This initiative did not at first enjoy complete success: in 1795–96 there were several infractions of the neutralised zone. But the creation of a 30,000-strong Army of Observation, dominated by Prussian troops but containing contingents from several smaller north-German states, to defend this neutrality and even more a second treaty with France (August 1796) established a pacific, Prussian-dominated north Germany. During the next decade, until its destruction in 1806, this brought the significant benefits of peace and prosperity to the area.

The creation of this neutralised zone fitted in with one strand in Frederick William II's complex foreign policy: the acquisition of regional security, against France and Austria. It had been one motive behind the military intervention in the Dutch Republic in 1787 and had surfaced periodically thereafter. Prussia's foreign minister at this period, Count Christian von Haugwitz, believed that the neutrality scheme was a realistic way of eventually extending Berlin's control over north-western Germany. In particular it placed Hanover under Prussia's influence, with implications for her future connection with Britain. It also embodied traditional opposition to Austria, who was the principal victim – and may also have been the main target – of these arrangements, which divided Germany (Vienna retained its established dominance in the south) and so contributed to the demise of the Holy Roman Empire a decade later. Above all, however, it demonstrated the impossibility of waging war on two fronts, which even Frederick William II acknowledged.

Neutrality was by now essential for Prussia. The adventurous policy pursued by the King since his accession in 1786 had all but bankrupted his state and, at the same time, revealed the fragile nature of Prussian power. The achievements of Frederick William II had been considerable, though these came after early failures. He secured more new territory than any ruler before him, extending Prussia by one third and her population by almost 60 per cent: from 5.5 million in 1786 to 8.7 million by the time of his death in 1797. Yet the costs of success had been even higher. The treasury was empty, the substantial cash reserve accumulated by Frederick the Great having been consumed in little more than a decade, and the public finances were in chaos. There was also real concern with the threat of French Revolutionary contagion, which appeared a direct challenge to the principles upon which Prussia's royal absolutism rested, and this would increase during the next few years. The destruction of the Polish buffer-state and the westward march of Russia weakened Berlin's international position and gave St Petersburg greater leverage upon its policy; while the Prussian administrative system was encountering serious difficulties in integrating the vast new Polish territories. Increasingly, Prussia's determination to uphold this neutrality became a policy of weakness, especially after the accession of the indecisive and pacific Frederick William III in 1797. It was to be 1806 before Prussia again fought France, technically as part of the Third Coalition, and 1813 before she made a significant military contribution to the struggle against Napoleon.

The Peace of Basel was viewed with particular concern in Vienna. Since spring 1793 Austria's foreign policy had been in the capable hands of Thugut, an established adversary of the Revolution. His opposition, however, was pragmatic rather than ideological. He recognised that in practice the *ancien régime* could not be restored fully, and he sought only to re-establish international peace and stability and make France less of a threat to her neighbours. Yet Thugut also represented traditional Habsburg opposition to Prussia, and this was strengthened by the settlement in spring 1795 and the Prussian advance which it represented. Thereafter he resented Berlin's abandonment of the coalition and feared its ascendancy in northern Germany, and he even conjured up periodically the spectre of a two-front war against France and Prussia. This was always improbable: the extent of the *rapprochement* was limited and trust was in short supply between Paris and Berlin. More importantly, Thugut was determined to restore Austria's relative international position by territorial annexations, which would also help to compensate Vienna for the enormous cost of the struggle. The loss of the Southern Netherlands, formally annexed by France in 1794, and the diminishing likelihood of substantial gains from Bavaria, meant that northern Italy was now the focus of Habsburg ambitions. Both in his search for such compensation and in his reluctance to allow opposition to the French Revolution to dictate Vienna's policy, Thugut typified the persistence of an older approach to international rivalry side-by-side with the struggle with France. It was also evident in his need for alliances, which he believed were essential to Austria's survival. Here, too, Prussia's defection created problems, increasing Vienna's dependence upon Russia, even though Catherine remained unwilling to join in the struggle against France.

The loss of Prussia was a considerable blow to the coalition, less because of her military strength than the strategic threat which she might have posed to the Revolutionary *régime*. Her neutrality removed any threat of an attack from the east against France's Dutch satellite or her new possession of Belgium, and for this reason it was welcomed in Paris. Spain immediately followed Berlin's example and abandoned the alliance, making peace in July 1795, while most minor German states also withdrew from the struggle. These peace settlements revealed that France's leaders were now prepared to come to terms with Europe's monarchical *régimes* and to divide their enemies by separate and still relatively moderate peace treaties, underlining the fact that continuities from the practice of international relations during the *ancien régime* survived in Paris too. By the middle of 1795, the only important members of the First Coalition still nominally at war were Austria, Britain and Sardinia. France, moreover, strengthened her international position considerably by alliances with the new revolutionary Dutch *régime* (now called the Batavian Republic) in 1795 and with Spain the following year, this last a revival of the traditional anti-British alignment overseas.

The considerable French successes in 1793–95 were not merely the consequence of the serious divisions within the First Coalition. They were also the product of a revolutionary transformation in the nature of warfare on land – one brought about by France. These changes were not a matter of new weapons, nor were they, primarily, produced by tactical innovations. The changes in tactics introduced had, for the most part, been widely discussed in France long before the wars of the Revolution. The really dramatic innovation was the appearance of the 'nation in arms'. It did not come about overnight. The initial campaigns were conducted, on both sides, with strict attention to the dogmas of eighteenth-century limited warfare. Opposing commanders concerned themselves, in 1792–93, with besieging and capturing key towns and fortresses. The new style of warfare was a response to the desperate internal and external situation faced by France. By the summer of 1793 it had become apparent that the necessary armies could no longer be supplied by volunteers, who supplemented the surviving veterans in the ranks. To meet this crisis, the *levée en masse* was decreed in August 1793, imposing near-universal conscription. Although many evaded the draft, the resulting expansion of the revolutionary armies was dramatic. By the following spring, France had 800,000 and possibly as many as one million men under arms. A military establishment of this size was wholly novel in modern history. Prussia, for example, though widely regarded by contemporaries as Europe's foremost military power, only had an army of around 200,000 men in 1786, while on the eve of the Revolution the French army had contained some 160,000 regulars. On the most generous estimate, the First Coalition could field some 460,000 men, around half the total available to France.

The size of the new revolutionary army and the emergency France faced meant that lengthy formal training was impossible. The consequent lack of discipline, however, was more than compensated for by the revolutionary enthusiasm of the conscript soldiers. The campaigns of 1793–95 were the heroic period of the revolutionary armies, when their immense numerical superiority and patriotism carried almost all before them. The new-found ardour was apparent in the more aggressive mobile tactics employed. Total victory was the object, ferocity part of the means to achieve it. The most important tactical innovation was the widespread use, after preliminary skirmishing, of attack by massed columns, rather than the traditional line formation. The concentration of France's greater numbers in this way proved highly effective against opponents who long remained wedded to the conventions of eighteenth-century warfare. Moreover, France's enemies were unable to increase their military establishments, which were everywhere a matter of precise financial calculation, to the size made necessary by the appearance of the 'nation in arms'. The poor performance of Austria and Prussia in the First Coalition, at one level, simply reflected their chronic financial difficulties and the inadequate size of their armies.

France's huge forces needed to be equipped and supplied, and their triumphs on the battlefield were, to a significant extent, made possible by the work of Carnot, the 'organiser of victories'. In 1793–94 a war economy was established and its decrees enforced by the guillotine. For a time the needs of the army were made the only object of French trade and production. Revolutionary France provided the first example of modern 'total war'. The enlarged military establishment, however, proved easier to create than to control, and war came to acquire its own momentum. In the past, demobilisation at the conclusion of fighting had often been accompanied by considerable dislocation, since it was not easy to integrate a substantial number of adult males into civilian society, particularly one experiencing the economic difficulties which often followed a war. This fundamental problem was considerably magnified by the unprecedented size of the revolutionary forces. After the victories of 1793–95 and the peace settlements which these produced, it proved very difficult to demobilise the swollen French army; but, equally, with the ending of the Reign of Terror (summer 1794) and the steady disintegration of the war economy, it was equally difficult to feed and equip the troops still serving. The attraction of further military adventures, which would enable the armies to live off occupied territory, as a means of postponing the problems of demobilisation and supplying the remaining troops, was considerable. Further territorial expansion came to be undertaken by subsequent French governments largely for this reason.

The principal target for these adventures after 1795 came to be Austria, since Britain (the other major remaining belligerent) retained her dominance at sea and was in practice safe from direct attack or from the invasion of Ireland which France long considered. Vienna had borne the brunt of the military struggle since 1793, and its fiscal and administrative infrastructure was struggling to cope. Austria had been continuously at war for a decade, first against the Ottoman Empire and then France, and, though impressive amounts of money and manpower had been mobilised, the strain was all too evident. A contemporary estimate was that, by the mid-1790s, average annual expenditure was running 40 per cent ahead of income, while interest payments consumed 15 per cent of revenue. The war-economy and the forcible mobilisation of resources which had made France so formidable since 1793 were anathema to Austrian officials, fearful of their social and political consequences within as fragile a polity as the Monarchy. In fact the army in Germany from 1796 onwards was requisitioning supplies in the style of French forces in order to survive and, within the Habsburg lands, conscription was expanded, but these measures were sanctioned with reluctance. Not the least of the challenges posed by the French Revolution to the established monarchies was to traditional thinking about how the home front could be organised to support a vastly expanded war-effort.

These pressures sapped Austria's will to continue the struggle. The political élite and even the high command were urging peace and, during a ministerial crisis in August 1796, Austria came close to withdrawing from the struggle. Thugut was the sole voice urging that the war should continue. Yet his control over policy remained intact, and at this point he won the Emperor's support. He was less able to resist France's massive military pressure during the winter of 1796–97.

The Directory, which ruled France after October 1795, launched its armies specifically against Austria, who was faced by a two-pronged attack in south Germany and in Italy. The Austrians put up surprisingly effective resistance in Germany, where the Archduke Charles – younger brother of the Emperor and already emerging as the Monarchy's leading commander – outmanoeuvred two substantial French invading armies, but their forces were hopelessly defeated in Italy. Command of the French army sent to the peninsula was given to the 26-year-old Napoleon Bonaparte. Born to a minor noble family in Corsica in the same year as the French annexation (1769), Bonaparte had received his military education in mainland France and had been commissioned into an artillery regiment during the final years of the *ancien régime*. The French army suffered from a shortage of officers during the 1790s, due to the large-scale emigration of noblemen and the accompanying political upheavals. This had ensured rapid advancement for the young Bonaparte who first came to prominence in 1793, when he led the forces which recaptured Toulon. His decisive part in commanding the troops who had defeated a royalist insurrection in Paris on 5 October 1795 (13 *Vendémiaire* IV: the legendary 'whiff of grapeshot') had further enhanced his standing.

A series of victories in Italy first brought Bonaparte to real prominence. He rapidly forced Sardinia to make peace (April 1796) and, within a year, destroyed Habsburg primacy in the northern half of the peninsula. These French successes culminated in his decisive victory at Rivoli near Lake Garda in early 1797. This opened the central European lands of the Habsburgs to invasion, and the victorious Bonaparte seized the opportunity in the kind of swift and dynamic campaign which would become his trademark. By April he had prised the peace preliminaries of Leoben, negotiated in a mere four days, out of Austria. The veteran Austrian diplomat sent to handle these talks encountered for the first time the French commander's distinctive style of negotiation: not traditional diplomacy with give-and-take on both sides, but hectoring demands, temper tantrums and thinly-veiled threats of worse terms if these demands were not instantly accepted. Though Thugut wanted to continue the military struggle, the Emperor Francis II – against a background of collapsing morale and a run on the banks in early April – insisted on peace.

Austria's foreign minister had intended to use this agreement, and the detailed talks which would accompany it, as a breathing space during which the military and financial problems could be tackled. Instead Vienna found itself facing remorseless military pressure which expanded the terms of Leoben, as the victorious Bonaparte led his forces rapidly through the Monarchy's southern provinces to within one hundred miles of the capital. When Thugut's last remaining hope, that of a more accommodating French *régime*, was dashed by the *coup* of 17–18 *Fructidor* (3–4 September 1797), which purged the Directory of the remaining moderates, Austria accepted the inevitability of defeat and signed the political obituary of the First Coalition at Campo Formio (present-day Campo Formido lying between Udine and Passariano).

The Peace of Campo Formio (October 1797), and the dramatic changes in Italian frontiers which accompanied it, were the work of the personally ambitious French commander, not of his political masters in Paris. The Directors were presented by Bonaparte with a *fait accompli* which they reluctantly endorsed. They were particularly unhappy at the way his blueprint for Italy involved the destruction of the independent states of Genoa, Modena and Venice, though none of these had been at war with France. By the peace of Campo Formio, the Habsburgs effectively recognised the extension of France's eastern frontier to the left bank of the Rhine and the French annexation of Belgium. Austria secured in return the expectation of the Archbishopric of Salzburg (coveted by Joseph II a dozen years before) and a small area in eastern Bavaria, gains which would strengthen the Monarchy's western frontier.

In the Italian peninsula, Austria's position was substantially weakened. She secured lands, but at the price of reduced political influence. Vienna was given substantial Venetian territory, including Venice itself and the lands on the Dalmatian coast, both as compensation for the loss of Milan, Brescia and Mantua (to France) and as an inducement to accept the creation of French satellite republics in northern Italy. Contrary to the specific instruction of the Directory, Bonaparte had used military force (April 1797) to carry out the destruction and partition of the neutral republic of Venice which made this possible. The French share (the lands west of the Adige) was united with Milan, Modena and the former Papal territories of Ferrara, Bologna and the Romagna (seized from the Pope in February 1797) to form the nominally independent Cisalpine Republic. Austria's traditional dominance in Italy had thus been undermined, though the Venetian territories and the improved access to the Adriatic which they conferred, were some compensation. France also took what was left of Venice's former eastern empire, the Ionian Islands, while Bonaparte completed his redrawing of the political map of Italy by creating the Ligurian Republic out of the independent state of Genoa (June 1797). These changes made the northern half of the peninsula predominantly republican and French while southern Italy remained solidly monarchical and nominally independent, a division which was clearly unstable. In the month after the peace was signed, Thugut penned a memorable jeremiad: 'Peace! Peace! But where is it? I do not see it in the treaty; at least if a rapid reading has not misled me. I find no security for us, and the execution of it will perhaps be only a second volume of the preliminaries'. The next few years would more than justify his pessimism.

The settlement which Bonaparte imposed on Italy in 1797 represented a significant change in relations between the French Revolution and Europe. Until this point, France had attempted to spread the doctrines of the Revolution by establishing satellite *régimes*, though her success had been limited. Modest territorial gains had been made by outright annexation, in the tradition of eighteenth-century limited warfare. French acquisitions could be justified, to a considerable extent, by the doctrine of 'natural frontiers'. There was some ambiguity, and even more debate, about what these actually were, but in general the theory appeared to justify expansion as far as the Pyrenees, the Alps and the river Rhine, and in this way facilitate the restoration of French hegemony in western Europe. In accordance with this principle, Belgium – occupied briefly in 1792–93 and permanently from June 1794 onwards – had been formally annexed in October 1795. No attempt had been made, however, to annex fully the Dutch Republic (now the Batavian Republic) after the French takeover early in 1795. The territorial changes in Italy in 1797 went far beyond these comparatively limited gains. The scale of the alterations in political geography was matched by the new political *régimes* which were set up, the so-called satellite republic. This was a radical policy of direct, aggressive expansion, exporting the Revolution by military conquest. The victorious general showed scant regard for Italian sovereignty in his remodelling of political geography, and the Directory soon followed his example. This signalled the first serious breach in the traditional approach – that of respecting most territorial arrangements and even many existing *régimes* – which had prevailed throughout the War of the First Coalition, but which had been overthrown by the settlement at Campo Formio.

The French Revolution and European diplomacy

Diplomats had long been the main source of information for their governments, and this remained the case during the 1790s. Though the expanding newspaper press contained reports of the dramatic events in France, and intrepid travellers and particularly *émigrés* provided even more, representatives in Paris continued to send extensive and even first-hand accounts, and these contributed to the fear and hostility which the French Revolution inspired. Diplomats and their families were occasionally caught up in the upheavals. The wives of the Sardinian and Spanish diplomats were insulted by a Paris mob because their servants still wore noble livery, though this had been abolished in France in 1790. The simultaneous abolition of coats-of-arms was a further source of friction, since diplomats usually displayed their royal master's arms and sometimes their own on the portals of their residences, provoking derision and hostility. Overenthusiastic mobs and over-zealous authorities caused minor problems: the papal and Portuguese ambassadors were temporarily detained as late as 1798. But such incidents were surprisingly rare, and foreign representatives in Paris continued to enjoy diplomatic immunity throughout these years. The strongly legalistic political culture of the Revolution contributed to this. But it was primarily a recognition of the need for reciprocity which led successive *régimes* to accept that diplomats must be protected, though this was exactly the kind of privilege which the Revolution aimed to destroy. France recognised that allies were desirable and herself maintained a wide-ranging network of representatives throughout the 1790s and beyond, though the warfare of these years did reduce its scale.

The actions of French representatives were a further source of friction. The new political order ushered in after 1789 clashed at many points with the world of Old Europe. Revolutionary diplomats, in defiance of established practice, intervened in the internal politics of the countries to which they were accredited, and often did so particularly blatantly acting as conduits of radical literature and propaganda. Even such apparently simple actions as the flying of the new revolutionary flag, the red, white and blue tricolour, over French diplomatic missions was a serious source of friction and often a target for reprisals: as it would be for Bernadotte in Vienna (see below, p. 288). French diplomats were murdered by mobs in Rome in 1793 and 1797, while in April 1799, as the Rastatt conference broke up, two of France's representatives were killed by Austrian soldiers, an episode which was widely condemned by the international community. Increasingly, as the *régime* in Paris became more and more radical, its representatives were shunned by their fellow diplomats and by the host governments, and came to feel themselves totally isolated. Everywhere seen as actual or potential conspirators against the old order, they disdained the established courtesies as legacies of the monarchical and aristocratic world which they wished to overthrow, and instead proclaimed themselves citizens and retreated further into the laager of revolutionary purity.

This gulf came to be most evident in the practice of diplomacy, though here, too, there were significant continuities. The early years of the Revolution had seen the *philosophe* critique of eighteenth-century international relations (see above, p. 141) influence politicians and even leaders of the Constituent Assembly, one of whom called in 1790 for France to spearhead the establishment of a 'new diplomacy'. Rejecting what they believed was the secrecy, cynicism and brutality of contemporary power politics, the *philosophes* had argued for contacts between states to be based on peace and the expansion of trade, which would benefit all countries and peoples, rather than war and political rivalry, which would benefit the ruler of one. National, rather than merely dynastic, interests would shape foreign policy, in an age when the people were sovereign.

When the Constituent Assembly turned its attention to external relations for the first time, in spring 1790, these ideas were taken up by an influential minority of speakers. The radicals – including Robespierre and the future Director Reubell – preached the necessity of a newly 'enlightened' approach. During these debates the comte de Mirabeau, who was emerging as an unofficial joint foreign minister (through his dominance in the Assembly and links with the court), looked forward to 'the time . . . when we shall have only friends and no allies, when there will be universal freedom of trade and when Europe will form one great family'. The Constituent Assembly's decree of 22 May 1790, renouncing foreign war and territorial conquest, embodied this idea of universal brotherhood, and was intended to inaugurate an era of international peace and cooperation. But Mirabeau was also realistic enough to see that France was forced to live in a world dominated by traditional power politics, and that it would not be prudent 'to trust to chance the influence which other powers exert on us and which we can exert on other powers'.

During the early years of the Revolution, the need for allies and, after 1792, the desperate struggle for survival forced its leaders into a series of compromises, which mitigated the sense of a clear-cut break with France's past and with the current diplomatic practices of other states. Yet the new political order which the Revolution embodied was always an obstacle to easy relations with other European countries, especially after France became a republic in autumn 1792. Its whole approach to the conduct of foreign policy was a challenge to established practices. In October 1790 the Constituent Assembly, in an attempt to promote the more open conduct of negotiations which the *philosophes* had advocated, established a permanent diplomatic committee which was able to interrogate France's foreign minister. Instructions to representatives abroad and negotiations with foreign countries now began to receive far more publicity. Eventually, the foreign ministry itself was temporarily abolished (April 1794), being replaced by a Commission for Foreign Relations responsible to the Committee of Public Safety.

Revolutionary purity was particularly evident – as would be expected – under the Committee of Public Safety between September 1793 and early 1795. The logic that France could only maintain full diplomatic relations with fellow republics and not with despised monarchies, led to a widespread downgrading of posts to the level of *chargé d'affaires*, with ministers or ambassadors only being sent to the young American republic, Switzerland and Venice. This proved temporary, however, and exemplified the instability which the upheavals of revolutionary politics imparted to the conduct of diplomacy. Though anyone who had served the monarchy before 1789 was automatically suspect – and, indeed, Dumouriez had carried through a complete cull of aristocratic and therefore experienced ambassadors during his brief period in office (see above, p. 259) – a significant number of diplomats and successive foreign ministers were former noblemen: exactly as Dumouriez himself was! This only began to change during the second half of the 1790s. In the aftermath of the *Fructidor* coup (September 1797) anyone who had served the Bourbon monarchy or been born into the nobility was dismissed. By the following year, no less than ten important diplomatic posts were filled by former regicides.

The same tension between new aspirations and old realities permeated the French Revolution's approach to diplomatic practice. Here, the Constituent Assembly's formal abolition of nobility in 1790 and, in a broader sense, the attack on aristocracy, were crucial to the widening divisions. The diplomacy of the *ancien régime* – and, therefore, of the powers fighting France – had been deeply aristocratic both in personnel and in tone: Europe's diplomatic culture was in essence the social culture of its élite, who provided most ambassadors and envoys. The representatives of the Revolution self-consciously distanced themselves from this world, both in appearance and style. As the Revolutionary garb of simple coats and trousers became established, replacing silk coats, ornate waistcoats, breeches and stockings, French diplomats were visibly different from their aristocratic counterparts. This impression was confirmed by the way in which France's representatives strode purposely into meetings, rather than pacing their steps in a choreographed way.

Protocol and precedence meant nothing, especially once the Bourbon monarchy had been overthrown, while the kind of genuflecting before ruling sovereigns central to formal audiences was out of the question. There could, however, be a difference between the firm attitude adopted by the régime in Paris, and the necessary compromises imposed on French agents by the particular contexts within which they operated. France's relations with the North African residencies, and her need to import grain from the Maghreb during the wars of the 1790s, imposed a series of concessions on her diplomats. In particular the French consul at Tunis continued to kiss the hand of the *bey* as provided for by the 1742 treaty (see above, pp. 126–7), though this agreement had been immediately rejected by the Committee of Public Safety, and the practice did not die out until 1836. The clear compromise was disguised in a rhetoric about how an act of submission was now a mere act of courtesy, but the extent of the French concession was clear.

Revolutionary diplomats were quite distinct in numerous ways. While appearances were important, however, there was far more to it than this. It was exemplified by the conduct of Treilhard, the French representative at the conference which met in autumn 1797 at Rastatt (see below, p. 280), to arrange the details of a German settlement. The Austrian delegates were appalled and affronted by his shouting during sessions of the conference and banging the table to emphasise a point. The gulf was especially evident to the Earl of Malmesbury who, as James Harris, had been Britain's leading diplomat during the later 1770s and 1780s. In autumn 1796 and again in summer 1797, he was sent to France in unsuccessful attempts to negotiate peace with the Directory. His comments, informed by a quarter-century's experience, highlighted the very different diplomatic world created by the Revolution. In the first place there was now an almost complete absence of the social gatherings of traditional diplomacy, at which informal negotiations could be conducted and diplomacy pursued by other means. Instead diplomacy was now almost entirely a matter of formal conferences. Even more strikingly, Malmesbury immediately noted the very different methods and practices of the revolutionaries. While the outward forms of the old diplomacy were observed, the blunter, less flexible style of the republican negotiators, who set out and then stuck to their demands, was a shock to the veteran British diplomat, used to the give-and-take of negotiations and to settlements reached through discussion and compromise. Already, the victories of French armies in 1795–97 had made such compromise far less necessary, as the Austrian negotiators had discovered at Leoben and Campo Formio, and the scope and, indeed, need for this would disappear altogether during the years to come, as France's military power waxed ever stronger.

CHAPTER 10

France's expansion in Europe, 1797–1807

In autumn 1797 the exhaustion and domestic problems of the leading belligerents had produced a settlement but did not guarantee a secure or extended peace. Contemporaries recognised that Campo Formio was no more than a truce, while the parallel Anglo-French negotiations at Lille had broken down as a result of the same *coup* of *Fructidor* which convinced Austria to accept Bonaparte's terms, and the maritime war continued. Within a year, a new and enlarged alliance had resumed the military struggle. In October 1798 a combined Russo-Ottoman force – itself a testimony to one of the more remarkable diplomatic revolutions of these years – attacked the French garrison of the Ionian Islands and began the War of the Second Coalition (1798–1802).

A radicalisation of French aims, as the new Directors sought to survive through further conquests and believed they could give the law to Europe, elicited a more vigorous and organised response from the leading powers. The Peace of Campo Formio had referred the details of the German settlement to a separate conference at Rastatt. When this met in late 1797, the new scale of French ambitions, in the Rhineland and in Europe more generally, immediately became evident. Indeed, in the instructions drawn up for their representatives, the Directors had bluntly announced their intention to ignore the provisions of Campo Formio. Instead they intended to annex the left bank of the Rhine and so deny Austria the compensation in Germany promised as an inducement to accept the disadvantageous Italian settlement.

The nature of the struggle was changing rapidly. France's earlier willingness to seek moderate settlements with individual states (see above, pp. 274–5) now gave way to an increasingly intransigent confrontation with the European powers. The reasons were incisively set out by Talleyrand, the foreign minister of the Directory, in late autumn 1797:

*Given the situation of the [French] republic in Europe, which has
raised itself in the teeth of the monarchies and on the ruins of several
of them, and which rules the continent now by the terror inspired by
its principles and its arms, can it not be said that the treaty of Campo
Formio and all the other treaties we have signed are nothing more than
just military agreements, some more advantageous than others? The
dispute which has been lulled for the time being by the surprise and
dismay of the vanquished has in no way been finally resolved by the
arms which must always be at the ready so long as hatred persists.*

The novel nature and intensity of the struggle was also evident to France's
opponents. In February 1798 the Archduke Charles commented to his
brother the Emperor, 'We are dealing with an enemy who works relentlessly for the destruction of religion, the overturning of all thrones, and
above all for the revolution, and whose ideas spread with such frightening
rapidity'. By 1797–98 such a conclusion appeared inescapable, especially
given the *régimes* friendly to France which had now been set up (see
above, pp. 274–5). All states aimed to secure new territory and so
increase their power, but the appetite of France and, more important, her
capacity to satisfy it far exceeded those of her rivals. It was the principal
reason why war was resumed so quickly.

French political and territorial expansion did not cease with the Peace
of Campo Formio: on the contrary, it gathered pace. In the same month
that the treaty was signed, Spain entered the war on the side of France,
with whom she had concluded an alliance two months earlier, restoring
the anti-British axis in the colonial sphere and making French influence
preponderant in Madrid. In February 1798 France – or rather General
Bonaparte – imposed an offensive and defensive alliance on the Cisalpine
Republic, thereby breaking the terms of Campo Formio, which had guaranteed its neutrality. Military intervention in Switzerland led to the proclamation of the Helvetic Republic (22 March 1798) and to the outright
annexation of two territories, Geneva and Mulhouse, parts of the Swiss
confederation. The enthusiasm of Swiss radicals provided a convenient
pretext for actions which the Directors believed necessary to protect
France's south-eastern frontier and to secure military communications
with northern Italy. The instability of the Italian settlement itself contributed to further French expansion in the peninsula. Disturbances in
the Papal States led to military intervention and the proclamation of the
Roman Republic (15 February 1798), which remained occupied by French
troops, with the Pope going into exile in France, where he was effectively

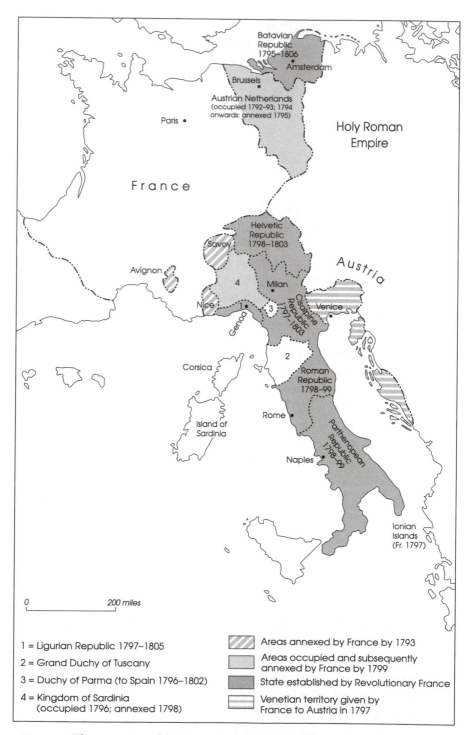

MAP 9 *The expansion of Revolutionary France, 1789–99*

Source: D. McKay and H.M. Scott, *The Rise of The Great Powers, 1648–1815*
(Longman Group Limited, 1983), p. 367

a prisoner of the Directory. In mid-1798 the French army completed the military occupation of Piedmont (the mainland part of the Kingdom of Sardinia), while remorseless levying of resources continued in the Ligurian Republic. These months also saw an intensification of the Directory's control over the satellite republics, which had all been set up by French arms and were expected to implement France's wishes. The Batavian Republic, for example, experienced further French intervention and the imposition of a new constitution (April 1798). The advance was renewed in the following winter. In December the French seized control of the kingdom of Sardinia, its ruler abdicating, while in the very next month (January 1799) the Parthenopean Republic was established at Naples, once again by French military power. Everywhere the Revolution appeared to be on the march and France's renewed expansion appeared irresistible. For, with the collapse of the First Coalition, Britain was the only major state still at war with her.

Britain's struggle with Revolutionary France

The War of the First Coalition had revealed the shortcomings of Britain's traditional strategy in the new circumstances of the 1790s. Her intervention had been both belated and reluctant. It had been widely assumed, as on the continent, that the war would be short, and at first Pitt had hoped to limit involvement. The British cabinet had believed that France's serious financial problems and the military might of her enemies would together bring about a rapid allied victory. By the final phase of the First Coalition they had to recognise that this would not be so. It was one reason why their commitments had steadily increased, as the junior partner of 1793 became the director of the alliance by 1795–96. British diplomacy had created such coherence as the First Coalition possessed, while loans to Austria and subsidies to some smaller German states, to Sardinia and eventually to Prussia had sustained the military struggle.

Britain's strategy throughout the First Coalition had remained the traditional formula of 'colonial' warfare, that is, tying France down in Europe while defeating her overseas. The struggle which began in 1793, unlike earlier Anglo-French conflicts, had purely European origins, but it had been fought on the high seas and in the colonies. Pitt's strategy had closely resembled that of his father during the Seven Years War (see above, pp. 110–13), while the renewed fighting had initially been seen as an opportunity to make good British losses during the War of American Independence. Continuing naval dominance enabled Britain to maintain an incomplete but effective blockade of France's Channel coastline, which bottled up the French fleet in Brest and slowly strangled French commerce. In mid-1794 Howe had intercepted a returning grain convoy and secured a hard-won tactical victory in a five-day engagement fought some 400 miles west of Ushant (Ile d'Ouessant, lying off the western-most tip of Brittany), the so-called 'Glorious First of June'. Though the French fleet fought bravely, it suffered heavy losses.

British supremacy was facilitated by the upheavals in the French navy brought about by the Revolution. By the early 1790s, after a decade of energetic reconstruction, France's fighting navy had reached maximum size, in terms of tonnage, during the entire sailing ship era. Yet this achievement rested upon fragile foundations. *Matériel* and finance were in short supply, while the lack of seafarers – especially by comparison with its British rival – was a permanent obstacle to manning such an enlarged fleet. Revolutionary politics exacerbated these problems. The impact upon the naval officer *corps* was even more serious than in the army: by 1793 almost two-thirds had left. During the eighteen months between October 1790 and March 1792 no less than five Naval ministers held office, while the established problems of *matériel* and finance worsened as administration broke down completely. Wide-ranging discontent among the crews and periodic mutinies completed the undermining of French sea power. In late August 1793 a *coup* against the Jacobin leadership in Paris had handed over the great southern naval base of Toulon and its sizeable fleet to a British squadron. Though the occupation was temporary, before the British garrison was forced to abandon the port and town, it destroyed the substantial timber stocks, making France's shortages of *matériel* even more serious, together with some of the capital ships. The whole episode epitomised how the initiative had passed decisively to Britain.

These developments magnified Britain's established mastery and highlighted her structural advantages. In the early 1790s, after a decade-long naval race, the combined French and Spanish fleets had enjoyed a clear lead in tonnage, perhaps even 30 per cent, over their British rival, but this quickly evaporated. Britain's established superiority in infrastructure, *matériel*, manpower and, above all, finances, soon became decisive, permitting a building and repair programme throughout the first two Coalitions. The waning of French sea power was matched by a steady increase in the number of capital ships Britain could send to sea. In absolute terms the royal navy only increased by around 20 per cent in total size during the first decade of fighting, but this lead was magnified by the parallel disintegration of the French fleet. It was the basis of London's strategic approach of concentrating its war effort outside Europe during the First Coalition.

This strategy enabled Britain to make gains at France's expense in India and especially the Caribbean, and thus to weaken still further her commercial and naval potential. France's West Indies colonies, especially Saint-Dominigue, were crucial for her foreign trade and ocean-going shipping. They therefore became the focus of British strategic planning during the War of the First Coalition. A series of large-scale expeditions were sent to the West Indies and, despite suffering enormous losses of manpower due to the tropical climate and to disease, gradually conquered most French possessions there: Martinique, St Lucia, St Vincent, Grenada and much of Saint-Dominigue – though not Guadeloupe – were seized and held. The same colonial strategy was directed against states forced into alliance with France. The creation of the Batavian Republic in 1795 was followed by a British onslaught on the Dutch colonial empire: the Cape of Good Hope, Malacca, Trincomalee and Colombo were all captured during the next 12 months, while in 1799 Surinam and Curaçao were added to this list. In 1796–97 Spain's switch of sides was followed by a British expedition against her Caribbean colonies, though only Trinidad was seized.

Britain's colonial gains were substantial, but did nothing to counteract French military successes, particularly in 1795–97. The resulting collapse of opposition to France on the continent undermined the prospects for the negotiated settlement aimed at by British strategy. Extended peace negotiations both in 1795–96 and 1797 were unsuccessful, largely because of what were viewed in London as France's extravagant terms. As French gains on land multiplied, moreover, British sea power had become dangerously over-extended in the attempt to counter them. Spain's alliance with France had been followed by a British naval withdrawal from the Mediterranean. The fighting since 1793 had thus revealed that a naval and colonial conflict of the traditional kind would not be sufficient. If the impressive progress of the Revolution were to be checked, a new strategic initiative was essential. It was by no means clear that Britain, though the only major undefeated state in the First Coalition, could launch this.

Britain's own situation in 1797, the year of the peace of Campo Formio, was to become very serious, with a financial crisis followed by naval mutinies. The disintegration of the First Coalition had deprived her of a bridgehead on the continent and made direct military intervention – even if the cabinet had been inclined to attempt this – all but impossible. The Low Countries were firmly under French control, while Hanover was neutralised and effectively dominated by neighbouring Prussia. It was one reason why London long supported the royalist insurgents in western France and helped to keep their resistance going until 1800, in spite of considerable misgivings about their aims. Though British propaganda since 1793 had necessarily emphasised the ideological dimension of the struggle, there was no willingness to restore Bourbon absolutism. The French royalists were in any case deeply split over the restored monarchy, and Britain always supported the constitutionalist faction. Pitt denied any 'intention to wage war against opinion' and aimed only to destroy the Revolution. The British government never officially recognised the comte de Provence after Louis XVI's execution, and its support for the counter-revolution was tactical and even opportunistic, and always a low priority. In any case, Britain's army could not contribute significantly to campaigns in Europe. The West Indian expeditions and the high losses there consumed much of the available manpower, while both military administration and fighting effectiveness were at a low ebb. The duke of York's appointment as commander-in-chief in 1795 was to prove a turning point, as the shortcomings began to be tackled energetically. Yet it would be the final stages of the War of the Second Coalition before these improvements were evident on the battlefield.

A French invasion could not totally be discounted, though British mastery at sea seemed to guarantee that England would not have to face a direct attack. Ireland remained an inviting target, and Irish dissatisfaction with English rule had grown to the point of rebellion. Within England the war was widely unpopular, while the radical movement continued to enjoy significant support. In 1797, moreover, the twin pillars of Britain's success in her eighteenth-century struggle with France – the distinctive system of public finance and the royal navy – both appeared to crumble. There was a severe financial crisis and, for a moment, it seemed as if the government's credit might collapse, with a run on the Bank of England and a suspension of the convertibility of its notes in February. These problems were symptomatic of the wholly new strains the struggle had placed upon government finance. Pitt had paid for the War of the First Coalition in the traditional way, by borrowing and increasing the national debt, which rose from £240 million (in 1792) to £427 million six years later. This reflected the massive cost of the conflict, which was more than twice that (in constant prices) of the previous Anglo-French War. Initially Pitt increased taxation to cover the extra costs incurred, and this contributed to a near doubling of interest rates in the six years after 1792 and to the significant depletion of the Bank of England's gold reserves, which was one element in the crisis early in 1797. In the longer perspective, these difficulties would lead to a changed approach to public finance, which would depend much more heavily upon taxation during the remainder of the struggle with France. Income tax, introduced in 1799, was added to the host of indirect taxes and quickly transformed the government's finances. Between 1800 and 1815, 70 per cent of the cost of the fighting would be paid by taxation, now consuming one-fifth of national income.

The threat to the royal navy was more acute and unexpected. In the spring and early summer the fleet was temporarily paralysed by mutinies at Spithead and the Nore, caused principally by rates of pay, unchanged since the mid-seventeenth century and seriously eroded by inflation. Victories over the two states forced into alliance with France did something to restore British confidence. In February 1797 Jervis had defeated the Spanish navy at Cape St Vincent which discouraged it subsequently from putting to sea, while in October Duncan destroyed the Dutch fleet (which had been rebuilt impressively and might have been used in any invasion) at Camperdown. Britain gradually recovered from her desperate plight, but the initiative clearly lay with France.

The origins of the Second Coalition, 1797-98

The solution sponsored by the foreign secretary, Lord Grenville, and endorsed by Pitt, was the formation of a new and all-powerful alliance which would defeat France, dictate a satisfactory peace and then maintain this settlement through regular meetings of the great powers. It obviously foreshadowed the alliance of 1814 and the Congress System, though its probable inspiration was the Grand Alliance against Louis XIV. Grenville's scheme rested upon a sound appreciation of the basic weakness of the First Coalition: the lack of agreement over political aims and military strategy. This shortcoming, however, proved easier to identify than to eradicate. The 'strategy of overthrow' pursued by London in 1798–99 ultimately foundered on many of the same problems which had undermined the First Coalition.

Grenville sought close political and military cooperation between Britain and the three eastern powers, Austria, Prussia and Russia, an anti-French coalition in form as well as in name. The barriers to any quadruple alliance were considerable. The main one was always that of reconciling old antagonisms and internal tensions in order that a common strategy could be adopted. Poland no longer remained to distract and divide the continental powers, yet the suspicion and acrimony its destruction had engendered along with the traditional rivalries in eastern Europe, in particular between Vienna and Berlin, reduced effective cooperation. Neither Austria nor Prussia was as yet fully convinced of the novel extent and nature of the French threat. Both believed France's power should be restrained by the traditional formula of territorial forfeits after a limited war. Relations between London and Berlin were notably cool, because of Prussia's early desertion of the First Coalition and her equivocal neutralism since 1795. There was also friction over George III's Electorate of Hanover, part of the neutralised zone in northern Germany set up after the Peace of Basel. It eventually proved impossible for Grenville to persuade the new Prussian King, Frederick William III (1797–1840), to join the Second Coalition.

Austria initially was no more willing. Thugut recognised that Campo Formio was a mere truce and viewed France's continuing expansion in 1797–98 with real concern. This anxiety was strengthened by the provocative behaviour of General Bernadotte, the new *régime's* first ambassador to the Habsburg court. His mission culminated in the flying of the revolutionary tricolour from his official residence, inciting a riot and the tearing down of the French flag. The Austrian government sought to calm the situation, but Bernadotte inflamed matters by leaving Vienna. Yet while Thugut recognised that no stable peace was possible with Revolutionary France, he remained concerned with Prussian power and determined to strengthen Austria's capacity to handle it. In 1798–99 considerable – though not altogether successful – efforts were made to overhaul the army and prepare for the anticipated renewal of fighting. After a decade of continuous and expensive warfare and with the defeats of 1796–97 fresh in his mind, however, Thugut was resolved not to renew the struggle until Austria's alliances were more secure and the prospects of success significantly improved.

Two of these objectives – political and financial aid – were imperilled by a complex and long-running dispute with London, from mid-1797 until the end of 1799, over a British loan and Vienna's refusal to ratify an agreement providing for repayment. It had its origins in Austrian borrowing in London in the mid-1790s, as Austria struggled to finance her extensive military commitments. Though Britain refused a subsidy, Pitt had finally accepted that the British government should guarantee a loan. When Austria refused to ratify the convention, on the grounds that the Leoben preliminaries had made this unnecessary, a dispute began which would long damage relations. Each side believed the other guilty of bad faith. Vienna resented British miserliness, and the way additional and wholly inadequate financial help appeared conditional on a further expansion of its military commitments, while the dispute also strengthened British resentment, already aroused by Austria's unilateral peace at Campo Formio. The quarrel denied the Habsburg government much-needed financial assistance, as London in reprisal cut off all payments, and disrupted efforts to negotiate a treaty: it was to be 1800 before a formal agreement could be concluded, when the convention was finally ratified after concessions by both sides, in order to allow Austria to join the Second Coalition.

These obstacles to a wide-ranging alliance gradually became apparent in 1798–99. Matters were delayed by the difficulty of conducting complex negotiations over vast distances, particularly during a very severe winter, with Channel storms and ice-bound roads. The diplomats also struggled to keep up with a rapidly changing military situation. The Second Coalition which eventually emerged was far removed from Grenville's original conception, and owed less to British diplomacy than to Bonaparte's Egyptian expedition of 1798–99 (see below, pp. 296–8). It proved to be a loose series of bilateral alliances, scarcely more of a coalition than its predecessor. Two of its prospective members, Prussia and Austria – while discussing the quadruple alliance with Britain – were simultaneously negotiating with the intended enemy. The uncertain outcomes were not speedily resolved. Prussia vacillated into neutrality, while Austria eventually rushed into a war with France and only then sought the further British financial support necessary to fight it. These developments highlighted Grenville's inability to mould continental politics to his own pattern. It was even more apparent in the case of Russia, who at first rejected Britain's approaches but within two years would become the leading member of the new coalition.

A central element in London's military strategy was the active participation of Russia, who until now had played no effective part in the struggle. Britain also believed that Russian intervention might encourage Austrian and Prussian involvement. Throughout the First Coalition, Catherine II had remained aloof, indifferent to repeated appeals for aid, despite being a firm ideological opponent of the Revolution. A token squadron to reinforce Britain's North Sea fleet was as far as she had been prepared to go. She remained preoccupied with the destruction of Poland until the final year of her life. At long last, however, she was now becoming seriously concerned at the scale of French successes, particularly in Italy. The Empress's vast gains from the Ottoman Empire had given the eastern Mediterranean and, in particular, the Italian peninsula, a new importance in Russian foreign policy. Direct access to the Black Sea, together with the right of her merchant ships to pass through the Straits after 1774, had led to the development of a flourishing export trade with the Mediterranean region, particularly in grain. At the same time, Russia's annexations from Poland had brought substantial numbers of Roman Catholic subjects, and this gave relations with the Papacy a new significance. For the Empress, as for her successors, French expansion in the Italian peninsula was a challenge to Russian interests and made her more inclined to join the struggle against France, underlining that Europe's political fault-lines were beginning to close. When Catherine died in November 1796, negotiations with Britain for a Russian army to fight in western Europe in return for a subsidy had been concluded, and a 60,000-strong force was preparing to join the Austrians.

Her son and successor, the mercurial and idealistic Paul I (1796–1801), immediately reversed this policy, refused to send troops to the Rhine and recalled the squadron serving with the British fleet. Russian troops were simultaneously withdrawn from Persia. Catherine II's final years had seen intervention there, in response to a Persian attack on St Petersburg's client Georgia in 1795, and a degree of control had been established over the eastern Caucasus. Within a month of Paul's accession that force had also been recalled, as his mother's expansionist policies were decisively rejected. Russia's new ruler genuinely wished to spare his people further war, with the burdens it imposed, and instead to introduce social and administrative reforms. The early months of his reign saw wide-ranging measures, introduced at breakneck speed and in the face of strong resistance to the apparent 'Prussianisation' of army, state and society, and this further inhibited external military commitments.

Paul initially hoped to prevent the continental war spreading into areas where Russia's security was involved. There were obvious echoes of the 'Northern System' of his former tutor and political adviser, Nikita Panin, in his idea of defensive alliances to protect Russian interests in eastern Europe and in his immediate abandonment of Catherine's expansionist policies. Yet Paul's own hostility towards the French Revolution was undoubted. He feared its challenge to the traditional order in Europe and detested its brutal assault on the sacred institution of monarchy. His approach to foreign affairs was strongly ideological. For a time, he believed Bonaparte would tame the Revolution; legitimacy mattered less to him than good order. Initially, Paul's moderation was reinforced by his domestic priorities, but it came to be undermined by the progress of events. By autumn 1797 – after a year on the throne – the military recruitment cancelled at his accession had been reinstated. By the following

February Russia was re-arming to cope with the French advance in the Mediterranean.

Paul's realisation that it was impossible to live at peace with the Revolution was not a response to British urgings nor to continued French expansion in western Europe. He was principally alarmed by Bonaparte's conquests in Italy, and was affronted by France's sweeping gains at Campo Formio and the accompanying partition of neutral Venice. Russia's ruler particularly resented France's seizure of Malta and annexation of the Ionian Islands. The crusading Order of the Knights of St John had taken refuge on Malta after the loss of Rhodes to the Ottomans in the 1520s. By the eighteenth century the Order was clearly in decline, though it continued to maintain a rather futile hostility towards Islam, while its international and aristocratic membership gave it continuing political influence. The confiscation of its rich properties in France in 1791–92 deprived it of two-fifths of its income and had been a severe blow. Its strategic potential for France's enemies, together with the lure of the Order's remaining wealth led Bonaparte to occupy the island on his way to Egypt in June 1798, encountering only token resistance.

The Order now found an improbable new champion in Paul I. Ever since his youth, he had been attracted by the chivalric ideal which the Order embodied and had made a detailed study of it. He had recently given more tangible proof of his sympathy. A priory belonging to the Knights in Volhynia had been part of Russia's share of the second partition of Poland, but Catherine II had refused to restore its income. Paul did not merely hand back the revenues very shortly after his accession, he actually increased them and backdated these payments to the second partition. The priory was also transferred to St Petersburg, enlarged and henceforth entirely financed by him. In gratitude, the Order declared Paul its protector in autumn 1797. The cause of the Knights slowly merged with Paul's almost messianic notion of a crusade against liberal and revolutionary movements everywhere, but especially in France. This link was strengthened by his irregular election as grand master (November 1798). His predecessor, Baron Hompesch, had been deposed – on the pretext of his supposed culpability for Malta's fall – by the Russian priory, which then nominated Russia's ruler as his successor: actions which were of dubious legality. While there was little enthusiasm, far less support, for this in the wider Order, it was difficult for Rome to resist developments which might bring support to the beleaguered Papacy. Russia's Orthodox Emperor now set about transforming the Catholic Order, opening membership to all faiths. Paul intended that the Knights, based in Russia and reinforced by a massive influx of Russian noblemen, would be the sword bearers in his crusade. He now assumed the role of champion of the Knights and unsuccessfully demanded that the French evacuate Malta.

By 1798, Paul I's actions were indicating his commitment to the struggle with the Revolution. The *émigrés* and their army, displaced by French expansion, were offered refuge in Russia together with financial support, while the future Louis XVIII was installed at Mittau (Jeglava) in the former duchy of Courland, annexed by Russia in 1795. When, in February 1798, French troops occupied Rome, Paul offered Pope Pius VI asylum, which he declined. The Russian Emperor was now the leading ideological opponent of the Revolution among Europe's crowned heads. Always prone to think in terms of moral absolutes, his deeply ideological approach to the struggle with France – which contrasted sharply with his pragmatism over relations with the Ottoman Empire, Georgia and Persia – convinced him he should act as the standard bearer in a crusade against the Revolution.

A more wholly political concern for Russia was provided by Bonaparte's seizure of the Ionian Islands from Venice and their formal incorporation into the French Republic in 1797. They lay off the western coast of Ottoman-controlled Greece and were of considerable strategic value. France's annexation was as a powerful challenge to Russia's growing interests in the eastern Mediterranean and even to her dominance of the Black Sea, since it was assumed that the islands would be used by France to extend her influence in the Balkans. Strategy thus merged with chivalry and ideology to make Paul increasingly concerned at the French advance. This, together with a general unease about the instability of southern and central Europe after Bonaparte's victories in Italy, finally convinced him he should declare war.

French expansion also brought the Ottoman Empire into the struggle. Selim III had remained aloof throughout the First Coalition, preoccupied with internal problems and content to pursue a pro-French neutrality: France was the Porte's traditional ally and an important source of technical aid to the Ottoman army. The French annexation of the Ionian Islands, which brought French influence very close to the Sultan's territories, fatally undermined this harmony. Well-founded anxiety about the precarious nature of Constantinople's control over its outlying provinces, together with concern at French expansion into south-eastern Europe, produced a swift reversal of the diplomatic alignments which had prevailed since 1792. It was facilitated by Paul's desire for a *rapprochement* with the Sultan. Bonaparte's invasion of the Ottoman dependency of Egypt in the summer of 1798 (see below, pp. 297–8) crystallised this concern.

It halted, at least temporarily, the vital food supplies which the densely populated and volatile city of Constantinople secured from Egypt. The Sultan now declared war on France (September 1798), concluding alliances with Russia and Britain. These new political alignments brought immediate military success. Early in 1799 a Russo-Ottoman force evicted the French from the Ionian Islands. The alliance of two such traditional and bitter enemies was the most remarkable of the diplomatic revolutions produced by the need to contain a resurgent France. It also underlined the growing incorporation of the Ottoman Empire into the European states-system.

The War of the Second Coalition, 1798–1802

The complex and rather divergent diplomacy of 1798–99 produced a ramshackle coalition. By spring 1799, Britain, Austria, Russia and the Ottoman Empire were at war with the Directory, as were Naples and Portugal, and were linked by a series of bilateral alliances. Treaties were signed between Austria and Naples (May 1798), between the Ottoman Empire and Russia and Britain (January 1799), and between Britain and Russia (December 1798), while Portugal was the established ally of Britain. But Russia and Austria were only allies by virtue of their earlier agreements, principally those of 1792 and 1795, while there was not, as yet, an alliance between London and Vienna, though this axis was likely to be central to any military struggle. There was thus no overall coalition. There was also no agreement on a unified strategy, and Grenville's efforts to sponsor one were unsuccessful.

These obvious shortcomings did not prevent the Second Coalition from considerable initial military success. Early in 1799, France took the initiative, sending her forces across the Rhine and then declaring war on Austria (March). Before long, the French were being pushed back in each theatre-of-war. Russian forces were sent to fight alongside the Austrians, first in Italy and then in Switzerland. The venerable if eccentric Suvorov, whose genius had earlier transformed the brave but stolid Russian troops into a mobile and aggressive army with offensive tactics which anticipated Napoleon, was recalled from retirement at Vienna's request, prompted by a British diplomat. Now almost 70, and a veteran of campaigns against the Ottoman Empire and in Poland, he was given command of the combined Austro-Russian forces in Italy, where his triumphant advance effectively cleared the French out of the north of the peninsula. In the south, meanwhile, a counter-revolution assisted by Nelson evicted the French from Naples. Simultaneously, the Austrians pushed forward in Switzerland, while in Germany the French had been forced back across the Rhine. By autumn 1799, the coalition appeared to be on the point of launching an invasion of France from Switzerland which, it was hoped, would end the war. This south-eastern front was one dimension of the allied offensive. The other was an ill-fated Anglo-Russian landing in Holland.

After the French overthrow of the Dutch Republic in 1795, Britain had lacked a bridgehead for her troops on the continent. In autumn 1799 a determined attempt was made to establish a second front at Den Helder in North Holland, which British ministers believed the most vulnerable part of French defences in western Europe. It was hoped that the expedition might provoke a Dutch rising against the French and their client Batavian *régime*, and in favour of the deposed House of Orange. Grenville believed that it could also force Berlin back into the war: a decade before Prussian soldiers had played the crucial role in an Orangist restoration (see pp. 241–2). Both hopes proved unfounded, and the expedition was little short of a fiasco. A British force did effect a landing, a considerable feat in the context of eighteenth-century combined operations, and it was reinforced by Russian troops. But the Anglo-Russian army encountered stiffer opposition than anticipated, since the French leaders were determined to retain their Belgian gains and defended Holland vigorously. The joint force faced the inevitable problems of supply, disease was soon rife, while the arrival of French reinforcements meant that the allies were soon outnumbered. These factors, together with a hesitation in following up the success in breaking through the French cordon, condemned the expedition to failure. Amidst bitter recriminations and with the onset of winter, the force secured an armistice, and the allied troops were evacuated at the end of October 1799. The fact that this agreement had been obtained unilaterally by the British commander worsened relations. Paul's resentment was considerable, and he was further alienated by London's continuing refusal to allow Russian troops to share in garrisoning Malta, recaptured by a British fleet in September 1798.

A second and even more severe setback was the almost simultaneous collapse of the campaign in the east and the abandonment of the planned invasion of France. The prospect of victory proved as divisive as defeat had earlier been, underlining the fragility of the Second Coalition. Problems arose principally from Vienna. Thugut was determined to avoid any repeat of 1796–97, when (he believed) Austria had been exposed to defeat by the self-interested conduct of her allies. He also intended that the massive Habsburg military contribution – in 1799 some three-quarters of the coalition's forces were Austrian – should be accompanied by firm political direction. This was resented by Suvorov, who disliked Vienna's control of operations and particularly the decision to deploy his army in Switzerland. It was also why the Archduke Charles, unlike in earlier campaigns, was subjected to direction by the foreign minister, who dictated military strategy.

Austria's wider aims complicated Thugut's relations with London and St Petersburg. He resented Britain's parsimony over financial aid, and apparent intentions over the Southern Netherlands, which Vienna wished to abandon but London wanted to strengthen under Austrian rule. Thugut was even more fearful and envious of Russia's successes in Italy; Austro-Russian military cooperation had never been very smooth. Though Suvorov had been made an Austrian field-marshal, in an attempt to reduce disputes, there had been a series of clashes with members of the high command and the political élite in Vienna. His adventurous and at times foolhardy strategy was one source of these disagreements, challenging as it did the more cautious approach favoured by the Habsburgs, who remained wedded to a traditional war of position. Further problems were caused when Suvorov began to implement Paul I's plans for the peninsula. Before he left Russia, he had been told that his mission was 'to restore thrones and altars', but his efforts to do this and, specifically, his clear intention to bring about the restoration of the King of Sardinia and his counterpart in Naples, led to the Emperor Francis II formally instructing him to desist.

Suvorov's actions threatened both Austria's own plans for Italy and her view of the conflict's wider purpose. Ministers in Vienna did not yet share Britain's assumption that it was simply a struggle to extinguish the Revolution. The notion of total victory was no part of their thinking. On the contrary, the Habsburgs remained devoted to the limited warfare of the *ancien régime*, assuming that military successes could be turned to immediate account through territorial acquisitions. In keeping with this doctrine, Austria hoped to use the victories over France to make substantial gains both in northern Italy and in western Germany. Still distrustful of Berlin, she was also anxious to deny Prussia any significant acquisitions. Habsburg ministers had long feared that their traditional rival would demand a share in any territorial readjustments in Germany after a French defeat.

Vienna's territorial ambitions exemplified the way individual aims undermined the coalition during the second half of 1799. Paul's view of Russian interests in the eastern Mediterranean also made him hostile to

Austrian expansion in Italy, though until now this attitude had been softened by the pressure of events. He intended that the expulsion of the French from the peninsula, achieved by the summer of 1799, would be followed by the restoration of the former rulers. But it became clear that Vienna had designs on France's Italian satellites. The Habsburgs refused to take part in an invasion of France and instead diverted their troops to the pursuit of their own territorial aims in Italy. The Russians, abandoned by the Austrians, were defeated by the French at the second battle of Zürich (September 1799). Suvorov's retreat, by a brilliant passage of the Alps into Germany in the late autumn, was only accomplished with heavy losses.

Russia's ruler had been disillusioned by the conduct of his allies and, to a lesser extent, the defeats suffered by his own armies. The formal breach was occasioned by Vienna's efforts to monopolise the capture of Ancona, an important port on Italy's north-east coast, which had been seized by a combined Austro-Russian army and a Russo-Ottoman fleet. Paul felt himself betrayed by Austria and now (November 1799) withdrew from the Second Coalition which, he wrote to the Emperor Francis, had become a war for Habsburg aggrandisement. In January 1800 Suvorov was ordered to return home. This decision also ended the short-lived Anglo-Russian *entente*. London had to decide between the two eastern powers and its automatic preference was Austria, who by tradition, geography and recent performance was a more dependable ally against France – though Grenville's diplomacy since 1797 had suggested otherwise. This choice, rather than Paul's resentment over Malta or the North Holland expedition, was the real cause of the Anglo-Russian breach which was evident by the beginning of 1800. The Second Coalition had collapsed. The breach, however, did finally facilitate an Austro-British reconciliation, as Vienna ratified the loan convention and London provided much-needed financial aid. By the second half of June 1800 a formal alliance had been restored.

The disintegration of the allied war effort during the second half of 1799 could not completely disguise the reverses which the Directory had suffered, particularly in Italy. France could also derive scant consolation from the Egyptian expedition of 1798–99. The command of this had been given to Napoleon Bonaparte, the rising star of French military life. His successes in the Italian peninsula (see above, pp. 272–4), carefully publicised by his own propaganda, had established his fame. Bonaparte's military talents had always been accompanied by intense political ambition and a willingness to play for the highest stakes. By 1797, when he returned victorious from Italy, he enjoyed considerable political influence, and he certainly possessed the ambition and ability to exploit this: particularly since the Directory was more and more dependent on the army to resist its political opponents.

Though the potential threat to the Ottoman Empire and Egypt's value as a base for further French expansion were significant, the Egyptian expedition was primarily intended to further the struggle against Britain. The only major state still fighting France after the Peace of Campo Formio, she was largely safe from direct attack. Though an invasion of England was seriously considered in 1797–98, France's lack of sea power made it impracticable, exactly as it had contributed to the failure of Irish expeditions in 1796 and 1798. It was only when this scheme was shelved that the Directory determined on the Egyptian expedition. French strategists had long considered the acquisition of Egypt, nominally part of the Ottoman Empire but effectively ruled by the Mamelukes, and this project was currently being canvassed by the foreign minister, Talleyrand. Bonaparte, aware that inactivity could be fatal to his political ambitions, took up the scheme and secured its adoption by the Directors, who were not sorry to see such a successful and ambitious general leave Paris. They believed that the capture of Egypt would be a blow to Britain's trade and prosperity, as well as a threat to her possession of India: ideas which seem rather grandiose, but were at the heart of French policy. The romantic streak in Bonaparte and his lifelong fascination with the 'East' led him to see the conquest of Egypt as the prelude to further eastern adventures, with himself cast in the role of a latter-day Alexander the Great.

The French force landed in Egypt on 1 July 1798, having easily captured the island of Malta (see above, p. 291) and then fortuitously avoided Nelson's squadron. Bonaparte soon occupied Alexandria, routed the Mameluke army at the battle of the Pyramids (21 July 1798) and captured Cairo. This gave the French control over Lower Egypt, but the promising opening was not sustained. Nelson's destruction of the French fleet at Aboukir Bay (Battle of the Nile, 1 August 1798) left Bonaparte and his army stranded and, incidentally, deprived them of news from Europe. This British success was, in its own way, as decisive as Nelson's more celebrated later victory at Trafalgar in 1805 (see below, p. 309). British victories in 1797 had given the royal navy a degree of control over the North Sea, Channel and Atlantic, and Aboukir Bay added the Mediterranean to this list. It also undermined French efforts to challenge Britain at sea, as Bonaparte himself acknowledged in its immediate aftermath.

France's initial hopes that the expedition would not antagonise the Sultan were shattered by his declaration of war (September 1798). Bonaparte now tried to advance northwards into Syria to consolidate his position. This strategy was initially successful and led to the capture of an Ottoman garrison at Jaffa, but the failure to take Acre (March–May 1799) forced him to retreat with heavy casualties. The intervention of a British fleet commanded by Sir Sidney Smith proved decisive; above all, it deprived Bonaparte of his siege artillery. The French army fell back to Egypt, suffering heavy losses from plague, but its commander was still able to defeat an Ottoman force sent against him (battle of Aboukir, 25 July 1799).

The expedition had now become a military and political cul-de-sac, above all for its leader. News of French defeats at the hands of the Second Coalition and of the volatile state of domestic politics then sent Bonaparte hurrying back to France. Abandoning his army, he left Egypt on 22 August 1799 and reached France early in October. The failure to negotiate the evacuation of the expeditionary force meant that the French occupation of Egypt continued until September 1801, when the troops – weakened by food shortages and disease – were finally forced to leave by an Anglo-Ottoman army. In the next year the Sultan Selim III made peace with France, as part of the general settlement at Amiens, and Constantinople now resumed a watchful neutrality towards the European conflict, facilitated by the staged withdrawal of the British expeditionary force, completed in March 1803.

By the autumn of 1799, the political situation in Paris was becoming critical, while the successes of the Second Coalition had made France's military situation acute. The Directory had ruled since 1795, but its hold on power was slipping fast. It had failed to overcome the political fragmentation after the ending of the Terror. Its own political base had always been dangerously narrow and it had a peculiarly chequered existence. The complex political structure set up in 1795 was, in itself, inherently defective, while it faced considerable problems. Plagued by a permanently critical economic situation and the endless financial difficulties produced by war, confronted by opposition from across the political spectrum, the Directory had survived increasingly through a series of *coups d'état*. The search for political stability was finally undermined by the financial strain of renewed war and by the defeats inflicted by the Second Coalition. By autumn 1799, it was apparent that the Revolution's only hope of survival was the army, and some politicians were searching for a general to carry out a further *coup*. Bonaparte's return to Paris in mid-October was opportune. Within a month he had carried through the *coup* of 18–19 *Brumaire* (9–10 November 1799) which established the Consulate. It had been intended that he should merely be the instrument for another change of government personnel but, to the surprise of his fellow conspirators, the ambitious Bonaparte emerged as the dominant figure in the new *régime*, through his post of first consul.

France's new ruler faced enormous internal problems. The economy was in disarray, the country weary of war, while there was also a long-standing rebellion in the Vendée, where a royalist counter-revolution could not be defeated. Bonaparte's own survival would depend on how he handled these difficulties, and this meant that peace was essential, particularly as the French armies were now in poor shape. The first consul made considerable efforts to negotiate a settlement with Vienna and London during the winter of 1799–1800, but these failed. The Habsburgs, having made substantial territorial gains in Italy, were unwilling to return to the position established by Campo Formio, while the British government remained unwilling to sign a peace that left Holland and Belgium under French control. Each state had its own view of what was an equitable settlement and these proved incompatible; yet neither side had won the decisive victory which would enable it to dictate terms. Peace, Bonaparte concluded, could not be negotiated; it would have to be imposed after further French victories.

The difficulties of the Second Coalition during the final months of 1799 had provided a welcome respite, but France's strategic position remained serious. Russia had withdrawn from the alliance in the previous year and Britain could not be attacked directly; the campaign of 1800 was therefore directed against Austria. The first consul grasped that Switzerland and northern Italy were the key military arena, though French armies also pressed forward in Germany. Characteristically, he took the initiative himself, leading the small and hastily improvised 'Army of the Reserve' in a decisive, if ill-managed, march across the Alps into Italy, outmanoeuvring the Austrians (lacking the leadership of the Archduke Charles, who had resigned after the previous campaign) and defeating them at Marengo (June 1800).

This defeat, together with the French advance in Germany, forced Vienna to conclude an armistice, though the subsequent negotiations proved inconclusive. But a decisive French victory at Hohenlinden in Bavaria (December 1800) finally ended Habsburg participation in the Second Coalition. The Austrian army was by now in very poor condition and when the Archduke Charles was recalled after the military defeats, he

quickly advised that further resistance was impossible. Vienna was forced
to accept the Peace of Lunéville (9 February 1801), which was a severe
reverse. It restored and extended French gains at Campo Formio four
years earlier. Austria was obliged to recognise France's possession not
merely of Belgium but of the left bank of the Rhine. The Habsburg
dependency in Italy, the Grand Duchy of Tuscany, was lost. With the
re-establishment of the Cisalpine Republic the French secured effective
control over northern and central Italy, though Austria was allowed to
keep Venetia. Habsburg power in the Italian peninsula had been destroyed,
while her influence in Germany had been further undermined. Vienna was
also obliged to recognise the satellite republics. Austria's defeat and the
harsh peace terms were the more bitter because of the initial optimism
generated by the Coalition's successes in 1799, and it brought about the
fall of Thugut and his discredited policies.

Bonaparte was less successful elsewhere in 1800–1. His efforts to
create a Franco-Russian *entente* by exploiting Paul's resentment towards
Britain and Austria ultimately failed. The First Consul and his foreign
minister, Talleyrand, wanted Russia's cooperation and perhaps even an
alliance to exclude British trade from northern Europe. France's conquests
had closed many continental ports to English goods, and this protean
'Continental System' needed St Petersburg's support to complete it by the
closure of the Baltic. A combination of French diplomacy and the widespread resentment among neutral states at Britain's high-handed enforcement of her own interpretation of maritime law had led to the formation
of a league of Armed Neutrality in December 1800, in which Russia was
joined by Denmark, Sweden and Prussia. This second Armed Neutrality
for a time intensified Britain's economic difficulties by cutting her off from
the vital Baltic and German markets, and it contributed to her increasing
willingness to negotiate with Bonaparte, as well as underlining her predicament after nearly a decade fighting France. Exactly as two decades
before (see above, p. 230) the neutral league was emblematic of Britain's
failure, after eight years of fighting, to get to grips with her French adversary. But the league crumbled swiftly after Nelson's bombardment of the
Danish fleet off Copenhagen (2 April 1801).

The final year of Paul I's reign (1800–1) saw a sharp deterioration in
relations with Britain, as the Emperor arrested English merchants, planned
a far-fetched military expedition to attack British India and encouraged
Prussia to occupy Hanover (see below, p. 312). This was matched by a
parallel improvement in relations with France, facilitated by the expulsion
of 'Louis XVIII' from his refuge at Mittau and the precipitate withdrawal

of financial support (January 1801). By this period the pragmatic Russian Emperor was more willing to come to terms with Bonaparte than with earlier French *régimes*, believing he would tame the Revolution and restore social and political order. Yet in the final months of his life, Paul, whose sanity was more and more doubted, entertained far more wide-ranging ambitions than merely a settlement with France. He dreamed of achieving his long-established aims of restoring monarchical order and peace to Europe and protecting the smaller states, through an armed mediation. Its component elements would be a Northern Alliance, based on his established links with Prussia, cooperation with the Armed Neutrality, and a *rapprochement* with France. Behind this grandiose scheme can be glimpsed the kind of Franco-Russian condominium over Europe achieved six years later at Tilsit. It was already stillborn when events intervened. The murder of Paul I (March 1801) and the succession of his son Alexander I (1801–25) ended Bonaparte's own lingering hopes of a Franco-Russian *rapprochement*, at least for the moment. On the credit side, both Portugal, nominally at war with France since 1793, and Naples came to terms in 1801.

Only Britain remained at war. Her sea power still prevented the realisation of French invasion plans. After a decade of fighting, however, the nation's will to carry on was waning. Overseas trade, Britain's life-blood, had been affected severely. The closure of the French market in 1793 itself had been significant, since trade had expanded after the commercial treaty in 1786. France's territorial expansion during the 1790s, moreover, had closed many of the traditional outlets for British commerce, particularly in the Low Countries and the Mediterranean. The war-weariness which these economic difficulties induced was strengthened by the direct taxation which Pitt had introduced to finance the struggle against France. Above all, the Peace of Lunéville had left Britain without a major ally. There was, by 1801, no obvious way she could influence events on the continent. The political crisis over Irish emancipation indirectly increased London's willingness to negotiate. George III's long-standing refusal to countenance any improvement in the position of Roman Catholics in Ireland led to the resignation early in 1801 of Pitt, who for a decade had directed and sustained Britain's war effort. The new ministry, led by Addington, wanted peace and listened eagerly to French offers to negotiate. The discussions were protracted, largely because Bonaparte hoped to hang on to Egypt. Peace preliminaries were eventually signed in London in October 1801. The Peace of Amiens (27 March 1802) provided for French garrisons to leave the Papal States and Naples. Britain returned all her conquests made during the war, except for the islands of Ceylon (which had been captured from the Dutch) and Trinidad (seized from Spain). Egypt was to be restored to the Ottoman Empire and Malta to the Knights.

The peace treaties of 1801–2 were intrinsically unstable; they were, in reality, mere truces, exactly like the earlier settlements. After a decade of almost continuous warfare, peace was welcomed by all the belligerents, but the agreements at Lunéville and Amiens were once again the product of exhaustion, not reconciliation. Austria resented the destruction of her dominant position in northern Italy and the challenge to her traditional authority in the German lands. She would clearly welcome an early opportunity of overturning the Peace of Lunéville. Britain, for her part, had sought an agreement in 1801 partly in the belief that the Revolution had run its course and that it might now be possible to live at peace with the French Republic; but the peace negotiations with France disillusioned them. They convinced British ministers of Bonaparte's 'inordinate ambition', as the foreign secretary Lord Hawkesbury (subsequently the second Lord Liverpool) described it. There could be little hope of an enduring peace with such a regime and such a ruler, particularly as the treaties of 1801–2 left France's hegemony in western and southern Europe substantially intact.

Napoleon and the European States-System

The 1790s had seen a decisive French challenge to what contemporaries called 'the Public Law of Europe'. In 1796, Burke, that inveterate opponent of the Revolution, claimed that the French were establishing 'a new description of empire, which is not grounded on any balance, but forms a sort of imperious hierarchy, of which France is to be the head and guardian'. France's massive territorial gains in 1797–1802 appeared to confirm his analysis. This expansion continued and, indeed, accelerated during the next decade. By 1812 Napoleon – as the First Consul was known after he became Emperor in 1804 – would rule a vast empire and control Europe to an extent unparalleled since Roman times. The creation and then the disintegration of this supremacy dominated international relations between the Peace of Amiens and the Congress of Vienna.

There were important continuities from the 1790s. The success of the revolutionary leaders in advancing the French frontier into the Low Countries, to the Rhine and into northern Italy, inevitably dictated the framework of Napoleon's policy. In a similar way, his ability to win decisive military victories magnified a tendency already evident. Territory was now taken from the major states and not, as before 1789, from those in decline. The limited warfare of the *ancien régime* and the balance of power it upheld had been integral to territorial stability. Prussia's seizure of Silesia from Austria had been the principal transfer of territory between great powers during the eighteenth century. In the decade after the peace of Campo Formio, by contrast, substantial amounts of land were taken from Prussia and Austria. These and similar seizures were made possible by the overwhelming victories won by French armies, particularly over the Third Coalition in 1805–7.

Napoleon's unique impact on the international system was primarily military. The decisive victories left his enemies completely at his mercy and made the diplomats largely irrelevant. In the early phase of his career Napoleon had been prepared to exploit diplomacy for tactical ends. He had been directly involved in the negotiation of the peace preliminaries with Austria in spring 1797 and in the final settlement at Campo Formio, revealing an imperious and bullying style which he retained, while in 1799–1800 and again in 1801–2 he had employed peace feelers to London to secure the period of repose he believed essential. As his position within France was consolidated and the potential of the French army enhanced, diplomacy became less and less necessary for the Emperor. Negotiation was impossible for Prussia after her shattering defeat in 1806, or for Austria after the disastrous war of 1809. Each power was incapable of further resistance and therefore handed over the territory he demanded.

Napoleon's approach to international relations always remained that of a general rather than a foreign minister. His impatience meant that he had little time for the delay and the give-and-take which were part of all negotiations, and he frequently censured the dilatoriness of the diplomats. He also shared the French Revolution's negative view of diplomacy and its practitioners (see above, pp. 276–9) and particularly disliked the notion of diplomatic immunity, one foundation of the diplomacy of the eighteenth century. By 1805 he could write that 'Ministers of foreign countries are, in plain words, accredited spies. It is as well to keep them at arm's length.' In accordance with this attitude, Napoleon flouted the conventions of international law and diplomacy, further alienating continental opinion.

Two early illustrations came at the Rastatt conference, which met in 1797–98 to arrange the settlement for Germany. Napoleon evicted both the delegate from the Bishopric of Würzburg, on the grounds that he was a cleric, and Sweden's representative, the ubiquitous Hans Axel von Fersen, thrown out since he had been an *émigré* agent. France's own representatives were murdered by Austrian hussars (see above, p. 276), underlining that it was not simply Napoleon who disregarded the conventions of international law. Yet his breaches were far more numerous. Six years later, in 1804, particular revulsion was caused by the kidnapping and execution of the duc d'Enghien (see below, p. 313). In 1803, after the resumption of the Anglo-French war, several British tourists still on the continent were arrested, along with three English diplomats and their staffs. In the following year the seizure of another British diplomat, Sir George Rumbold, was even more flagrant. In late October 1804, French troops – acting on Napoleon's direct orders – seized Rumbold and his papers from his villa and took him to Paris, where he was imprisoned. This action violated both diplomatic immunity and the Prussian neutrality zone. Frederick William III sent a stiff letter of protest and this may have contributed to the envoy's release after three weeks, although Rumbold's papers were retained. Such flagrant breaches of international law contrasted sharply with the action of the British government in 1806, when it imprisoned a man who offered to assassinate Napoleon and actually informed France of this. This highlighted the gulf between the established powers and the *régime* in Paris; it also helps explain why Napoleon's France never became fully accepted as a member of the international community. Most European governments were in any case irreconcilably opposed to the Emperor whom they soon saw as the heir to the hated French Revolution.

Napoleon did contribute to one significant long-term development: the appearance of military attachés. The French Revolution and especially the Napoleonic state used soldiers as diplomats far more than during the *ancien régime*: some 20 diplomatic missions were headed by generals from 1789 to 1814. In keeping with Napoleon's view of ambassadors as 'accredited spies', embassies were used systematically to assemble information on the armies of likely opponents. In 1806 several French officers were sent to Berlin to report on the Prussian army in anticipation of a war launched that autumn (see below, pp. 318–19), while, in the same year, the French embassy in Vienna contained a captain responsible solely for collecting information on Austria's forces. Military and naval intelligence had long been assembled through embassies, but not as extensively and systematically as under Napoleon. By 1805 the French foreign ministry contained a designated bureau responsible for handling information on rival armies and navies. These developments anticipated the establishment of military attachés in the embassies of all major states during the nineteenth century.

Except for his personal aggrandisement, Napoleon's foreign policy lacked a central theme. But the dominant elements in his strategy can be discerned: opposition to England, control of Germany and Italy, supremacy for France in the Mediterranean and in the Balkans and, increasingly, recognition by the other European powers of his own achievements and those of the Bonaparte dynasty. At various times one or more of these aims was uppermost; but Napoleon's capacity to win decisive military victories meant that he was never forced to make a choice over priorities almost to the end. The Napoleonic empire itself arose piecemeal from these victories; the imperialism was not so much planned as unavoidable. The personal elements was very important. Napoleon's unique energy and spirit, together with his own ambition which verged on megalomania, gave a decisive twist to French policy in these years. These ambitions, which increased with each new military triumph, provided the nearest thing to a unified explanation of his foreign policy. He was essentially an opportunist who sought to exploit the existing jealousies and suspicions among his enemies. In so far as Napoleon had any consistent diplomatic strategy it was to retain at least one great power as a partner or satellite: Prussia up to 1806, Russia after Tilsit, Austria after her humiliation in 1809. Each was lured by the promise of subsequent gains but none secured these. Napoleon's use of alliances was always tactical; diplomacy continued to be subservient to military strategy. All problems, he believed, were capable of a military solution. In this he was mistaken. Each new victory in the years after 1803 created the same basic problem; how to produce a stable political settlement between France and Europe. Each time Napoleon sought a military solution, and ultimately he would overextend himself.

The renewal of the Anglo-French War and the formation of the Third Coalition, 1802–1805

London's attitude to the settlement at Amiens was ambivalent. George III had referred to it as an 'experimental peace', as Britain attempted to coexist with France. After a decade of expensive war and mounting economic difficulties the treaty was welcomed as a breathing-space. The prime minister, Addington, quickly abolished the wartime expedient of income tax and even cut expenditure in the hope that it might prove enduring. This contrasted with the increase in the pace of French naval construction, indicating that Napoleon viewed the settlement as temporary, and underlined the British optimism and even naïvety. Yet there was also widespread if grudging recognition in London that the treaty had ignored many fundamental issues and had done nothing to diminish the underlying rivalry. The Addington ministry had bought peace through substantial concessions; within a few months the extent of these became evident.

France's continued control of the mouths of the Scheldt and the Rhine was unacceptable, as was Napoleon's dominance over the continent. The settlement failed to restore the anticipated prosperity to Britain, or to reopen the markets of France and her dependencies to British goods because of continuing protectionist policies. The First Consul, for his part, disliked the hostile tone of *émigré* and British journalists writing in British newspapers, complained about their activities and resented the Addington ministry's failure to curb them. The enduring suspicion and bad feeling, on both sides of the Channel, was soon evident in disputes over the execution of the treaty, and from the late autumn of 1802, relations deteriorated rapidly. In the event, the breathing-space secured at Amiens would last for only 14 months.

The deterioration was produced principally by Napoleon's continued ambitions and by consequent British resentment at breaches of the spirit and, sometimes, even the letter of the peace of Amiens and the earlier settlement at Lunéville. Talleyrand later remarked that 'Hardly was the peace concluded when moderation commenced to abandon Bonaparte', and there was ample evidence of this in these months. Britain feared further French colonial expansion which lay behind the sending of troops to the former Spanish colony of Santo Domingo (Haiti) in the Caribbean (the eastern end of the island, also containing the former French colony of Saint-Dominigue, ceded to its French ally by Madrid) to crush a slave revolt, and apparent in the earlier forced cession of Louisiana (1801). The First Consul's unsuccessful efforts to force his Spanish ally to transfer Florida as well to France's control indicated the scale of the threat which Britain might soon face in the Caribbean from a revived French empire. In the event, the French units on Haiti were devastated by disease and had to be withdrawn, forcing the abandonment of Napoleon's ambitious plans and leading to the sale of Louisiana to the American Republic in 1803. Yet in the short term, these actions caused tension with London. Napoleon's energetic and large-scale reconstruction of the French navy similarly alarmed ministers in London, since it struck at the heart of Britain's security.

Napoleon's continued annexations in Europe and apparent ambitions in the Near East caused most alarm, especially as there was now little resistance on the continent to further French expansion. The First Consul's acquisitions in peace were almost as impressive as his gains by war, and his aggressive policy was widely supported in the French military and civil *élite*. His schemes for the reorganisation of Germany (see pp. 327–8), his military intervention in October 1802 to shore up the Swiss Helvetic Republic and his new acquisitions in Italy (Piedmont – the remaining mainland part of the kingdom of Sardinia – Parma and the island of Elba were formally annexed to France in autumn 1802), and the harsh treatment meted out to the Dutch Batavian Republic and Spain as satellites, were all viewed in London as breaches of the settlements of 1801–2. Even more anxiety was aroused by fears of a new French attack on Egypt and an eventual challenge to British power in India. The appearance of Colonel Horace Sébastiani's report in the *Moniteur* on 30 January 1803 appeared to confirm this view. Sébastiani was a French agent who had been sent to the Near East. His report emphasised the weakness both of the Ottoman Empire and the remaining British force in Egypt and concluded that an army of merely 6,000 men could reconquer the latter. His conclusions, and their appearance in an official newspaper, confirmed Britain's belief that Napoleon would reoccupy Egypt as soon as they observed the terms of the peace of Amiens and withdrew their forces from the Mediterranean. France's foreign minister Talleyrand frankly told the British ambassador that this would soon be carried out, though in fact Napoleon does not seem to have intended it at this time.

The Addington ministry eventually decided, in a belated show of strength, to retain Malta, Britain's one remaining Mediterranean base. It was legally a breach of the peace treaty, but by the final weeks of 1802 there was little doubt that the struggle would soon be resumed. London's new-found firmness was also evident in demands that France should evacuate Switzerland and the Batavian Republic. Napoleon, for his part, believed this novel stubbornness could be overcome by intimidation – a belief encouraged by British weakness during the peace negotiations. Relations became increasingly acrimonious in the early months of 1803 and, on 18 May, Britain declared war. The First Consul's actions had done much to provoke a renewal of fighting, but in the final weeks of peace both he and Talleyrand had by turns pleaded with and threatened the departing British ambassador in an attempt to delay war. France may have anticipated resuming the struggle only in 1805, by which time her navy would be appreciably stronger.

The fighting soon resumed the familiar pattern. Britain's dominance at sea, and the effective naval blockade of France's Channel and Atlantic ports, enabled her to seize a series of French and Dutch colonies; but the same strategic stalemate which had been evident since the First Coalition and had contributed to the peace of Amiens remained. Neither British mastery at sea nor French supremacy on land was itself sufficient to secure a decisive victory for either side. Until the formation of the Third Coalition in 1805, Britain fought alone and only her navy saved her from defeat at a period when the strategic initiative had passed to France. Napoleon, free from continental enemies, seriously contemplated the invasion of England long envisaged by French strategists. A vast force – the 'Army of Invasion' – was maintained at Boulogne from late 1803 until autumn 1805, but no descent could be attempted because Britain retained the initiative at sea.

The royal navy made an enormous contribution to France's defeat during the Revolutionary and Napoleonic Wars. The scale of the emergency Britain faced was reflected in unprecedented naval expansion. Personnel had increased from some 16,000 in the early 1790s to around 141,000 men by 1809, as more and more ships were commissioned. The first decade of the struggle saw a series of British naval victories and the destruction of the fleets of Britain's rivals which established a supremacy which was quite unprecedented. By 1810 Britain's share of global naval tonnage was to be around 50 per cent, an increase of two-thirds on the figure two decades before, when it had been around 30 per cent. Captured ships had been reflagged, while the material destruction inflicted on her rivals had been considerable. France's continuing inferiority at sea was confirmed by Britain's superior tactics and leadership. The traditional 'line-ahead' formation of the eighteenth century was steadily abandoned, as British commanders came to prefer the more aggressive tactics of the *mêlée*, close combat aimed at isolating and destroying individual ships or sectors of the opposing fleet. In encounters of this kind, superior British gunnery and shiphandling were always likely to prove decisive. British leadership was also far better. The age of Nelson saw the emergence of a number of able, professional and aggressive commanders – Nelson himself, Howe and St Vincent, Cornwallis and Collingwood. The French fleet, by contrast, continued to lack experience of sea and combat, while its leadership and administration had been all but destroyed during the early years of the Revolution and manning was a permanent problem. Though it was rapidly being rebuilt, particularly after 1804, France's fleet continued to be confined to port.

Napoleon's planned invasion of England required at least temporary French control at sea, so that the 'Army of Invasion' could be transported across the Channel. But this was prevented by the British blockade of the principal French naval bases, which stopped a major fleet being assembled at sea. Central to this stranglehold was the 'close' blockade of Brest maintained with difficulty from May 1803 until November 1805 when, at the battle of Trafalgar, Nelson destroyed a combined Franco-Spanish fleet when it came out of Cadiz (Spain had entered the war on France's side in December 1804). The British victory confirmed the abandonment, two months earlier, of French invasion plans, which Napoleon never revived, effectively conceding naval dominance to Britain. This mastery was used to secure a powerful position in the Baltic, to facilitate British trade especially in naval stores, and it enabled the royal navy to re-establish its control over the Mediterranean, where periodic sorties were conducted against outlying French positions. Sea power, however, remained an essentially defensive weapon which in itself could not bring about the defeat of France. It could and did prevent invasion, but it was unable to give much support to London's continental allies or even to deliver an effective blow against French power. These limitations were certainly apparent to Pitt, who had become prime minister again in May 1804. Shortly after his return to office, he began a series of diplomatic initiatives which led to the formation of the Third Coalition.

Pitt's realisation that victory could only be secured on land made him willing to provide subsidies on an unprecedented scale, in itself a significant modification of British policy. Subsidies had, hitherto, been given reluctantly and selectively. They had been paid either in return for troops or, occasionally, in an attempt to retain a country in the coalition. Henceforth, Britain would subsidise any ally, and this was to be very important during the final decade of the struggle. Subsidies, however, were still to be the limit of London's commitment. Pitt wanted a coalition but not direct military involvement on the Continent, and this was resented by potential allies who had to face Napoleon's armies directly.

The new attitude to subsidies indicated Pitt's desire to form a coalition quickly in 1804–5, since he believed the strategic initiative lay with France. Military assistance on the scale needed to defeat Napoleon could only come from one or more of the major continental powers. It was now acknowledged that this war could only be won in Europe: except for the period 1806–7, London now saw the struggle in continental terms. But after a decade of expensive and unsuccessful hostilities, France's enemies were reluctant to join a new alliance. They were as afraid of the peace terms which a victorious France might impose as of further military defeat. Twice already – in 1797 and in 1801 – Napoleon had redrawn the political map and demolished traditional institutions at the end of a successful war. Monarchical Europe always feared more fighting might lead to its own final destruction. It was why, in contrast to the rapid resumption of the Anglo-French war, fighting did not begin again on the continent until 1805, as only with considerable difficulty could a new coalition be assembled.

Austria, Britain's partner during the 1790s, was for a long time unwilling to resume the struggle. Her armies had suffered heavy defeats during the final stages of the War of the Second Coalition, while she had had to shoulder the main burden of the continental war after Prussia's withdrawal in 1795. Inadequate resources had always been her Achilles' heel and, by 1802, after 15 years of near-continuous warfare, her finances were in chaos. Vienna had funded this fighting by further substantial borrowing and by issuing increasing amounts of paper currency. Between 1792 and 1801, on the best available figures, the public debt had increased by 57 per cent, from around 390 million florins to 613 million, sharply increasing the proportion of current income devoted to servicing this borrowing. The switch to a paper currency had worked reasonably well during the 1790s, but the volume of notes in circulation doubled between 1799 and 1801, setting off substantial inflation as the face value of this currency came to be discounted. The settlement at Lunéville was followed by a 60 per cent cut in the military budget. This was only one – albeit the most serious – of the war's domestic consequences. Habsburg territory had been laid waste by French forces, the struggle had become increasingly unpopular and it had proved difficult to recruit enough soldiers, while the reduced army urgently needed to be overhauled.

The Emperor Francis was consequently determined to avoid an early renewal of the fighting, and for the next few years peace and domestic reform were Austria's twin goals. Foreign policy was nominally in the hands of a career diplomat, Count Ludwig Cobenzl, though the Emperor's former tutor and now his trusted adviser and Cabinet Secretary, Franz von Colloredo-Wallsee, was at least as influential. The resumption of the Anglo-French war in spring 1803 appeared to threaten Vienna's neutrality. Cobenzl believed that naval power would give Britain the upper hand in this struggle, and feared that a defeated France might seek compensation by attacking Austria. This analysis led to a speeding-up of military reforms already under way, and to a covert policy of alliance with Russia, intended to provide a deterrent and concluded in secret in December 1804. The paradox involved did not escape Cobenzl's critics in Vienna, who were headed by the Archduke Charles and Colloredo: the alliance could not be disclosed in case it provoked a French attack, yet it was intended to deter that same aggression. Austria's policy at this time highlighted the extreme difficulty of any secure peace with France, as Napoleonic imperialism gathered pace. Yet there was considerable friction between Vienna and Paris. Austria feared renewed French expansion in Germany and the Mediterranean, and resented the imposition in 1803 of an Imperial Deputation, which destroyed the Holy Roman Empire and traditional Habsburg influence in Germany, and led to important territorial changes (see below, pp. 327–8). While relations were further soured by Napoleon's assumption of the title of emperor in May 1804, Austria's policy remained firmly pacific.

Prussia was even less likely to join a new coalition. Her army's enduring reputation ensured she was courted by both sides, and successive Kings had skilfully exploited this since 1795. Prussia's policy was still to stand aloof, to incline slightly towards Paris and to try to increase her territory and consolidate her influence in northern Germany. This approach was realistic and defensible, and peace had served her well since her withdrawal from the First Coalition. Berlin had enjoyed a period of modest prosperity, and secured minor gains from successive French territorial reorganisations of Germany, while political tradition ensured that Austria's eclipse was not wholly unwelcome. Frederick William III had successfully retrenched and paid off some of the debts built up by his financially-reckless predecessor. By 1806 these would stand at 36 million *taler*, a fall of almost 20 million since 1795, while a reserve of 17 million had also been accumulated.

International events, however, were undermining Prussia's stance, and by 1803 the north German neutrality zone had been completely compromised. France's occupation of Hanover on the resumption of war with Britain and, in a wider sense, French territorial and political expansion, ended the neutralisation of the region, and reduced Berlin to a client. Prussia was now sandwiched between expansionist powers both to the west and to the east. Just as significant as France, in the longer perspective, was Russia's growing importance for Frederick William III's foreign policy. The destruction of Poland during the 1790s had removed a valuable buffer state: after 1795 Prussia had a frontier with Russia which was more than 500 kilometres long, enabling her powerful neighbour to exert increasing leverage on her.

The King's famous meeting with Alexander I at Memel (Klaipeda) in June 1802 testified to St Petersburg's new importance and forged a personal alliance which would endure for the next two decades. Thereafter, though his emotional commitment to the allied cause was becoming evident, it was several years before it influenced his foreign policy. Though the geopolitical constraints on Prussian policy were much greater by 1803, Berlin's diplomatic outlook remained neutralist. The same was true of the intensifying struggle for power in the entourage of the indecisive King, as ministers and courtiers championed rival solutions to Prussia's predicament but could not bring about a change in policy. The war party, who urged the folly of leaving Napoleon a free hand in the political reorganisation of the continent, was by 1803–4 gaining strength and confidence, but was not strong enough to push the country into further fighting. The future acquisition of Hanover remained central to Prussian thinking, and it was carefully cultivated by the French. There was very little chance, therefore, at this time, that she would abandon her so-far profitable neutrality and join Pitt's coalition.

A new Anglo-Russian alliance did not, initially, seem any more likely. Indeed, for some time after his accession in 1801, Alexander I appeared as hostile towards Britain as towards Napoleonic France, largely because of British naval action against neutral shipping in the Baltic and, in particular, Nelson's raid on Copenhagen in 1801. London's continuing refusal to hand over Malta to Russia was another significant source of friction. At the same time, internal reforms carried out by France's first consul attracted the Russian ruler, who nurtured similar aims. In October 1801, a Franco-Russian peace settlement had been worked out and thereafter Alexander had sought good relations with Napoleon. He wanted to concentrate on internal reforms and, in the early years of his reign, Russia continued to remain aloof from the struggle. There was, so far, little reason for any serious tension, especially as Napoleon's territorial ambitions did not yet impinge directly on Russian interests. Consequently, by 1802–3, Alexander's foreign policy had become distinctly isolationist.

Yet it became increasingly difficult for St Petersburg to sustain its neutrality, due to anxieties about French ambitions in the eastern Mediterranean (see below, pp. 313–14). Essentially the same fears which induced Britain to resume the war in May 1803 eventually persuaded Russia to re-enter the struggle. The Ottoman Empire, where there had been serious internal disturbances in 1802–3, seemed on the point of disintegration. Alexander and his advisers, who believed Russia alone should control the future of south-eastern Europe, were alarmed that France would exploit this instability. French expansion there would threaten Russia's security and her fast-expanding Black Sea trade. It would undermine the value of Catherine II's territorial acquisitions and might even imperil access to the Mediterranean through the Straits. In a similar way, Napoleon's increasingly expansionist policies in central Europe inspired fears that France could threaten Russia's new-found possessions in Poland.

These anxieties produced a significant deterioration in Russo-French relations, and this was exacerbated by other disputes. In the summer of 1803 Russia attempted to mediate in the renewed Anglo-French war, but Napoleon considered Alexander's intervention pro-English and rejected it out of hand. The French leader made matters worse by delivering a public dressing-down to the Russian ambassador who was promptly withdrawn. From the autumn of that year there was a serious Franco-Russian quarrel over the Ionian Islands – nominally an independent republic since the expulsion of the French by a Russo-Ottoman force in 1799. The d'Enghien affair in March 1804 did much to alienate Alexander, as it did monarchical Europe as a whole. The duc, a member of the former French royal family, was abducted by Napoleon's agents from neutral Baden, taken back to France, tried before a military tribunal and summarily executed. Alexander was outraged at what he considered murder. Even worse, the abduction had been from his wife's homeland. In reprisal, diplomatic relations with France were broken off in autumn 1804, shortly before Napoleon caused even more offence by crowning himself emperor. His adoption of the imperial title was disliked because it seemed to legitimise the hated French Revolution and the principles it embodied.

The deterioration in relations was facilitated by the growing influence in St Petersburg of the Polish nobleman, Prince Adam Czartoryski, a personal friend of Russia's young ruler and, for a time, the lover of Alexander's wife Elizabeth, with whom he remained infatuated. Czartoryski had come to the Russian court shortly after the third partition and had made his career there. In 1799 he had been sent as ambassador to Turin. His two years in Italy gave him a first-hand view of French expansion and created a strong suspicion of Bonaparte and his ambitions which coloured his future attitudes. Recalled in mid-1801 by Russia's new ruler, Czartoryski had become a leading voice in the so-called 'Unofficial Committee', the informal brains trust which advised Alexander I during the early part of his reign.

The Russian Emperor's upbringing had emphasised domestic issues, and he was ill-prepared to handle foreign policy. He was therefore receptive to the ideas put forward by Czartoryski, whose role increased during the next few years. From the autumn of 1802 he helped formulate Russian policy; after February 1804 he was Alexander's principal diplomatic adviser and *de facto* foreign minister with more influence than any of his successors during the reign. Under his guidance, Russia again became fully involved in European affairs. He encouraged the Emperor's growing concern at French expansion, especially in the Balkans, and suggested how Napoleon might be restrained. His plan, set out in a famous memorandum of 1803, blended *Realpolitik* with idealistic theorising about a future political settlement for Europe and even a system of collective security rooted in enforceable international law. Central to it was inevitably the re-establishment in some shape of the former Kingdom of Poland. But the deeply patriotic Czartoryski knew such talk would arouse the suspicions of the Russian court, and it was only in 1805 that a reborn Poland under St Petersburg's tutelage could be publicly canvassed.

Alexander I's thinking about foreign policy was, at this early point in his career, vague and imperfectly formed. He was clearly sympathetic to Czartoryski's ideas. Idealistic, the Emperor regarded diplomacy not in terms of particular alliances or rivalries (as most contemporaries did) but in vaguer and more theoretical concepts. The 'balance of power' and the 'community of Europe' were always central to his thinking, while he also had some sympathy for Polish aspirations: this had been one foundation of his friendship with Czartoryski. The fact that his minister aimed to make Russia supreme in the Balkans and in central Europe was a further recommendation. Consequently, these plans became the official basis of Russian diplomacy in 1804–5. An alliance of Russia, Austria and Prussia was to be formed, initially to restrain Napoleon's continuing expansion through an ultimatum. Only if this failed would the eastern powers consider war. In this eventuality, British participation and, more important, British gold would be essential.

This rather Utopian scheme fell far short of the new coalition Pitt hoped to create. Although alliance negotiations were begun by a British approach to Russia in 1804, by early the next year the prospective partners were still far apart. In particular, London's refusal to hand over Malta caused friction. Alexander had no wish to see another British base in the Mediterranean, since this could become as serious a threat to Russian interests there as that currently posed by France. He also resented the fact that Britain would still commit only money, not men, to the fighting on the continent. An Anglo-Russian subsidy agreement was actually signed in April 1805 in St Petersburg, but Britain was at first unwilling to ratify the terms forced on her representative by Alexander's ministers. Pitt, though he desired a new coalition, would still not make the concessions needed to bring it about.

Napoleon's unbridled ambitions now created the alliance which had eluded the diplomatic efforts of both Britain and Russia. On 18 May

1805 he took the throne of the former Cisalpine Republic, which now became the kingdom of Italy. The following month (6 June) he annexed Genoa (the Ligurian Republic) to France. These two actions, and the vast ambitions to which they testified, created in two months the coalition which two years of diplomacy had failed to produce. In July 1805 Britain ratified the April treaty with Russia, whose troops were dispatched in the following month to aid Austria, who had also decided to fight. Austrian support was essential, given Prussia's continuing neutrality, if Russian troops were to reach the central European battlefields. This decision in Vienna was taken against a background of government breakdown, with serious disagreements between the Emperor's leading advisers, and food shortages, leading to riots in the city in July. Yet the Austrians recognised that they had little alternative. Napoleon's actions in Italy infringed the Austro-French settlement at Lunéville (1801) and made clear that no enduring peace with France could be concluded.

The Austrian Emperor Francis I, as he had become in autumn 1804 when Vienna formally acknowledged the demise of the Holy Roman Empire (see below, p. 327), formally entered the war in August 1805 by adhering to the Anglo-Russian treaty, having successfully forced an increase in Britain's subsidy to him. Britain similarly paid a hefty subsidy to Sweden, in October, so that Russia could use the remaining strip of Swedish Pomerania as a base for operations in Germany. Naples became the coalition's final member through her treaty with Russia (September 1805). The extent of Napoleon's dominance in Germany was reflected in the fact that most of the smaller German states, many of whom had joined the two previous coalitions, now remained aloof. Prussia, for the moment, clung to her neutrality despite appeals for assistance from all sides, but Baden, Bavaria and Württemberg, three of the principal bene-ficiaries from the Imperial Deputation of 1803 (see below, p. 327) actu-ally joined Napoleon.

The destruction of the Third Coalition, 1805–1807

The Third Coalition satisfied neither Britain nor Russia. Neither Alexan-der's dreams of a crusade to restore peace nor Pitt's vision of an all-embracing coalition were answered by the military alliances hurriedly created in summer and autumn 1805 in response to Napoleon's escalating ambitions. Though the alliance's resources were considerable, the reluct-ant partners still viewed the war in different, occasionally contradictory, ways. The fighting which followed quickly demonstrated the fragility of this newly-created unity, as the speed of France's armies overwhelmed the ill-coordinated opposing coalition.

The campaign of 1805, launched precariously against the background of a severe financial crisis in France, proved a triumph for Napoleon. Austria was not yet ready for the war she had declared and in little more than three months suffered a complete defeat. The military reforms introduced by the Archduke Charles had barely begun to take effect. Vienna was still intent on retrieving its position in Italy and mistakenly sent large numbers of troops there, believing France would attack it. Napoleon, however, advanced rapidly in Germany, surprised and outmanoeuvred General Mack, latest in a long line of inept Austrian commanders, and forced a humiliating surrender at Ulm (20 October 1805). The French went on to occupy Vienna in mid-November before Napoleon advanced east in pursuit of his retreating enemies and brilliantly defeated a combined Austro-Russian army at Austerlitz in Moravia (2 December 1805). This shattering reverse was witnessed at first hand by Alexander I and Czartoryski, who had to flee the battlefield. Its impact on the Emperor's fragile self-confidence was to be considerable, particularly since he had countermanded his general's advice to retreat rather than risk annihilation.

Austria now withdrew from the Third Coalition and signed the treaty of Pressburg (Bratislava) on 26 December 1805, acknowledging her exclusion from Italy and the complete destruction of Habsburg authority in Germany. In return for minor gains from Bavaria, Austria lost Venetia, Istria and Dalmatia (to the Kingdom of Italy), the Tyrol and the Vorarlberg (to Bavaria) and the Breisgau (to Württemberg and Baden). These eclipsed all her earlier territorial losses, and underlined the scale of her defeat. She was also forced to pay a substantial indemnity and to recognise Napoleon's German clients, Bavaria and Württemberg, as independent kingdoms; a third, Baden, was raised to the status of a Grand Duchy. With hindsight the Treaty of Pressburg can be recognised as a decisive moment for Austria, after which her statesmen could either accept the satellite status created by military defeat, or rebel against the French yoke and risk further losses.

A similar choice faced Prussia, whose security and the North German neutrality zone upon which it rested had been undermined by France's dynamic expansion. This was evident by 1803 (see above, p. 311) and was to become even clearer. Prussia's pro-French neutrality was reducing her to a Napoleonic satellite, but alignment with Russia offered as many dangers: subservience to French military imperialism might well be replaced by subservience to Russian political expansion. Strategic vulnerability had always been central to Prussian foreign policy, and never more so than now. The resulting debates and manoeuvres at the Prussian court were intensified by the impact of a structural change in Prussian government, which had its roots in the growth of a more personalised monarchy during Frederick the Great's reign and became particularly important during the early 1800s.

Formally, Prussian foreign policy was conducted by the King working in partnership with the *Kabinettsministerium*. During and after the Seven Years War, however, Prussia's ruler had relied increasingly on a small group of secretaries in the *Kabinett* who resided with him at Potsdam. As a result, ministers and their departments had been marginalised and supplanted. Until his death in 1786 Frederick's remarkable abilities and towering personality had ensured that the members of the *Kabinett* remained scribes and only occasionally unofficial advisers. It was to be a very different story under his two less forceful and able successors. During the next twenty years two parallel but rival systems of government existed. There was a vacuum at the heart of the Prussian state, as political authority came to be contested by *Kabinett* secretaries, courtiers, military commanders and official ministers, all struggling to influence the weak and indecisive King. While the outward appearance of orderly government continued, behind this façade an atavistic struggle for supremacy developed in the 'antechamber of power', as the King's entourage has been styled.

These political rivalries shaped Prussia's response to the threats in the west and east. They became particularly important as Prussia's options narrowed with French expansion and Russia's growing involvement in central Europe, through the Third Coalition. Count Christian von Haugwitz had been the main influence upon Prussian foreign policy since 1792. He had been closely associated with the neutrality policy ever since its inception and strongly supported cooperation with Paris. In June 1806 he declared that 'France is all-powerful and Napoleon is the man of the century; what have we to fear if united with him?' France, moreover, could now offer the enticing bait of Hanover to reward continued Prussian neutrality. Its acquisition would confirm Prussia's dominance in north Germany, while an appreciation of her military vulnerability made Berlin's policy strongly pacific and appeared to recommend Haugwitz's approach. His principal rival was Karl August von Hardenberg who favoured alliance with Russia to challenge France. In August 1804 – four months after a secret Prusso-Russian alliance – Hardenberg became foreign minister. But Haugwitz continued to be consulted by the King and, a year later, he was recalled to Berlin from his exile. By this point the difficulties for Prussian policy, trapped in a vice between France and Russia, were particularly clear.

In October 1805 Haugwitz was formally appointed joint foreign minister alongside Hardenberg. This arrangement mirrored Prussia's predicament, but it could only intensify the instability and manoeuvring in Berlin, as Frederick William III's options narrowed even further. By this point Prussia, under continuous diplomatic pressure from Russia, Austria and Britain, was inching towards joining the Third Coalition and in November 1805 signed a treaty undertaking to do this. Prussian policy was thrown into reverse, however, by France's overwhelming victory at Austerlitz. Haugwitz now negotiated the Treaty of Schönbrunn (15 December 1805) with France, by which Prussia secured the coveted cession of Hanover, which was occupied by her troops. It would be a long time before this transaction was forgotten at the Habsburg court – or, indeed, in London.

Despite this gain, Prussia was completely at Napoleon's mercy, as Frederick William III quickly discovered. By the treaty of Paris (15 February 1806) he was forced to promise troops for the continuing French war against Russia, to join the Continental System (Napoleon's economic blockade against Britain – see below, pp. 333–6) and to close its ports to British shipping, moves which ended a period of Prussian economic prosperity. Britain responded to this and to the occupation of Hanover by declaring war (11 June) and attacking Prussian shipping. Frederick William III was soon afraid that Hanover might even now be snatched away, for in summer 1806 Napoleon was rumoured to be offering to return the electorate to George III for peace with Britain. By now Prussia's policy, recognising the impossibility of enduring cooperation with Napoleon, was more and more focussed upon Russia. In March Hardenberg was forced to resign, but immediately became Frederick William III's secret minister, charged with negotiating an alliance with Alexander I. The King and the political and military élite recognised that war had become unavoidable. Prussia had been reduced to a Napoleonic satellite and her future would be determined by the French Emperor. Her powerlessness to challenge the further reorganisation of Germany which would produce the Confederation of the Rhine (see below, p. 327) underlined this impotence. Even Haugwitz, long the champion of cooperation with France, recognised that this was impossible and began secret preparations to fight. By the autumn his policy had converged with that being pursued by his arch-rival. Prussia's humiliation was complete, and war was seen as the only possible solution.

The decision to fight was taken in late June, and mobilisation was ordered on 6 August. At the beginning of October Frederick William III issued an ultimatum – intended to be rejected – demanding the return of some Prussian territories and the recall of French troops from Prussia's borders. It was the worst possible moment for a display of resolution. Having comprehensively defeated Austria and forced Russia to retreat, Napoleon ignored the demands and launched an attack against an isolated Prussia. In a swift and brilliantly improvised campaign lasting only a week Napoleon smashed the Prussians at the twin battles of Jena–Auerstädt (14 October 1806) and overran the central Hohenzollern territories. The King and his entourage fled to East Prussia, while the French occupied Berlin and captured one fortress after another. This catastrophic defeat shattered the myth of Prussian invincibility created by Frederick the Great's victories, and paved the way for important internal reforms.

Prussia's defeat had a wider significance. In 1806 the strongest army of the *ancien régime* was shattered by the new-style warfare of the Revolution now perfected by Napoleon. The victories over the Third Coalition, achieved by short and relentless campaigns, demonstrated the decisive role of warfare at this time. Napoleon's principal achievement in military history was to restore the primacy of battle. In the eighteenth century, it had usually been seen as a last resort. With one or two significant exceptions, commanders had preferred to conduct manoeuvres and sieges, rather than risk the destruction of their expensive armies and precious trained manpower in battle. The first real challenge to this limited and defensive warfare had come in the mid-1790s, when the revolutionary armies, with their abundant manpower and novel enthusiasm, had successfully adopted the offensive (see above, pp. 270–1). Napoleon now refined and perfected these changes. There were important continuities from the revolutionary decade, particularly where recruitment was concerned. Napoleon's field armies were significantly smaller than the swollen forces created by the *levée en masse* and the accompanying republican and patriotic ardour of the 1790s, and with the creation of a French empire contained significant numbers of soldiers – over 60 per cent at its peak – recruited outside France. Within French territory the so-called Jourdan Law (1798) established annual and systematic conscription and consolidated the French advantages in manpower conferred by the 1793 *levée*. Further modifications were made in the early 1800s. Until the final phase of the empire, this system ensured a reliable supply of recruits and conferred an advantage over Napoleon's enemies.

In other respects, however, Napoleon's army was very different from its revolutionary predecessor. The French armies which had fought and, eventually, defeated the Second Coalition were disorganised and dispirited by the time fighting on the continent ended in 1801. These problems were addressed in the camps maintained along France's Channel coast in 1803–5. Though the projected invasion of England never took place, the continual drilling and exercising improved both the army's morale and its professionalism, and created the military machine which destroyed the Third Coalition. The Grand Army was more disciplined than its revolutionary predecessor, and was deployed in a very different way. Central to Napoleon's approach was the ending of the traditional distinction between strategy (the overall conduct of a campaign) and tactics (the actual fighting of battles). The Emperor fused these two elements: a decisive battle was always his principal objective. His ability to move his troops over long distances at high speeds and then to concentrate them against a vulnerable enemy was unsurpassed. Basic to this was Napoleon's subdivision of his troops into separate corps, usually of some 25,000–30,000 men. Each corps consisted of several infantry and cavalry divisions, together with their own artillery and support units. This reform, introduced in 1800, created far more operational and strategic flexibility. It made possible the deployment of the army over a much wider front, which somewhat reduced the problem of securing provisions and, more important, hid from the enemy the ultimate objective until the last moment. The various corps could be quickly assembled just before a battle. Speed was central to Napoleonic warfare: swift, forced marches gave the Emperor the crucial advantage of surprise, which could usually be turned into victory.

On the battlefield, after initial skirmishing and an artillery bombardment, massed infantry columns attacked to probe for a weakness in the enemy's position: Napoleon usually enjoyed numerical superiority as well. Further artillery fire and infantry reserves were directed against this weak spot until the enemy's line collapsed, giving the French first a decisive local superiority and then total victory. Finally, cavalry was sent to scatter the fleeing troops and demoralise the civilian population. These basic tactics, together with a willingness to improvise and an ability to conceive of a battle as a whole and act accordingly, largely explain Napoleon's remarkable series of victories. In the course of his career he fought no less than sixty battles and lost only three: Aspern–Essling, Leipzig and Waterloo. This near-unbroken record of success was the basis of his impact upon the other European states as well as the foundation of his own career. Not the least of his qualities as a commander was a remarkable ability to inspire his troops and look after their welfare – though the disaster in Russia (see below, pp. 348–50) was an obvious exception – and was rewarded with unquestioned obedience. Morale was aided by the system of promotion through the ranks on merit rather than seniority or social status, the Revolution's 'career open to all the talents'.

Napoleon's system of warfare did have weaknesses, however, and these became more evident during his final campaigns. The cavalry was never up to the standard of the other arms: poorly-mounted, it was inferior to that of its adversaries. The destruction of the Third Coalition had rested on the reorganisation of the French army in the years of peace on the continent after 1801. Napoleon's Grand Army was simply too strong and well-organised for the Austrians and Prussians, who both underestimated the power of France's reformed army. This achievement proved impossible to sustain. The central problem was to produce adequately-trained replacements for losses suffered, a difficulty compounded by the almost continuous campaigns after 1805 and by the Napoleonic army's ever-increasing commitments. Though there were usually plenty of new soldiers, the demand for immediate replacements was too great, particularly after 1806, to give these recruits any prolonged training.

Experience in the field, in short, replaced training and Napoleon was consequently forced to modify his tactics. Attack by massed column proved steadily less successful and came decisively to grief against the Austrians at Aspern–Essling in 1809; thereafter the Emperor compensated for the shortcomings of his infantry by heavier reliance on increased numbers of cannon; but the victories gained by extended artillery duels proved even more costly in casualties. And while the provision of recruits for Napoleon's armies became increasingly difficult, particularly after 1812, his enemies who had responded to France's mass armies by their own greater dependence on conscripts, proved able to put larger armies into the field. A further, increasing problem was the provisioning of the French armies. Napoleon's emphasis on speed meant supply trains could not keep up with the advancing army. His forces therefore had to live off the land like the armies of the Thirty Years War, plundering and raising 'contributions' as they marched. It was an additional reason for Napoleon's relentless pursuit of further conquests since ideally populations supposedly friendly to France should be spared these horrors. The intended solution to this logistical problem was a rapid victory after which the enemy's magazines or supply bases could be captured and its population forced to support the French army. However, when Napoleon extended his operations into the less fertile lands on the periphery of Europe, Spain, Poland

and, in 1812, Russia, the basic problem of supply became even more pressing. In these areas the vulnerability of a strategy based on rapid *Blitzkrieg*, would become all too evident; it was already apparent during Napoleon's campaign against Russia in 1807.

St Petersburg's diplomatic activity in 1804–5 had not been transferred to the battlefield. After the Austro-Russian defeat at Austerlitz (December 1805), the Russian forces had retreated out of Napoleon's reach. The impact of this immediate reverse on Alexander's complex personality was considerable. His earlier confidence evaporated and, for much of 1806, he took refuge in inactivity and waiting on events. Czartoryski's unusually close relationship with the Emperor was damaged by the reverses, his influence upon policy waned and he was dismissed in June. As he was to do at several critical moments, the Russian ruler now acted as his own foreign minister. Russia's options in foreign policy remained the same as since the later 1790s: an interventionist war, or peace through non-involvement. Alexander, characteristically, could not decide and, for much of 1806, contrived to pursue both strategies simultaneously. Negotiations were conducted in Paris and, as Napoleon wanted peace, an agreement was signed (Oubril treaty, July 1806). But it was not ratified by Alexander who disliked the terms: he was not yet prepared to recognise Napoleon's dominance in Germany nor French control of Dalmatia (ceded by Austria in 1805). At the same time, Alexander's personal commitment to Prussia's Frederick William III, forged at Memel in 1802, remained strong. When Napoleon attacked in October 1806, Russian troops were sent to Prussia's assistance, though these contingents were as usual slow moving westwards and had no influence on the military struggle.

By this point (November 1806) Russia was also involved in a new war against the Ottoman Empire, which had sided with France in the second half of 1806. This ended a period of indecisive Ottoman foreign policy which stretched back to 1802. The French invasion of Egypt in 1798 had destroyed the traditional Franco-Ottoman alignment. In the War of the Second Coalition, the Ottoman Empire had fought on the side of France's enemies. However, an armistice had been concluded with Paris in 1801 and a formal peace treaty in June the following year. Thereafter Selim III sought neutrality, but the growing weakness of his own state together with the dynamism of French policy made this impossible. The Sultan's internal problems were immense and appeared to suggest that the disintegration of the Ottoman Empire might be finally on hand. Constantinople's control over its outlying provinces was now nominal, and this inevitably weakened its foreign policy. After 1802 the Ottoman government had tried to restore the traditional alliance with France, who was anxious to recover her previous economic and political influence throughout the Near East. Russia seemed the greatest danger, since she clearly wanted to consolidate and, if possible, expand recent gains from the Ottoman Empire, which had built on the position established during Catherine II's reign. These were considerable: access into the Mediterranean through the Straits (under the alliance concluded with the Porte in 1799), a protectorate over the Ionian Islands and, in more general terms, naval mastery in the eastern Mediterranean as well as in the Black Sea. In 1802, the Sultan was forced to accept Russian control over the appointment of the local rulers (hospodars) of Moldavia and Wallachia; thereafter these Danubian principalities acted as a conduit for increasing Russian influence within the Ottoman Empire itself. Such dependence was irksome to Selim III, who also resented Russia's recent push into the Caucasus and eastern Anatolia.

Napoleon continually urged a firm anti-Russian policy on Selim III and, specifically, tried to persuade him to close the Straits to Russian warships. But these efforts proved unsuccessful, and by 1805 the French Emperor sought only Ottoman neutrality and was instead interested in alliance with Persia, directed both against Russia and against British power in India. However, Napoleon's military successes in the closing months of 1805 (see above, p. 316) led to the recovery of France's influence in Constantinople. Selim III, on hearing of French triumphs at Ulm and Austerlitz, reversed Ottoman policy and sought to save his empire through alliance with Napoleon. The prospect of recovering territory previously lost to Russia and, in particular, the Crimea, had been emphasised by French diplomacy, and this now became the Sultan's objective, by means of a war fought in partnership with France and Persia. Matters came to a head in the autumn of 1806. The Sultan replaced the hospodars of Moldavia and Wallachia by men sympathetic to France and then declared the Straits closed to foreign warships, thereby preventing the Russian Black Sea fleet reinforcing the Ionian Islands. These actions further antagonised St Petersburg, where an influential group had long urged renewed southward expansion. In early November, Russian troops invaded the Danubian principalities, and the following month Selim III formally declared war.

By late 1806, Alexander was fighting on two fronts, as French troops moved eastwards to attack Russia. Napoleon had not wanted hostilities, but his attitude changed on reaching Berlin after defeating the Prussians. Captured state papers revealed the closeness of Russo-Prussian contacts in the summer of 1806. Alexander I had clearly been playing a double game by encouraging Prussia's resistance while negotiating peace with

France. Napoleon now determined on war and, at the same time, decided against a unilateral peace with the defeated Prussia. French forces advanced into Poland in December 1806, winning an expensive technical victory in the snow at Eylau on 8 February 1807. But by this point Napoleon's military situation was precarious: food was short, reinforcements were needed and his lines of communication were dangerously exposed and harried by guerrillas. The diplomatic situation was also insecure. France's Emperor was not wholly confident that Austria would remain at peace, while he also feared an increased British commitment to the war in Europe. His complex diplomacy aimed in 1806–7 to combat the menace of a reinvigorated Third Coalition, although he overestimated the threat it posed. He tried to divide his enemies, and at the same time to intimidate Austria into remaining neutral. These months provide perhaps the clearest illustration of Napoleon's view that diplomacy should always be subordinate to military strategy. Consequently in 1806–7 his 'peace tactics' reflected his difficult military position: he aimed less at establishing a durable settlement for the continent than at reinforcing and supplying his army, which was trapped in a Polish winter.

Austria now had a new, anti-French foreign minister in Count Johann Philipp Stadion, who had taken office in December 1805. A member of the Imperial nobility, Stadion was the first aristocrat from the former Holy Roman Empire to control Austria's entire foreign policy. His appointment signalled Francis's nostalgic commitment to a German role and gave his policy an anti-French tone. However, the other leading figure in Vienna, Archduke Charles, and the increasingly influential ambassador in Paris, Clemens Lothar Wenzel von Metternich, believed Russia, not Napoleon, was Austria's greatest foe and favoured cooperation with France. These divided counsels would be important during the next few years. For the moment, not even Stadion's hatred of Napoleon could overcome Vienna's fear of another disastrous war, especially after the collapse of Prussia in October 1806. Britain seemed even more insular than usual. The 'Ministry of All the Talents' which came into office on the death of Pitt (January 1806) was indecisive, slow and parsimonious. It reacted against Pitt's subsidy policy of 1804–6 and generally drew back from continental commitments. Consequently, London's relations with potential allies worsened. Neither the British military diversion nor the Austrian intervention materialised, and when the campaign reopened in the spring of 1807, Russia faced Napoleon's armies alone. Within two months the issue had been decided: on 14 June the Russian army suffered a major defeat at Friedland.

Tilsit and the Franco-Russian rapprochement

It was now quite clear to Alexander that Russia had lost her war with France. Yet this was less apparent to Napoleon, who had been impressed by the bravery and tenacity of Russian forces at Eylau and Friedland and knew he had only defeated an army in the field and not occupied Russia. It was not the kind of overwhelming victory secured over Prussia or even Austria in 1805–6. He could not therefore dictate terms, and had no wish for a prolonged campaign in Russia, with all the accompanying problems of supply. Napoleon was anxious to leave eastern Europe to complete the reorganisation of Italy and Germany, and, more especially, to concentrate on the struggle with Britain. He therefore wanted a speedy settlement with Russia; he also saw short-term advantages in an alliance with her. Alexander, for his part, was similarly anxious for a quick peace, particularly when he was fighting the Ottoman Empire. Politically isolated, he was disillusioned with his partners in the Third Coalition, and especially resented Britain's inactivity in 1806–7 and meanness over subsidies. The help which Russia needed and expected never came, as British troops were not committed to the continent but sent overseas to mop up French colonies. What the *Edinburgh Review* called 'our love of sugar islands' played a considerable part in alienating Russia. London's refusal to consider a substantial loan or provide significant subsidies, together with the familiar maritime disputes which were the product of Britain's view of neutral rights, had reduced relations to a low ebb by the summer of 1807. Alexander I had also been disappointed by Austria's inactivity and even more by Prussia's supine conduct in 1806–7; there were to be considerable Russo-Prussian recriminations over each other's military performance. The Russian ruler's psychological make-up was also important. Having suffered a decisive military defeat, he was offered the opportunity to repair his own damaged reputation by an apparent diplomatic triumph. This dimension was cleverly exploited by Napoleon in a series of private conversations which began on 25 June 1807, initially on a raft in the middle of the Niemen (as no neutral territory was easily available), and then in the town of Tilsit (Sovietsk).

The Russian emperor quickly accepted the proffered alliance with Napoleon. But the real significance of Tilsit is not the Franco-Russian *rapprochement*, important as this undoubtedly was. Nor is it Alexander's willingness to commit himself to imposing peace on Britain, reviving the anti-British policy of his father seven years before. It is rather Russia's abandonment of Prussia, which Napoleon achieved through his personal mastery in their private talks. Alexander surrendered more completely than he had intended, and Prussia was the victim of this, though 'out of regard for the Emperor of the Russias' (in the words of the formal treaty) Napoleon did allow Frederick William III to keep his throne and part of his kingdom. Prussia's ruler was actually present at Tilsit, but excluded from the discussions which he watched – in the pouring rain – from the banks of the Niemen, underlining the low point to which Prussian power had been reduced.

The series of treaties signed at Tilsit (7–9 July 1807) consisted of a general territorial settlement, a Franco-Russian alliance and a Franco-Prussian peace treaty. Though defeated on the battlefield, Russia's losses were comparatively slight: her recent gains in the Adriatic, Cattaro (a military outpost in Dalmatia) and the Ionian Islands, were both ceded to France, while in return Alexander gained a fragment of Prussian Poland, the province of Bialystok. The two emperors had vaguely discussed joint action against the Ottoman Empire, but no formal agreement emerged. Alexander, however, did have to accept French mediation in his war with the Sultan. Finally, as part of Napoleon's broader strategy of isolating Britain, Russia promised first to mediate and, if this failed, to declare war and to join the Continental System. It was also agreed to compel Sweden, Denmark and Portugal to do the same. Tilsit appeared to divide the continent into two spheres of influence between two triumphant emperors: France dominated western and, increasingly, central Europe, while Russia was supreme in the Baltic, in the east and in the south-east. But, in reality, Tilsit and the wider political and territorial changes in 1806–7 created significant barriers to future Russian expansion. Russia had lost its foothold in the Mediterranean and was threatened by Napoleon's gains in Germany and by the creation of the Grand Duchy of Warsaw (see below, p. 327). The political settlement at Tilsit was thus fundamentally unstable, for Napoleon never intended Alexander to be his equal.

The two principal victims were Prussia and Austria. Prussia's defeat in 1806 had been total. French armies had occupied all her territories except East Prussia. Alexander's intercession enabled Frederick William III to retain his throne, but the King lost over one-third of his territory and half his subjects, while the Prussian army was reduced to a sixth of its previous size. Napoleon intended that a truncated Prussia should become a buttress against Russia, while being no competitor to France in Germany. Frederick William III's Rhineland provinces were therefore given to the newly formed Kingdom of Westphalia (see below, p. 332) while all Prussia's gains from the Polish partitions (except a thin strip of West

Prussia) became the new, French-dominated Grand Duchy of Warsaw. Finally, French troops were to occupy key Prussian fortresses and provinces until a massive war indemnity (set at 16 times the monarchy's *annual* revenue) was paid.

In many ways Austria lost even more by the Tilsit agreement and by the political changes which accompanied Napoleon's rout of the Third Coalition. Her territorial losses in 1805, together with the subsequent remodelling of the continent, undermined traditional Habsburg influence both in the Balkans and in Germany (Austria had already been expelled from Italy). Her decline was symbolised by the formal abolition of the Holy Roman Empire in 1806. This was the culmination of a political and territorial revolution in Germany over the previous decade in which Napoleon had played the decisive part. The mosaic of territories which made up the Empire had traditionally been dominated by Austria and latterly by Prussia. This was now replaced in the west by the Confederation of the Rhine, established in July 1806, comprising several enlarged secular states controlled by France. The origins of this transformation lay in the victories of the Revolutionaries in the 1790s and the establishment of France's frontier in the Rhineland, which opened the way for the further growth of French influence in Germany and made the fate of the Holy Roman Empire dependent on Paris. Napoleon's defeat of the Second Coalition confirmed France's dominant role, and enabled him to complete the reconstruction of Germany (excluding the north-west, where the Kingdom of Westphalia would be formed in 1807 – see below, p. 332). After protracted and complex negotiations, first at Rastatt (1797–99) and then at Regensburg (1801–3), a decision was issued in February 1803 from an Imperial Deputation (a special commission of the *Reichstag*) and accepted by Austria in April. This destroyed the old constitution of the Holy Roman Empire, cut the number of ecclesiastical princes dramatically, from 81 to 3, and the Imperial cities from 51 to 6. In the accompanying territorial redivision the principal beneficiaries were Prussia and Nassau, together with those states which were the basis of the later Confederation of the Rhine, already taking shape in Napoleon's mind. The Holy Roman Empire was thus effectively dead by 1803, as Francis II, now Emperor Francis I of *Austria*, acknowledged in the following year (August 1804). It was not to be buried until 1806.

The defeat of Austria in 1805 prepared the way for the German Empire's final eclipse. Napoleon now divided the remaining small states in 1805–6 between the four principal French clients: Bavaria, Baden, Hesse-Darmstadt and Württemberg. It was accompanied by the establishment of the Confederation of the Rhine (July 1806), essentially a political alliance between Napoleon and his four German satellites, which were placed firmly under French control. A series of dynastic marriages between the Bonaparte family and these German princely families then followed. Finally, on 6 August 1806 the Austrian Emperor Francis I, at Napoleon's instigation, formally abdicated as Holy Roman Emperor and so brought the Empire to an end. In all this, the aim of defeating Austria was uppermost in Napoleon's mind. The political and territorial transformation of Germany which followed was largely spontaneous, a series of responses to the situation created by each new military victory: exactly as in the creation of the Napoleonic Empire as a whole.

CHAPTER 11

Napoleonic Europe, 1807–1815

Napoleon's power was at its zenith in the years after Tilsit. The territories under his control had doubled in extent since 1802, and the scale of his dominance over the continent, established by his victories, was unprecedented. A successful military challenge to Napoleon's Grand Empire was, for the moment, unthinkable. The French Emperor was 'the only man in Europe who wills and acts', according to Metternich who observed him at first hand as Austria's ambassador in Paris. Napoleon was now free to carry out the political reorganisation of Europe and to enforce the Continental System. Writing of the years after Tilsit, Albert Sorel famously declared that France had 'only allies and victims'. This verdict was doubly true: the French Emperor no longer had to contend with political rivals, on the continent at least; he also tended to regard all his allies as potential future victims, so complete had his power become and so unrestrained his ambition.

Diplomacy was far less important during the next few years. The assumption of political near-equality upon which it rested simply did not apply when all the continental great powers had been so recently and so heavily defeated. It was also true in a second respect. Napoleon, as part of his attempt to turn the continent against Britain, forced Russia, Prussia and Austria to declare war on her during the winter of 1807. The formal disruption of diplomatic relations cut London off from its potential partners. Unable to create a new coalition by diplomacy Britain was forced to make a more direct military commitment, since it was now fully accepted by her statesmen that no stable or permanent settlement could be concluded with France's imperious ruler.

The Grand Empire

Napoleon's policy acquired two new and clearly linked characteristics during these years. In the first place, he became increasingly concerned with establishing the monarchical respectability of his family and with securing and perpetuating his own achievement and that of the dynasty he hoped to establish. In the Tilsit agreement he had extracted from Alexander I recognition not merely of all France's territorial annexations but of his own imperial title and of the royal status of his three brothers. Stendhal subsequently commented that 'Napoleon had the defect of all parvenus, that of having too great an opinion of the class into which he had risen'. The Emperor never secured the acceptance by the established dynasties which he craved, largely because of his successful military imperialism and the origins of his own power in the hated French Revolution, with which he was permanently associated. Napoleonic usurpation was a new phenomenon, the memory of which continued to alarm the other great powers long into the nineteenth century.

Secondly, the Emperor became increasingly ruthless and despotic as his successes piled up. Metternich declared in October 1807 that 'there has recently been a total change in the methods of Napoleon: he seems to think . . . moderation is a useless obstacle'. One example was the dismissal of his foreign minister, Talleyrand, in the previous August. Talleyrand was a supreme political survivor and an extremely ambiguous figure whose precise influence on the Emperor's policy is unclear: even after 1807 he continued to be consulted, though he was also a skilled self-publicist, prone to exaggerate his own importance. At this period his independence and occasional criticism were no longer welcome to Napoleon, whose increasing lack of restraint was evident in a further series of annexations: Tuscany, Parma and Piacenza were all integrated into the French Empire in 1808. The Papal States were formally annexed in May 1809, and when Pope Pius VII responded by excommunicating Napoleon he was imprisoned and not released until 1814.

Napoleon's ruthlessness was also apparent in the organisation of the Grand Empire, which was now brought to completion. Its unique extent posed considerable problems of government. The Emperor disliked the semi-independence formerly enjoyed by the satellite republics, which were now replaced by vassal kingdoms. The system of subject states had been made possible by Napoleon's victories in 1805–7, though some important modifications were subsequently made. The experiment rested on the

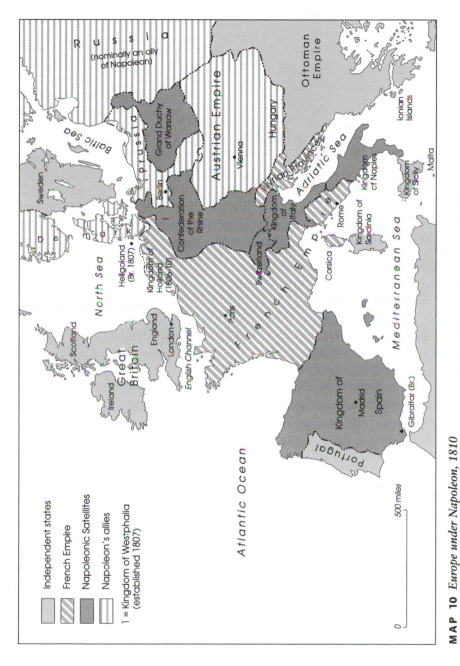

MAP 10 *Europe under Napoleon, 1810*

Source: D. McKay and H.M. Scott, *The Rise of The Great Powers, 1648–1815* (Longman Group Limited, 1983), pp. 368–9

considerable loyalty of the other Bonapartes who were, in essence, to be royal prefects. The Grand Empire was to be at one level a gigantic family enterprise. Each kingdom was ruled by a relative of Napoleon, who was intended to provide the obedience to centralised direction hitherto lacking. In particular, these sub-kings were expected to implement the Continental System (see below, pp. 334–6) and to generate the resources upon which the whole edifice of Napoleonic power depended.

The kingdom of Italy had been the first satellite. It was created in spring 1805 and ruled, as viceroy for the absent King (Napoleon himself) by Prince Eugene de Beauharnais, the son by her first marriage of the Emperor's wife Josephine. A second Italian satellite was established a year later: the kingdom of Naples, ruled by the Emperor's brother, Joseph, from 1806 to 1808 and then (when he was transferred to Spain) by Napoleon's brother-in-law, Joachim Murat. The kingdom of Holland was also created in 1806 from the Batavian Republic and ruled by Louis Bonaparte. But from the first it was beset by financial problems, while King Louis proved rather too 'Dutch' for his brother's liking. His perceived failings in dealing with the Walcheren expedition (see below, p. 343), together with a wish to reinforce the Continental System, eventually led Napoleon to force his abdication (July 1810) and to incorporate Holland into France. In 1807 the Kingdom of Westphalia had been created out of territories seized from Napoleon's opponents in 1806–7 and some of his German clients: in particular Hesse–Cassel, Brunswick, part of Hanover and Prussia west of the Elbe. Ruled by Jerome Bonaparte, it became part of the Confederation of the Rhine (see above, pp. 327–8) which it was intended to dominate. Finally, the satellite kingdom of Spain was inaugurated in summer 1808 with Joseph Bonaparte as king, but a revolt against French rule was already under way and his brother's authority was never to be fully established in the peninsula (see below, pp. 338–41). Spain was certainly the least successful satellite, if indeed it ever was one in the way the other kingdoms were.

Although Napoleon expected unquestioned obedience from his relatives, they inevitably acquired new, national interests with their crowns and were unable to disregard these completely. The consequent tensions, together with the need to intensify the Continental System, made Napoleon by summer 1810 contemplate dissolving the satellite kingdoms and replacing them by a European-wide government resembling that of imperial Rome. But the breakdown in relations with Russia saved them, with the single exception of Holland, and most struggled on to be destroyed, along with their creator, in 1814–15.

The expansion evident at this period changed the nature of the French Empire. Until 1806–7 its centre of gravity – what Michael Broers has styled the 'inner empire' – was a coherent region bounded by three of Europe's great rivers, the Rhine, Meuse and Rhone, together with the Alps and the valley of the Po. The core consisted of France, the Southern Netherlands, western Germany and the northern Italian peninsula, an area possessing real economic unity and a degree of political coherence. It was also the lands given to Lothar when Charlemagne's empire had been partitioned in 843, and Napoleonic propaganda highlighted this. The Emperor, ever alert to suitable historical precedents, played upon the Carolingian resonances. After 1807, however, the Continental System created an imperative to expand and a second, 'outer', empire came into being. Direct French control was extended into other regions – Holland, Spain, central and southern Italy, Germany – with a consequent adjustment to its centre of gravity and a loss of strategic and economic coherence.

The system of satellite kingdoms was not a total failure. All except Spain benefitted to some extent from important domestic reforms and together they made a significant military contribution to French imperialism. Two-thirds of the Grand Army which invaded Russia in 1812 was non-French; the kingdom of Westphalia was a particularly important reservoir of conscripts. Around half the cost of military expenditure between 1804 and 1814 was extracted from the conquered territories. Napoleon had intended that the satellite kingdoms should be financially self-sufficient and even contribute to the French treasury; but Spain in particular was a considerable drain on his own exchequer. What is more, although only Spain contributed significantly to Napoleon's downfall (see below, pp. 338–41), increasing resentment was aroused in all the kingdoms by conscription, taxation and the economic distress produced by the Continental System, which was the main aim of French policy from 1807 onwards.

The satellites were expected to play a key role in Napoleon's economic blockade of Britain. This Continental System was a determined attempt to defeat his rival economically, pursued from 1806 until its collapse in 1812–13. Commercial rivalry was always one dimension of the Revolutionary and Napoleonic Wars, as in earlier Anglo-French conflicts. Throughout the 1790s, successive French régimes had tried, without much success, to exclude British goods from France and, increasingly, from those areas under their control, while Britain attempted as usual to employ her navy to stop neutrals trading with France and her satellites. Resentment of high-handed British behaviour may have aided the initial acceptance of

Napoleon's schemes. After 1806 economic warfare was pursued far more systematically than ever before and therefore became much more prominent. Its real novelty lay in its geographical extent, seen in the very name, 'Continental System'. The unprecedented scale of Napoleon's conquests and the resulting control of Europe's coastline made it possible to attempt to close *all* continental ports to British trade.

The economic ideas behind the blockade were extremely primitive and mired in the mercantilist thinking which was becoming outmoded by this period. They were also incompatible. The central notion was that Europe should cease importing British goods while continuing to export its own manufactures to Britain. In accordance with a basic tenet of mercantilism, Britain would be forced to pay for imported goods in gold, rather than in her own manufactures, and so would face economic ruin. Aimed only at British exports, the Continental System was essentially a boycott or self-blockade. Napoleon believed that since Britain's credit system depended ultimately on her trade, a contraction of her exports, coupled with a need to pay for imports in bullion, would make her unable to finance further campaigns or subsidise allies. In time, London would be forced to accept peace on France's terms. Economic, or rather financial, strangulation would achieve what the Emperor's army could not accomplish because of British sea power.

The Continental System, however, had a second and arguably more important purpose: to make France Europe's leading economic and industrial power. England's decline would obviously contribute to this, but a strengthening of France's own economic potential was more important. Other continental countries were to provide raw materials and captive markets for France's industries, and in this way act as colonies for her dominant economy. It was why the Emperor forced the satellites to accept one-sided arrangements by which they were open to French goods, but could not in return export their own products to France. Both purposes were at bottom political objectives – defeating Britain and consolidating French power – and it proved predictably difficult to realise these by economic means.

Napoleon had attempted to create an embryonic Continental System in 1800–1 (see above, p. 300) and thereafter the trade war against England was pursued more vigorously. But it was only in 1806–7 that he could establish the blockade systematically. The Berlin Decrees (21 November 1806) codified the Continental System. Subsequent edicts, particularly the Second Milan Decree (December 1807), extended and strengthened the boycott. Its geographical scope was subsequently widened. Russia joined at Tilsit, while later in the same year (1807) Napoleon forced Portugal to close her ports temporarily to British goods. The Emperor now found himself driven to further territorial expansion in a vain attempt to make the Continental System watertight. As the blockade failed to work, he intensified it. This was why France annexed those territories lying on the North Sea coastline as far north as the Baltic in 1810–11. Earlier, the principal state not involved in the blockade, Sweden, had been attacked by Russia and her mentally unstable king, Gustav IV (1792–1809), deposed; he was soon replaced by the French Marshal Bernadotte. In January 1810 Sweden was forced to join the Continental System, but her membership was nominal since in practice British trade with her continued uninterrupted.

The Continental System was potentially a serious threat to Britain, but it was never applied for long enough to be effective. It was only enforced rigorously from July 1807 to July 1808, and from spring 1810 until the Russian campaign of 1812. During these two periods, Britain did experience severe economic difficulties and, in 1810, a real shortage of bullion. Her exports to the continent, particularly manufactured goods, fell significantly. At other times, however, British traders showed considerable enterprise in adjusting to the changing circumstances. Smuggling was always widespread, while new markets were successfully opened up. The royal navy assisted in defeating the blockade, which in any case was not rigorously implemented. One example was that Napoleon never sought to prevent the export of grain to Britain, though this would have intensified her difficulties as she was now obliged to import foodstuffs due to the rapid growth of population. Indeed, in 1809 and again in 1810 he actually sold licences to French merchants allowing them to export corn to England. In 1811 continental grain averted widespread famine there. The failure to apply the blockade rigorously and continuously, was largely due to Napoleon's political miscalculations, in particular over the Iberian peninsula and, later, Russia. Intervention in Portugal and the flight of the royal family to Brazil which followed opened up that vast market to British goods, while the subsequent Spanish revolt of 1808 (see below, p. 338) greatly extended markets in Spain and Spanish America. It also increasingly diverted French troops to the Iberian peninsula and this, in turn, made breaches of the blockade easier in the all-important Baltic region where Britain had already had notable success against it.

The Baltic was important both for grain imports and as the principal source of vital naval stores, also allowing British goods to enter Europe as a whole. Britain's navy was successful in keeping the Baltic open to her commerce. Concern that Denmark would abandon her previous neutrality, move into the French orbit and imperil British trade by closing the Sound, led to the pre-emptive bombardment of Copenhagen and seizure of the Danish fleet in the late summer of 1807. This ruthless action, together with the enhanced French military presence in northern Germany, south of the Danish peninsula, increased Copenhagen's dependence upon Paris. She was to be a French satellite for the next six years, as a consequence losing Norway to her rival, Sweden, who would take over the province at the end of the Napoleonic Wars. As Denmark became one of the strongest supporters of the Continental System, a fleet was sent to the Baltic each year until 1813, to protect British trade, particularly against Danish privateers. British squadrons instituted a convoy system for merchant shipping and patrolled the Mediterranean as well as the Baltic trade routes.

Napoleon's economic warfare was defeated both by its inherent flaws and by the strength and adaptability of the British economy and its ability to open up new markets. London's formal response – the attempt to impose a system of licences on the neutrals by Orders in Council – was less important, though it did lead to an insignificant and inconclusive Anglo-American War of 1812–14. Ultimately, the Continental System was undermined by the increasing lack of enthusiasm for its enforcement by the allied and vassal states which made up the Napoleonic Empire. Support had never been very widespread, and it was quickly diminished by the undoubted economic hardship which the blockade caused the participants. The Continental System ultimately contributed significantly to undermining the Napoleonic Empire.

Challenges to the Napoleonic Empire, 1808–1812

The increasing demands the Grand Empire placed upon France's new subjects aroused widespread resentment and, at times, open opposition. There was, for example, a long-running peasant revolt in Calabria, in southern Italy, which took five years and significant military forces to suppress (1806–11). Such outright resistance was unusual, however, and could normally be contained: it was not a serious threat to the continuation of French power, which could only come from one of the major continental states. Napoleon's dominance after Tilsit was to be challenged directly on three occasions: by a Spanish rising which began in 1808, by an Austrian attack in 1809 and then by Russia's growing independence which culminated in war in 1812. Individually these were serious challenges, and collectively they would prove fatal for Napoleonic Europe.

The first serious military resistance came from Spain, and the failure to suppress this rebellion would ultimately prove immensely significant. After initial hostility to the French Revolution, Spain had been forced by her own weakness to leave the First Coalition in 1795 and the following year to ally with France (Treaty of San Ildefonso). Thereafter she had become a tool of French policy. She had been obliged to fight on France's side from 1796 to 1802 and again after December 1804, although she had been slow to re-enter the renewed Anglo-French War. Spain's military contribution had been negligible and even her navy – though rebuilt impressively during the 1780s and 1790s – had been of little use against Britain. The extended period of warfare after 1793, however, together with accelerating inflation had created financial problems for the Spanish treasury. Despite the substantial income which the colonies still generated, warfare had been accompanied by growing deficits and extensive external borrowing. By 1808 expenditure was twice income, while the accumulated debt was ten times annual revenue. Yet the illusion of Spanish power was hard to dispel given her glorious past and extensive empire, and Napoleon persisted in regarding Spain as potentially a great power, whose resources could help sustain his empire.

The Spanish monarchy had repeatedly disappointed the Emperor: as a naval power at Trafalgar, as a source of wealth (its empire, principally in South America, failed to yield silver on the scale anticipated) and finally as a member of the Continental System, which it did not enforce rigorously. By 1807, factional strife at the Spanish court was further reducing her value as a satellite. Charles IV had been king since 1788, but the real ruler had long been the Queen's favourite, Manuel de Godoy, who supported the French alliance. Though he had pursued reformist policies, Godoy's *régime* was unpopular. His own modest origins in the provincial nobility together with the nature of his power – as the old-style favourite of the royal couple and even the reputed lover of the Queen – were disliked by ministerial and aristocratic opinion, while his foreign policy with its growing subservience to France, was widely attacked. Though the favourite understood the dangers of a French alliance and the accompanying satellite status, Spanish weakness made this the only obvious course of action. Godoy was trapped between his external and internal enemies, and his overthrow appeared increasingly likely.

Napoleon now decided to create another satellite kingdom in order to control Spanish resources and policy directly. The lure of overthrowing a

Bourbon monarchy and replacing it by another Bonapartist King, together with a wish to tighten the Continental System, also influenced him. In the final months of 1807, under cover of a joint war to place Portugal under France's control and so strengthen the economic blockade, French troops were sent to the Iberian peninsula. The following spring saw a full-scale French takeover, aided by a simultaneous political upheaval within Spain. In mid-March 1808, a Madrid mob, encouraged and directed by Godoy's opponents, brought about first his dismissal and then the abdication of the complaisant Charles IV, whose son became king as Ferdinand VII. But two months later at Bayonne Napoleon forced both father and son to surrender the throne which was given to the Emperor's own brother, Joseph Bonaparte, who transferred to Spain from Naples (5 May 1808).

This latest satellite kingdom was unstable from the first. A patriotic rising against the occupying French army commanded by Joachim Murat had already begun in Madrid (2 May) and was intensified by news of Ferdinand VII's forced abdication. The insurrection gathered strength and secured widespread popular support. With the emergence of juntas throughout Spain, leadership passed from the hesitant court aristocracy and ministers to local notables, officials and clerics, who directed resistance to the French for the next six years. In July Spanish regulars forced a French army to surrender at Bailén. In purely military terms this striking success was misleading: the French forces were raw recruits and the Spaniards now exaggerated their prowess in pitched battles. Thereafter, Spain's regular army (which Napoleon deemed the worst in Europe) suffered a series of humiliating defeats by the experienced French units sent to the peninsula. The Spanish turned instead to a strongly localised and increasingly ferocious guerrilla war, particularly in the rural north, which the French were unable to defeat. The supreme junta which coordinated resistance also sought international support, particularly from London.

By 1807, Britain had been effectively shut out from Europe by the rout of the Third Coalition. The Spanish revolt provided an immediate, and ultimately important, way back, an arena for the direct military intervention sought by London. The Spanish junta's appeal for British aid was immediately answered: in early August 1808 Sir Arthur Wellesley (later Duke of Wellington) landed in Portugal with 15,000 men. This expedition, and the eventual successes in the peninsula to which it led, were the product of a decisive change in British policy, now controlled by more forceful and imaginative figures. Canning, foreign secretary from 1807 to 1809, together with his political rival Castlereagh, the secretary of war, gave new momentum to Britain's war-effort, and transformed the strategy upon which it rested. London now announced that, in effect, it would underwrite any European revolt against the Grand Empire. Napoleon's destruction of the Third Coalition in 1805–7 had finally convinced British statesmen that the established, and essentially traditional, approach of attacking France's commerce and colonies while subsidising allies in Europe would not bring victory. Britain would have to increase her commitment and her troops would have to fight on the continent. Hitherto, Britain's military effort had been limited to clearly-defined areas of interest in north-western Europe; but they were now to be sent in increasing numbers elsewhere on the continent. Canning also supervised a fundamental, though gradual, change in the nature of this aid. Previous ministries had concluded what were essentially troop-hiring treaties in which payment was carefully supervised and measured against the number of soldiers actually provided. These treaties had aroused resentment, with widespread accusations of penny-pinching, among her hard-pressed allies, who were expected to face the Napoleonic military machine in return for relatively modest subsidies. Canning now sought to increase British aid to Napoleon's enemies. At the same time, this ceased to be a matter of simple cash payments. The duration and cost of the struggle and, more recently, the operation of the Continental System had left Britain short of bullion. Canning therefore inaugurated what became the pattern for the final years of the war: he reduced the amount of money and instead sent arms and equipment, especially clothing, which industrial Britain could provide and which continental allies needed almost as much as cash.

Wellesley's army quickly achieved his initial aim to secure a base in Portugal. An immediate victory at Vimiero (August 1808) boosted morale, but the first invasion of Spain (in 1808–9) was a failure; a second British force under Sir John Moore narrowly avoided disaster and was forced to retreat to Corunna, from where it was shipped home. Portugal, however, remained secure, and the importance of this base which could be supplied by the fleet was increased by the events of 1809. Austria's defeat by Napoleon (see below, pp. 343–4) and the failure of Britain's Walcheren expedition (see below, p. 343) left the peninsula as the only European arena where Britain could continue the struggle. In 1809, Wellesley invaded Spain and in July won a victory at Talavera (and the title of Viscount Wellington for himself), before again being forced to retreat. In the next year the French made a determined attack on Portugal which Wellington halted in the winter of 1810–11 at the lines of Torres Vedras, outside Lisbon. Only in 1812 could the British commander abandon his defensive strategy and go over to the attack.

For several years his campaigns had not produced any decisive vict-ories, as his critics in the British cabinet and in parliament did not fail to emphasise. The enduring and eventually increased commitment to the peninsula owed much to Wellington's eldest brother, Marquess Richard Wellesley, who was briefly ambassador in Spain in 1809 and then Foreign Secretary from that December until February 1812. Wellesley had returned to London convinced that the struggle in the peninsula was 'the last hope of continental Europe'. During the next two years he successfully cham-pioned an enlarged British commitment against his sceptical and hostile ministerial colleagues. The increased resources which resulted were used by his younger brother Wellington to enlarge his army to around 100,000 men. With this he won a series of decisive victories in 1812–13, particu-larly Salamanca (July 1812), and secured effective control of southern Spain. The conquest was completed by a triumph at Vittoria in June 1813. Early the following year Wellington was able to advance into France.

British victories in the peninsula were significantly helped by Portu-guese auxiliaries (who made up around half of Wellington's troops) and Spanish insurgents. Cooperation, however, was far from smooth, particu-larly with the Spanish provisional régime. It was difficult to agree a com-mon military strategy, while Britain's allies resented that more resources were not sent to the Iberian Peninsula, instead being put into the Walcheren expedition and London's other strategic priorities. Particular problems arose with the revolt of the Spanish South American colonies after 1808. The rebels looked to Britain for support, which they were prepared to purchase through commercial concessions, but Spain expected her to assist in defeating the independence movements and to spurn the trading opportunities. The failure of British merchants to respect Spain's block-ade of the insurgents was resented by the Spanish régime. These and similar issues complicated Wellington's task and made his eventual suc-cess more remarkable. His achievement was primarily that of survival, which proved decisive.

His campaigns, together with the Spanish guerrilla war, were a consid-erable, and increasing, drain on French manpower and resources. Already by the beginning of 1809 France had suffered more losses in the peninsula than in all of the battles since Napoleon became first consul a decade before, and this total increased in the desperate fighting which followed. By 1812 France was maintaining as many as 300,000 troops south of the Pyrenees. Most were in garrisons or fighting guerrillas, so that the French could never concentrate more than 70,000 men against Wellington. The 'Spanish ulcer' eventually cost Napoleon around 250,000 casualties and perhaps four billion francs, and it inflicted significant damage upon France's military reputation. These were the first serious setbacks suffered by Napoleonic armies, and they encouraged other European nations to challenge French hegemony. The Peninsular War was also part of a larger change in Britain's relations with the continental states: it undermined the widespread belief that London was only interested in colonial gains and indifferent to the continent, and raised the previously low prestige of the British army. These campaigns possessed a political and diplomatic importance for the European struggle which transcended their military significance.

Britain had initially seen the Peninsular War as diversionary. Her statesmen hoped that by increasing Napoleon's difficulties they would encourage Alexander I to abandon the alliance concluded at Tilsit, believing he had only accepted it out of necessity and wanted to escape it as soon as practicable. It was also assumed that the rest of northern Europe (Sweden, Denmark and Prussia) would follow the Emperor into war with France. The first challenge to Napoleon, however, came not from Russia but from Austria, though France's difficulties in Spain were certainly an indirect factor in the Habsburg decision to declare war in April 1809.

Austria's eclipse in 1805 had been complete. Her army was defeated and demoralised, her treasury empty, her ministers discredited. She had been powerless to resist Napoleon's damaging territorial reorganisation in 1806–7. Her influence in Germany, declining for a decade, had been finally destroyed, while the Franco-Russian agreement at Tilsit deprived her of any influence in the Balkans. After a temporary period of *rapprochement* with France, however, observers in Vienna soon concluded that coexistence with Napoleon was impossible and that to be France's ally was also to be her future victim.

After the humiliation at Austerlitz, younger and more vigorous spirits came to the fore, above all the Archduke Charles and Stadion, who had become foreign minister in December 1805. Stadion was a Rhinelander and a career diplomat, whose undoubted personal hatred of Napoleon was strengthened by the French confiscating his family estates. He championed a war of revenge, a peoples' war in Germany and Austria which would defeat Napoleon. To achieve this, he believed that social and political reforms were first essential to arouse enthusiasm and encourage Germany to rise. Only in the military sphere were significant reforms actually accomplished. Archduke Charles began a major reorganisation of the Habsburg regular army and particularly its administration, while in 1808 a provincial militia (*Landwehr*) was established. Austrian finances, however, were still in disarray. The war of 1805, like its predecessors, had been financed by printing money and inflation was rampant. The international situation also seemed unfavourable for further fighting with France, since it was not clear who might help the Habsburgs.

Throughout 1808, however, the war party at the Austrian court steadily gained the ascendancy. It was assisted by the Emperor Francis's third marriage to Maria Ludovica of Este at the beginning of that year. The new Empress enthusiastically adopted Stadion's ideas of a German national rising against the Napoleonic Empire and became a forceful advocate of renewed fighting, as did the Emperor's mother-in-law, who resented the loss of her own duchy of Modena. Stadion supervised a vigorous propaganda campaign, promoting Austrian patriotism and the central role of the Habsburg monarchy and dynasty in upholding this. Its impact, however, was qualified by the failure to introduce all the radical reforms which the foreign minister believed essential but could not persuade the Emperor to sanction.

France's difficulties in Spain in the summer of 1808 and the news of Bailén indirectly strengthened the war party in Vienna, by highlighting both the dangers for a dynasty of passive acceptance of satellite status, and the potential of resistance. Further support came from Austria's ambassador in Paris, Metternich, who was becoming increasingly hostile towards the French Emperor, as he realised the scope of his ambitions. But the ambassador also recognised that Austria could not fight another war until the Habsburg state was stronger and there was some realistic chance of foreign assistance, and urged coexistence in his dispatches. However, his exaggerated reports of mounting domestic opposition to Napoleon and his assessment of France's vulnerability because of her extensive military commitments, arrived in Vienna at a critical time and may have contributed to the decision to fight. By the autumn of 1808, the Archduke Charles had emerged as an opponent of renewed fighting. Aware that his army reforms were incomplete, he pleaded in vain for a delay. But he was now an isolated voice. War was widely seen in Vienna as inevitable. As Metternich observed from Paris, it was viewed as the only way to preserve political independence. Two further arguments reinforced the hardening attitude: a growing belief that Austria should fight before Napoleon could resolve the Spanish situation – the French Emperor travelled south in late 1808 to take command of French forces in person – and the knowledge that funds would run out in March 1809, after which mobilisation would be more difficult. By the closing weeks of 1808 nothing could stop the war-party, now reinforced by the Archduke Charles (who had again changed his mind), and the decision to fight was taken in an extended series of conferences between 8 and 23 December. Military preparations were stepped up in the early months of 1809 and, on 9 April, war was formally declared on France.

The fighting in 1809 lasted barely three months and became another entry in the catalogue of Habsburg military disasters. The army was, as the Archduke Charles had feared, unequal to the task, preparations for a new conflict had not included drawing up a military strategy to fight it, and no international support materialised. There was no German national rising, while neither Russia, nor Prussia, nor the German princes provided assistance. Only Britain gave any support, and that was limited, fortuitous and too late: a subsidy and eventually a diversionary attack in the southern Netherlands. Britain's attempt in the summer of 1809 to seize the island of Walcheren at the mouth of the Scheldt and to destroy the French naval base there was a fiasco, and in any case had been undertaken for purely British reasons. A large-scale combined operation involving 70,000 men was wrecked by divided and hesitant command and by the fever which soon became rife among the soldiers, and withdrew with heavy losses. By this time, the continental war was over, for Austria alone was no match for the might of Napoleon's armies. By the middle of May (a month after war was declared) the French Emperor had occupied Vienna and though the Archduke Charles won a brave, and costly, victory at Aspern–Essling (May 1809) he could not press home his advantage. The campaign was decided by another impressive Napoleonic victory at Wagram (6 July 1809) and an armistice was signed a week later.

The peace settlement of Schönbrunn which followed (14 October 1809) was effectively dictated by Napoleon and brought further humiliations for the Habsburgs. Austria was forced to make substantial territorial cessions to French satellites or clients: in particular she had to cede her share of the Polish partitions (largely to the Grand Duchy of Warsaw), the strip of the Dalmatian coast she had retained on the Adriatic along with Carniola and Istria (to the kingdom of Italy), parts of Bohemia (to Saxony) and areas round Salzburg and Berchtesgaden and some of Upper Austria (to Bavaria). Vienna was forced to join the Continental System (though it now had no ports to close to British trade!), the Austrian army was limited to 150,000 and, though Habsburg finances were in ruins, an indemnity of 200 million francs was exacted. The impact of French financial demands was particularly serious. In the following December, Vienna, in order to pay the indemnity, was forced to confiscate all the silver in private hands throughout its territories (with the exception of Hungary) and by early in 1811 the state was effectively bankrupt. The sole consolation was that the Austrian Emperor was not actually forced to abdicate, though he now ruled fewer than four million subjects when Hungary is excluded.

Defeat inevitably ended the influence of both Stadion and Archduke Charles, coldly dismissed by his brother in July 1809. The new foreign minister, or chancellor, appointed early in October, was Metternich, who would remain in power until 1848. The new Chancellor was fundamentally as hostile towards Napoleon as Stadion had been, but in the aftermath of the disastrous war of 1809 his policy was necessarily that of coexistence. In August 1809, he defined Austria's future policy as being 'tacking, wiping away the past and collaboration' and he argued to the Emperor in the same month that 'we can seek our security only in adapting ourselves to the triumphant French system'. The adoption of such principles was a significant turning point in Vienna's foreign policy and in the history of the wars of 1792–1815. Austria – often single-handed – had sustained the military struggle against France for 17 years, but had now embraced coexistence for the foreseeable future. Ultimately, Metternich aimed to supplant Russia as Napoleon's major ally. Diplomacy might revive Austria's fortunes in a way her armies manifestly could not. He put great store on recovering influence through marriage-diplomacy, a traditional Habsburg stratagem. The French Emperor was known, because of his dynasticism, to want to divorce his first wife, Josephine (who had not provided him with a son) and remarry to perpetuate his achievement. Metternich intended that Napoleon's new wife should be the Archduchess Marie Louise, the eldest and favourite daughter of the Emperor Francis. The attractions of such a match were considerable and in spring 1810 Napoleon, after divorcing Josephine, married his Habsburg Archduchess. But Metternich's hoped-for political recovery failed to materialise. Austria remained a French satellite, as was particularly clear during the war with Russia in 1812, though she – like Prussia – was always more independent than Bavaria or the Kingdom of Westphalia, who were totally subservient to Paris.

The Franco-Russian *rapprochement* at Tilsit had been a matter of temporary expediency on both sides (see above, p. 325). Yet the alliance endured, at least nominally, until the French invasion of Russia in 1812. Napoleon's desire after 1807 to concentrate on the political reorganisation of his conquests, the Continental System and the struggle with Britain made him favour a period of cooperation with Russia, and this had been strengthened by the Spanish revolt after 1808 and the Austrian war in 1809. Alexander's public support for the Tilsit agreement was reflected in his appointment as foreign minister of N.P. Rumiantsev, who supported cooperation with France. Rumiantsev believed that Russian involvement in central and western Europe distracted attention from what should be their primary aim, renewed expansion to the south, and supported the French alliance because he believed (wrongly) it demonstrated Napoleon would leave them a free hand against the Ottoman Empire. In reality, the French Emperor was always determined to prevent Russia seizing Constantinople, and his refusal to sanction her expansion in south-eastern Europe effectively wrecked any chance of a stable and permanent alliance.

In any case, Rumiantsev was a cover for Alexander's real objectives. The foreign minister's well-known support for the French alliance would reassure Napoleon, while he would be a convenient scapegoat within Russia, where the alignment was widely unpopular both at court and among the nobility. The Emperor was actively involved in foreign policy, often corresponding directly with Russian diplomats abroad. This was necessary since Alexander intended to prepare for a future war against France. The spell cast by Napoleon at Tilsit had soon evaporated, as he appreciated the alignment's unpopularity in Russia and French opposition to further Russian gains. Alexander defined his policy after Tilsit as being 'to gain a breathing-space and, during this precious interval, build up our resources'. He therefore aimed to strengthen the Russian army, overhaul the administration and improve Russia's international position. The Emperor was largely successful in disguising his real intentions. It was only in 1811 that Napoleon fully admitted that a war against Russia would be necessary, and he always underestimated the Russian ruler's astuteness and determination. France's mounting difficulties in Spain and, in 1809, the war with Austria, were exploited by Alexander to reassert his own political independence. Napoleon was forced to withdraw French troops from Germany to deal with these problems, and this increased both his need of Russian support and St Petersburg's freedom of action. In 1808 Russia had attacked Sweden and seized Swedish Finland, which was formally united to Russia the next year, with Alexander ruling as grand duke. This gain did much to eradicate traditional Russian fears about their vulnerable north-western frontier, though the war with Sweden (undertaken on French urging to force her to enter the Continental System) was unpopular since it also demonstrated Russia's subservience to France.

The meeting of the two emperors at Erfurt in late autumn 1808 showed the cracks which had appeared in the alliance since Tilsit, and these became more evident when the Austro–French War began in 1809. Napoleon immediately requested the military assistance Russia was required to provide under an agreement concluded at Erfurt. Though he formally declared war, Alexander secretly informed Vienna that Russia would remain neutral. He delayed so long in dispatching aid that Russian soldiers played no part in Austria's defeat: there were only two Russian casualties in the campaign of 1809. This enraged Napoleon, who now lost all confidence in the Tilsit alliance. But he also had sufficient problems without provoking Russia. To retain Alexander's friendship he allowed him to make minor territorial gains in eastern Galicia from the peace settlement with Austria in October 1809. The Franco-Russian axis was henceforth to be increasingly fragile, and for his part, Napoleon only supported what he styled a 'phantom alliance' after 1809 because of his mounting difficulties elsewhere.

The Grand Duchy of Warsaw, created by Napoleon in 1807 from Prussia's Polish lands, was the major source of friction. Ruled *in absentia* by a French client, the King of Saxony, the duchy was governed by a French-dominated regency and was an outpost of Napoleonic influence in eastern Europe. Alexander feared that it might become the nucleus of a reborn, independent and pro-French Polish state which would threaten Russia's own recent gains from the partitions of Poland. These anxieties grew after the defeat of the Habsburgs in 1809, when the addition of most of Galicia considerably increased the duchy's size: it doubled its territory and population. The enlarged Grand Duchy, far from being merely a territorial annex of the Kingdom of Saxony as St Petersburg had anticipated, now contained the heartlands of the vanished state, with the historic capitals of Cracow and Warsaw, and was an embryonic reborn Poland. Although Alexander wanted a reborn Polish state, he intended it should be within the Russian Empire and firmly under his own control, a revival of the idea earlier put forward by Czartoryski, who had continued to retain some influence with Russia's ruler. His suspicions over Poland reflected the mutual lack of trust which characterised Franco-Russian relations. The Polish nobility themselves believed, or at least hoped, that France intended to re-establish their homeland; in 1812 they were to contribute nearly 100,000 men to the force which invaded Russia, the largest single national contingent. But they were mistaken, for Napoleon was entirely opportunistic in his dealings with the Poles.

The *rapprochement* with France had always been unpopular in Russia, especially because it involved entry into the Continental System, in November 1807. Trade with England was long established and had proved very profitable for Russian merchants and many nobles, but it was now ended, at least officially. The Continental System, though its economic impact on

Russia has often been exaggerated, did produce severe commercial difficulties in 1808 and early 1809. Though Russo-British trade recovered
almost to its former level, it again declined notably after mid-1810 and
remained at this low ebb throughout the next two years. The impact was
especially severe on Russia. Many noble families relied on the export of
the all-important naval stores produced on their estates, while much
Russian commerce was handled by British merchants, whose exclusion
was keenly felt. Customs receipts fell sharply, worsening the government's
financial plight. Alexander I's *régime* had printed notes on a large scale to
remain solvent, and after 1807 it did so to an unparalleled extent, as the
deficit soared. The value of the paper rouble fell by over 60 per cent
between 1807 and 1811. Though there were several causes, within Russia
the Continental System was widely held responsible.

Its importance, however, was more political than economic, a symbol
of the subservience involved in the French alliance, which had fewer and
fewer supporters. On 31 December 1810 Russia in effect withdrew from
the Continental System by introducing a new tariff which discriminated
against French commerce. This was partly a response to Napoleon's seizure of territories along the North Sea coastline in the closing months of
1810 and to the implied threat to the Duchy of Oldenburg, which France
formally annexed on 22 January 1811. Oldenburg was ruled by Alexander's relatives and its independence had been guaranteed at Tilsit. Its
annexation worsened relations, as did the simultaneous seizure of Lübeck,
since this seemed to foreshadow a French challenge to Russia's dominance of the Baltic. Alexander also disliked the continued French occupation of Prussian fortresses on the Oder, while further friction was produced
by Napoleon's search for a new wife (see above, p. 344). Alexander in
effect declined to give the Emperor one of his sisters as a bride and this
was resented in Paris, while the Austrian marriage similarly aroused
resentment at the Russian court, principally because of its anti-Russian
implication.

There were thus ample sources of friction, particularly by 1810–11.
By early 1811, it was clear to Alexander that he would soon be at war
with France. For his part, Napoleon determined to fight to re-establish the
control he seemed to have secured at Tilsit and thereby shore up the
Continental System. He also hoped that a decisive victory over Russia
might bring Britain to her knees, for Alexander was now the main hope
of statesmen in London. Napoleon was planning for an invasion of
Russia from autumn 1811 onwards. Both sides tried simultaneously to
strengthen their diplomatic positions. Alexander sought support from

Austria (including – remarkably – the offer of both Ottoman dependencies of Moldavia and Wallachia) and Prussia, but Napoleon successfully intimidated both states into supporting, or at least not actively opposing him. However, early in 1812 the French Emperor failed to secure an alliance with the Ottoman Empire, which had been involved in war with Russia since 1806 (see above, pp. 322–3). The Sultan, in fact, soon made peace with Russia.

The imminence of war with France had made Russia equally determined to end the conflict with the Ottoman Empire, especially as the intermittent campaigning had been indecisive. The Tilsit agreement had anticipated a Russo-Ottoman armistice and this had duly been concluded in August 1807; but it had foundered on St Petersburg's desire to retain the Danubian principalities (substantially occupied by Russian troops), and at Erfurt in 1808 Napoleon had been forced to consent to this eventual gain. But the Ottoman Empire was as stubborn as ever about actually ceding territory. As war with France loomed, however, Alexander became increasingly determined to extricate himself from the indecisive struggle in the Balkans. Serious peace negotiations began in October 1811, but they were prolonged and St Petersburg's bargaining position grew steadily weaker as Napoleon's preparations to invade Russia became evident. Neither a major Russian military victory early in 1812, nor a peace mission could prise a settlement out of Constantinople. Initially, the Russians had been prepared to buy peace through the return of Wallachia to Constantinople's nominal control, but they were eventually forced to evacuate Moldavia as well. The Russo-Ottoman War was ended by the peace of Bucharest (17 May 1812) by which Russia acquired most of Bessarabia, a significant gain which brought her as far south as the Danube, but far less than she had once seemed likely to secure.

The defeat of Napoleon, 1812–1815

Napoleon crossed the Niemen in the final week of June 1812 without any formal declaration of war. He had assembled 600,000 men in Poland, of whom only 250,000 were French, and some 500,000 of these launched the invasion of Russia. This massive force far outnumbered the Russian armies which had to retreat ever deeper, fighting courageous small-scale rearguard actions and continually harrying the advancing army, but avoiding a major battle. Napoleon was certainly aware of the unique logistical problems involved in campaigning in Russia and made more extensive preparations than for any other campaign. But his military strategy was undermined by his failure to bring the Russians to a pitched battle, while he lacked a political strategy to force Alexander to conclude a peace settlement. In contrast to earlier campaigns the invading army was large and unwieldy. It proved unable to move rapidly enough to catch and then defeat the retreating Russians. Moreover, many of Napoleon's most experienced troops were in Spain; war on two widely separated fronts ultimately led to failure in both. The French units in the invading force inevitably contained many new conscripts alongside the leavening of veterans, while the foreign contingents were very uneven in quality. There was widespread desertion and indiscriminate plundering, instead of the systematic requisitioning the army needed for its food. These supply problems were intensified by the very extended lines of communication and by the scorched earth tactics adopted by the retreating Russians.

On 7 September 1812 Napoleon won a technical but costly victory at Borodino. It was not the decisive victory needed, for though the French were able to occupy Moscow in mid-September, the Russian army withdrew from the battlefield in good order and remained a threat. Even the occupation of Moscow did not, as Napoleon expected, force Alexander to make peace. The Russian ruler would not – and indeed could not – negotiate. The patriotic enthusiasm produced by the French invasion made any concession impossible. Napoleon never appreciated that a second Tilsit, a second surrender to France, was unthinkable and might even imperil Alexander's throne. Ignoring warnings about the severity of a Russian winter – the autumn of 1812 was in fact unusually mild – the Emperor lingered in Moscow until 19 October. Only then did the retreat begin, slowed by the army's loot, its casualties and its 600 guns. There was also continual harassing by Cossacks, partisans and some Russian regulars units, which made foraging all but impossible, and the army was soon disintegrating through hunger. Its sufferings were increased by snow early in November and severe frosts in December. By the end of 1812 only 40,000 men – less than 10 per cent of the original army – crossed back into Poland.

The costs of Napoleon's Russian campaign were immense: 270,000 dead and 200,000 prisoners. The further loss of around 200,000 horses and 1,000 guns seriously weakened the French cavalry and artillery in subsequent campaigns. Material losses, however, were only a small part of the story. The disaster in Russia, together with French setbacks in the Peninsular War, shattered the myth of Napoleonic invincibility and, in only six months, transformed the European situation. Russia's role was pivotal. Her ruler was anxious to drive the French back from Central

Europe and re-establish a Russian glacis of the traditional kind: already he was listening to renewed urgings from Czartoryski to restore Poland under St Petersburg's control. Alexander I therefore decided in December to pursue the retreating French forces and to carry the struggle far beyond Russia's own borders. This was a crucial decision and one with moment-ous consequences. By the end of 1812 Napoleon was fighting for his own survival, not – as previously – for further conquests. The Grand Empire was to collapse with surprising speed.

The French defeat eventually led to a general reversal of diplomatic alignments. It was begun by the convention of Tauroggen (30 December 1812), an armistice between Prussia – or, rather, General Yorck, com-manding Prussian units covering Napoleon's left flank in 1812, who acted completely without authorisation – and the advancing Russian army. This agreement allowed the Russians to occupy East Prussia and forced the French to pull further back. Alexander now offered an alliance to Frederick William III, who still hesitated but was forced into war primarily by popular pressure. Since the collapse of 1806, Prussian patriotism had been fostered by an impressive, though incomplete and short-lived, series of administrative, social and military reforms and there was consider-able support for the war of 1813, not only in Prussia but throughout Germany. The King was also driven to act by the independent conduct of many military commanders in the aftermath of Tauroggen: by the time the decision for war was made, two-thirds of the Prussian army was not under direct royal control. On 28 February 1813 Russia and Prussia signed the treaty of Kalisch (Kalisz), a military alliance against France, and in mid-March Berlin formally entered the war.

Alexander now saw himself as the Liberator of Europe. The dark days of 1812 had imbued him with a sense of his Christian mission to defeat Napoleon and to free Europe from French domination. His mystical fervour, and a parallel desire to extend Russian power, provided a major impetus behind the new allied coalition which was now formed. By the middle of 1813 the Fourth Coalition, consisting of Russia, Prussia, Britain, Sweden, Spain and Portugal, had been created, though Austria still remained aloof. Its principal foundations were the bilateral Anglo-Russian and Anglo-Prussian alliances signed at Reichenbach (June 1813). Britain provided the allies with much-needed munitions and her armies had begun to drive back the French in Spain, but her main contribution was financial. In 1813 British subsidies (principally to Russia, Prussia and Sweden) amounted to £11 million, almost equal to the *total* paid out during the first two coalitions of 1793–1802.

The early months of 1813 saw a triumphant allied advance across central Europe, as Napoleon hastily scraped together another army in France. Though the recruiting system worked surprisingly well, the quality of these conscripts was poor and the French infantry contained large numbers of youths, veterans and invalids, while the enormous losses of horses in Russia meant France was now critically short of cavalry. At the end of April 1813 the French counter-attacked, and in May Napoleon drove the allied armies back through Saxony, winning two indecisive victories at Lützen and Bautzen. But France was still engaged in a war on two fronts and needed to provide soldiers for Spain, where Wellington's decisive advance had begun (see above, p. 340). This undermined the French advance in central Europe, and in June Napoleon eagerly accepted an Austrian-inspired armistice and the summoning of a peace congress at Prague. He had no wish for a negotiated settlement, but he hoped – exactly like the allies – to strengthen his military position during the lull in the fighting.

Austrian foreign policy had only slowly adjusted to the changing situation after Napoleon's disaster in Russia. Vienna's progress towards armed intervention and membership of the Fourth Coalition was slow and reluctant, reflecting the complexities of its position by this point. The allies and especially Alexander made determined efforts to bring Austria into the embryonic coalition, but without success. Metternich was uncertain how the struggle might end, wanted to support the winning side, and also saw real dangers for Austria in the destruction of Napoleon's Grand Empire. The Chancellor was alarmed by the patriotic and popular tone of the Russo-Prussian campaign: the appeal for a German national crusade against the French could have anti-Habsburg implications. Moreover, Napoleon's marriage to the Austrian archduchess, Marie Louise, made Vienna – still nominally France's ally – more willing for a settlement which kept either Napoleon or his son, the King of Rome (born in March 1811), on the French throne. But the real concerns of Habsburg policy in 1813–14 were an overwhelming desire for peace and anxieties about the nature of the future settlement, particularly in Germany.

Metternich and the Emperor Francis were both deeply suspicious of Alexander's ambitions. In one sense, the Chancellor feared Russia's growing ascendancy more than he had Napoleon's dominance, and wished to maintain a powerful France to balance Russian strength and to uphold the independence of central Europe. Austria had no wish to see Russian dominance of Germany replace that of France, while Alexander's ambitions towards Poland and the Balkans also seemed to threaten Habsburg interests. She was also concerned to prevent Prussia stealing a march on her: old rivalries had not been extinguished in Vienna where there was a consequent wish to ensure the cohesiveness of the 'Third Germany' of smaller states. From late in 1812 Metternich aimed principally to defend Austrian interests at any subsequent peace, first by armed neutrality, then by mediation and finally by joining the Fourth Coalition. His essential moderation was evident in a series of Austrian-inspired attempts to conclude a negotiated settlement. Only Napoleon's continuing refusal to negotiate, together with the news of Wellington's victory at Vittoria (marking the effective end of French control over Spain), finally drove Vienna to declare war on France on 12 August 1813. Significantly, this was the first occasion on which *all* the great powers – Britain, Austria, Prussia and Russia – had fought Napoleon; it was also the first time since 1795 that Austrian and Prussian troops cooperated against France. But even now there was no formal alliance, only a military convention, between Vienna and the other members of the Fourth Coalition. The treaty of Teplitz (9 September 1813) bound Austria, Russia and Prussia to maintain 150,000 men each in the field. Metternich would not underwrite the emerging Russo–Prussian plans for a future settlement, nor would he sign a treaty to prevent a negotiated agreement with France, however unlikely this had become.

Napoleon could have secured peace on reasonable terms in the summer of 1813 and remained ruler of France. The negotiations might also have divided his opponents, not least because of Austria's ambivalence. Europe was exhausted and war-weary, and might have concluded a moderate settlement. Indeed, the peace terms outlined by the allies at Reichenbach would have left Napoleon as ruler of France, and French military power superior to that of any other single state. But he resolutely refused to make the necessary concessions and, characteristically, sought military salvation, rather than explore the path of diplomacy which he so disdained. Aiming for total victory he risked complete defeat. In part, this reflected his established preference for military solutions. Napoleon also believed that a negotiated settlement would mean the end of his own authority, for he was not a hereditary sovereign. He was now well aware of the unpopularity of his *régime* in France, where opposition had reached dangerous proportions. An unsuccessful conclusion to the long and burdensome years of warfare would spell the end of the Bonaparte dynasty, whatever the allies might do. Equally, however, his generalship in the autumn of 1813, on which he staked everything, was strangely indecisive and hesitant, reflecting his own personal exhaustion.

The end of the armistice in mid-August led to fighting being resumed. The armies of the Fourth Coalition enjoyed a clear numerical superiority and by mid-October this produced a decisive if costly victory at Leipzig (the 'Battle of the Nations', 16–19 October). This defeat destroyed Napoleon's influence in Germany, and as he retreated across the Rhine at the close of 1813, his satellites deserted him and the Grand Empire collapsed. The extent to which Napoleonic hegemony had always depended on military supremacy now became fully apparent. Napoleon had received little real support from the peoples he conquered, except perhaps from the middle classes and public officials in parts of western Germany and northern Italy, while there had been increasing revulsion against the burdens his *régime* imposed. His victories and conquests aroused nationalist feelings everywhere, especially in Spain and Russia. But, though there were patriotic risings against him, these played a limited part in his final defeat. That was accomplished by the professional armies of the great powers, whose numerical superiority was overwhelming.

The allies, remembering the defeats of the First Coalition when it had invaded France two decades before, hesitated and their forces made only slow progress in the winter of 1813–14. But the Fourth Coalition was given a new sense of purpose early in 1814 by the arrival at allied headquarters of Viscount Castlereagh, British foreign secretary since March 1812. Castlereagh was determined to bring down Napoleon, and to restore France to the rule of the Bourbons and to her pre-Revolutionary position in Europe. He was anxious to secure Britain's established aims – security in the Low Countries, recovery of Hanover, colonial gains – and he did so. But in his pursuit of London's particular interests he was to show an unusual willingness to listen to other points of view and to compromise with his allies. He quickly imposed the alliance of Chaumont (9 March 1814) on the members of the Fourth Coalition, which committed them not to conclude a separate peace and outlined a future settlement for western Europe. It also provided that the great powers would cooperate for the next 20 years, in order to uphold this settlement.

Napoleon enjoyed a successful final fling in the early months of 1814, winning some impressive if small-scale victories as the allies invaded France. He was by now critically short of men and munitions, for his latest attempt to rebuild his shattered army had encountered considerable resistance. A renewed allied advance captured Paris at the very end of March 1814 and on 6 April Napoleon formally abdicated. Alexander, alone of the allied leaders, was now in the French capital, and could decide the fate of France and her Emperor. But the Russian Emperor determined to play the magnanimous victor, and ensured that Napoleon received surprisingly lenient treatment. The treaty of Fontainebleau (11 April 1814) gave him a revenue of two million francs from French funds, the title of emperor and sovereignty over the Mediterranean island of Elba, of which he took possession early in May 1814. The Empress Marie Louise was given Parma and the reversion of the duchy to her son.

In the months that followed, Napoleon kept a close watch on the negotiations between the victorious allies, who were soon seriously divided over the terms of a general peace settlement (see below, pp. 355–61). He was equally interested in the performance of the new government in France, where Louis XVIII had been restored on British insistence. The King and his advisers behaved ineptly and it was soon apparent that the French people were unreconciled. Napoleon was aware of this and made a final bid for power (the 'Hundred Days'). Landing on the mainland on 1 March 1815, he quickly won support as the Bourbon *régime* collapsed, and by the 20th he was in Paris and again ruler of France. But allied armies were immediately sent against him, and, after a rapid campaign in the Southern Netherlands, he was narrowly defeated at the battle of Waterloo (18 June 1815). Napoleon abdicated for the second time four days later, and at Castlereagh's insistence, lived out the rest of his life as a British prisoner on the island of St Helena in the distant South Atlantic.

The Vienna settlement, 1814–1815

The European settlement was accomplished in two stages. That for western Europe, largely shaped by Castlereagh, was embodied in the First Peace of Paris (30 May 1814); it was subsequently modified after the 'Hundred Days' by a second and more severe treaty in November 1815. The more complex reconstruction of central and eastern Europe, where Alexander I's views largely prevailed, was the work of the Congress of Vienna, which met between October 1814 and June 1815. The task confronting the galaxy of crowned heads and foreign ministers who assembled in the Austrian capital was daunting, and it came to be tackled not in formal sessions but in private meetings – often at the abundant social and cultural events which occupied the participants – and ad hoc committees set up to deal with particular issues. The term 'Congress of Vienna' is in fact a misnomer: the conference's opening was postponed indefinitely and it only met to sign the final act. The presence of so many political leaders in one city, however, was highly unusual and may have been unique, and it certainly facilitated the conclusion of a settlement, which was dictated by the victorious great powers.

The stabilisation of Europe after more than two decades of near-continuous war was a time-consuming and complex business. The rapid collapse of Napoleon's Grand Empire had left numerous problems to be solved, particularly of frontiers. The map of Europe, several times re-drawn during the last quarter-century, had to be revised again. The allied negotiators were also constrained in important ways by previous obliga-tions, by certain *faits accomplis* and by military realities, especially in eastern Europe where Russian troops occupied much of the territory which had to be redistributed and which Alexander had no intention of yielding. On one occasion he boasted that there were 200,000 of his soldiers in the territories of the former Polish Kingdom. During the final phase of the fighting, several minor states had abandoned Napoleon in return for allied promises to respect their sovereignty, and these obligations also pre-empted the peace settlement, particularly in Germany. Such practical con-siderations were always more important than any ideology. In the event the Vienna settlement emerged piecemeal out of the negotiations, treaties and military campaigns of 1813–15 and out of the aspirations of the various national interests.

The dominant desire among the allies was to avoid another generation of political and social upheaval on the scale of 1789–1815 and to create a lasting basis for peace. The Vienna settlement was designed to prevent not only future revolution and constant warfare but also the domination of one state, to create an enduring equilibrium, which it was believed would be the best guarantee of future peace. But since each state perceived this in different terms, the details of the settlement proved a fertile source of disagreements, especially as the peacemakers were suspicious of each other and inevitably pursued their own interests. Apart from a very general desire to establish a political equilibrium and to safeguard against future challenges to the political *status quo*, the allies – with the single exception of the Russian Emperor – were little influenced by ideology. Although the ubiquitous Talleyrand, now the servant of the restored Bourbons in France, preached the doctrine of legitimacy, it was not consistently applied. It was invoked to justify the return of the exiled Bourbons to France, Spain and, after the 'Hundred Days', to Naples (from which Murat was expelled after rallying to Napoleon in spring 1815), but it was frequently ignored elsewhere. Indeed, some of Napoleon's work was tacitly accepted, par-ticularly the suppression of a large number of smaller states. In Germany, his destruction of the ecclesiastical principalities was confirmed and the number of sovereign units brought together under a new confederation reduced from over 300 to 38.

Ideas for a general settlement had been expressed at several points during the military struggle, notably by Czartoryski in his famous memorandum of 1803 and by Pitt during the Anglo-Russian alliance negotiations of 1805. The British notions were similar to the thinking behind the 1713–14 settlement at the end of the Spanish Succession War. France was to be contained by a ring of states around her frontiers. But instead of the feeble neighbours which had collapsed so completely in 1792–93, strong buffer states were to guard against future French aggression. Such thinking underlined that the settlement was Janus-faced: it looked forward to newer dispensations which were to shape nineteenth-century international relations, but also back to eighteenth-century doctrines and precedents and, specifically, to the containment of France by a 'Barrier', albeit of a rather different kind, in western Europe. It was Britain who argued primarily for this. Her financial and military contribution to the Final Coalition, and the presence of Castlereagh on the continent in 1814–15, together ensured that British diplomacy played the key role. The Foreign Secretary secured his barrier of strengthened states and, at the same time, ensured that the Low Countries (and the Scheldt in particular) should be in friendly hands: a long-established British concern because of the strategic importance of the region. The new kingdom of the Netherlands (made up of Holland and Belgium and ruled by the House of Orange) together with Prussia, which was given extensive Rhineland territories, stood guard on France's northern and north-eastern borders. In the south the chief sentries were the strengthened Kingdom of Sardinia (comprising the island of Sardinia, Savoy, Nice, Piedmont and Genoa) and Austria, with her new-found dominance in Italy. In this way the areas which France had most frequently threatened in the past were strengthened against any future aggression. The 1815 settlement in western Europe was dominated by the idea of containment and, as such, coincided with British interests.

London was primarily concerned in 1814–15 with Europe's political and territorial reorganisation, but Castlereagh was careful also to defend British colonial and naval supremacy. The Vienna settlement confirmed and extended Britain's dominance overseas. During the war against France, Britain had mopped up her colonies and those of her satellites, especially the Dutch. Though Castlereagh's preoccupation with the continent led to many of these being returned at the peace, Britain did retain some conquests to protect her trade and communications. The addition of Tobago, St Lucia and part of Guyana (Trinidad had been secured in

1802) significantly strengthened her in the West Indies. The acquisition of Mauritius and Cape Colony to add to Ceylon (also acquired in 1802) provided a firmer foothold in the East and protected communications with India, increasingly seen as the jewel in her empire. In Europe, Britain obtained Heligoland off the coast of Hanover, which was itself returned to George III, and a protectorate over the 'Septinsular Republic' of the Ionian Islands, which together with Malta (which was retained) and Gibraltar secured her naval position in the Mediterranean.

The Vienna settlement further strengthened Britain's economic, colonial and maritime supremacy, the foundations of her position as a great power. The wars of 1792–1815 had weakened her Dutch, Spanish and particularly French rivals overseas, and her dominance was now greater even than in 1763. From the later eighteenth century, moreover, the Industrial Revolution was adding a formidable new dimension to British power, which had always depended heavily on her commercial and financial strength. Though Britain's emergence since the end of the seventeenth century had been spectacular, it had not been accompanied by a permanent commitment to continental politics. Despite the links with Hanover, Britain's situation as an island often enabled her – unlike the other great powers – to abstain from European alliances and diplomacy, and this was both a source of strength and a cause of suspicion. Periodically Britain had played the role of a great land power, especially when the Low Countries or Hanover were threatened. She sent troops to the continent while simultaneously pursuing her own maritime and colonial interests overseas. But such involvement had been interspersed with extended periods of insularity, if not outright isolation, and – despite Castlereagh's role in 1814–15 – there was no reason to believe that her ambivalent membership of the European states-system had given way to permanent involvement. Continental states could not ignore Britain, but British statesmen could relegate European issues to a subsidiary position: this was part of the explanation for Britain's political rise.

Britain's traditional rival, France, was the principal loser by the wars of 1792–1815, and in western Europe the settlement was specifically directed against any resurgence of French power. But after two decades of war which France herself had largely provoked, her losses were less than might have been expected and were limited to her territorial conquests during the Revolutionary and Napoleonic Wars. Anxious not to make the second Bourbon restoration more difficult than it was already, the great powers treated the defeated France comparatively leniently. Although Prussia in particular wanted to partition French territory, the other allies resisted this in case it weakened the position of the restored Louis XVIII: monarchy was seen as the best defence against revolution. The Second Peace of Paris (20 November 1815) was certainly more severe than its predecessor of May 1814. France was punished for her support of Napoleon during the 'Hundred Days', by a reduction of her frontiers to those of 1790 (instead of 1792 which the allies had previously been prepared to allow: her most significant losses were the Saar to Prussia and part of Savoy to the kingdom of Sardinia); by a five-year allied occupation of northern France (this could be, and was, reduced to three); and by a massive indemnity of 700 million francs, imposed on a country whose economy lay in ruins after more than two decades of warfare. But France's former territorial integrity was confirmed and she remained a great power.

The allies believed the French had a role to play in the European states-system. Metternich in Austria, menaced by Russian expansion westwards and a Russo–Prussian alignment, was already anxious to encourage France's re-emergence as a major state able to counteract Russia. The 1815 settlement enabled France to recover her international position, and she remained potentially a very strong state because of her abundant economic and demographic resources, probably second only to Russia on the continent in 1815. Despite this and her favourable strategic position, however, France remained trapped between the demands of the continental struggle and her world-wide rivalry with Britain, and there was no indication in 1815 that this problem had been resolved.

Russia gained most from the Revolutionary and Napoleonic Wars. Her central role in the final defeat of France was reflected in her gains at Vienna. In 1814–15 Alexander was determined to realise his pet scheme for a reborn Poland under Russian control, one which should include as much as possible of Austria's and Prussia's Polish lands. Though Czartoryski was again part of his entourage in Vienna, his direct influence upon the Emperor's policy was slight. Instead Russian policy was firmly controlled by Alexander, who at this period acted as his own foreign minister and even arranged much of the detail of the settlement. Since Russian troops occupied Poland it was not easy to resist his demands. But early in 1815, under the threat of an alliance between Austria, Britain and France, the Russian Emperor made some modest concessions and an agreement was reached. Prussia received the western fringe of the Napoleonic Grand Duchy of Warsaw (including Posen and Thorn) and Austria retained Galicia, while Cracow became a free city. The rest of the Grand Duchy was given as a kingdom ('Congress Poland') to Alexander and was promised a constitution, to be determined solely by its new Russian ruler.

Poland's destiny was now permanently linked to that of Russia. The Vienna settlement amounted to a fourth partition, though one which gave St Petersburg a disproportionate share of the spoils. This immense Russian gain, when added to that of Finland (from Sweden in 1809) and Bessarabia (from the Ottoman Empire in 1812), marked Russia's greatest westward expansion so far.

The emergence of Russia as a great power had been the central political development of the second half of the eighteenth century, and the wars of 1792–1815 made her the continent's dominant one. The appearance of Russian armies in western Europe and their contribution to the defeat of Napoleon ensured that Russia's vast manpower and military might would be feared for a generation. Her challenge to the Ottoman Empire was more apparent than ever. Nor were Austria or Prussia alone able to resist further Russian encroachments: fear of Russia already dominated Metternich's foreign policy. The only constraints on Russia's dominance were her own extensive commitments, in Asia as well as in Europe, her limited economic resources and restricted ability to mobilise these, and the extent her foreign policy depended on the whim of her ruler. Throughout the wars of 1792–1815, Russia had alternated – as indeed throughout the eighteenth century – between absorption in her own affairs and involvement in the European power struggle. Alexander's mystical devotion to the 'Liberation of Europe', and the successes of his armies in 1812–14, had given his state a dominant voice among the peacemakers, particularly in the settlement of eastern and central Europe. But there was no certainty that Russia would continue this role after 1815.

Prussia's military role in the final campaigns against Napoleon allowed the allies conveniently to overlook her earlier neutralism, and she made substantial gains, which made her territory better able to support the role of a great power than previously. She received considerable territory in Westphalia (part of the Rhenish 'barrier' against France), Swedish Pomerania, Posen and two-fifths of Saxony, which was punished severely for its loyalty to Napoleon. The Saxon lands in particular were compensation for Prussian losses to Russia as part of 'Congress Poland'. Prussia's acquisitions in 1815 made her once again a comparatively strong state and significantly enhanced her economic potential. She was now clearly dominant in northern Germany and at least the equal of Austria within the new German Confederation. Prussia's geopolitics had changed fundamentally: from being a central and eastern European power she had become a more western-orientated European state. But the shattering defeat of 1806 had revealed the fundamental weaknesses of the Prussian monarchy and the reform era which followed had only partly remedied these. For a generation to come, Prussia remained – with Austria – the weakest of the great powers. Both were menaced by Russia's dominance, a threat Prussia tried to solve by a close association with St Petersburg.

Austria's relative position among the great powers had also been weakened by the recent wars. Superficially, Habsburg recovery was complete. Despite successive defeats at the hands of France, Austria recovered and, in some measure, expanded her territories. She retained Galicia, and Bavaria returned those territories acquired in 1805 and 1809 (Bavaria, which had deserted Napoleon in autumn 1813, received Würzburg, Frankfurt and part of the Lower Palatinate as compensation). Austria also made very significant territorial and political gains in Italy, principally to compensate for Russian and Prussian annexations elsewhere and to replace Belgium (now part of the enlarged 'Kingdom of the Netherlands'). She received Venetia and regained Lombardy as well as securing influence over the other restored Italian rulers: an alliance now linked Vienna with Turin, while the Bourbon ruler of the Kingdom of the Two Sicilies looked to Austria for guidance and the Papacy was also on good terms with her. In the remaining smaller independent territories in northern Italy (Tuscany, Parma and Modena) Habsburg rulers had been established or re-established. These arrangements gave Vienna virtual control over the whole peninsula after 1815, the final realisation of Austria's eighteenth-century ambitions there.

Austria retained the status of a great power until the First World War, more due to her geographical extent and European role than her own intrinsic strength. Up to the Crimean War she was also seen by the western powers as a barrier against Russia, and by the latter as a barrier against France. The central problem remained, however, and was actually more acute. Austria's commitments outran her resources, and the 1815 settlement increased these, particularly in Italy. Elsewhere, Habsburg interests were also adversely affected. In Germany, Austria was now at best the equal of Prussia; together they dominated the new German Confederation established in June 1815 with Austria as permanent chairman. But Berlin's gains in western Germany finally signalled the end of Austria's traditional role as defender of the Rhine against France and they were to help the growth in Prussian power and Austria's ultimate expulsion from Germany. The Habsburgs had increasingly to concern themselves with both Italy and eastern Europe. Since the 1770s, if not earlier, Vienna had struggled to prevent or at least control the growth of Russian power in the latter. The Vienna settlement reflected a further political reverse for

Habsburg policy. Metternich believed his primary task was to resist the Russian challenge, though he still feared the resurgence of French power. Russia's dominance of Poland, her close links with Prussia, her strengthened position on the Danube (through the acquisition of Bessarabia in 1812) and the danger she posed to the Ottoman Empire all threatened Habsburg interests, but it was not clear how a weak Austria could resist Russia. Austria thus remained, as she had been ever since her seventeenth-century political emergence, a state with the responsibilities of a great power but with an exposed and precarious strategic situation which she lacked the means to defend.

At the Congress of Vienna decisions had been taken by the four allies together with France (quickly readmitted on a limited basis to the ranks of the major powers) and then simply imposed on the other states. This political leadership was confirmed by the Quadruple Alliance of 20 November 1815, a treaty between Britain, Russia, Prussia and Austria which provided for regular meetings of allied rulers or their ministers and was to be the basis of the so-called 'Congress System' of 1815–23. In this way the major powers claimed and exercised the right to supervise developments throughout the Continent, even to intervene militarily in a state's internal affairs. The European states-system restored in 1815 was in intention a collection of great powers, approximately equal in strength – though Russia and Britain were clearly far stronger than the others, and France had the potential to be so – and together completely dominant within Europe. Such a system had emerged in the later eighteenth century, but had then been overturned by France's bid for hegemony. The defeat of Napoleonic military imperialism marked the completion of the birth of a great power system which had taken place since 1740.

Conclusion: The eighteenth-century origins of the nineteenth-century Great Power System

The comparative peace and stability of the century after 1815 have been widely admired and scarcely less widely analysed. It was unprecedented in terms both of the previous and subsequent history of Europe's international system. There was to be no war involving all the great powers before 1914 and no conflict between two or more great powers for four decades both at the beginning (1815–53) and at the end (1871–1914) of the period. While the 1850s and 1860s did see five wars involving two or more great powers, these were to be relatively restricted in scope and far less destructive than previously. In all respects the nineteenth century was – in Europe, if not its overseas colonies or on its own periphery: both important limitations – to be far more peaceful than its predecessor. It was true both in terms of the number of years when conflicts were in progress, and in the total casualties during this fighting. When overall population is taken into account, at least seven times as many Europeans died in eighteenth-century wars as in their nineteenth-century equivalents.[1]

The century after 1815 was also an era of unusual stability in the membership of Europe's international élite. After 1870 the newly-unified Kingdom of Italy joined the ranks of the great powers, while Prussia was subsumed into Germany: otherwise the leading states who concluded peace at Vienna remained dominant 100 years later, which was unique in the development of the modern international system. The sixteenth century had seen the rise of the Spanish Monarchy in Europe and America, the seventeenth that of the French Bourbons; the eighteenth century had witnessed the emergence of Britain, Russia and Prussia. But the hundred

---

[1] Paul W. Schroeder, 'The Nineteenth Century International System: changes in the structure', *World Politics* 39 (1986), p. 11, calculated from the figures in Jack S. Levy, *War in the Modern Great Power System, 1495–1975* (Lexington, KY, 1983).

years after 1815 saw no such political upheaval, only the addition of Italy, who long remained the weakest of the great powers. While the relative ranking of the leading states changed during the nineteenth century, in some cases more than once, the great power system itself was remarkably stable.

The explanation has usually been found in the skill and imagination of the peacemakers who assembled in Vienna in 1814–15, and that must clearly be a large part of any answer. In important respects the nineteenth-century political world created differed from its *ancien régime* predecessor. It is particularly clear where the reciprocal guarantees embodied in the settlement were concerned: guarantees which covered not merely territorial integrity but military security and political status. These legal obligations were acknowledged by all the great powers and were to be defended by them throughout the next generation and beyond. In a second respect, moreover, the post-1815 international system differed from its predecessor: this was in how the disruptive effects of overseas rivalry were contained and exerted less influence on European international relations until the later nineteenth century, when this would change with momentous consequences.

Whether the third element in this new political order, a distinction between the traditional concern with the 'balance of power' (based upon conflict and fear) and the new-found attempt to construct a 'political equilibrium' (rooted in enlightened self-interest), is quite as sharp as the main proponent of that view, Paul W. Schroeder, believes, has been questioned. But the importance of the Vienna settlement in constructing a political world relatively free from recurrent warfare is undoubted and constitutes the major achievement of the diplomats who shaped it. This was brought about by the great powers exerting a quite novel degree of control over the wider international system. Their own ascendancy was itself an important source of the stability of nineteenth-century international relations. Again, however, there were important eighteenth-century precedents in how the role of smaller states and, even more, their political independence had declined from the middle decades of that period onwards. Bavaria, Sardinia and Denmark would all be examples of this trend. The Napoleonic hegemony was in this, as in other respects, a reversion to an earlier pattern: Bavaria was the leading example of a smaller state which had briefly flourished during the French *imperium*. It had secured territory, not political power, and had never been more than a French client, though in 1815 it made territorial gains which ensured it did not return completely to its former insignificance. The degree of control which the five great powers exercised after the Congress of Vienna was novel in its extent, not its nature.

In this as in other respects, the nineteenth-century international system grew organically out of its eighteenth-century predecessor. One central thesis of the present study has been that while the emergence of a modern great power system has been a gradual and evolutionary process, its key period was from the Prussian invasion of Silesia until the conclusion of the Vienna settlement. While some of the developments involved have important origins and even crucial phases before 1740, its central components can all be located within the decades covered by this book. The most obvious way in which it was true was in establishing Europe's political geography down to the end of the First World War. One feature of the nineteenth century would be the relative absence of major territorial changes, particularly in comparison to the dramatic alterations during the following hundred years. There were significant modifications, above all the political unification of Italy and Germany which had remained geographically divided in 1815. These were less important, however, than the fact that the map of Europe in 1914 was recognisable from what it had been a hundred years before, which was unusual in itself.

By contrast the decades between 1740 and 1815 had seen fundamental changes in political geography: above all the continuing retreat of Ottoman power, the removal of Poland from the map, less dramatically the territorial and political reorganisation of the Italian peninsula and the Holy Roman Empire, and, temporarily, the vast expansion of France in Europe. The most enduring legacy of this period resulted from the first two of these changes: the political advance of Russia into eastern and south-eastern Europe, which would dominate nineteenth-century international relations. The other crucial legacy of these decades was the rise of Britain's colonial and economic power, which would accelerate after 1815 and was accompanied by a decidedly ambivalent attitude to continental Europe and its political problems.

The generation before the Congress of Vienna had also seen the political reunification of Europe, which would prove to be enduring. At least from the end of the Seven Years War, if not earlier, fault lines had divided the continent into two distinct political worlds. During the three decades after 1763 the major western states had exercised little influence in eastern Europe and *vice versa*, as the continent fractured into separate diplomatic systems. The revival of French power during the 1790s, after a generation of decline, and in particular Napoleon's vast imperial designs, reversed this fragmentation. It did not do so overnight: Russia and, to a lesser extent, Prussia had concentrated on the extinction of Poland during the 1790s, not the struggle against France. But the sheer dynamism of French military imperialism and the novel scale of Napoleonic pretensions made diplomatic cooperation essential for survival and forced Europe's major states to cooperate in ways and to an extent which were novel. This cooperation was at its height during the Final Coalition and the peace negotiations which followed, and it would prove an important and enduring legacy of this period.

These decades had been crucial in a second respect. One point which is rightly made is the ability of the five great powers after 1815 to solve difficult problems through diplomacy rather than by resorting to armed confrontation: itself a testimony to the Pentarchy's dominance as well as one main source of the long periods of peace which nineteenth-century Europe would enjoy. Certainly the list is impressive: beginning with the ending of the Allied military occupation of France, which was readmitted into the ranks of the great powers in 1818; running through the handling of a series of revolts during the 1820s (Naples, Sardinia, Spain and Greece), together with the peaceful recognition of the political independence granted to the Latin American colonies which had successfully revolted against Spain after 1808; including the way in which acute Russo-Ottoman tension was for a time damped down and, when fighting eventually broke out, shortened by international intervention. The list could be extended by including the successes of international diplomacy during the 1830s and 1840s, headed by the independence of Belgium and the partition of the new Kingdom of the Netherlands, needed to bring this about. What is clear is that the generation after 1815 and in a more general sense the entire nineteenth century – with the obvious exception of 1853–71 – was characterised by a novel ability of the leading states to prevent major issues escalating into war. The so-called 'Congress System' was obviously a manifestation of this, but the newly-creative role of diplomacy extended far beyond the formal end of these regular meetings of the great powers.

Once more this nineteenth-century trend had important eighteenth-century antecedents. These were twofold. The first was the expansion of international society to include two major states on Europe's eastern and southern periphery, which facilitated the solution of problems there through diplomacy. The full incorporation of Russia into the diplomatic network under Catherine II and her periodically enlarged political role thereafter were central developments. Without these, and Russian military power, Alexander I's decisive intervention at the Congress of Vienna would have been impossible. And, though the earliest Ottoman diplomatic missions to

European capitals under Selim III did not become permanent at first, the crucial breakthrough had taken place. The principle that the Empire should be part of this network had been established and its full incorporation would be renewed and completed during the second quarter of the nineteenth century. It would be formalised by the Ottoman Empire's admission to international society in 1856, at the end of the Crimean War.

In a second and wider sense, the Congress of Vienna and the regular meetings of the great powers which followed exemplified the role of discussion and compromise, leading to the peaceful solution of problems, and influenced subsequent practice. This was a fundamental change. Up to 1740 and, to a considerable extent, far beyond, diplomacy had been overwhelmingly reactive and had responded to problems when these arose. By the nineteenth century, largely due to shared experience during the military struggle against French power, and made possible by the completion of the network of embassies and other missions, diplomacy was becoming much more constructive and proactive, seeking to identify problems and so defuse crises before they arose.

The decades between the 1740s and the 1780s had seen a further consolidation of the diplomatic society which had begun to emerge during and immediately after the reign of Louis XIV. The French Revolution and the Napoleonic era were characterised by a pause in this process, both because these *régimes* to some extent disdained the concessive and slow-moving world of diplomacy and also due to the widespread warfare of these decades. In this perspective the Congress of Vienna was a return to older diplomatic forms, an assertion of the value of a style of negotiation which was slow-moving, achieved through compromise and involved social events at which informal negotiations could be conducted, as well as formal meetings of a conference. The Vienna settlement was important for the organisation of diplomacy, accompanied as it was by an extended agreement on protocol. Two established problems were definitively regulated, simplifying future practice. The first was the decision to divide all diplomats into three classes, increased to four at the Congress of Aix-la-Chapelle (Aachen) three years later. These divisions were: ambassadors; envoys and ministers plenipotentiary; ministers resident; and *chargés d'affaires*. The vexed question of precedence, which had earlier gone primarily by the hierarchy of rulers' titles (the representative of an Emperor outranked a King and so on) and had been the source of numerous disputes, was definitively resolved by agreement that, within these four classes, the date at which a diplomat had arrived at a particular court would determine precedence. These agreements, together with those reached on a host of minor issues, testified to the growing importance of diplomacy and at the same time simplified such relations in the future.

These decades, and particularly the 1790s and 1800s, were significant in a third way, which has not always been noted. Throughout this period continuous and determined, though not completely successful, efforts were being made to overhaul domestic infrastructures. The more effective mobilisation of economic and demographic resources which characterised nineteenth-century great powers originated in these efforts. The internal foundations of great power status had become more important from the mid-eighteenth century onwards. In the three eastern monarchies, these decades had seen a succession of schemes to increase the prosperity of the country and its inhabitants, and so boost the wealth of the state, accompanied by efforts to recruit and tax more efficiently. These attempts were redoubled during the Revolutionary and Napoleonic Wars: France's remarkable success in extracting resources from her own subjects and from the territories she controlled, together with the wealth of these lands, forced her opponents to similar exertions. Britain's formidable economic and financial strength ensured this mobilisation took the unusual form of new taxation, Pitt's income tax, and while this was not without internal repercussions, the social élite accepted – as they had done since the close of the seventeenth century – that they should bear a disproportionate share. The stresses placed upon France's other opponents were far greater and proved to be enduring.

One reason for extended peace after 1815 was a need to restore shattered infrastructures after a prolonged period of large-scale fighting. France's defeat, however narrow it had seemed on the battlefield of Waterloo, was actually complete and this influenced the peace settlement and subsequent international relations. Like treaties concluded at the end of earlier decisive wars – 1763 and 1713–14 would be other examples – the Vienna settlement ushered in a period when the main priority of all European governments was internal reconstruction, for which peace was an essential precondition. The new challenge to the old order, everywhere restored and in some places triumphant in 1815, from the widespread liberal and national movements of these years, strengthened this preoccupation and the accompanying domestic repression. It is part of any explanation of the relative international stability and the enduring peace, particularly immediately after 1815.

That stability was consciously fostered by the peacemakers at Vienna. In another sense, however, it was restored after the international anarchy of the 1790s and 1800s. Here the perspective of Georg Friedrich von

Martens (1756–1821), German jurist, Göttingen professor, and compiler of a well-known and widely-used series of handbooks of international law and diplomacy, is revealing. Writing in April 1801, in the 'Preface' to his latest compilation, he reflected on the eventful decade and more since he had first planned his work, which seems to have been in the later 1780s or even as late as 1790. Then, he reflected, Europe had been enjoying relatively widespread peace, which had been re-established at Lunéville two months earlier. In Martens' eyes, the eighteenth-century system had been relatively stable. Instability, he believed, was the product of the French Revolution, which had turned the political world upside down but which he hoped Bonaparte would tame and reverse: a widespread view after the *Brumaire coup*.[2] Martens' reflections are an important reminder that the wars of 1792–1815 were seen by many contemporaries as having disrupted a relatively stable political order. That world, created by the peace of Utrecht almost a hundred years before and with long periods of general peace between 1715 and 1739, and again from 1763–87, was itself a vast improvement on the seventeenth century, when there had been only three calendar years without fighting somewhere in Europe or involving a continental state. Though the growing stability which had developed during the eighteenth century had been interrupted by the upheavals of the French Revolutionary and Napoleonic periods, it would be resumed after the Congress of Vienna.

[2] G.F. von Martens, *Cours diplomatiques, ou Tableau des Relations Extérieures des Puissances de l'Europe* (3 vols.; Berlin, 1801), iii. x.

Chronology of principal events

1713		Treaty of Utrecht
1714		Treaty of Rastatt
1715		Death of Louis XIV, King of France since 1643
1726		Cardinal Fleury becomes first minister in France
1733–38		War of the Polish Succession
1735		Beginning of Russo-Ottoman War
1737		Austria declares war on the Ottoman Empire
1739	September	Peace of Belgrade ends war between the Ottoman Empire, and Russia and Austria
	October	Anglo-Spanish War (1739–48) begins
1740	May	Death of Prussia's Frederick William I; accession of Frederick II ('Frederick the Great')
	October	Death of Emperor Charles VI and accession of Maria Theresa in the Habsburg Monarchy; death of Russian Empress Anna
	December	Frederick the Great invades Silesia
1741	January	Most of Silesia occupied by Prussia
	April	Battle of Mollwitz
	May–June	Anti-Austrian alliance (the 'League of Nymphenburg') formed; includes France, Spain, Prussia, Bavaria and Saxony
	July	Sweden declares war on Russia
	December	Accession of Russia's Empress Elizabeth
1742	January	Sir Robert Walpole resigns; Bavaria's Elector, Charles Albert, elected Emperor Charles VII
	May	Battle of Chotusitz

	June	Provisional Austro-Prussian peace agreement at Breslau
	July	Treaty of Berlin ends Prussia's First Silesian War
1743	January	Death of Cardinal Fleury
	August	Peace of Åbo ends Russo-Swedish War
	September	Treaty of Worms between Britain, Austria and Sardinia
	October	Second Family Compact signed between France and Spain
1744	March	France declares war on Britain
	August	Prussia re-enters the war against Austria
1745	January	Charles VII dies
	April	Austria and Bavaria make peace by the Treaty of Füssen
	May	Battle of Fontenoy
	June	Battle of Hohenfriedberg
	July	Jacobite rebellion begins in Scotland
	September	Francis Stephen elected Emperor; battle of Soor
	December	Battle of Kesselsdorf; separate peace between Austria and Prussia, the Treaty of Dresden, ends the Second Silesian War
1746	April	Battle of Culloden
	June	Signature of Austro-Russian defensive alliance, renewing one concluded in 1726
	October	Battle of Rocoux; peace negotiations begin at Breda
1747	May	Orangist revolution in the Dutch Republic
	July	Battle of Laufeldt
	September	French capture of Bergen-op-Zoom
1748	March	Negotiations begin at Aix-la-Chapelle
	Oct.–Nov.	Peace of Aix-la-Chapelle signed
1752		Treaty of Aranjuez between Austria, Spain and Sardinia
1753		Kaunitz becomes State Chancellor
1753 onwards		Unofficial Anglo-French confrontation in North America
1755		Sending of British regular soldiers to North America under Braddock; British seizures of French merchantmen

	September	Convention of St Petersburg between Russia and Britain; never ratified
1756	January	Anglo-Prussian Convention of Westminster
	May	First Treaty of Versailles between France and Austria; British declaration of war on France begins the Anglo-French Seven Years War
	August	Frederick the Great's invasion of Saxony begins the continental Seven Years War
1756–63		Seven Years War
1757	Jan.–Feb.	Russia joins the anti-Prussian coalition
	March	Sweden joins the anti-Prussian coalition
	May	Second Treaty of Versailles between France and Austria; battle of Prague
	June	Battle of Kolin
	August	Battle of Gross Jägersdorf
	November	Battle of Rossbach
	December	Battle of Leuthen
1758	August	Battle of Zorndorf
	December	Duc de Choiseul becomes French foreign minister
1759	March	Third Treaty of Versailles between France and Austria, backdated to December 1758
	July	Battle of Kay
	August	Accession of Charles III in Spain; battle of Kunersdorf
1760		Surrender of French Canada
	August	Battle of Liegnitz
	November	Battle of Torgau
1761	August	Third Family Compact
1762	January	British declaration of war on Spain; death of Empress Elizabeth of Russia, succeeded by Peter III
	May	Russia makes peace with Prussia
	July	Peter III swept from the Russian throne; succeeded by his wife who becomes Catherine II
1763	February	Peace treaties of Paris (10th) and Hubertusburg (15th)
	October	Death of Augustus III of Saxony–Poland

1764	April	Conclusion of Russo-Prussian alliance treaty
	September	Stanislas Poniatowski becomes King of Poland
1765	March	Russo-Danish alliance treaty
1766		Anglo-Russian commercial treaty
1768	May	France agrees to buy Corsica from the Republic of Genoa
	October	Ottoman declaration of war on Russia
1768–74		Russo-Ottoman War
1770–71		Second Anglo-Bourbon confrontation over the Falklands
1772	August	Signature of treaties partitioning Poland for the first time; Gustav III's *coup* restores the powers of the Swedish monarchy
1773		Final Russo-Danish agreement over the duchy of Holstein
1774	July	Treaty of Kutchuk-Kainardji ends Russo-Ottoman War
1775	May	Austria seizes the Bukovina from the Ottoman Empire
1775–83		Revolt of North American colonies against Britain
1777	December	Death of Bavarian Elector
1778	January	Agreement between Charles Theodore of the Palatinate, heir to Bavaria, and Austria; followed by Austrian occupation of Lower Bavaria
	February	Franco-American treaties signed; France committed to intervention in Britain's war with her former colonists
	July	Anglo-French War formally begins; War of Bavarian Succession begins, with Prussia and Saxony fighting Austria
1779		Convention of Aynali Kavak: Ottoman Empire acknowledges Russian control over the Crimea
	April	Franco-Spanish Convention of Aranjuez commits Spain to intervene on the side of France and the Americans

	May	Peace of Teschen, mediated by France and Russia, ends the War of the Bavarian Succession
1780		League of Armed Neutrality, consisting of Russia, Sweden, Denmark, Austria, Prussia, the Kingdom of the Two Sicilies and the Dutch Republic
	November	Death of Maria Theresa
	December	British declaration of war on the Dutch Republic
1781	May–June	Informal defensive alliance between Russia's Catherine II and Austria's Joseph II
1783	April	Russian annexation of the Crimea
	September	Definitive peace treaties signed at Versailles, ending the American War
1784–85		Failure of Austria's attempt to acquire Bavaria by means of an exchange involving the Austrian Netherlands
1785	July	League of German Princes (*Fürstenbund*), formed under Frederick the Great's leadership
1786	August	Death of Frederick the Great; accession of Frederick William II
	September	Franco-British Commercial treaty ('Eden Treaty')
1787	January	Franco-Russian Commercial treaty
	August	Ottoman declaration of war on Russia
	September	Prussian troops restore Stadtholder William V
1788	February	Austrian declaration of war on the Ottoman Empire
	July	Gustav III declares war on Russia
	April–Aug.	Triple Alliance between Britain, Prussia and the Dutch Republic
1788–91		"Four–Years' Diet" in Poland
1789	January	Formal summoning of Estates–General
	May	Estates–General convenes
	July	Fall of the Bastille; 'Great Fear'
	August	Abolition of feudalism and privileges; Declaration of Rights of Man and Citizen
1790	Jan.–Oct.	Anglo-Spanish confrontation over Nootka Sound

	February	Death of Joseph II; succeeded by Leopold II
	March	Prusso-Polish defensive alliance concluded
	May	Constituent Assembly renounces foreign conquests
	June	Constituent Assembly abolishes nobility in France
	July	Civil Constitution of the Clergy; Convention of Reichenbach between Austria and Prussia
	August	Russo-Swedish War concluded by the peace of Verela
1791	Mar.–Apr.	Failure of British ultimatum to Russia over Ochakov
	June	Flight to Varennes and temporary suspension of Louis XVI
	July	Padua Circular; reinstatement of Louis XVI
	August	Austro-Ottoman Peace signed at Sistova; Declaration of Pillnitz
	October	Legislative Assembly meets for the first time; Brissot's first call for war
1792	January	Russo-Ottoman Peace signed at Jassy; French ultimatum to Austria
	February	Austro-Prussian defensive alliance
	March	Death of Leopold II; accession of Francis II
	April	France declares war on Austria
	June	Prussia declares war on France
	July	Brunswick Manifesto
	August	Overthrow of French monarchy; Prussian troops invade France
	September	September Massacres; French victory at Valmy; proclamation of the French Republic
	November	Battle of Jemappes; 'Fraternity and Assistance' decrees
	December	Decree on Occupied Territories
1793	January	Trial and execution of Louis XVI; Second Partition of Poland, carried out by Russia and Prussia
	February	French declare war on Britain and the Dutch Republic
	March	French declare war on Spain
	August	Decree of *levée en masse*

	Aug.–Dec.	British occupation of Toulon
	October	Declaration of revolutionary government
1793–97		War of the First Coalition
1794	Mar.–Oct.	Polish rising against Russia and Prussia
	June	'Glorious First of June'; battle of Fleurus
	December	Invasion of Dutch Republic
1795	April	Franco-Prussian peace of Basel
	May	Establishment of Batavian Republic
	July	Franco-Spanish peace treaty
	October	Annexation of Belgium; Third Partition of Poland between Russia, Austria and Prussia
	November	Establishment of Directory in France
1796	April	French army under Bonaparte invades Italy
	August	Franco-Spanish alliance
1797	January	Battle of Rivoli
	April	Preliminaries of Leoben
	May	French occupation of Venetian Republic
	June	Establishment of Cisalpine Republic
	September	Fructidor *coup*; collapse of Franco-British peace talks
	October	British naval victory at Camperdown; peace of Campo Formio
	November	Rastatt conference opens
1798	February	Proclamation of Roman Republic; French alliance with Cisalpine Republic
	May	Departure of Egyptian expedition
	June	French capture of Malta
	August	Battle of the Nile
	September	Ottoman declaration of war on France
1798–1802		War of the Second Coalition
1799	January	French capture Naples and proclaim the Parthenopean Republic
	March	Austria declares war on France
	August	Bonaparte leaves Egypt
	Aug.–Oct.	Failure of Anglo-Russian expedition to North Holland
	November	Directory overthrown by Bonaparte in the *coup d'état* of Brumaire
1800	May	Bonaparte crosses the Alps
	June	Battle of Marengo

	December	Battle of Hohenlinden; second Armed Neutrality of Russia, Denmark, Sweden and Prussia
1801	February	Peace of Lunéville
	March	Assassination of Russia's Paul I, ruler since 1796
	April	Battle of Copenhagen
	October	Franco-British peace preliminaries signed; Russia makes peace with France
1802	March	Peace of Amiens between Britain and France
	June	Alexander I and Frederick William I meet at Klaipeda
	Sept.–Oct.	Further French annexations in Italian peninsula
	October	French military intervention to shore up the (Swiss) Helvetic Republic
1803	January	Colonel Sébastiani's report published in the *Moniteur*
	February	Imperial Deputation destroys the constitution of the Holy Roman Empire
	May	British declaration of war on France; French occupation of Hanover
1803	June–	French 'Army of Invasion' maintained at Boulogne, until October 1805
1804	March	Seizure of the duc d'Enghien
	May	Napoleon assumes the title 'Emperor'
	August	Francis II becomes 'Emperor of Austria' as 'Francis I'
	December	Spain enters war on the side of France
1805–07		War of the Third Coalition
1805	April	Anglo-Russian subsidy treaty
	May	Napoleon takes the throne of the former Cisalpine Republic
	June	French annexation of the Ligurian Republic (Genoa)
	July	Anglo-Russian agreement to form the Third Coalition
	August	Austria enters war against France
	October	Austrian surrender at Ulm; Nelson's victory over a Franco-Spanish fleet at Trafalgar

	December	French victory at Austerlitz; Austria makes peace at Pressburg; Prussia secures annexation of Hanover by the Treaty of Schönbrunn
1806	June	Creation of Kingdom of Holland with Louis Bonaparte as ruler; Britain declares war on Prussia
	July	Formation of Confederation of the Rhine
	August	Prussian mobilisation and ultimatum to France; formal dissolution of Holy Roman Empire
	October	Prussia routed at Jena–Auerstädt; French army enters Berlin
	November	Berlin decrees codifying the Continental System
	December	Ottoman declaration of war against Russia; French troops advance against Russia
1807	January	British Orders in Council respond to the Continental System
	February	Battle of Eylau
	June	Battle of Friedland
	July	Treaties of Tilsit; formal establishment of Grand Duchy of Warsaw
	September	British bombardment of Copenhagen
	Nov.–Dec.	First and Second Milan decrees extend the Continental System
1808	February	Russia invades Finland
	Mar.–May	Spanish rising against French; Joseph Bonaparte becomes King of Spain
	July	French defeat at Bailén
	August	British expeditionary force lands in Portugal
	Sept.–Oct.	Meeting between Napoleon and Alexander I at Erfurt
1809	April	Austrian declaration of war against France
	May	Austria defeats French at Aspern–Essling
	July	Napoleon's victory over Austrians at Wagram; British victory at Talavera
	Aug.–Dec.	Failure of British Walcheren expedition
	October	Metternich becomes Austrian Chancellor; Franco-Austrian peace of Schönbrunn

1810	July	French annexation of Holland, after abdication of Louis Bonaparte
	December	France annexes the Hanseatic towns, Oldenburg, and parts of Berg and Hanover; Russia withdraws from Continental System
1812	May	Peace of Bucharest ends Russo-Ottoman War
	June	French invasion of Russia begins
	July	Wellington's victory at Salamanca
	September	French victory at Borodino
	October	French retreat from Moscow begins
	December	Prusso-Russian Convention of Tauroggen
1813–14		War of the Fourth Coalition
1813	February	Treaty of Kalisch, Russo-Prussian military alliance
	March	Prussia formally enters war against France
	June	Anglo-Russian and Anglo-Prussian alliances signed at Reichenbach; Wellington's victory at Vittoria
	August	Austria declares war against France
	September	Treaty of Teplitz
	October	Allied victory in 'Battle of the Nations' at Leipzig; French retreat begins
1814	March	Treaty of Chaumont; allies capture Paris
	April	Napoleon abdicates
	May	First peace of Paris
1814	October–	Congress of Vienna
1815	March	Napoleon lands in France; beginning of the 'Hundred Days'
	June	Napoleon defeated at Waterloo and abdicates for the second time
	November	Second peace of Paris

Bibliographical essay

This bibliography is intended both as a guide to further reading and as an indication of the scholarship upon which I have principally drawn in writing this book. It concentrates on works in English and includes numerous articles, since some of the most important recent contributions have been published in journals and edited collections, and shorter surveys are often especially valuable in teaching. The majority of the works listed themselves contain extensive bibliographies. Books in English are published in London unless indicated otherwise.

General

Though this guide focusses upon Anglophone books and articles, some of the most important items are in foreign languages. The most authoritative and up-to-date surveys of the eighteenth-century states system are Lucien Bély, *Les relations internationales en Europe XVIIe–XVIIIe siècles* (Paris, 1992; 2nd edn., 1998) and two volumes in the 'Handbuch der Geschichte der Internationalen Beziehungen', Heinz Duchhardt, *Balance of Power und Pentarchie: Internationale Beziehungen 1700–1785* (Paderborn, 1997) and Michael Erbe, *Revolutionäre Erschütterung und erneuertes Gleichgewicht (1785–1830)* (Stuttgart, 2004); all three contain excellent bibliographies of works in several languages. Among older studies, the vintage Max Immich, *Geschichte des europäischen Staatensystems von 1660 bis 1789* (1905; repr. Munich, 1967) and A. Wahl, *Geschichte des europäischen Staatensystems im Zeitalter des französischen Revolution und der Freiheitskriege, 1789–1815* (1912; repr. Munich, 1967) remain unsurpassed as sources of information, while Jacques Droz, *Histoire diplomatique de 1648 à 1919* (2nd edn., Paris, 1959) is an imaginative analytical survey of a longer period. A recent French view is Jean-Pierre Bois, *De la paix des rois à l'ordre des empereurs 1714–1815* (Paris, 2003). In English, Jeremy Black, *The Rise of the European Powers, 1679–1793*

(1990) and the same author's subsequent *European International Relations 1648–1815* (2002) have useful insights, while E. Luard, *The Balance of Power: the System of International Relations, 1648–1815* (1992) is an intelligent attempt to analyse the assumptions behind the conduct of diplomacy. Studies of contemporary thinking about peace and war include Peter Wilson, 'War in German Thought from the Peace of Westphalia to Napoleon', *European History Quarterly* **28** (1998), 5–50, an exemplary investigation of the kind that it would be valuable to have for other countries, and the notably incisive Richard Tuck, *The Rights of War and Peace: Political Thought and the International Order from Grotius to Kant* (Oxford, 1999). In a class of its own, particularly for the detailed narrative it provides of the period after 1787, is Paul W. Schroeder, *The Transformation of European Politics 1763–1848* (Oxford, 1994), which single-handedly has revived the study of international history; a special issue of *International History Review* **16**:iv (1994) saluted its appearance, with admiringly critical essays by fellow specialists and a dignified response by the author. The rise, fall and rebirth of one crucial paradigm, that of the 'primacy of foreign policy', is re-examined in a special issue of *German History* **21** (2003), with a key historiographical essay by Brendan Simms: 'The Return of the Primacy of Foreign Policy', pp. 275–91.

For the foreign policies of individual states, Britain is best served for surveys of long periods. D.B. Horn, *Great Britain and Europe in the Eighteenth Century* (Oxford, 1967) remains authoritative, although the arrangement of chapters makes it difficult to use. P. Langford, *The Eighteenth Century, 1688–1815* (1976) is a sound and much more accessible guide; while there is also Jeremy Black, *A System of Ambition?: British Foreign Policy 1660–1793* (1991; 2nd edn., Stroud, 2000) and J.R. Jones, *Britain and the World, 1649–1815* (1980), together with an incisive essay by N.A.M. Rodger, 'The Continental Commitment in the eighteenth Century', in *War, Strategy and International Politics: Essays in honour of Sir Michael Howard*, eds L. Freedman, P. Hayes and R. O'Neil (Oxford, 1992), pp. 39–55. For French policy, helpful introductions are: Jeremy Black, *From Louis XIV to Napoleon: the fate of a great power* (1999) and P. Rain, *La Diplomatie Française, i: D'Henri IV à Vergennes, ii: De Mirabeau à Bonaparte* (2 vols., Paris, 1945–50). For the Dutch Republic, there is A.C. Carter, *Neutrality or Commitment: the evolution of Dutch foreign policy, 1667–1795* (1975), which should be read with J.W. Smit, 'The Netherlands and Europe in the seventeenth and eighteenth centuries', in *Britain and the Netherlands in Europe and Asia*, ed. J.S. Bromley and E.H. Kossmann (1968), pp. 13–36. There is nothing comparable for other

European states, though an authoritative and notably informative military and diplomatic perspective on Austria's rise is provided by Michael Hochedlinger, *Austria's Wars of Emergence 1683–1797* (London, 2003), while one dimension of Habsburg policy is skilfully surveyed by Karl A. Roider, Jr., *Austria's Eastern Question 1700–1790* (Princeton, 1982). For Russia, John P. Le Donne, *The Russian Empire and the World 1700–1917: the geopolitics of expansion and containment* (New York, 1997) and his later and complementary *The Grand Strategy of the Russian Empire, 1650–1831* (New York, 2004) are informative but idiosyncratic and make too much of their geopolitical premises, while William C. Fuller, Jr., *Strategy and Power in Russia 1600–1914* (New York, 1992) provides a balanced military perspective on Russia's westward advance. Finally, Peter H. Wilson, *German Armies 1648–1806* (London, 1998) provides an informative political and military perspective on the crucial Central European conflicts of these decades, which are also examined in the notably lively Brendan Simms, *The Struggle for Mastery in Germany, 1779–1850* (1998).

Colonial rivalries are outlined by J.H. Parry, *Trade and Dominion: the European Overseas Empire in the Eighteenth Century* (1971) and G. Williams, *The Expansion of Europe in the Eighteenth Century* (1966), and their diplomatic repercussions for one area by the final chapters of M. Savelle, *The Origins of American Diplomacy: the International History of Anglo-America 1492–1763* (New York, 1967) and by G.S. Graham, *Empire of the North Atlantic: the Maritime Struggle for North America* (1958). The key British perspective is furnished by the large-scale P.J. Marshall, ed., *The Eighteenth Century*, vol. 2 of 'The Oxford History of the British Empire' (Oxford, 1998), a series of authoritative chapters by individual scholars which provide much important detail but which – like so many composite volumes – does so at the expense of the overall picture, and the notably lively and much more accessible Bruce Lenman, *Britain's Colonial Wars 1688–1783* (2001). On naval rivalry, the most important recent work is the remarkable study by Jan Glete, *Navies and Nations: Warships, Navies and State Building in Europe and America, 1500–1860* (2 vols., Stockholm, 1993). Whatever reservations may be felt about the validity of his approach to calculating relative naval strength, it constitutes the essential starting point. Its conclusions are skilfully integrated into the reliable synthesis by Richard Harding, *Seapower and Naval Warfare 1650–1830* (1999), while for Britain there are Richard Harding, *The Evolution of the Sailing Navy 1509–1815* (1995), P.M. Kennedy, *The Rise and Fall of British Naval Mastery* (1976), J.R. Hill, ed., *The Oxford*

Illustrated History of the Royal Navy (Oxford, 1995), with relevant and substantial chapters by John B. Hattendorf ('The Struggle with France, 1690–1815') and Daniel A. Baugh, ('The eighteenth-century Navy as a National Institution, 1690–1815') and now N.A.M. Rodger, *The Command of the Ocean: a Naval History of Britain, 1649–1815* (2004), a large-scale and vastly-informative work which immediately becomes the starting point for future research; and for France the old-fashioned E.H. Jenkins, *A History of the French Navy* (1973) and the more up-to-date perspectives of M. Vergé-Francheschi, *La marine française au XVIIIe siècle* (Paris, 1996), and Martine Acerra and André Zysberg, *L'essor des marines de guerre européennes 1680–1790* (Paris, 1997), which is considerably more francocentric than it proclaims. Reliable and up-to-date studies of land warfare include: M.S. Anderson, *War and Society in Europe of the Old Regime, 1618–1789* (1988); Jeremy Black, *European Warfare 1660–1815* (1994); and Christopher Duffy, *The Military Experience in the Age of Reason* (1987).

Chapter 1

There are three excellent and up-to-date textbooks: the authoritative and wide-ranging M.S. Anderson, *Europe in the Eighteenth Century 1713–1783* (4th edn., 2000), the notably lively William Doyle, *The Old European Order 1660–1800* (2nd edn., Oxford, 1992) and the outstanding collective work edited by T.C.W. Blanning, *The Eighteenth Century* (2000). The essential domestic context to international rivalries, and important information on the foreign policies of individual states, are contained in the following national histories: for France, the informative political survey ed. William Doyle, *Old Regime France 1648–1788* (Oxford, 2001), a detailed narrative by Colin Jones, *The Great Nation: France from Louis XIV to Napoleon* (2002) and Daniel Roche, *France in the Enlightenment* (1993; Engl. trans., Cambridge, MA, 1998), a notably original approach to eighteenth-century French history; Spanish history can be studied in the sturdy John Lynch, *Bourbon Spain 1700–1808* (Oxford, 1989), the final chapters of Henry Kamen, *Spain's Road to Empire: the making of a World Power, 1492–1763* (2002), and the same author's *Philip V of Spain* (2001), while its Iberian neighbour is the subject of David Francis, *Portugal 1715–1808* (1985). Britain is particularly well-served, with several up-to-date surveys: much the best is Paul Langford, *A Polite and Commercial People 1727–1783* (Oxford, 1989), while over a larger time-span there are Wilfrid Prest, *Albion Ascendant: English History 1660–1815* (Oxford, 1998), a notably fresh account, and the composite work ed. Paul Langford, *The Eighteenth Century 1688–1815* (2002). The nature of Britain's eighteenth-century emergence and, in particular, the 'fiscal-military' state which made it possible, has inspired considerable debate. It was inspired by John Brewer, *The Sinews of Power: War, Money and the English state 1688–1783* (1989), and can be followed up in Lawrence Stone, ed., *An Imperial State at War: Britain from 1689 to 1815* (1994) and H.V. Bowen, *War and British Society 1688–1815* (Cambridge, 1998). For the second of the Maritime Powers there is the vast and informative Jonathan I. Israel, *The Dutch Republic: its rise, greatness and fall 1477–1806* (Oxford, 1995), part IV of which provides a detailed treatment of the eighteenth century; for Austria, Charles Ingrao, *The Habsburg Monarchy 1618–1815* (1994; 2nd edn., Cambridge, 2000), a model survey, and the more recent Paula Sutter Fichtner, *The Habsburg Monarchy 1490–1848* (2003). For the German-speaking lands there is now an outstanding and up-to-date survey: Peter H. Wilson, *From Reich to Revolution: German History, 1558–1806* (Basingstoke, 2004) while Prussia is best approached through the essays in ed. Philip G. Dwyer, *The Rise of Prussia 1700–1830* (2000); for Russia, Simon Dixon, *The Modernisation of Russia 1676–1825* (Cambridge, 1999) is sparkling and up to date, and important detail can be quarried from Michael T. Florinsky, *Russia: a history and an interpretation*, I (New York, 1947). Poland's eclipse is best approached through Jerzy Lukowski, *Liberty's Folly: the Polish Lithuanian Commonwealth in the Eighteenth Century* (1991) and R. Butterwick, ed., *The Polish–Lithuanian monarchy in a European context c. 1500–1795* (Basingstoke, 2001). For Sweden, there is Michael Roberts, *The Age of Liberty: Sweden 1719–1772* (Cambridge, 1986); for Denmark there are some helpful articles, above all Ole Feldbaek, 'Eighteenth-century Danish neutrality: its diplomacy, economics and law', *Scandinavian Journal of History*, 8 (1983), pp. 3–21, and the same author's 'Denmark and the Baltic, 1720–1864', in *In Quest of Trade and Security: the Baltic in Power Politics, 1500–1990, I: 1500–1890*, eds. Göran Rystad, Klaus-R. Böhme, Wilhelm M. Carlgren (Lund, 1994), pp. 257–93; and Hans Bagger, 'The role of the Baltic in Russian foreign policy, 1721–1773', in *Imperial Russian Foreign Policy*, ed. Hugh Ragsdale (New York, 1993), pp. 36–72; while for the second half of the period there is an informative parallel survey of the two Scandinavian kingdoms by H. Arnold Barton, *Scandinavia in the Revolutionary Era 1760–1815* (Minneapolis, 1986). There is no satisfactory general study of the eighteenth-century Ottoman Empire, but Virginia H. Aksan, *An Ottoman Statesman in War and Peace: Ahmed Resmi Efendi*

1700–1783 (Leiden, 1995), explores the central themes in an informative way and some material can be quarried from Donald Quataert, *The Ottoman Empire 1700–1922* (2000). The past generation has seen important research on the fiscal dimension of state power, and this is effectively consolidated in *Economic Systems and State Finance*, ed. Richard Bonney (Oxford, 1995), the outstanding volume in the otherwise uneven sequence produced by the European Science Foundation project on 'The Origins of the Modern State in Europe, 13th–18th Centuries'. Bonney has now edited a valuable companion collection, *The Rise of the Fiscal State in Europe, c. 1200–1815* (Oxford, 1999), which contains much important information. A complementary series of articles is W.M. Ormrod, Margaret Bonney and Richard Bonney eds., *Crises, Revolutions and Self-Sustained Growth: Essays in European Fiscal History, 1130–1830* (Stamford, 1999); see in particular T.J.A. Le Goff, 'How to Finance an Eighteenth-century War' (pp. 377–413), which is illuminating on the mounting economic problems of the French Bourbon monarchy.

The best account of international rivalry during the period 1714–39 is provided by Pierre Muret, *La prépondérance anglaise, 1715–1763* (Paris, 1937). Developments in the Italian peninsula are sketched by Guido Quazza, 'Italy's role in the European problems of the first half of the eighteenth century', *Studies in Diplomatic History: Essays in Memory of David Bayne Horn*, ed. R.M. Hatton and M.S. Anderson (1970), pp. 138–54, which summarises a much larger study in Italian; in greater detail in G. Hanlon, *The Twilight of a Military Tradition: Italian aristocrats and European conflicts 1560–1800* (1998), chapter 8; the same author's *Early Modern Italy 1550–1800* (Basingstoke, 2000), part III; and from Turin's perspective by an incisive short study by Christopher Storrs, 'Ormea as Foreign Minister: the Savoyard State between England and Spain 1732–1745', in *Nobilità e Stato in Piemonte: I Ferrero d'Ormea* ed. A. Merlotti (Turin, 2003), pp. 231–48. British policy is best approached through Jeremy Black, *British foreign policy in the age of Walpole* (Edinburgh, 1985); Daniel Szechi, *The Jacobites, Britain and Europe* (Manchester, 1994), and Rebecca Wills, *The Jacobites and Russia, 1715–1750* (East Linton, 2002), while on Fleury, there is A. McC. Wilson, *French foreign policy during the administration of Cardinal Fleury* (Cambridge, MA, 1936), a classic work which is updated by Jeremy Black, 'French Foreign Policy in the Age of Fleury Reassessed', *English Historical Review*, 103 (1988), pp. 359–84. Rohan Butler, *Choiseul*, vol. I: *Father and Son 1719–1754* (Oxford, 1980), part 1, offers a panoramic view of European diplomacy during the 1720s and 1730s and important detail on Lorraine.

The waning of one alliance is the subject of an important study by Hugh Dunthorne, *The Maritime Powers 1721–1740: a study of Anglo-Dutch Relations in the Age of Walpole* (New York, 1986) while Austria's political, financial and dynastic problems are explored in K.A. Roider, Jr., *The Reluctant Ally: Austria's Policy in the Austro-Turkish War, 1737–1739* (Baton Rouge, LA, 1972) and C.W. Ingrao, 'The Pragmatic Sanction and the Theresian Succession', in *Theresian Austria*, ed. W.J. McGill (Washington, PA, 1981).

Chapters 2, 3 and 4

The best introductions to the period 1739–63 are the vintage W.L.Dorn, *Competition for Empire 1740–1763* (New York, 1940) and Part 4 of Muret, *La prépondérance anglaise, 1715–1763*. A recent British perspective is Jeremy Black, *America or Europe?: British Foreign Policy 1739–63* (1998), while there is much of interest in the standard biography of the minister who dominated British diplomacy, Reed Browning, *The Duke of Newcastle* (New Haven, CT, 1975). Richard Pares, 'American versus Continental Warfare, 1739–1763', *English Historical Review*, 51 (1936), pp. 429–65 is fundamental; it is reprinted in the same author's *The Historian's Business and other Essays* (Oxford, 1961), pp. 130–72. Two reliable studies of the warfare of the 1740s are available: M.S. Anderson, *The War of the Austrian Succession 1740–1748* (1995), which is crisp and comprehensive, and Reed Browning, *The War of the Austrian Succession* (Stroud, 1994), which adds important detail from a mildly Anglocentric perspective. The origins of the Anglo-Spanish war have been recently the subject of a major revisionist study by Philip Woodfine, *Britannia's Glories: the Walpole Ministry and the 1739 war with Spain* (1998), the conclusions of which were anticipated and summarised in the same author's 'The Anglo-Spanish War of 1739', in J. Black, ed., *The Origins of War in Early Modern Europe* (Edinburgh, 1987), pp. 185–209. The commercial disputes which preceded the war are the subject of E.G. Hildner, 'The role of the South Sea Company in the diplomacy leading to the War of Jenkins' Ear 1729–1739', *Hispanic American Historical Review*, 18 (1938), pp. 322–41; Geoffrey J. Walker, *Spanish Politics and Imperial Trade, 1700–1789* (1979); and Jean O. McLachlan, *Trade and Peace with Old Spain 1667–1750* (Cambridge, 1940). The best account of Anglo-Bourbon rivalry is Richard Pares, *War and Trade in the West Indies 1739–1763* (Oxford, 1936). On the war of 1739–48 there are some valuable articles: R.H. Harding, 'Sir Robert Walpole's Ministry and the Conduct of the War with Spain, 1739–41', *Historical Research* **60** (1987), pp. 299–320; Philip Woodfine, 'Ideas of naval power and the conflict with Spain, 1737–1742', in J. Black and P. Woodfine, eds., *The British Navy and the Use of Naval Power in the eighteenth century* (Leicester, 1988), pp. 71–90; J.C.M. Oglesby, 'England versus Spain in America, 1739–48: the Spanish side of the hill', *Canadian Historical Association: Historical Papers* (1970), pp. 147–57; and the same author's 'Spain's Havana Squadron and the preservation of the Balance of Power in the Caribbean, 1740–1748', *Hispanic American Historical Review*, **49** (1969), pp. 473–88.

Prussia's decisive impact between 1740 and 1763 is outlined by H.M. Scott, 'Prussia's Emergence as a European Great Power', in Philip Dwyer, ed., *The Rise of Prussia: Rethinking Prussian History 1700–1830* (2000), pp. 153–76, and can be taken further in D.B. Horn, *Frederick the Great and the Rise of Prussia* (1964); T. Schieder, *Frederick the Great* (Engl. trans., 2000), and Dennis E. Showalter, *The Wars of Frederick the Great* (1996); while that of Russia is best studied in Eugeny V. Anisimov, *Empress Elizabeth: Her Reign and Her Russia 1741–1761* (Engl. trans., Gulf Breeze, FL, 1995). The warfare and diplomacy of the 1740s are viewed from a French perspective in the large-scale Butler, *Choiseul*, parts II and III. Despite its title, Sir Richard Lodge, *Studies in Eighteenth-Century Diplomacy 1740–1748* (1930) is an Anglocentric and very detailed study of diplomacy and peacemaking 1743–48; a more recent British perspective is Chapter 3 of N.A.M. Rodger, *The Insatiable Earl: a life of John Montagu, Fourth Earl of Sandwich 1718–1792* (1993); while one key issue is dealt with by Jack M. Sosin, 'Louisburg and the Peace of Aix-la-Chapelle, 1748', *William and Mary Quarterly* **14** (1957), pp. 516–35.

On Anglo-French relations after 1748, Max Savelle, *The Diplomatic History of the Canadian Boundary, 1749–1763* (New Haven, CT, 1940) remains informative, but the fundamental article which revises older views is T.R. Clayton, 'The Duke of Newcastle, the Earl of Halifax and the American Origins of the Seven Years' War', *Historical Journal*, **24** (1981), pp. 571–603; see also M. Savelle, *The Origins of American Diplomacy: the International History of Anglo-America 1492–1763* (New York, 1967) and L.H. Gipson, 'British diplomacy in the light of Anglo-Spanish New World issues 1750–1757', *American Historical Review*, **51** (1946), pp. 627–48. A masterly introduction to the mid-century 'reversal of alliances' is D.B. Horn, 'The Diplomatic Revolution', *New Cambridge Modern History* vii, ed. J.O. Lindsay (Cambridge, 1957), 440–64; the standard full-scale study remains R. Waddington, *Louis XV et le renversement des alliances* (Paris, 1896). M. Braubach, *Versailles und Wien von Ludwig*

XIV. bis Kaunitz (Bonn, 1952) has been widely praised as a study of the origins of the Diplomatic Revolution, but it is deterministic and selective in its use of evidence. Uriel Dann, *Hanover and Great Britain 1740–1760* (Leicester, 1991) is brief and to the point. There are also some relevant articles on the years 1749–56: H.M. Scott, '"The True Principles of the Revolution": the Duke of Newcastle and the Idea of the Old System', in J. Black, ed., *Knights Errant and True Englishmen: British Foreign Policy, 1660–1800* (Edinburgh, 1989), pp. 55–91; W. Mediger, 'Great Britain, Hanover and the rise of Prussia', in *Studies in Diplomatic History*, eds. Hatton and Anderson pp. 199–213; W.J. McGill, 'The Roots of Policy: Kaunitz in Vienna and Versailles 1749–1753', *Journal of Modern History*, 43 (1971), pp. 228–44; R. Browning, 'The British orientation of Austrian foreign policy 1749–54', *Central European History*, 1 (1968), pp. 299–323 and the same author's 'The duke of Newcastle and the imperial election plan, 1749–1754', *Journal of British Studies*, 7 (1967), pp. 28–47; and D.B. Horn, 'The Duke of Newcastle and the origins of the Diplomatic Revolution', in *The Diversity of History*, eds. J.H. Elliott and H.G. Koenigsberger (1970), pp. 245–68. D.B. Horn, *Sir Charles Hanbury Williams and European Diplomacy 1747–58* (1930) remains a distinguished study of continental diplomacy in the mid-1750s. Lothar Schilling, *Kaunitz und das Renversement des Alliances* (Berlin, 1994) is an illuminating exploration of the Chancellor's approach to international relations. The debate on the responsibility for the Seven Years War is examined by H. Butterfield, *The Reconstruction of an Historical Episode* (Glasgow, 1951), reprinted in the same author's *Man on his Past* (Cambridge, 1955). The role of Russia is examined, and exaggerated, by the unconvincing H.H. Kaplan, *Russia and the Outbreak of the Seven Years' War* (Berkeley, 1968).

There are good brief accounts of the continental Seven Years War from an Austrian perspective in Franz A.J. Szabo, *Kaunitz and enlightened absolutism 1753–1780* (Cambridge, 1994), chapter 7, and from a Prussian in Schieder, *Frederick the Great*, chapter 4, and Showalter, *The Wars of Frederick the Great*, chapters 4–6. Vienna's war-effort is anatomised by Christopher Duffy, *Instrument of War* (Rosemount, IL, 2000), the first part of a detailed and authoritative two-volume study of *The Austrian Army in the Seven Years War*. Aspects of Russia's war are examined in two articles by John Keep: 'The Russian Army in the Seven Years War', in E. Lohr and M. Poe, eds., *The Military and Society in Russia 1450–1917* (Leiden, 2002), pp. 197–220 and 'Feeding the Troops: Russian Army Supply Policies during the Seven Years War', *Canadian Slavonic Papers*, 29 (1987), pp. 24–44; see also Carol S. Leonard, *Reform and Regicide:*

the Reign of Peter III of Russia (Bloomington, IN, 1993). The reasons for French military failure are sketchily surveyed by Lee Kennett, *The French Armies in the Seven Years' War* (Durham, NC., 1967) and the problems of the navy are evident from James S. Pritchard, *Louis XV's Navy: a study of organisation and administration* (Kingston and Montreal, 1987); the financial constraints upon both are apparent from James C. Riley, *The Seven Years War and the Old Regime in France: the economic and financial toll* (Princeton, NJ, 1986), though some of its conclusions are controversial. War-time diplomacy is examined by L.J. Oliva, *Misalliance: a Study of French Policy in Russia during the Seven Years' War* (New York, 1964), a study of one troubled alliance, while the relations of two other temporary partners are authoritatively dealt with by P.F. Doran, *Andrew Mitchell and Anglo-Prussian Diplomatic Relations during the Seven Years War* (New York, 1986) and Karl W. Schweizer, *Frederick the Great, William Pitt and Lord Bute: the Anglo-Prussian alliance 1756–1763* (New York, 1991); F. Spencer, 'The Anglo-Prussian breach of 1762', *History*, **41** (1956), pp. 100–12, remains an important brief discussion of their celebrated break-up.

Valuable brief accounts of the Anglo-French struggle are provided by the latest and also the best biography of Pitt, that by Marie Peters, *The Elder Pitt* (1998), chapter 3, and from a naval perspective by Harding, *Seapower and Naval Warfare*, chapter 8. Thinking about Britain's war-effort has been transformed by the impressive study of Richard Middleton, *The Bells of Victory: the Pitt-Newcastle ministry and the Conduct of the Seven Years' War, 1757–1762* (Cambridge, 1985), together with the same author's articles: see in particular 'Pitt, Anson and the Admiralty, 1756–1761', *History*, **55** (1970), pp. 189–98; 'Naval Administration in the Age of Pitt and Anson, 1755–1763', in Black and Woodfine, eds., *The British Navy and the Use of Naval Power*, pp. 109–27; and 'British Naval Strategy, 1755–62: the Western Squadron', *Mariner's Mirror*, **75** (1989), pp. 349–67. A modern study of the Anglo-Spanish War of 1762–63 is badly needed, though the journal *Mariner's Mirror* contains some significant articles: see in particular David F. Marley, 'A Fearful Gift: the Spanish Naval Build-up in the West Indies, 1759–1762', **80** (1994), pp. 403–17; the same author's 'Havana Surprised: Prelude to the British Invasion, 1762', **78** (1992), pp. 293–305; Nicholas Tracy, 'The Capture of Manila, 1762', and David Syrett, 'The British Landing at Havana: an example of an eighteenth-century combined operation', both in **55** (1969): respectively pp. 311–22 and 325–31. Dr. Tracy has now published a more detailed account: *Manila Ransomed: the British Assault on Manila in the*

Seven Years War (Exeter, 1995). Finally, there is a solid introduction to the Anglo-French peace negotiations by Z.E. Rashed, *The Peace of Paris 1763* (Liverpool, 1951).

The fighting's international and domestic legacies are set out in chapters 2 and 3 of H.M. Scott, *The Emergence of the Eastern Powers 1756–1775* (Cambridge, 2001). The declining fortunes of one state are evident from A.C. Carter, *The Dutch Republic in Europe in the Seven Years War* (1971) and, from a British perspective, from H.M. Scott, 'Sir Joseph Yorke and the Waning of the Anglo-Dutch Alliance, 1747–1788', in R. Moore and H. van Nierop, eds., *Colonial Empires Compared: Britain and the Netherlands, 1750–1850* (Aldershot, 2003), pp. 11–31.

Chapter 5

There is now a first-class introduction by M.S. Anderson, *The Rise of Modern Diplomacy 1450–1919* (1993). Even more wide-ranging and equally informative, if episodic, is Linda S. Frey and Marsha L. Frey, *The History of Diplomatic Immunity* (Columbus, OH, 1999), which is more broadly conceived than the title might suggest. Daniela Frigo, ed., *Politics and Diplomacy in early modern Italy* (Cambridge, 2000) contains some informative essays, in particular Christopher Storrs, 'Savoyard diplomacy in the eighteenth century (1684–1798)' (pp. 210–53). The kind of quarrels which arose between diplomats are illustrated by L. Wolff, 'A Duel for Ceremonial Precedence: the Papal Nuncio versus the Russian Ambassador at Warsaw, 1775–1785', *International History Review*, 7 (1985), pp. 235–44. The evidence for the mid-eighteenth century changes in the nature of the international system and in the language of international relations is set out in the 'Introduction' to Scott, *The Emergence of the Eastern Powers 1756–1775*, while the workings of this great-power system are still best described in the writings of two nineteenth-century masters: Leopold von Ranke, 'The Great Powers', first published in 1833 and reprinted in English translation in *The Theory and Practice of History* ed. Georg G. Iggers and K. von Moltke (New York, 1973), pp. 65–101; and Albert Sorel, *Europe and the French Revolution: the political traditions of the Old Régime* (Engl. trans., 1969), the first volume of a classic work. Denmark's pursuit of neutrality can be followed in Ole Tuxen, 'Principles and Priorities: the Danish View of Neutrality during the Colonial War of 1755–63', *Scandinavian Journal of History*, 13 (1988), pp. 207–32, and Gunner Lind, 'The Making of the Neutrality Convention of 1756', *ibid.*, 8 (1983), pp. 171–92. Important theoretical discussions include J. Viner,

'Power versus plenty as objectives of foreign policy in the seventeenth and eighteenth centuries', *World Politics*, 1 (1948), pp. 1–29; M.S. Anderson, 'Eighteenth-century theories of the balance of power' in *Studies in Diplomatic History*, eds. Hatton and Anderson, pp. 183–98; F. Gilbert, 'The "new diplomacy" of the eighteenth century', *World Politics*, 4 (1951), pp. 1–38, reprinted in the same author's collected essays: *History: Choice and Commitment* (Cambridge, MA, 1977), pp. 323–50; and F.H. Hinsley, *Power and the Pursuit of Peace* (Cambridge, 1963); while M. Wright, ed., *Theory and Practice of the Balance of Power, 1486–1914* (1975) is a useful collection of documents.

Valuable information on Russia's eighteenth-century discovery of European diplomacy can be quarried from V.E. Grabar, *The History of International Law in Russia, 1647–1917: a bio-bibliographical study*, translated and edited by W.E. Butler (Oxford, 1990), while D. Altbauer, 'The Diplomats of Peter the Great', *Jahrbücher für Geschichte Osteuropas*, new series 28 (1980), pp. 1–16, and Avis Bohlen, 'Changes in Russian diplomacy under Peter the Great', *Cahiers du monde russe et soviétique*, 7 (1966), pp. 341–58, examine the creation of Russia's own diplomatic network. On the Ottoman case, a valuable perspective is J.C. Hurewitz, 'Ottoman diplomacy and the European state system', *Middle East Journal*, 25 (1961), pp. 141–52; and the topic can be taken further in three overlapping articles by Thomas Naff: 'The Ottoman Empire and the European States System', in H. Bull and A.Watson, eds., *The Expansion of International Society* (Oxford, 1984), pp. 143–69; 'Ottoman Diplomatic Relations with Europe in the Eighteenth Century', in T. Naff and R. Owen, eds., *Studies in Eighteenth Century Islamic History* (Carbondale, IL, 1977), pp. 88–107; and 'Reform and the conduct of Ottoman diplomacy in the reign of Selim III, 1789–1807', *Journal of the American Oriental Society*, 83 (1963), pp. 295–315; and two by Carter V. Findley, 'The Legacy of Tradition to Reform: Origins of the Ottoman Foreign Ministry', *International Journal of Middle Eastern Studies*, 1 (1970), pp. 334–57, and 'The Foundation of the Ottoman Foreign Ministry', *ibid.*, 3 (1972), pp. 388–416. The problems and delays involved in all negotiations in Constantinople are graphically illustrated by Dan H. Andersen, 'Denmark's treaty with the Sublime Porte in 1756', *Scandinavian Journal of History*, 17 (1992), pp. 145–66, which examines the conclusion of a commercial agreement. *Mubadele: an Ottoman-Russian Exchange of Ambassadors*, edited and translated by N. Itzkowitz and M. Mote (Chicago, IL, 1970), a translation of contemporary accounts, is informative on both states' diplomacies.

Only the diplomatic services and foreign offices of Britain and France have, as yet, been treated adequately. For Britain see D.B. Horn's authoritative introduction, *The British Diplomatic Service, 1689–1789* (Oxford, 1961), which is updated by Jeremy Black, *British Diplomats and Diplomacy 1688–1800* (Exeter, 2001), and C.R. Middleton, *The Administration of British Foreign Policy 1782–1846* (Durham, NC, 1977); for France, Jean-Pierre Samoyault, *Les Bureaux du secrétariat d'état des affaires étrangères sous Louis XV* (Paris, 1971); F. Masson, *Le Département des affaires étrangères pendant la Révolution, 1787–1804* (1897) and E.A. Whitcomb, *Napoleon's Diplomatic Service* (Durham, NC., 1979). France's diplomatic contacts with the North African 'states' are explored from an anthropological perspective in the large-scale and important study by Christian Windler, *La diplomatie comme expérience de l'autre: consuls français au Maghreb (1700–1840)* (Geneva, 2002); his principal conclusions can be found in a series of articles in English: 'Diplomatic History as a Field for Cultural Analysis: Muslim–Christian Relations in Tunis, 1700–1840', *Historical Journal* 44 (2001), pp. 79–106; 'Tributes and Presents in Franco-Tunisian diplomacy', *Journal of Early Modern History* 4 (2000), pp. 168–99; and 'Representing a State in a Segmentary Society: French Consuls in Tunis from the Ancien Régime to the Restoration', *Journal of Modern History* 73 (2001), pp. 233–74. The machinery for Austria's foreign policy is described by Szabo, *Kaunitz*, chapter 2, and for her German rival by H.M. Scott, 'Prussia's Royal Foreign Minister', in Robert Oresko, G.C. Gibbs and H.M. Scott, eds., *Royal and Republican Sovereignty in early Modern Europe* (Cambridge, 1997), pp. 500–26. A good general study of Torcy's 'School for Ambassadors' is by H.M.A. Keens-Soper, 'The French Political Academy, 1712', *European Studies Review*, 2 (1972), pp. 329–55, while a more specialised initiative is the subject of Karl A. Roider, Jr., 'The Oriental Academy in the Theresienzeit', *Topic*, 34 (1980), pp. 19–28. H.M. Scott, 'The Rise of the First Minister in eighteenth-century Europe', in T.C.W. Blanning and David Cannadine, eds., *History and Biography: Essays in Honour of Derek Beales* (Cambridge, 1996), pp. 21–52, provides a wider perspective on Europe's leading statesmen. O.T. Murphy, 'Charles Gravier de Vergennes; profile of an old regime diplomat', *Political Science Quarterly*, 83 (1968), pp. 400–18, examines how this late-eighteenth-century figure, although perhaps an untypical one, viewed the European system. The Papacy's reduced role is evident from the final chapters of A.D. Wright, *The Early Modern Papacy: from the Council of Trent to the French Revolution 1564–1789* (Harlow, 2000), while its vulnerability to pressure from Europe's Catholic states in one crucial episode is the subject of H.M. Scott, 'Religion and *Realpolitik*: the duc de Choiseul, the Bourbon Family Compact, and the Society of Jesus, 1758–1773', *International History Review* **25** (2003), pp. 37–62. Finally, J.W. Thompson and S.K. Padover, *Secret Diplomacy: Espionage and Cryptography, 1500–1815* (1937), a lurid and unconvincing book, is the only general treatment of an important subject.

Chapter 6

A solid, informative outline of developments after the Seven Years War is provided by M.S. Anderson, 'European Diplomatic Relations 1763–90', *New Cambridge Modern History* viii, ed. A. Goodwin (Cambridge, 1965), pp. 252–78. The interpretation advanced in this chapter, together with a narrative of events from 1763 to 1775, is set out in detail in Scott, *Emergence of the Eastern Powers*. France's long-term trajectory is examined by Daniel A. Baugh, 'Withdrawing from Europe: Anglo-French Maritime Geopolitics, ca. 1750–1800', *International History Review* **20** (1998), pp. 1–32, and from a rather different perspective, by H.M. Scott, 'The Decline of France and the Transformation of the European States System, 1756–1792', in Peter Krüger and Paul W. Schröder (sic), eds., in cooperation with Katja Wüstenbecker, *'The Transformation of European Politics 1763–1848': Episode or Model in Modern History?* (Münster, Hamburg and London, 2003), pp. 105–28. That of Prussia is examined by two articles in *German History* **12:3** (1994): H.M. Scott, 'Aping the Great Powers: Frederick the Great and the Defence of Prussia's International Position, 1763–86' (pp. 286–307) and Dennis E. Showalter, 'Hubertusburg to Auerstädt: the Prussian Army in Decline' (pp. 308–33); while Russia's changed European role is the subject of H.M.Scott, 'Russia as a European Great Power', in R. Bartlett and J.M. Hartley, eds., *Russia in the Age of Enlightenment: Essays for Isabel de Madariaga* (1990), pp. 7–39; Hugh Ragsdale, 'Russian Foreign Policy, 1763–1815: Does it Exemplify Paul Schroeder's Theses', in Krüger, Schröder and Wüstenbecker, eds., *'The Transformation of European Politics'*, pp. 129–51; and Martin Malia, *Russia under Western Eyes: from the Bronze Horseman to the Lenin Mausoleum* (Cambridge, MA, 1999), especially pp. 15–84.

The introduction to *The Fourth Earl of Sandwich: Diplomatic Correspondence 1763–1765* ed. F. Spencer (Manchester, 1961), is useful on the early years of peace, while the reduced role of France is explored by H.M. Scott, 'France and the Polish Throne, 1763–1764', *Slavonic and East European Review* **53** (1975), pp. 370–88. The genesis of the most important post-war alliance is re-examined by H.M. Scott, 'Frederick II, the Ottoman Empire and the Origins of the Russo-Prussian Alliance of April 1764', *European Studies Review* 7 (1977), pp. 153–75. D.M. Griffiths provides a convenient outline of 'The Rise and Fall of the Northern System', *Canadian–American Slavonic Studies* 4 (1970), pp. 547–69; the best account of the Empress's foreign policy is that contained in the magisterial survey by Isabel de Madariaga, *Russia in the Age of Catherine the Great* (1981); see also the specialised articles published in part I of the proceedings of a major annivesary conference: *Katharina II., Russland und Europa: Beiträge zur internationalen Forschung* ed. Claus Scharf (Mainz, 2001). Lawrence J. Baack, 'State Service in the eighteenth century: the Bernstorffs in Hanover and Denmark', *International History Review* 1 (1979), pp. 323–48, is a convenient brief introduction to Denmark's impressive foreign minister, whose policy after 1763 is also illuminated by Michael Roberts, 'Great Britain, Denmark and Russia 1763–70', in Hatton and Anderson, eds., *Studies in Diplomatic History*, pp. 236–67. Roberts' large-scale political biography of Sir John Goodricke, *British Diplomacy and Swedish Politics 1758–1773* (1980), together with the same author's 'Great Britain and the Swedish Revolution 1772–73', *Historical Journal* 7 (1964), pp. 1–46 [reprinted in *idem., Essays in Swedish History* (1967), pp. 286–347] are the best introduction to Sweden's role in post-war diplomacy; over a shorter period there is the detailed study of Michael F. Metcalf, *Russia, England and Swedish Party Politics 1762–1766* (Stockholm and Totowa, NJ, 1977).

Developments in Poland are best approached through Adam Zamoyski, *The Last King of Poland* (1992), a well-written political biography of Poniatowski, and especially the authoritative writings of J.T. Lukowski: see his *Liberty's Folly*, chapters 7–8, his detailed monography, *The Szlachta and the Confederation of Radom, 1764–1767/68* (Antemurale, xxi; Rome, 1977), and two illuminating articles, 'Towards Partition: Polish Magnates and Russian Intervention in Poland during the Early Reign of Stanislaw August Poniatowski', *Historical Journal* 28 (1985), pp. 557–74, and 'Guarantee or Annexation: A Note on Russian Plans to Acquire Polish Territory Prior to the First Partition of Poland', *Bulletin of the Institute of Historical Research* 106 (1983), pp. 60–5. A longer perspective, strongly nationalist and even determinist, is Zofia Zielinska, 'Poland between Prussia and Russia in the eighteenth century', in Samuel Fiszman, ed., *Constitution and Reform in eighteenth-century Poland: the Constitution of 3 May 1791* (Bloomington and Indianapolis, IN, 1997), pp. 87–111. The best introduction to the diplomacy of the Russo-Ottoman War of 1768–74 remains

Albert Sorel, *The Eastern Question in the eighteenth century* (Engl. trans., 1898), while for the settlement which ended it see R.H. Davidson, ' "Russian Skill and Turkish Imbecility": the Treaty of Kuchuk Kainardji Reconsidered', *Slavic Review* 35 (1976), pp. 463–83. The Ottoman side of the war can be studied in the path-breaking writings of Virginia Aksan: see her *Ottoman Statesman*, chapter 3; 'The One-eyed Fighting the Blind: Mobilization, Supply and Command in the Russo-Turkish War of 1768–74', *International History Review* 15 (1993), pp. 221–38; and 'Feeding the Ottoman Troops on the Danube, 1768–1774', *War and Society* 13 (1995), pp. 1–14. Zbigniew Kulak, 'The Plans and Aims of Frederick II's Policy towards Poland', *Polish Western Affairs* 22 (1981), pp. 70–101, is informative though rather nationalistic in tone. On the first partition there is now a reliable guide: J.T. Lukowski, *The Partitions of Poland: 1772, 1793, 1795* (1999), chapters 1–3. Finally, Austrian policy is best approached through the impressive Derek Beales, *Joseph II, vol. I: In the Shadow of Maria Theresa 1741–80* (Cambridge, 1987), chapter 9, and two informative and overlapping studies by Karl A. Roider, Jr., *Austria's Eastern Question 1700–1790* (Princeton, 1982), chapters 6–8, and *Baron Thugut and Austria's Response to the French Revolution* (Princeton, 1987), chapter 2.

Chapter 7

The best introductions to Russia's decisive advance are the authoritative and large-scale survey by Madariaga, *Russia in the Age of Catherine the Great*, chapters 23–28, and Simon Sebag Montefiore's effervescent life of the Empress's larger-than-life consort: *Prince of Princes: the Life of Potemkin* (2000), whose role in southern expansion was earlier reassessed by Marc Raeff, 'In the Imperial Manner' in Raeff, ed., *Catherine the Great: a Profile* (1972), pp. 197–246, and in an overlapping series of articles by Hugh Ragsdale, incorporating the results of new research in Russian and European archives: 'New Light on the Greek Project', in R.P. Bartlett, A.G. Cross and Karen Rasmussen, eds., *Russia and the World of the Eighteenth Century* (Columbus, OH, 1988), pp. 493–501; 'Montmorin and Catherine's Greek Project', *Cahiers du monde russe et soviétique* 27 (1986), pp. 27–44; 'Evaluating the Traditions of Russian Aggression: Catherine II and the Greek Project', *Slavonic and East European Review* 66 (1988), pp. 91–117; 'Russian Projects of Conquest in the Eighteenth Century', in Ragsdale, ed., *Imperial Russian Foreign Policy* (Cambridge, 1993), pp. 75–102. Thomas Freller, 'In Search of a Mediterranean Base:

the Order of St John and Russia's Great Power Plans during the rule of Tsar Peter the Great and Tsarina Catherine II', *Journal of Early Modern History* 8 (2004), pp. 3–30, provides useful background. The informative article by Vasilios N. Makrides, 'Orthodoxie und Politik: die russisch-griechischen Beziehungen zur Zeit Katharinas II.', in Scharf, ed., *Katharina II., Russland und Europa*, pp. 85–119, is important for the religious context of the Greek Project. The same collection contains (pp. 183–225) the best study of the Empress's Austrian alliance: Michael Hochedlinger, ' "Herzensfreundschaft" – Zweckgemeinschaft – Hypothek?: das russisch-österreichische Bündnis von 1781 bis zur zweiten Teilung Polens'. Isabel de Madariaga, 'The secret Austro–Russian Treaty of 1781', *Slavonic and East European Review* 38 (1959–60), pp. 114–45, examines the conclusion of this treaty and Catherine's use of it in 1783 when Russia annexed the Crimea. A.W. Fisher, *The Russian Annexation of the Crimea 1772–1783* (Cambridge, 1970) is invaluable for the complex internal struggle within the Khanate, but the international dimension is covered best by M.S. Anderson, 'The Great Powers and the Russian annexation of the Crimea, 1783–4', *Slavonic and East European Review* 37 (1958–59), pp. 17–41. Case studies of Russia's southwards expansion include Muriel Atkin, *Russia and Iran, 1780–1828* (Minneapolis, 1980), George F. Jewsbury, *The Russian Annexation of Bessarabia 1774–1828* (Boulder, CO, 1976) and Nikolas K. Gvosdev, *Imperial Policies and Perspectives towards Georgia, 1760–1819* (Basingstoke, 2000), while the Ottoman response is apparent from Aksan, *An Ottoman Statesman*, chapter 4; the French from Orville T. Murphy's sturdy biography, *French Diplomacy in an Age of Revolution: Charles Gravier, Comte de Vergennes* (Albany, NY, 1982); and the Austrian from an important article by Harvey L. Dyck, 'Pondering the Russian Fact: Kaunitz and the Catherinian Empire in the 1770s', *Canadian Slavonic Papers* 22 (1981), pp. 451–69; Roider, *Austria's Eastern Question*, chapters 9–10; and the outstanding and all-too-brief T.C.W. Blanning, *Joseph II* (1994), chapter 5, which provides the most satisfactory available introduction to Habsburg policy during the later 1770s and 1780s.

An exemplary brief account of Austria's first attempt to acquire Bavaria is Beales, *Joseph II*, I, chapter 13; the old study by Harold Temperley, *Frederic the Great and Kaiser Joseph* (1915) remains useful. The failure of the second attempt is best approached through a seminal article by T.C.W. Blanning, ' "That Horrid Electorate" or "Ma Patrie Germanique"?: George III, Hanover and the *Fürstenbund* of 1785', *Historical Journal* 20 (1977), pp. 311–44, while its cultural politics are illuminated by Maiken

Umbach, 'The Politics of Sentimentality and the German *Fürstenbund* 1779–1785', *ibid.*, **41** (1998), pp. 679–704, and the same author's stimulating and wide-ranging *Federalism and Enlightenment in Germany 1740–1806* (2000). P.P. Bernard, *Joseph II and Bavaria* (The Hague, 1964), is a comprehensive study of the two episodes, but it is inaccurate over details and unconvincing in its wider diplomatic perspective, and must be used with caution.

An informative study from a British perspective, particularly on the war of 1787–92, is A.I. Bagis, *Britain and the Struggle for the Integrity of the Ottoman Empire: Sir Robert Ainslie's Embassy to Istanbul 1776–1794* (Istanbul, 1984), while incidental light is cast on the origins of that conflict in Jeremy Black, 'Sir Robert Ainslie: His Majesty's Agent-provocateur? British foreign policy and the international crisis of 1787', *European History Quarterly* **14** (1984), pp. 253–83. On the fighting, see M.S. Anderson, *The Eastern Question 1774–1923* (1966), chapter 1, and three detailed studies from Vienna's perspective: the richly-informative Michael Hochedlinger, *Krise und Wiederherstellung: Österreichische Großmachtpolitik zwischen Türkenkrieg und "Zweiter Diplomatischer Revolution" 1787–1791* (Berlin, 2000); two important and well-researched articles by Matthew Z. Mayer, in *International History Review* **27** (2004): 'The Price for Austria's Security: Part I – Joseph II, the Russian Alliance, and the Ottoman War, 1787–1789' (pp. 257–99) and 'Part II – Leopold II, the Prussian Threat, and the Peace of Sistova, 1790–91' (pp. 473–514); and Karl A. Roider, Jr., 'Kaunitz, Joseph II and the Turkish War', *Slavonic and East European Review* **54** (1976), pp. 538–56. Leopold II's foreign policy is also illuminated by T.C.W. Blanning, 'An old but new biography of Leopold II', in Blanning and Cannadine, eds., *History and Biography: Essays in Honour of Derek Beales*, pp. 53–71. This provides an introduction to the major and entirely neglected study by Paul von Mitrofanov, *Leopold II avstriiskii: vneshniaia politika* (Petrograd, 1916), which I have been able to consult thanks to the generosity of Professor Blanning, who loaned me his extensive notes on it.

The ambitions of Gustav III and international relations in the Baltic region are explored in the following articles: R.J. Misiunas, 'The Baltic question after Nystad', *Baltic History* **1** (1974), pp. 71–90, a stimulating survey which covers the whole eighteenth century; H.A. Barton, 'Gustav III of Sweden and the East Baltic, 1771–1792', *Journal of Baltic Studies* **7** (1976), pp. 13–30; S.P. Oakley, 'Gustavus III's plans for war with Denmark in 1783–84', in *Studies in Diplomatic History*, ed. Hatton and Anderson, pp. 268–86; and H.A. Barton, 'Russia and the problem of Sweden–

Finland, 1721–1809', *East European Quarterly* 5 (1972), pp. 431–55. The most accessible introduction to the Russo-Swedish War of 1788–90 is now the articles by Jan Glete and Lars Ericson in the lavish exhibition catalogue, *Catherine the Great and Gustav III* (Helsingborg, 1999), pp. 174–215. There are valuable accounts of the confrontation over Ochakov in M.S. Anderson, *Britain's Discovery of Russia 1553–1815* (1958), chapter 6, and John Ehrman, *The Younger Pitt, ii: the reluctant transition* (1983), chapter 1; while Alan Cunningham, 'The Ochakov Debate', in *idem., Ottoman Encounters in the Age of Revolution: Collected Essays* ed. Edward Ingram (2 vols., 1993), I. pp. 1–31, and Paul L.C. Webb, 'Sea Power in the Ochakov Affair of 1791', *International History Review* 2 (1980), pp. 13–33, are helpful articles.

The most accessible studies of the extinction of Poland are Lukowski's authoritative *The Partitions of Poland*, chapters 5–7, and the detailed and lively Zamoyski, *The Last King of Poland*. The problems over implementing the first partition are examined from a Prussian perspective by Jerzy Topolski, 'The Polish–Prussian Frontier during the period of the First Partition (1772–1777)', *Anglo-Polish Western Affairs* 10 (1969), pp. 81–110. On the diplomacy, R.H. Lord, *The Second Partition of Poland* (Cambridge, MA, 1915) is a classic detailed study, while the same author's 'The Third Partition of Poland', *Slavonic and East European Review* 3 (1924–25), pp. 481–98, is a valuable sketch. There are also two informative articles by J. Lojek, 'The international crisis of 1791: Poland between the Triple Alliance and Russia', *East-Central Europe* 2 (1975), pp. 1–63, and 'Catherine II's armed intervention in Poland . . . 1791–92', *Canadian–American Slavic Studies* 4 (1970), pp. 570–93.

Chapter 8

The continuing lack of an adequate study of Choiseul's ministry remains a considerable barrier to the full understanding of Anglo-Bourbon relations after the Seven Years War. J.F. Ramsey, *Anglo-French relations 1763–70: a Study of Choiseul's Foreign Policy* (Berkeley, 1939) is a sketchy outline which relies too heavily on British material; L. Blart, *Les Rapports de la France et de l'Espagne après le pacte de famille, jusqu' à la fin du ministère du duc de Choiseul* (1915) is a far better guide. For the origins of the Franco-Spanish alliance, see D. Ozanam, 'Les origines du troisième pacte de Famille (1761)', *Revue d'histoire diplomatique* 75 (1961), pp. 307–40 and R.D.O. Butler, 'The Secret Compact of 1753 between the Kings of France and Naples', in Oresko *et al.*, eds., *Royal and*

Republican Sovereignty, pp. 551–79; while its nature is analysed by M.V. López-Cordón Cortezo, 'Pacte de famille ou Intérêts d'Etat: la monarchie française et la diplomatie espagnole au XVIIIe siècle', and H.M. Scott, 'Choiseul et le troisième Pacte de Famille', both in Lucien Bély, ed., *La Présence des Bourbons en Europe, xvie–xxie siècles* (2003), pp. 185–205 and 207–220. M. Roberts, *Splendid Isolation 1763–1780* (Reading, 1970) is a magisterial short survey of British foreign policy; a detailed narrative is provided by H.M. Scott, *British Foreign Policy in the Age of the American Revolution* (Oxford, 1990), the main conclusions of which are summarised in the same author's 'Britain as a European Great Power in the Age of the American Revolution', in H.T. Dickinson, ed., *Britain and the American Revolution* (1998), pp. 180–204. The essential naval dimension is provided by Nicholas Tracy, *Navies, Deterrence and American Independence: Britain and Seapower in the 1760s and 1770s* (Vancouver, 1988), which consolidates and summarises a well-researched if rather Anglocentric series of articles which are referred to in his bibliography; and, for a French perspective, by H.M. Scott, 'The Importance of Bourbon Naval Reconstruction to the Strategy of Choiseul after the Seven Years War', *International History Review* **1** (1979), pp. 17–35. There is a helpful article by Jeremy Black, 'Anglo-French Relations, 1763–1775', *Francia* **18** (1991), pp. 89–114, while the attempt at a Franco–British rapprochement in the early 1770s is outlined in B. du Fraguier, 'Le duc d'Aiguillon et l'Angleterre', *Revue d'histoire diplomatique* **26** (1912), pp. 607–27, and placed in context by Roberts, 'Great Britain and the Swedish Revolution, 1772–73', in his *Essays in Swedish History*. The War of American Independence is seen from a British standpoint in the superb study of P. Mackesy, *The War for America 1775–1783* (1964); this is valuably updated by Stephen Conway, *The War of American Independence 1775–1783* (1995), now the best introduction, the conclusions of which are summarised in the same author's 'British Governments and the Conduct of the American War', in Dickinson, ed., *Britain and the American Revolution*, pp. 155–79. Rodger, *Sandwich*, chapters 13–15, is the most important recent study of the political side of Britain's war. French policy is best examined in Murphy's biography of Vergennes, *French Diplomacy in the Age of Revolution*, the perceptive (and book-length) introduction to John Hardman and Munro Price, eds., *Louis XVI and the comte de Vergennes: correspondence, 1774–1787* (Oxford, 1998), and a pathbreaking study by J.R. Dull, *The French Navy and American Independence* (Princeton, N.J., 1975). The same author's *A Diplomatic History of the American Revolution* (New Haven, CT, 1985) is now the standard work and largely supersedes the more patriotic S.F. Bemis, *The Diplomacy of the American Revolution* (New York, 1935). R.W. Van Alstyne, *Empire and Independence: the International History of the American Revolution* (New York, 1965) provides an incisive American perspective, but is not always reliable on the European dimension; by far the best account of continental diplomacy is I. de Madariaga, *Britain, Russia and the Armed Neutrality of 1780* (1962). A modern study of the Anglo-Dutch War of 1780–84 is badly needed; the best available is probably P.J. Blok, *History of the People of the Netherlands*, vol. v (New York, 1912), chapters 9 and 10. New findings on the war's origins are presented in H.M. Scott, 'Sir Joseph Yorke, Dutch Politics and the Origins of the Fourth Anglo-Dutch War', *Historical Journal* 31 (1988), pp. 571–89. J.W. Schulte Nordholt, *The Dutch Republic and American Independence* (Chapel Hill, NC, 1982) has some useful material on foreign policy, while helpful sidelights on the Anglo-Dutch hostilities are the articles by Jan van Zijverden and Jan Parmentier (pp. 186–205, pp. 206–26) in *Pirates and Privateers: New Perspectives on the War on Trade in the Eighteenth and Nineteenth Centuries* ed. D.J. Starkey, E.S. van Eyck van Heslinga and J.A. de Moor (Exeter, 1977).

There is no reliable single volume on the peace settlements of 1783–84. The most important recent accounts are the overlapping articles in the special issue of *International History Review* 5:iii (1983) and the anniversary collection edited by R. Hoffman and P.J. Albert, eds., *Peace and the Peacemakers: the Treaty of 1783* (Charlottesville, VA, 1986), along with the fine monograph by Andrew Stockley, *Britain and France at the Birth of America: the European Powers and the Peace Negotiations of 1782–83* (Exeter, 2001). Among older studies, the account in V.T. Harlow, *The Founding of the Second British Empire 1763–1793, i: Discovery and Revolution* (1952) was the starting point for modern reassessment of the Peace of Versailles, though Harlow claims too much for Shelburne and takes a rather insular view of the discussions, while R.B. Morris, *The Peacemakers: the Great Powers and American Independence* (New York, 1965) is rambling and discursive, but provides much important detail.

The standard work on the post-war decade is the detailed and large-scale Jeremy Black, *British Foreign Policy in an Age of Revolutions 1783–1793* (1994), while John Cannon, 'The Loss of America', in Dickinson, ed., *Britain and the American Revolution*, pp. 233–57, is notably lively and balanced. The French perspective is apparent from Orville T. Murphy, *The Diplomatic Retreat of France and Public Opinion on the Eve of the French Revolution 1783–1789* (Washington, DC, 1998). Britain's continuing naval dominance is explained by Paul L.C. Webb, 'The Rebuilding and Repair of the Fleet, 1783–93', *Bulletin of the Institute of Historical Research* 50 (1977), pp. 194–209. A good general account of Pitt's foreign policy before 1790 is J. Ehrman, *The Younger Pitt: the Years of Acclaim* (1969), chapters 16 and 17; Ehrman has also written a dense monograph on *The British Government and Commercial Negotiations with Europe, 1783–93* (Cambridge, 1962) and there is a useful study of 'The Anglo-French Commercial Treaty of 1786' by W.O. Henderson in *Economic History Review*, 2nd series, 10 (1957–58), pp. 104–12; and an informative series of articles by M.M. Donaghy: see in particular 'Calonne and the Anglo-French Commercial Treaty of 1786', *Journal of Modern History* 50 (1978), on demand supplement, pp. 1157–84; 'The Maréchal de Castries and the Anglo-French Commercial Negotiations of 1786–87', *Historical Journal* 22 (1979), pp. 295–312; and 'The Exchange of Products of the Soil and Industrial Goods in the Anglo-French Commercial Treaty of 1786', *Journal of European Economic History* 19 (1990), pp. 377–401. Events in the Dutch Republic are admirably described by S. Schama, *Patriots and Liberators: Revolution in the Netherlands 1780– 1813* (1977), while a lively study of Sir James Harris's activities is provided by A. Cobban, *Ambassadors and Secret Agents* (1954). The confusions and eventual disintegration of French policy can be followed in Munro Price, 'The Dutch Affair and the Fall of the *Ancien Régime*, 1784–1787', *Historical Journal* 38 (1995), pp. 875–905 and in the same author's more widely conceived *Preserving the Monarchy: the comte de Vergennes, 1774–1787* (Cambridge, 1995), while N.C.F. van Sas, 'The Patriot Revolution: New Perspectives', in M.C. Jacob and W.W. Mijnhardt, eds., *The Dutch Republic in the Eighteenth Century: Decline, Enlightenment and Revolution* (Ithaca, NY, 1992), pp. 91–122, is a stimulating introduction. For Anglo-Prussian relations in the later 1780s there is only the old study by R. Lodge, *Great Britain and Prussia in the Eighteenth Century* (Oxford, 1923).

Chapter 9

The proliferation of research and publication on the Revolutionary period continues to neglect international relations and there are still some significant gaps. Older studies often remain the best guides. Chief among these is the great work of Albert Sorel, *L'Europe et la Révolution française* (8 vols., 1885–1905), which is unsurpassed for factual information, though its thesis is controversial. The crucial book for this and the two subsequent chapters is Paul W. Schroeder's magnificent *The Transformation of European Politics*, which has influenced the text at many points; while T.C.W. Blanning, 'Europe and the French Revolution', in C. Lucas, ed., *Rewriting the French Revolution* (Oxford, 1991), pp. 183–206, is an incisive brief discussion. A compact if now rather dated introduction is Steven T. Ross, *European Diplomatic History 1789–1815: France against Europe* (New York, 1969), which is unfortunately difficult to obtain. A. Fugier, *La Révolution française et l'empire napoléonien* (1954) provides a reliable, if Francocentric, survey; G. Lefebvre, *The French Revolution* (Engl. trans., 2 vols., 1964) contains a judicious account of international relations. The best recent survey is William Doyle, *The Oxford History of the French Revolution* (Oxford, 1989; 2nd edn., 2002), by a scholar who is admirably aware of the international dimension, as is Bailey Stone, who has written two studies, *The Genesis of the French Revolution: a global–historical interpretation* (Cambridge, 1994) and *Reinterpreting the French Revolution: a Global–Historical Perspective* (Cambridge, 2002) which are timely if not altogether convincing reinterpretations. The changing attitudes to international rivalry in France are explored by Jeremy J. Whiteman, *Reform, Revolution and French Global Policy, 1787–1791* (Aldershot, 2003) and by Linda and Marsha Frey, ' "The Reign of the Charlatans is Over": the French Revolutionary Attack on Diplomatic Practice', *Journal of Modern History* 65 (1993), pp. 706–44; while important continuities are emphasised by the illuminating article by Gary Savage, 'Favier's Heirs: the French Revolution and the *Secret du Roi*', *Historical Journal* 41 (1998), pp. 225–58, and in two well-researched articles by Thomas E. Kaiser, 'Who's afraid of Marie-Antoinette?: Diplomacy, Austrophobia and the Queen', *French History* 14 (2000), pp. 241–71, and 'From the Austrian Committee to the Foreign Plot: Marie-Antoinette, Austrophobia, and the Terror', *French Historical Studies* 26 (2003), pp. 579–617. The best account of the Nootka Sound crisis is that contained in Warren L. Cook, *Flood Tide of Empire: Spain and the Pacific Northwest, 1543–1819* (New Haven, CT, 1973), chapters 4–6, which is also the only easily accessible study of Anglo-Bourbon relations from Madrid's perspective for the entire generation after 1763. For the confrontation over Nootka there are also some helpful articles: Paul L.C. Webb, 'The Naval Aspects of the Nootka Sound Crisis', *The Mariner's Mirror* 61 (1975), pp. 133–54; C. de Parrel, 'Pitt et l'Espagne', *Revue d'histoire diplomatique* 64 (1950), pp. 58–98; H.V. Evans, 'The Nootka Sound controversy in Anglo-French diplomacy – 1790', *Journal of Modern History* **46** (1974), pp. 609–40; and J.M. Norris, 'The Policy of the British Cabinet in the Nootka Crisis', *English Historical Review* **70** (1955), pp. 562–80.

The impact of Revolutionary France on Europe is examined by the vastly informative J. Godechot, *La Grande Nation* (2 vols., 1956), and the now rather dated R.R. Palmer, *The Age of the Democratic Revolution, ii: The Struggle* (Princeton, 1964), while T.C.W. Blanning, *The French Revolution in Germany* (Oxford, 1983) is an exemplary case study of a key area. The activities of the *émigrés* are outlined in part two of J. Godechot, *The Counter-Revolution: Doctrine and Action 1789–1804* (1972), and in the valuable recent collection ed. Kirsty Carpenter and Philip Mansel, *The French Émigrés in Europe and the Struggle against the Revolution, 1789–1814* (1999): see in particular Mansel's own essay, 'From Coblenz to Hartwell: the Émigré Government and the European Powers, 1791–1814' (pp. 1–28), and by Philippe Boutry, 'Les Bourbons en exil (1789–1814)', in Bély, ed., *La présence des Bourbons*, pp. 233–54. Discussions of the initial European response include Jean-René Aymes, 'Spain and the French Revolution', *Mediterranean Historical Review* **6** (1991), pp. 62–85, J.W. Marcum, 'Catherine II and the French Revolution: a Reappraisal', *Canadian Slavonic Papers* **16** (1974), pp. 187–200, and, on a much larger scale, the early chapters of Michael Broers, *Napoleonic Imperialism and the Savoyard Monarchy 1773–1821: State-building in Piedmont* (Lampeter, 1997). Munro Price, *The Fall of the French Monarchy: Louis XVI, Marie Antoinette and the Baron de Breteuil* (2002) and the same author's 'Louis XVI and Gustavus III: Secret Diplomacy and Counter-Revolution, 1791–1792', *Historical Journal* **42** (1999), pp. 435–66, are important for the court's links with the conservative powers; on the same topic and the Swedish King's counter-revolutionary schemes see H.A. Barton, *Count Hans Axel von Fersen* (Boston, 1975), chapters 4–6.

There is now an admirable study of the path to war by T.C.W. Blanning, *The Origins of the French Revolutionary Wars* (1986); the same author's broadly-conceived *The French Revolutionary Wars 1787–1802* (1996) is the best guide to the fighting which followed. A contrasting perspective is provided by P.C. Howe, 'Charles-François Dumouriez and the Revolutionising of French Foreign Affairs in 1792', *French Historical Studies* **14** (1986), pp. 367–90, while for the revival of French military power John A. Lynn, *The Bayonets of the Republic: Motivation and Tactics in the Army of Revolutionary France, 1791–1794* (Urbana, IL, 1984; repr. Boulder, CO, 1996) is fundamental. S.S. Biro, *The German Policy of*

Revolutionary France: a study of French diplomacy during the war of the First Coalition 1792–1797 (Cambridge, MA., 1957), is vastly informative. Detailed studies of Britain's involvement in the War of the First Coalition include: Black, *British Foreign Policy in an Age of Revolution*, chapters 7–9; John Ehrman, *The Younger Pitt, ii: The reluctant transition* (1983); and Jennifer Mori, *William Pitt and the French Revolution, 1785–1795* (Edinburgh, 1995). Austria's role is the subject of Michael Hochedlinger, 'Who's afraid of the French Revolution?: Austrian Foreign Policy and the European Crisis, 1787–1797', *German History* 21 (2003), pp. 293–318, of an important and notably well-researched monograph by Martin C. Dean, *Austrian Policy during the French Revolutionary Wars 1796–1799* (Vienna, 1993), of A. Roider, *Baron Thugut and Austria's Response to the French Revolution*, and Alan J. Reinerman, 'The Papacy, Austria, and the anti-French struggle in Italy, 1792–1797', in *Austria in the Age of the French Revolution 1789–1815*, eds. Kinley Brauer and William E. Wright (Minneapolis, 1990), pp. 47–68; while Prussia's is explored in two informative articles by Philip Dwyer: 'The Politics of Prussian Neutrality 1795–1805', *German History* 12 (1994), pp. 351–73, and 'Prussia during the French Revolutionary and Napoleonic Wars, 1786–1815', in Dwyer, ed., *The Rise of Prussia*, pp. 239–58, and her problems incorporating the new Polish gains in an illuminating study by William W. Hagen, 'The partitions of Poland and the crisis of the old regime in Prussia, 1772–1806', *Central European History* 9 (1976), pp. 115–28.

Chapter 10

The origins of the War of the Second Coalition are examined by Blanning, *Origins*, chapter 6, and its course in the same author's *French Revolutionary Wars*, chapters 6–7. Britain's contribution to this phase of the fighting has inspired much high-quality recent scholarship: see in particular the final volume of the magisterial John Ehrman, *The Younger Pitt, iii: The consuming struggle* (1996) and the judicious (and much briefer) Michael Duffy, *The Younger Pitt* (2000). More generally, there is a ponderous but informative study of London's financial contribution by J.M. Sherwig, *Guineas and Gunpowder: British foreign aid in the Wars with France, 1793–1815* (Cambridge, MA, 1969), while for Britain's support of the Counter-Revolution there are three fine monographs: W.R. Fryer, *Republic or Restoration in France, 1794–1797?* (Manchester, 1965), H. Mitchell, *The Underground War against Revolutionary France* (Oxford, 1965), and the vastly-detailed Maurice Hutt, *Chouannerie and Counter-Revolution:*

Puisaye, the Princes and the British Government in the 1790s (2 vols., Cambridge, 1983). The valuable collection edited by H.T. Dickinson, *Britain and the French Revolution 1789–1815* (1989) contains informative and notably accessible essays on diplomacy (Michael Duffy), strategy (Piers Mackesy) and public finance (P.K. O'Brien), while the tangled skein of Anglo-Austrian financial relations during the 1790s is unravelled by K.F. Helleiner, *The Imperial Loan* (Oxford, 1965).

The War of the Second Coalition is seen from Britain's viewpoint in a series of studies: A.B. Rodger, *The War of the Second Coalition, 1789–1801* (Oxford, 1964), idiosyncratic but with some penetrating comments, and a trilogy by P. Mackesy, *Statesmen at War: the strategy of overthrow 1789–99* (1974); *War without Victory: the downfall of Pitt 1799–1802* (Oxford, 1984); and *British Victory in Egypt, 1801: the end of Napoleon's conquest* (1995), with their masterly grasp of the interplay between strategy and politics. Its ending is the subject of John D. Grainger, *The Amiens Truce: Britain and Bonaparte, 1801–1803* (Woodbridge, 2004), a breezy, Anglophone narrative which adds detail to the established account, and of Simon Burrows, 'Culture and Misperception: The Law and the Press in the Outbreak of War in 1803', *International History Review* **18** (1996), pp. 793–818. The need for an Austro-Russian counterpoint to the view from London provided by Mackesy in particular is rightly emphasised by Paul W. Schroeder, 'The Collapse of the Second Coalition', *Journal of Modern History* **59** (1987), pp. 244–90, an important article which exaggerates in order to make a crucial point. This corrective is supplied (for Austria) by Dean, *Austrian Policy*, chapter 5, and Roider, *Baron Thugut*, chapters 10–11, and two articles by Roider: 'The Habsburg Foreign Ministry and Political Reform, 1801–1805', *Central European History* **22** (1989), pp. 160–82, and 'Austria's Road to Austerlitz', in *Austria in the Age of the French Revolution*, eds. Brauer and Wright, pp. 11–24; and (for Russia) by Roderick E. McGrew, *Paul I of Russia 1754–1801* (Oxford, 1992), especially chapters 7–9. Significant material on the Russian Emperor's foreign policy is also contained in *Paul I*, ed. H. Ragsdale (Pittsburg, PA, 1979); in H. Ragsdale, *Détente in the Napoleonic Era* (Lawrence, KS, 1980), which details Bonaparte's attempted *rapprochement* with Russia in 1800–1; in the same author's 'Russia, Prussia, and Europe in the Policy of Paul I', *Jahrbücher für Geschichte Osteuropas* NF **31** (1983), pp. 81–118; and in Ole Feldbaek, 'The Foreign Policy of Tsar Paul I, 1800–1801: an interpretation', *ibid.*, NF **30** (1982), pp. 16–36.

Feldbaek has also written an important and widely-conceived study of *Denmark and the Armed Neutrality 1800–1801: Small Power Policy in a World War* (Copenhagen, 1980) and an examination of 'The Anglo-Russian Rapprochement of 1801', *Scandinavian Journal of History* 3 (1978), pp. 205–27, while Christer Jorgensen, *The Anglo-Swedish Alliance against Napoleonic France* (Basingstoke, 2004) provides a detailed Baltic perspective on the first decade of the nineteenth century. Britain's unsuccessful search for a Russian alliance is the subject of Charles James Fedorak, 'In Search of a Necessary Ally: Addington, Hawkesbury and Russia 1801–1804', *International History Review* 13 (1991), pp. 221–45, while Russia's foreign policy under Alexander I can be approached through P.K. Grimsted, *The Foreign Ministers of Alexander I* (Berkeley, CA, 1969) and W.H. Zawadzki, *A Man of Honour: Adam Czartoryski as a Statesman of Russia and Poland 1795–1831* (Oxford, 1993), chapters 3–7; there are also serviceable biographical studies by A. Palmer, *Alexander I* (1974) and Janet M. Hartley, *Alexander I* (1994). Hartley has also written a helpful article, 'Is Russia part of Europe?: Russian Perceptions of Europe in the reign of Alexander I', *Cahiers du monde russe et soviétique* 33 (1992), pp. 369–86, while there is W.H. Zawadzki, 'Russia and the Re-opening of the Polish Question, 1801–14', *International History Review* 7 (1985), pp. 19–44.

Prussia's complex policies towards the rise of French power have inspired some important scholarship: see in particular the outstanding Brendan Simms, *The Impact of Napoleon: Prussian high policy, foreign policy and the crisis of the executive 1797–1806* (Cambridge, 1997), to which the same author's 'The Road to Jena: Prussian High Politics, 1804–6', *German History* 12 (1994), pp. 374–94, can be read as an introduction; Lothar Kittstein, *Politik im Zeitalter der Revolution: Untersuchungen zur preussischen Staatlichkeit 1792–1807* (Stuttgart, 2003), a large-scale work, the implications of which will take some time to digest; and an important series of well-researched articles by Philip Dwyer: 'The Politics of Prussian Neutrality, 1795–1805', *German History* 12 (1994), pp. 351–73; 'Prussia and the Armed Neutrality: the invasion of Hanover in 1801', *International History Review* 15 (1993), pp. 661–87; 'Two Definitions of Neutrality: Prussia, the European States-System, and the French Invasion of Hanover in 1803', *International History Review* 19 (1997), pp. 522–40; and 'Prussia during the French Revolutionary and Napoleonic Wars', in Dwyer, ed., *Rise of Prussia*, pp. 239–58. The old study by G.S. Ford, *Hanover and Prussia 1795–1803* (New York, 1903) remains an important source of detailed information. The Anglo-Prussian confrontation of 1806 is examined in the richly-documented article by Brendan Simms, '"An Odd Question Enough": Charles James Fox, the Crown and British policy during the Hanoverian Crisis of 1806', *Historical Journal* 38 (1995), pp. 567–96, while London's approach to the fighting is the subject of Christopher D. Hall, *British Strategy in the Napoleonic War 1803–15* (Manchester, 1992). The southern European dimension is provided by N.E. Saul, *Russia and the Mediterranean 1797–1807* (Chicago, 1970) and another fine study by P. Mackesy, *The War in the Mediterranean 1803–10* (1957).

The revolutionary changes in land warfare are outlined by M. Howard, *War in European History* (Oxford, 1976), chapter 5, and by G.E. Rothenberg, *The Art of Warfare in the Age of Napoleon* (1977); for Bonaparte as a military commander see the comprehensive and up-to-date studies by Charles J. Esdaile, *The Wars of Napoleon* (1995) and David Gates, *The Napoleonic Wars 1803–1815* (1997), which have superseded the study by D.G. Chandler, *The Campaigns of Napoleon* (1967), now important primarily for its detailed information. His leading opponent is the subject of G.E. Rothenberg, *Napoleon's Greatest Adversary: Archduke Charles and the Austrian Army 1792–1814* (1982; 2nd edn., Stapelhurst, 1995). Biographies of Bonaparte abound: the most balanced are F. Markham, *Napoleon* (1963) and G. Ellis, *Napoleon* (1997). The old volume by C.L. Mowat, *The Diplomacy of Napoleon* (1924) remains uniquely comprehensive, while the remarkable article by P. Muret, 'Une conception nouvelle de la politique étrangère de Napoléon Ier', *Revue d'histoire moderne et contemporaine* 18 (1913), pp. 177–200 and 353–80, discusses interpretations of his foreign policy. France's impact is best studied through Michael Broers, *Europe under Napoleon 1799–1815* (1996), some of the arguments of which are taken further in the same author's 'Napoleon, Charlemagne, and Lotharingia: Acculturation and the Boundaries of Napoleonic Europe', *Historical Journal* 44 (2001), pp. 135–54; Alexander Grab, *Napoleon and the Transformation of Europe* (2003) adds some national case studies and is up to date. There are important specialised works on aspects of Napoleonic ascendancy: H.C. Deutsch, *The Genesis of Napoleonic Imperialism* (Cambridge, MA, 1938), for the years 1800–5; H. Butterfield, *The Peace Tactics of Napoleon 1806–1808* (Cambridge, 1929); O. Connelly, *Napoleon's Satellite Kingdoms* (New York, 1965); and E.E.Y. Hales, *Napoleon and the Pope* (1962). Newer perspectives can be gleaned from the collections edited by Philip Dwyer, *Napoleon and Europe* (2001) and by Michael Rowe, *Collaboration and Resistance in Napoleonic Europe: State Formation in an Age of Upheaval* (2003). Rowe has also written a model study of one key region: *From Reich to State: the Rhineland in the Revolutionary Age, 1780–1830* (Cambridge, 2003).

Chapter 11

Many of the titles mentioned under the previous chapter are also relevant for the period 1807–15, particularly those on Napoleon, the French Empire and Russia. C.J. Bartlett, *Castlereagh* (1966) is a well-written political biography, while Rory Muir, *Britain and the Defeat of Napoleon 1807–15* (New Haven, CT, 1996) provides a detailed narrative. Charles Esdaile, *The Peninsular War* (2002) is up to date and conceived on a generous scale, while there is also D. Gates, *The Spanish Ulcer: a history of the Peninsular War* (1986). John K. Severn, *A Wellesley Affair: Richard Marquess Wellesley and the Conduct of Anglo-Spanish Diplomacy, 1809–1812* (Tallahassee, FL, 1981) is an illuminating study of the accompanying political problems. There are several informative studies of Habsburg foreign policy during the Napoleonic period, above all E.E. Kraehe, *Metternich's German Policy, i: The Contest with Napoleon, 1799–1814* (Princeton, 1963), which contains important information, though the interpretation is controversial; M.R. Falk, 'Stadion: adversaire de Napoléon (1806–1809)', *Annales historiques de la Révolution française* 34 (1962), pp. 288–305; Alan Palmer, *Metternich* (1972), a readable political biography; James A. Vann, 'Habsburg Policy and the Austrian War of 1809', *Central European History* 7 (1974), pp. 291–310; C.S.B. Buckland, *Metternich and the British Government from 1809–1813* (1932); and J. B. Stearns, *The Role of Metternich in Undermining Napoleon* (Urbana, IL, 1948). The Baltic dimension is explored in H.S. Andersen, 'Denmark between the Wars with Britain, 1801–7', *Scandinavian Journal of History* 14 (1989), pp. 231–38; an illuminating overview by Ole Feldbaek, 'Denmark in the Napoleonic Wars: a Foreign Policy survey', *ibid.*, 26 (2001), pp. 89–101; a detailed monograph by Sven G. Trulsson, *British and Swedish Policies and Strategies in the Baltic after the Peace of Tilsit in 1807* (Lund, 1976); and three shorter studies: R. Carr, 'Gustavus IV and the British Government, 1804–1809', *English Historical Review* 60 (1945), pp. 36–66; A.N. Ryan, 'The causes of the British attack upon Copenhagen in 1807', *ibid.* 68 (1953), pp. 37–55; and 'The defence of British trade with the Baltic, 1808–1813', *ibid.* 74 (1959), pp. 443–66. Economic warfare is examined in E.F. Heckscher's classic *The Continental System* (1922) and in a large-scale and rather technical study by F. Crouzet, *L'Economie britannique et le blocus continental (1803–1813)* (2 vols., Paris, 1958); perhaps more accessible is the article by Crouzet, 'Wars, blockade and economic change in Europe 1792–1815', *Journal of Economic History* 24 (1964), 567–88. This blockade's impact upon one key relationship is the subject of M.S. Anderson, 'The Continental System and Russo-British Relations during the Napoleonic War', in K. Bourne and D.C. Watt, *Studies in International History: Essays Presented to W. Norton Medlicott* (1967), pp. 68–80. On the final struggle with Napoleon, G.A. Craig, 'Problems of coalition warfare: the military alliance against Napoleon, 1813–14', in his *War, Politics and Diplomacy* (1966), is an important article and E.V. Gulick, 'The Final Coalition and the Congress of Vienna, 1813–1815', in C.W. Crawley, ed., *The New Cambridge Modern History, ix: War and Peace in an Age of Upheaval 1793–1830* (Cambridge, 1965), pp. 639–67, a serviceable political outline. On these years there are some important shorter studies: Philip G. Dwyer, 'The Two Faces of Prussian Foreign Policy: Karl August von Hardenberg as Foreign Minister, 1804–1815' in Thomas Stamm-Kuhlmann, *Freier Gebrauch der Kräfte: Eine Bestandsaufnahme der Hardenberg Forschung* (Munich, 2001), pp. 75–91, and Gordon A. Craig, 'Wilhelm von Humboldt as Diplomat', in Bourne and Watt, eds., *Studies in International History* (cited above), pp. 81–102, on the complexities of Prussia's position; Lars Tangeraas, 'Castlereagh, Bernadotte and Norway', *Scandinavian Journal of History* 8 (1983), pp. 193–223; and especially the illuminating Paul W. Schroeder, 'An Unnatural "Natural Alliance": Castlereagh, Metternich, and Aberdeen in 1813', *International History Review* 10 (1988), pp. 522–40. There is a valuable short discussion of the peace conference by D. Dakin, 'The Congress of Vienna, 1814–15, and its antecedents' in A. Sked, ed., *Europe's Balance of Power 1815–1848* (1979), pp. 14–33, but the best account is now Enno E. Kraehe, *Metternich's German Policy, ii: The Congress of Vienna 1814–1815* (Princeton, 1983); among older studies the following remain useful within their limits: C.K. Webster, *The Congress of Vienna 1814–15* (1919); H. Nicolson, *The Congress of Vienna* (1946); G. Ferrero, *The Reconstruction of Europe: Talleyrand and the Congress of Vienna* (New York, 1941); and E.V. Gulick, *Europe's Classical Balance of Power* (Ithaca, 1955). The nature of the settlement which resulted is explored by Paul W. Schroeder, 'Did the Vienna Settlement rest on a Balance of Power?', *American Historical Review* 97 (1992), pp. 683–706, with a series of short replies by fellow specialists: that by Enno E. Kraehe, 'A Bipolar Balance of Power' (pp. 707–15) is particularly noteworthy.

Conclusion

The nature of the nineteenth-century international system is explored in some incisive articles by Paul W. Schroeder: see in particular 'The European International System, 1789–1848: Is there a Problem? An Answer?', *Consortium on Revolutionary Europe: Proceedings* **15** (1985), pp. 2–26; 'The Nineteenth-century International System: Changes in the Structure', *World Politics* **39** (1986), pp. 1–26; and 'The 19th Century System: Balance of Power or Political Equilibrium?', *Review of International Studies*, **15** (1989), pp. 135–53. The same author's 'International Politics, Peace, and War, 1815–1914', in T.C.W. Blanning, ed., *The Nineteenth Century* (Oxford, 2000), pp. 158–209, is an admirable introduction, while fuller and more narrative accounts are provided by F.R. Bridge and Roger Bullen, *The Great Powers and the European States System* (2nd edn., 2004) and Norman Rich, *Great Power Diplomacy 1814–1914* (New York, 1992). Krüger and Schröder, eds., *"Transformation of European Politics, 1763–1848": Episode or Model?* and Sked, ed., *Europe's Balance of Power* both contain helpful essays on the post-1815 period, while a wider political perspective is provided by Michael Broers, *Europe after Napoleon: Revolution, reaction and romanticism, 1814–1848* (Manchester, 1996).

Index

Alliances are indexed alphabetically under 'Alliances'; treaties of peace under 'Treaties'; individual wars under 'Wars' and battles under 'Battles'. Single, passing mentions of individuals and places are usually not indexed.